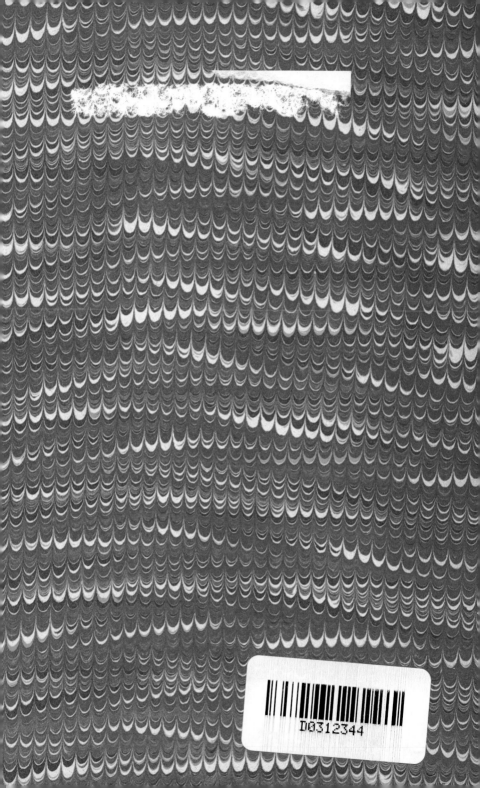

D0312344

Reprinted 1983 from the 1890 edition.
Cover design © 1981 Time-Life Books Inc.
Library of Congress CIP data following page 376.

This volume is bound in leather.

and graphic. Mr. DeLeon is the promising writer of the South. He knows his people and region thoroughly.—[*Chicago Times.*

A very romantic story. The book is sensational ; but the skill with which the story is told saves it from being ridiculous.—[*San Francisco Chronicle.*

Most successful descriptive and character studies. Animated from the very first chapter ; and once beginning, one can scarcely leave it.—[*New Orleans Bee.*

The sketch of moonshining life in the North Carolina mountains is, to say the least, clever. The author has made a distinct success in this.—[*Hartford Post.*

The devotion of the old negro for his "chile" and the affection springing up between her and Wilmot Browne are the features of the book.—[*North American.*

A highly exciting story of life, in widely differing circles. All of the bad characters are disposed of rapidly, but with a proper eye to effect.—[*New York Herald.*

Just the thing for the car or hammock ; a lively novel, introducing many odd characters in many odd situations of high and low life.—[*Minneapolis Housekeeper.*

Well written and full of "situations," many of them wrought up to a point of thrilling interest. The many characters are drawn in natural colors.—[*Brooklyn Citizen.*

Mr. DeLeon has written several novels which had a run ; but this one surpasses any in cleverness of plot, thrilling situations and general interest.—[*Salt Lake Herald.*

Brightness of dialogue and richness of incident. The suicide of the gambler is a startling effect ; worthy of the imagination and descriptive power of Zola !—[*Mobile Register.*

The same authority pronounces "the leading man of the Grand Duke's Opera House" the most original type in comic fiction since we met *Sam Weller.*—[*Denver Republican.*

Some situations, especially those in the slums of the "East Side," are intensely dramatic. *Juny* and the characters that surround her are exceedingly well drawn.— [*Philadelphia Times.*

"Juny" is bright and sensational. * * The Mobile novelist is especially happy in his southern scenes and characters ; but his plots have wide range and embrace high and low life.—[*Atlanta Constitution.*

T. C. DeLeon has recommended himself as a writer of talent and power. His latest work is perhaps his best, as his wit, his dramatic force and his striking ability for character drawing are all forcibly exhibited.—[*Columbus (O.) Journal.*

We have not read a better story for many a day. Mr. DeLeon has advanced rapidly to foremost rank among American novelists of the present day. The plot is skillfully framed and many thrilling, as well as humorous, situations keep the reader's mind alert.—[*Chicago Herald.*

T. C. DeLeon, whose "Rock or the Rye," a clever parody of Amelie Rives, was a decided success, has added "Juny" to the list of his novels ; the scene changing from a moonshiner's camp to New York, with the heroine a beautiful Octoroon girl.—[*San Francisco Argonaut.*

Southern authors are coming to the front. Among those named more and more frequently of late is T. C. DeLeon. The story is as full of plot as it can hold ; and if action plays as large a part in fiction, as Demosthenes averred it did in oratory, "Juny" should be a popular book.—[*Boston Commonwealth.*

Mr. DeLeon's "Creole and Puritan" proved most conclusively that he could write well ; and his satire on the "Quick or the Dead" was laughed over by the whole country. The story of "Juny" shows the creative power of the author. It is strong and his descriptive powers have full sway.—[*New Orleans Picayune.*

The old negro and the detective, Mr. Hunter Beagle, seem to have been taken from life and are carefully elaborated. * * The "Art Evolutionist" is a very clever portrayal of the creature who is made possible by, and subsists upon, the *fads* for which the present century must ever remain responsible.—[*Courier-Journal.*

FOUR YEARS

IN

REBEL CAPITALS:

AN INSIDE VIEW OF

LIFE IN THE SOUTHERN CONFEDERACY,

FROM BIRTH TO DEATH.

FROM ORIGINAL NOTES, COLLATED IN THE YEARS 1861 TO 1865,

BY T. C. DeLEON,

AUTHOR OF "CREOLE AND PURITAN," "CROSS PURPOSES," "JUNY," ETC.

" In the land where we were dreaming !"
—*D. B. Lucas.*

"I leave it to men's charitable speeches, to foreign
nations and to the next ages."
—*Francis Bacon.*

MOBILE, ALA.
THE GOSSIP PRINTING COMPANY.
1890.

TO MY VALUED FRIEND,

MRS. AUGUSTA EVANS WILSON,

AS ONE LITTLE TOKEN OF APPRECIATION OF A LIFE-WORK
DEDICATE TO HER SEX, TO HER SECTION
AND TO TRUTH,

THESE SKETCHES

OF LIFE BEHIND OUR CHINESE WALL
ARE INSCRIBED.

IN PLACE OF PREFACE.

Fortunate, indeed, is the reader who takes up a volume without preface; of which the persons are left to enact their own drama and the author does not come before the curtain, like the chorus of Greek tragedy, to speak for them.

But, in printing the pages that follow, it may seem needful to ask that they be taken for what they are; simple sketches of the inner life of " Rebeldom"—behind its Chinese wall of wood and steel—during those unexampled four years of its existence.

Written almost immediately after the war, from notes and recollections gathered during its most trying scenes, these papers are now revised, condensed and formulated for the first time. In years past, some of their crude predecessors have appeared—as random articles—in the columns of the Mobile *Sunday Times*, Appleton's *Journal*, the Louisville *Courier-Journal*, the Philadelphia *Times* and other publications.

Even in their present condensation and revision, they claim only to be simple memoranda of the result of great events; and of their reaction upon the mental and moral tone of the southern people, rather than a record of those events themselves.

This volume aspires neither to the height of history, nor to the depths of political analysis; for it may still be too early for either, or for both, of these. Equally has it resisted temptation to touch on many topics—not strictly belonging inside the Southern Capitals—still vexed by political agitation, or personal interest. These, if unsettled by dire arbitrament of the sword, must be left to Time and his best coadjutor, " sober second-thought."

Campaigns and battles have already surfeited most readers; and their details—usually so incorrectly stated by the inexpert—have little to do with a relation of things within the Confederacy, as they then appeared to the masses of her people. Such, therefore, are simply touched upon in outline, where necessary to show their reaction upon the popular pulse, or to correct some flagrant error regarding that.

To the vast majority of those without her boundaries—to very many, indeed, within them—realities of the South, during the war,

5

were a sealed book. False impressions, on many important points, were disseminated; and these, because unnoted, have grown to proportions of accepted truth. A few of them, it may not yet be too late to correct.

While the pages that follow fail not to record some weaknesses in our people, or some flagrant errors of their leaders, they yet endeavor to chronicle faithfully heroic constancy of men, and selfless devotion of women, whose peers the student of History may challenge that vaunting Muse to show.

To prejudiced provincialism, on the one side, they may appear too lukewarm; by stupid fanaticism on the other, they may be called treasonable. But—written without prejudice, and equally without fear, or favor—they have aimed only at impartial truth, and at nearest possible correctness of narration.

Indubitably the war proved that there were great men, on both the sides to it; and, to-day, the little men on either—" May profit by their example. If *this* be treason, make the most of it!"

The sole object kept in view was to paint honestly the inner life of the South; the general tone of her people, under strain and privation unparalleled ; the gradual changes of society and character in the struggling nation—in a clear, unshaded outline of *things as they were.*

Should this volume at all succeed in giving this ; should it uproot one false impression, to plant a single true one in its place, then has it fully equaled the aspiration of

THE AUTHOR.

Mobile, Ala., June 25, 1890.

TABLE OF CONTENTS.

FOUR YEARS IN REBEL CAPITALS.

CHAPTER I.

THE FOREHEAD OF THE STORM.

The cloud no bigger than a man's hand had risen.

It became visible to all in Washington over the southern horizon. All around to East and West was but the dull, dingy line of the storm that was soon to burst in wild fury over that section, leaving only seared desolation in its wake. Already the timid and wary began to take in sail and think of a port; while the most reckless looked from the horizon to each other's faces, with restless and uneasy glances.

In the days of 1860, as everybody knows, the society of Washington city was composed of two distinct circles, tangent at no one point. The larger, outer circle whirled around with crash and fury several months in each year; then, spinning out its centrifugal force, flew into minute fragments and scattered to extreme ends of the land. The smaller one—the inner circle—revolved sedately in its accustomed grooves, moving no whit faster for the buzz of the monster that surrounded and half hid it for so long; and when that spun itself to pieces moved on as undisturbed as Werther's Charlotte.

The outer circle drew with it all the outside population, all the "dwellers in tents," from the busiest lobbyman to the laziest looker-on. All the "hotel people"—those caravans that yearly poured unceasing into the not too comfortable *caravanserai* down town—stretched eager hands toward this circle; for, to them, it meant Washington. Having clutched an insecure grasp upon its rim, away they went with a fizz and a spin, dizzy and delighted—devil take the hindmost! Therein did the thousand lobbyists, who yearly came to roll logs, pull wires and juggle through bills, find their congenial prey.

Who shall rise up and write the secret history of that wonderful committee and of the ways and means it used to prey impartially upon government and client? Who shall record the "deeds without a name," hatched out of eggs from the midnight terrapin; the strange secrets drawn out by the post-prandial corkscrew? Who shall justly calculate the influence the lobby and its workings had in hastening that inevitable, the war between the states?

Into this outer circle whirled that smaller element which came to the Capital to spend money—not to make it. Diamonds flash, point lace flounces flaunt! Who will stop that mighty whirligig to inspect whether the champagne is real, or the turtle is prime?

Allons! le jeu est fait!

Camp-followers and hangers-on of Congress, many of its members from the West, claim agents from Kansas, husbandless married women from California and subterranean politicians from everywhere herein found elements as congenial as profitable. All stirred into the great *olla podrida* and helped to "Make the hell broth boil and bubble."

The inner circle was the real society of Washington. Half submerged for half of each year by accumulating streams of strangers, it ever rose the same—fresh and unstained by deposit from the baser flood. Therein, beyond doubt, one found the most cultured coteries. the courtliest polish and the simplest elegance that the drawing-rooms of this continent could boast. The bench and the bar of the highest court lent their loftiest intellects and keenest wits. Careful selections were there from Congress of those who held senates on their lips and kept together the machinery of an expanding nation; and those "rising men," soon to replace, or to struggle with them, across the narrow Potomac near by. To this society, too, the foreign legations furnished a strong element. Bred in courts, familiar with the theories of all the world, these men must prove valuable and agreeable addition to any society into which they are thrown.

It is rather the fashion just now to inveigh against foreigners in society, to lay at their door many of the peccadilloes that have crept into our city life; but the diplomats are, with rare exceptions, men of birth, education and of proved ability in their own homes. Their ethics may be less strict than those which obtain about Plymouth Rock, but experience with them will prove that, however loose their own code, they carefully conform to the custom of others; that if they have any scars across their morals, they have also the tact and good taste to keep them decorously draped from sight.

In the inner circle of Washington were those officers of the army and navy, selected for ability or service—or possibly "by grace of cousinship"—to hold posts near the government; and, with full allowance for favoritism, some of these were men of culture, travel and attainment—most of them were gentlemen. And the nucleus, as well as the amalgam of all these elements, was the resident families of old Washingtonians. These had lived there so long as to be able to winnow the chaff and throw the refuse off.

There has ever been much talk about the corruption of Washington, easy hints about Sodom, with a general sweep at the depravity of its social system. But it is plain these facile fault-finders knew no more of its inner circle—and for its resident society only is any city responsible—than they did of the court of the Grand Turk. Such critics had come to Washington, had made their "dicker," danced at the hotel hops, and been jostled on the Avenue. If they essayed an entrance into the charmed circle, they failed.

Year after year, even the Titans of the lobby assailed the gates of that heaven refused them; and year after year they fell back, baffled and grommelling, into the pit of that outer circle whence they came. Yet every year, especially in the autumn and spring, behind that Chinese wall was a round of entertainments less costly than the crushes of the critic circle, but stamped with quiet elegance aped in vain by the non-elect. And when the whirl whirled out at last, with the departing Congress; when the howling crowd had danced its mad *carmagnole* and its vulgar echoes had died into distance, then Washington society was itself again. Then the sociality of intercourse—that peculiar charm which made it so unique—became once more free and unrestrained.

Passing from the reek of a hotel ball, or the stewing soiree of a Cabinet secretary into the quiet *salon* of a West End home, the very atmosphere was different, and comparison came of itself with that old *Quartier Saint Germain,* which kept undefiled from the pitch that smirched its Paris, through all the hideous dramas of the *bonnet rouge.*

The influence of political place in this country has long spawned a social degradation. Where the gift is in the hands of a fixed power,

its seeking is lowering enough; but when it is besought from the
enlightened voter himself, "the scurvy politician" becomes a reality
painfully frequent. Soliciting the ballot over a glass of green corn
juice in the back room of a country grocery, or flattering the *cara
sposa* of the farmhouse, with squalling brat upon his knee, is scarcely
calculated to make the best of men more of "an ornament to society."
Constant contact with sharpers and constant effort to be sharper than
they is equally as apt to blunt his sense of delicacy as it is to unfit one
for higher responsibilities of official station. So it was not unnatural
that that society of Washington, based wholly on politics, was not
found wholly clean. But under the seething surface—first visible to
the casual glance—was a substratum as pure as it was solid and
unyielding.

Habitués of twenty years remarked that, with all the giddy whirl
of previous winters in the outer circle, none had approached in mad
rapidity that of 1860–61. The rush of aimless visiting, matinées and
dinners, balls and suppers, followed each other without cessation;
dress and diamonds, equipage and cards, all cost more than ever
before. This might be the last of it, said an uneasy sense of the
coming storm; and in the precedent sultriness, the thousands who
had come to make money vied with the tens who came to spend it in
mad distribution of the proceeds. Madame, who had made an immense investment of somebody's capital in diamonds and lace, must
let the world see them. Mademoiselle must make a certain exhibit
of shapely shoulders and of telling stride in the German; and time
was shortening fast. And Knower, of the Third House, had put all
the proceeds of engineering that last bill through, into gorgeous plate.
It would never do to waste it, for Knower meant business; and this
might be the end of the thing.

So the stream rushed on, catching the weak and timid ones upon
its brink and plunging them into the whirling vortex. And still the
rusty old wheels revolved, as creakily as ever, at the Capital. Blobb,
of Oregon, made machine speeches to the sleepy House, but neither
he, nor they, noted the darkening atmosphere without. Senator Jenks
took his half-hourly "nip" with laudable punctuality, thereafter rising
eloquent to call Mr. President's attention to that little bill; and all
the while that huge engine, the lobby, steadily pumped away in the
political basement, sending streams of hot corruption into every artery
of the government.

Suddenly a sullen reverberation echoes over the Potomac from the South. The long-threatened deed is done at last. South Carolina has seceded, and the first link is rudely stricken from the chain.

There is a little start; that is all. The Third House stays for a second its gold spoon; and, perhaps, a trifle of the turtle spills before reaching its mouth. Madame rearranges her parure and smoothes her ruffled lace; while Mademoiselle pouts a little, then studies her card for the next waltzer. Senator Jenks takes his "nip" just a trifle more regularly; and Blobb, of Oregon, draws a longer breath before his next period. As for the lobby-pump, its piston grows red-hot and its valves fly wide open, with the work it does ; while thicker and more foul are the streams it sends abroad.

For awhile there is some little talk around Willard's about the "secesh;" and the old soldiers wear grave faces as they pass to and fro between the War Department and General Scott's headquarters. But to the outer circle, it is only a nine-day wonder; while the dancing and dining army men soon make light of the matter.

But the stone the surface closes smoothly over at the center makes large ripples at the edges. Faces that were long before now begin to lengthen; and thoughtful men wag solemn heads as they pass, or pause to take each other by the buttonhole. More frequent knots discuss the status in hotel lobbies and even in the passages of the departments; careful non-partisans keep their lips tightly closed, and hot talk, *pro* or *con*, begins to grow more popular.

One day I find, per card, that the Patagonian Ambassador dines me at seven. As it is not a state dinner I go, to find it even more stupid. At dessert the reserve wears off and all soon get deep in the "Star of the West" episode.

"Looks mighty bad now, sir. Something must be done, sir, and soon, too," says Diggs, a hard-working M. C. from the North-west. "But, as yet, I don't see—what, exactly!"

"Will your government use force to supply Fort Sumter?" asks Count B., of the Sardinian legation.

"If so, it might surely drive out those states so doubtful now, that they may not go to extremes," suggested the Prussian *chargé ad interim.*

"Why, they'll be whipped back by the army and navy within ninety days from date," remarks a gentleman connected with pension brokerage.

"If part of the army and navy does not go to get whipped with them," growls an old major of the famed Aztec Club. And the scar across the nose, that he brought away from the Belen Gate, grows very uncomfortably purple.

"By Jove! I weally believes he means it! Weally!" whispers very young Savile Rowe, of H. B. M. legation. "Let's get wid of these politics. Dwop in at Knower's; soiwee, you know;" and Savile tucks his arm under mine.

Two blocks away we try to lose uncomfortable ideas in an atmosphere of spermaceti, hot broadcloth, jockey club and terrapin.

"Next quadwille, Miss Wose?"

"Oh, yes, Mr. Rowe; and—the third galop—let me see—the fifth waltz. And oh! isn't it nasty of those people in South Carolina! Why *don't* they behave themselves? Oh, dear! what a lovely color Karmeen Sorser has to-night! *Au revoir!*" and Miss Rose Ruche glides off, *à deux temps,* on the arm of the Turkish *chargé.*

As I stroll through the rooms, there is much glaring light and there are many nude necks. I am jostled by polking damsels and buttonholed by most approved bores. But, through the blare of the brass horns and over the steaming terrapin, the one subject rises again and again, refusing burial as persistently as Eugene Aram's old man.

"Try a glass of this punch," Knower chirps cheerily. "Devilish good punch! Good glass, too. See the crest and the monogram blowed in. Put Kansas Coal Contriver's Company proceeds into that glass. But things *are* looking blue, sir, devilish blue; and I don't see the way out at all. Fact is, I'm getting pretty down in the mouth!" And the lobbyist put a bumper of punch in the same position. "People may talk, sir, but my head's as long as the next, and I don't see the way out. Washington's dead, sir; dead as a hammer, if this secession goes on. Why, what'll become of our business if they move the Capital? Kill us, sir; kill us! Lots of southern members leaving already"—and Knower's voice sunk to a whisper—"and would you believe it? I heard of nine resignations from the army to-day. Gad, sir! had it from the best authority. That means business, I'm afraid."

And little by little the conviction dawned on all classes that it did mean business—ugly, real business. What had been only mutterings a few weeks back grew into loud, defiant speech. Southern men, in and out of Congress, banded under their leading spirits, boldly and emphatically declared what they meant to do. Never had excitement around the Capitol run half so high. Even the Kansas-Nebraska furore had failed to pack the Senate galleries so full of men and women, struggling for seats and sitting sometimes through the night. One after another the southern leaders made their valedictories— some calm and dignified, some hot and vindictive—and left the seats they had filled for years. One after another, known and honored names were stricken from the army and navy lists, by resignation. One after another, states met in convention and, by "ordinance of secession," declared themselves independent of the Federal Government. It was as though the train had been prepared and the action of South Carolina was but the lighting of the fuse. Within six weeks from Mr. Buchanan's New Year reception, six states had deliber• ately gone out of the Union.

When it was too late, the sleepy administration opened its eyes. Not liking the looks of things, it shut them again. When it was too late, there were windy declarations and some feeble temporizing; but all thinking men felt that the crisis had come and nothing could avert it. The earthquake that had rumbled so long in premonitory throes suddenly yawned in an ugly chasm, that swallowed up the petty differences of each side. One throb and the little lines of party were roughly obliterated; while across the gulf that gaped between them, men glared at each other with but one meaning in their eyes.

That solemn mummery, the "Peace Congress," might temporarily have turned the tide it was wholly powerless to dam; but the arch seceder, Massachusetts, manipulated even that slight chance of compromise. The weaker elements in convention were no match for the peaceful Puritan whom war might profit, but could not injure. Peace was pelted from under her olive with splinters of Plymouth Rock, and Massachusetts members poured upon the troubled waters oil—of vitriol!

When the "Peace Commissioners" from the southern Congress at Montgomery came to Washington, all felt their presence only a mockery. It was too late! they came only to demand what the government could not then concede, and every line they wrote was waste of ink, every word they spoke waste of breath. Southern congress- men were leaving by every train. Families of years residence were pulling down their household gods and starting on a pilgrimage to

2

set them up—where they knew not, save it must be in the South. Old friends looked doubtfully at each other, and wild rumors were rife of incursions over the Potomac by wild-haired riders from Virginia.   Even the fungi of the departmental desks, seeming suddenly imbued with life, rose and threw away their quills—and with them the very bread for their families—to go South.   It was the modern hegira!

A dull, vague unrest brooded over Washington, as though the city had been shadowed with a vast pall, or threatened with a plague. Then when it was again too late, General Scott—"the general," as the hero of Lundy's Lane and Mexico was universally known—virtually went into the Cabinet, practically filling the chair that Jefferson Davis had vacated.   Men felt that they must range themselves on one side, or the other, for the South had spoken and meant what she said.   There might be war; there must be separation!

I was lounging slowly past the rampant bronze Jackson in Lafayette Square when Styles Staple joined me.

"When do you start?" was his salutation.

"When do I start?"   Staple's question was a sudden one.

"Yes, for the South?   You're going, of course; and the governor writes me to be off at once.   Better go together.   Eh?   Night boat, 4th of March."

Now the governor mentioned was not presiding executive of a southern state, but was Staple *père*, of the heavy cotton firm of Staple, Long & Middling, New Orleans.   Staple *fils* had been for years a great social card in Washington.   The clubs, the legations, the avenues and the german knew him equally well; and though he talked about "the house," his only visible transaction with it was to make the name familiar to bill-brokers by frequent drafts.   So I answered the question by another:

"What are you going to do when you get there?"

"Stop at Montgomery, see the Congress, draw on 'the house,' and then t' Orleans," he answered cheerfully.   "Come with me. Lots to see; and, no doubt, about plenty to do.   If this sky holds, all men will be wanted.   As you're going, the sooner the better. What do you say?   Evening boat, March 4th?   Is it a go?"

It gave only two days for preparation to leave what had come nearer being home than any other place in a nomadic life.   But he was right.   I was going, and we settled the matter, and separated to wind up our affairs and take *congé*.

The night before President Lincoln's inauguration was a restless and trying one to every man in Washington. Nervous men heard signal for bloody outbreak in every unfamiliar sound. Thoughtful ones peered beyond the mist and saw the boiling of the mad breakers, where eight millions of incensed and uncontrolled population hurled themselves against the granite foundation of the established government. Selfish heads tossed upon sleepless pillows, haunted by the thought that the dawn would break upon a great change, boding ruin to their prospects, monetary or political. Even the butterflies felt that there was a something impending; incomprehensible, but uncomfortably suggestive of work instead of pleasure. So Washington rose red-eyed and unrefreshed on the 4th of March, 1861.

Elaborate preparations had been made to have the day's ceremonial brilliant and imposing beyond precedent. Visiting militia and civil organizations from every quarter—North, East and West—had been collecting for days, and meeting reception more labored than spontaneous. The best bands of the country had flocked to the Capital, to drown bad blood in the blare of brass; and all available cavalry and artillery of the regular army had been hastily rendezvoused, for the double purpose of spectacle and security. Still the public mind was feverish and unquiet; and the post commandant was like the public mind.

Rumors were again rife of raids over the Potomac, with Henry A. Wise or Ben McCullough at their head; nightmares of plots to rob the Treasury and raze the White House sat heavy on the timid; while extremists manufactured long-haired men, with air guns, secreted here and there and sworn to shoot Mr. Lincoln, while reading his inaugural.

All night long, orderlies were dashing to and fro at breakneck speed; and guard details were marching to all points of possible danger. Day dawn saw a light battery drawn up on G street facing the Treasury, guns unlimbered and ready for action; while infantry held both approaches to the Long Bridge across the Potomac. Other bodies of regulars were scattered at points most available for rapid concentration; squadrons of cavalry were stationed at the crossings of several avenues; and all possible precautions were had to quell summarily any symptoms of riot.

These preparations resembling more the capital of Mexico than that of these United States, were augury of the peace of the administration thus ushered in! Happily, they were needless. All who remember that inauguration will recall the dull, dead quiet with which the day passed off. The very studiousness of precaution took away from the enjoyment of the spectacle even; and a cloud was thrown over the whole event by the certainty of trouble ahead. The streets were anxious and all gayety showed effort, while many lowering faces peeped at the procession from windows and housetops.

It was over at last. The new man had begun with the new era; and Staple and I had finished our *chasse* at Wormley's dinner table, when that worthy's pleasant, yellow face peered in at the door.

As we jumped into the carriage awaiting us and Wormley banged the door, a knot of loungers ran up to say good-bye. They were all men-about-town; and if not very dear to each other, it was still a wrench to break up associations with those whose faces had been familiar to every dinner and drive and reception for years. We had never met but in amity and amid the gayest scenes; now we were plunging into a pathless future. Who could tell but a turn might bring us face to face, where hands would cross with deadly purpose; while the hiss of the Minié-ball sang accompaniment in place of the last galop that Louis Weber had composed.

"Better stay where you are, boys!"—"You're making a bad thing of it!"—"Don't leave us Styles, old fellow!"—"You'll starve down South, sure!"—were a few of the hopeful adieux showered at us.

"Thank you all, just the same, but I think we won't stay," Staple responded. "What would 'the house' do? God bless you, boys! Good-bye, Jim!"

CHAPTER II.

"THE CRADLE OF THE CONFEDERACY."

Evening had fallen as evening can fall only in early Washington spring. As we plunged into the low, close cabin of the Acquia Creek steamer of that day, there was a weak light, but a strong smell of kerosene and whisky. Wet, steamy men huddled around the hot stove, talking blatant politics in terms as strong as their liquor. So, leaving the reek below, we faced the storm on deck, vainly striving to fix the familiar city lights as they faded through the mist and rain; more vainly still peering into the misty future, through driving fancies chasing each other in the brain.

The journey south in those days was not a delight. Its components were discomfort, dust and doubt. As we rattled through at gray of dawn, Richmond was fast asleep, blissfully ignorant of that May morning when she would wake to find herself famous, with the eyes of all the civilized world painfully strained toward her. But from Petersburg to Wilmington the country side was wide awake and eager for news. Anxious knots were at every station and water tank, and not overclean hands were thrust into the windows, with the cry: "Airy paper?" Sometimes yellow faces, framed with long, lank hair, peered in at the doors; while occasional voices indescribably twanged: "You'uns got any news from thar 'nauggeration?"

Staple's ready, while not very accurate, replies were hungrily swallowed; proffered papers of any date were clutched and borne as prizes to the learned man of each group, to be spelled out to the delectation of open-mouthed listeners. For the whole country had turned out, with its hands in its breeches pockets, and so far it seemed content to gape and lounge about the stations. The men, to all appearance, were ready and eager; but at that time no idea of such a thing as preparation had entered their minds.

It is difficult, at best, to overcome the *vis inertiæ* of the lower-class dweller along the South Atlantic seaboard; but when he is first knocked in the head with so knotty a club as secession, and then is told to be up and doing, he probably does——nothing. Their leaders had not been among them yet, and the "Goobers" were entirely at sea. They knew that something had gone wrong, that something was expected of them; but how, where or what, their conception was of the vaguest. The average intelligence of the masses thereabout is not high; the change noticeable before crossing the Virginia line becoming more and more marked as one travels straight south. Whether the monotonous stretches of pine barren depress mentally, or frequent recurring "ager" prostrates physically, who shall say? But to the casual glance along that railroad line, was not presented an unvarying picture of bright, or intellectual, faces.

In Wilmington—not then the busy mart and "port of the Con‑federacy," she later grew to be—almost equal apathy prevailed. There was more general sense of a crisis upon them; but the escape valve for extra steam, generated therefrom, seemed to be in talk only. There were loud-mouthed groups about the hotel, sundry irate and some drunken politicians at the ferry. But signs of real action were nowhere seen; and modes of organization seemed to have interested no man one met. The "Old North State" had stood ready to dissolve her connection with the Union for some five weeks; but to the looker-on, she seemed no more ready for the struggle to follow her "ordinance of secession," than if that step had not been considered.

But it must be remembered that this was the very beginning, when a whole people were staggered by reaction of their own blow; and all seemed to stand irresolute on the threshold of a vast change. And when the tug really came, the state responded so bravely and so readily that none of her sisters might doubt the mettle she was made of. Her record is written from Bethel to Appomattox, in letters so bright that time can not dim, or conquest tarnish, them.

Through South Carolina and Georgia, men seemed more awake to the greatness of the change and to the imminence of its results. Inland Georgia, especially, showed keener and shrewder. Questions were more to the point; and many a quick retort was popped through the car windows at Staple's wonderful inventions. A strongly as-severated wish to do something, and that at the earliest moment, was generally clinched by a bouncing oath; but where, or how, that something was to be done was never even hinted. Briefly, Georgia seemed more anxious for preparation than her neighbors; withal she was equally far from preparation. It were manifestly unfair to judge the status of a whole people by glimpses from a railway carriage. But from that point of view, the earliest hours of revolution—those hours which, properly utilized, are most fruitful of result—were woefully and weakly wasted by "the leaders."

The people had risen *en masse*. The flame had spread among them like lava to their lowest depths. Told that their section needed them, they had responded like the Douglas, "Ready, aye, ready!" Beyond this they were told nothing; and during those most precious weeks they waited, while demagoguery flourished and action slept. The entire cotton growing region was in active fermentation; but, until the surface bubbles ceased, no practical deposit could be looked for.

"Devilish strong hands and pretty broad backs these, but I've yet to see the first head among them! I suppose we'll find *them* at Montgomery!"

After emitting which Orphic utterance at West Point, Styles Staple emptied the partnership's pocket-flask, and then slept peacefully until we reached the "Cradle of the Confederacy."

Montgomery, like Rome, sits on seven hills. The city is picturesque in perch upon bold, high bluffs, which, on the city side, cut sheer down to the Alabama river ; here, seemingly scarce more than a biscuit-toss across. From the opposite bank spread great flat stretches of marsh and meadow land, while on the other side, behind the town, the formation swells and undulates with gentle rise. As in most southern inland towns, its one great artery, Main street, runs from the river bluffs to the Capitol, perched on a high hill a full mile away. This street, wide and sandy, was in the cradle days badly paved, but rather closely built up. Nor was the Capitol a peculiarly stately pile, either in size or architectural effect. Still it dominated the lesser structures, as it stared down the street with quite a Roman rigor. The staff upon its dome bore the flag of the new nation, run up there shortly after the Congress met by the hands of a noted daughter of Virginia. Miss Letitia Tyler was not only a representative of proud Old Dominion blood, but was also granddaughter of the ex-President of the United States, whose eldest son, Robert, lived in the new Capital. All Montgomery had flocked to Capitol Hill in holiday attire; bells rang and cannon boomed, and the throng—including all mem-

bers of the government—stood bareheaded as the fair Virginian threw
that flag to the breeze. Then a poet-priest—who later added the
sword to the quill—spoke a solemn benediction on the people, their
flag and their cause; and a shout went up from every throat that
told they meant to honor and strive for it; if need be, to die for it.
What was the meaning of the pact, then and there made, had been
told by a hundred battle-fields, from Texas to Gettysburg, from Santa
Rosa to Belmont, ere the star of the South set forever, and her remnant of warriors sadly draped that "conquered banner."

On the whole, the effect of Montgomery upon the newly arrived
was rather pleasing, with a something rather provincial, quite in
keeping with its location inland. Streets, various in length, uncertain
in direction and impractical as to pavement, ran into Main street at
many points; and most of them were closely built with pretty houses,
all of them surrounded by gardens and many by handsome grounds.
Equidistant from the end of Main street and from each other, stood,
in these cradle days, the two hotels of which the Capital could boast.
Montgomery Hall, of bitter memory—like the much-sung "Raven of
Zurich," for uncleanliness of nest and length of bill—had been the
resort of country merchants, horse and cattle-men; but now the
Solon of the hour dwelt therein, with the possible hero of many a
field.   The Exchange—of rather more pretentions and vastly more
comfort—was at that time in the hands of a northern firm, who
"could keep a hotel." The latter was political headquarters—the
President, the Cabinet and a swarm of the possible great residing
there.

Montgomery was Washington over again; only on a smaller scale,
and with the avidity and agility in pursuit of the spoils somewhat
enhanced by the freshness of scent.

"The President is at this house?" I queried of the ex-member of
Congress next me at dinner.   "But he does not appear, I suppose?"

"Oh, yes; he's waiting here till his house is made ready.   But he
doesn't have a private table; takes his meals like an everyday mortal,
at the ladies' ordinary."

He had scarcely spoken when Mr. Davis entered by a side door
and took his seat, with only an occasional stare of earnest, but not
disrespectful, curiosity from the more recent arrivals.

Even in the few weeks since I had seen him, there was a great change. He looked worn and thinner; and the set expression of the somewhat stern features gavè a grim hardness not natural to their lines. With scarcely a glance around, he returned the general salutations, sat down absently and was soon absorbed in conversation with General Cooper, who had recently resigned the adjutant-generalship of the United States army and accepted a similar post and a brigadier's commission from Mr. Davis.

An after-dinner interview with the President of the Confederacy, to present the "very important" documents from one of the martyrs pining for hanging at Washington, proved them only a prolix report of the inauguration. Mr. Davis soon threw them aside to hear the verbal account from us.

At this time the southern chief was fifty-two years old—tall, erect and spare by natural habit, but worn thin to almost emaciation by mental and physical toil. Almost constant sickness and unremitting excitement of the last few months had left their imprint on face as well as figure. The features had sharpened and the lines had deepened and hardened; the thin lips had a firmer compression and the lower jaw—always firm and prominent—was closer pressed to its fellow. Mr. Davis had lost the sight of one eye many months previous, though that member scarcely showed its imperfection; but in the other burned a deep, steady glow, showing the presence with him of thought that never slept. And in conversation he had the habit of listening with eyes shaded by the lids, then suddenly shooting forth at the speaker a gleam from the stone-gray pupil which seemed to penetrate his innermost mind.

Little ceremony, or form, hedged the incubating government; and perfect simplicity marked every detail about Mr. Davis. His office, for the moment, was one of the parlors of the hotel. Members of the Cabinet and high officials came in and out without ceremony, to ask questions and receive very brief replies; or for whispered consultation with the President's private secretary, whose desk was in the same room. Casual visitors were simply announced by an usher, and were received whenever business did not prevent. Mr. Davis' manner was unvarying in its quiet and courtesy, drawing out all that one had to tell, and indicating by brief answer, or criticism, that he had extracted the pith from it. At that moment he was the very idol of the people; the grand embodiment to them of their grand cause;

and they gave him their hands unquestioning, to applaud any move soever he might make. And equally unthinking as this popular manifestation of early hero-worship, was the clamor that later floated into Richmond on every wind, blaming the government—and especially its head—for every untoward detail of the facile descent to destruction.

A better acquaintance with the Confederate Capital impressed one still more with its likeness to Washington toward the end of the session ; but many features of that likeness were salient ones, which had marred and debased the older city. The government just organizing, endless places of profit, of trust, or of honor, were to be filled ; and for each and every one of them was a rush of jostling and almost rabid claimants. The skeleton of the regular army had just been articulated by Congress, but the bare bones would soon have swelled to more than Falstaffian proportions, had one in every twenty of the ardent aspirants been applied as matter and muscle. The first " gazette " was watched for with straining eyes, and naturally would follow aching hearts ; for disappointment here first sowed the dragon's teeth that were to spring into armed opponents of the unappreciative power.

The whole country was new. Everything was to be done—to be made; and who was so capable for both, in their own conceit, as that swarm of worn-out lobbymen and contractors who, having thoroughly exploited " the old concern," now gathered to gorge upon the new. And by the hundred flocked hither those unclean birds, blinking bleared eyes at any chance bit, whetting foul bills to peck at carrion from the departmental sewer. Busy and active at all hours, the lobby of the Exchange, when the crowd and the noise rose to the flood at night, smacked no little of pandemonium. Every knot of men had its grievance ; every flag in the pavement was a rostrum. Slowness of organization, the weakness of Congress, secession of the border states, personnel of the Cabinet and especially the latest army appointments—these and kindred subjects were canvassed with heat equaled only by ignorance. Men from every section of the South defended their own people in highest of keys and no little temper ; startling measures for public safety were offered and state secrets openly discussed in this curbstone congress ; while a rank growth of newspaper correspondents, with " the very latest," swelled the hum into a veritable Babel. And the most incomprehensible of all was the diametric opposition of men from the same neighborhood, in their views of the same subject. Often it would be a vital one, of doctrine, or of policy; and yet these neighbors would antagonize more bitterly than would men from opposite parts of the confederation.

Two ideas, however, seemed to pervade the entire South at this time which, though arrived at by most differing courses of reasoning, were discussed with complacent unanimity. One was that keystone dogma of secession, "Cotton is king;" the second, the belief that the war, should there be any, could not last over three months. The causes that led to the first belief were too numerous, if not too generally understood also, to be discussed here afresh; and upon them, men of all sections and of all creeds based firmest faith that, so soon as Europe understood that the separation was permanent and a regular government had been organized, the power of cotton alone would dictate immediate recognition. The man who ventured dissent from this idea, back it by what reason he might, was voted no better than an idiot; if, indeed, his rank disloyalty was not broadly hinted at.

But the second proposition was harder still to comprehend. There had already been a tacit declaration of war, and overt acts were of frequent commission. As the states seceded, they seized the arsenals, with arms and munitions; the shipping, mints and all United States property, only permitting the officers to go on their parole.

The North was already straining preparation to resent these insults offered to the power and to the flag of the Union. The people were of one race, embittered by long-existent rivalries and jealousies as strangers can never be embittered; and the balance of numbers, of capital and of machinery were on the other side. These causes, as they were without fresh incentives that needs must follow war, seemed sufficient to convince reasoning men that if the storm burst, it would be as enduring as it was terrific. I could realize that to men saturated with pride of section, who knew little of facts and feelings beyond their boundaries, the idea of peaceful separation, or of a short war, could be possible. But that the citizens of the world now congregated at Montgomery, who had sucked in her wisdom as mother's milk, should talk thus, puzzled those who paused to query if they really meant what they said.

Up to this time Montgomery had been scarcely more than a great inland village; dividing her local importance between being the capital of Alabama, the terminus of her principal railroad, and the practical head of navigation for her greatest river. The society had been composed of some planters, cotton men, a few capitalists, some noted professionals and a large class connected with railroad and steamboat interests. There had always been considerable culture, more hospitality and still more ambition, social and civic; but there was still much lacking of what the world expects of a city. Now, however, a future loomed up before the town, which had never before crossed the dreams of its oldest inhabitant. Her choice as the "cradle of the Confederacy," the sudden access of population therefrom, the probable erection of furnaces, factories and storehouses, with consequent disbursement of millions—all these gave the humdrum town a new value and importance, even to its humblest citizen. Already small merchants saw their ledgers grow in size, to the tune of added cash to fall jingling into enlarged tills. In fact, the choice of the Capital had turned a society, provincially content to run in accustomed grooves, quite topsy-turvy; and, perhaps for want of some other escape-valve under the new pressure, the townspeople grumbled consumedly.

Tiring of experimental camping-out in a hotel, a few gentlemen hired a house and established a "mess." They were all notables— General Cooper, General Meyers, Dr. DeLeon, Colonel Deas and others, the three first being adjutant-general, quartermaster-general and surgeon-general of the new army. A chief of department, or two and this writer, completed the occupants of "the Ranche," as it was early christened by "the colonel;" and its piazza soon became the favorite lounging-place in the evening of the better and brighter elements of the floating population. There was sure to be found the newest arrival, if he were worth knowing; the latest papers and news "from across;" and, as the blue smoke of the Havanas floated lazily out on the soft summer night, many a jovial laugh followed it and a not infrequent prediction of scenes to come almost prophetic. And of the lips that made these most are now silent forever—stilled in the reddest glow of battle, with the war-cry hot upon them.

So far the news that came in from all quarters continued cheering. A vague sense of doubt and suspense would creep in when one stopped to think, but nothing terrible, or shocking, had yet happened anywhere. Though the nation was going down to battle, its banners were flaunting gaily and its bands were playing anything but dirges.

CHAPTER III.

CONGRESS AND CABINET.

The proposition that, shown who writes the ballads of a country, one may tell who makes its laws, is far from reversible in many instances; and assuredly the lawmakers of the Confederacy looked little like poets.

When the councils of a country are assembled for work, it is but natural to look for a body of grave and reverend—if not most potent — seigniors. And especially, when a new government is forming from selected fragments of the old, might one expect a pure and simple structure, free from those faults and weaknesses which sowed the seeds of disintegration in the elder fabric.

It was too much the fashion to believe that the Confederacy— having sprung full-grown from foam of the angry sea of politics— was full-armed as well. A revolution, unprecedented in the world's history, had already been achieved. A strongly cemented and firmly seated government had been disrupted; and a new one, built from the dissevered fragments, had been erected almost under the shadow of its Capitol. And no drop of blood had been spilled! Six millions of people had uprisen and, by a simple declaration of will, had in a few short weeks undone the work of near a century. Without arms in their hands; without a keel in their waters; without a dollar in their treasury, they arrayed themselves against the mother government with the serious purpose of not only asserting, but maintaining, their independence of it.

So far, all had been, accomplished without violence. But, whatever the simpler masses might expect, the initiated politician could scarce have believed that the older government would meekly submit to "Let the erring sisters go in peace." Hence, one might justly have looked to see the executive council of the new nation—to whom had been intrusted its safety and its hopes—with every thought bent, every nerve strained to the one vital point—preparation! One could only have expected measures simple as energetic; laws clear, concise and comprehensive; care only for the arming, organizing and maintenance of the people.

Blessed are they who expect nothing! One glance at the "Congress of the Confederate States of America," as it sat in the Capitol at Montgomery, told the whole story of its organization and of its future usefulness.

The states went out of the union, separately and at different periods, by the action of conventions. These were naturally composed of men who had long been prominently before the people, urging the measures of secession. As a matter of course, the old political workers of each section, by fair means and foul, were enabled to secure election to these conventions; and, once there, they so fevered and worked upon the public mind, amid rapidly succeeding events, that its after-thought could neither be reasonable nor deliberate. The act of secession once consummated, the state connected itself with the Confederacy and representatives had to be sent to Montgomery. Small wonder that the men most prominent in the secession conventions should secure their own election, as little regard to fitness as ability being had by the excited electors.

The House of Representatives at Montgomery looked like the Washington Congress, viewed through a reversed opera-glass. The same want of dignity and serious work; the same position of ease, with feet on desk and hat on head; the same buzzing talk on indifferent subjects; often the very same men in the lobbies—taking dry smokes from unlit cigars; all these elements were there in duplicate, if somewhat smaller and more concentrated. No point in Montgomery was remote enough—no assemblage dignified enough—to escape the swoop of the lobby vulture. His beak was as sharp and his unclean talons as strong as those of the traditional bird, which had blinked and battened so long on the eaves of the Washington edifice. When "the old concern" had been dismembered, limbs had been dragged whole to aid in the construction of the new giant; and scenting these from afar, he hastened hither fierce for his fresh banquet.

Glancing down from the gallery of the House, many were the familiar faces peering over the desks; and, even where one did not know the individual, it was easy to recognize the politician by trade among the rosy and uncomfortable novices. It was constant food for wonderment to thoughtful men, that the South had, in most cases, chosen party hacks to legislate for and to lead her in this great crisis, rather than transfused younger blood and steadier nerves into her councils; rather than grafted new minds upon the as yet healthy body. The revolution was popularly accepted as the result of corruptions and aggressions which these very men had been utterly helpless to correct, or to prevent; even had they not been able actors in them. Yet, worn-out politicians—who had years before been " promoted from servants to sovereigns and had taken back seats "—floated high upon the present surge. Men hot from Washington, reeking with the wiles of the old House and with their unblushing buncombe fresh upon them, took the lead in every movement; and the rank old Washington leaven threatened to permeate every pore of the new government.

It is small wonder that the measures of such a congress, when not vacillating, were weak. If the time demanded anything, that demand was the promptest organization of an army, with an immediate basis of foreign credit, to arm, equip and clothe it. Next to this was the urgent need for a simple and readily managed machinery in the different departments of the government.

Neither of these desiderata could be secured by their few earnest and capable advocates, who thrust them forward over and over again, only to be pushed aside by the sensation element with which the popular will of the new nation—or the want of it—had diluted her councils. There were windy dissertations on the color of the flag, or on the establishment of a patent office; and members made long speeches, bearing on no special point, but that most special one of their own re-election. There were bitter denunciations of " the old wreck ; " violent diatribes on the " gridiron " flag; with many an eloquent and manly declaration of the feelings and the attitude of the South. But these were not the bitter need. Declarations sufficient had already been made; and the masses—having made them, and being ready and willing to maintain them—stood with their hands in their pockets, open-mouthed, eager, but inactive. They were waiting for some organization, for some systematized preparation for the struggle even they felt to be surely coming. Not one in three of the congressmen dared look the real issue directly in the face; and these were powerless to accomplish anything practical. But their constant pressure finally forced from the reluctant legislature a few first steps toward reduction of the chaos.

The Government was to consist, after the President, of a vice-President and a secretary for each of the departments of State, War, Navy, Treasury, Post-Office and Justice ; the latter being a combination of the responsibilities of the Interior Department and the Attorney-General's office.

Alexander H. Stephens, of Georgia, had been elevated to the vice-Presidency, as reconciling the oppositions of "original secession" and "anti secession." He had long been a prominent politician ; was thoroughly acquainted with all the points of public life; and was, at this time, quite popular with people of all sections, being generally regarded as a man of exceptional capacity and great independence.

The portfolio of State was in the hands of another Georgian, Robert Toombs. In the present posture of affairs, little could be expected from it, as until the nations of Europe should recognize the South, she could have no foreign policy. The honorable secretary himself seemed fully to realize how little onerous was his position. One of the ten thousand applicants for any and every position approached him for a place in his department and exhibited his letters of recommendation.

"Perfectly useless, sir!" responded Mr. Toombs with a thunderous oath. Let us whisper that the honorable secretary was a profound swearer.

"But, sir," persisted the place hunter, "if you will only look at this letter from Mr. ———, I think you can find something for me."

"Can you get in here, sir?" roared the secretary fiercely, taking off his hat and pointing into it—with a volley of sonorous oaths— "That's the Department of State, sir!"

The Post-Office and Department of Justice were, as yet, about as useful as the State Department; but to the War Office, every eye was turned, and the popular verdict seemed to be that the choice there was not the right man in the right place. Mr. Leroy Pope Walker, to whom its administration was intrusted, was scarcely known beyond the borders of his own state; but those who did know him prophesied that he would early stagger under the heavy responsibility that would necessarily fall upon him in event of war. Many averred that he was only a man of straw to whom Mr. Davis

3

had offered the portfolio, simply that he might exercise his own well-known love for military affairs and be himself the *de facto* Secretary of War.

The selection of Mr. Mallory, of Florida, for the Navy Department, was more popular and was, as yet, generally considered a good one. His long experience as chairman of the committee on naval affairs, in the United States Senate, and his reputation for clearness of reasoning and firmness of purpose, made him acceptable to the majority of politicians and people. Of Mr. Reagan the people knew little; but their fate was not in his hands, and just now they were content to wait for their letters.

The Treasury Department was justly supposed to be the key to national success. It was at least the twin, in importance, with the War Office. Mr. Memminger, of South Carolina, was a self-made man, who had managed the finances of his state and had made reputation for some financiering ability and much common sense. He had, moreover, the advantage of being a new man; and the critics were willing to give him the benefit of common law, until he should prove himself guilty. Still the finance of the country was so vital, and came home so nearly to every man in it, that perhaps a deeper anxiety was felt about its management than that of any other branch.

The Attorney-General, or chief of the Department of Justice, had a reputation as wide as the continent—and as far as mental ability and legal knowledge went, there could be no question among the growlers as to his perfect qualifications for the position. Mr. Judah P. Benjamin was not only the successful politician, who had risen from obscurity to become the leader of his party in the Senate, and its exponent of the constitutional questions involved in its action; but he was, also, the first lawyer at the bar of the Supreme Court and was known as a ripe and cultivated scholar. So the people who shook their heads at him—and they were neither few nor far between—did it on other grounds than that of incapacity.

This was the popular view of that day at the new Capital. The country at large had but little means of knowing the real stuff of which the Cabinet was made. It is true, four of the six were old and thoroughly broken party horses, who had for years cantered around the Washington arena, till the scent of its sawdust was dear to their nostrils. But the people knew little of them individually and took their tone from the politicians of the past. So—as it is a known fact that politicians are never satisfied—the Cabinet and Congress, as tried in the hotel alembic, were not found pure gold.

So the country grumbled. The newspapers snarled, criticised and asserted, with some show of truth, that things were at a dead standstill, and that nothing practical had been accomplished.

Such was the aspect of affairs at Montgomery, when on the 10th of April, Governor Pickens, of South Carolina, telegraphed that the Government at Washington had notified him of its intention to supply Fort Sumter—"Peaceably if we can; forcibly if we must."

Bulletins were posted before the Exchange, the newspaper office and the "Government House;" and for two days there was intense suspense as to what course the South would pursue. Then the news flashed over the wires that, on the morning of the 12th of April, Beauregard had opened the ball in earnest, by commencing the bombardment of Fort Sumter. This caused the excitement to go up to fever heat; and the echo of that first gun made every heart in the breadth of the land bound with quickened throb. Business was suspended, all the stores in the town were closed, while crowds at the hotels and in the streets became larger and more anxious as the day wore on. Various and strange were the speculations as to the issue of the fight and its consequences; but the conviction came, like a thunder clap upon the most skeptical, that there was to be war after all!

CHAPTER IV.

"THE AWAKENING OF THE LION."

When tidings came of the fall of Fort Sumter, there was wild rejoicing throughout the South and it culminated at her Capital. All the great, and many of the little men of the Government were serenaded by bands of the most patriotic musical persuasion. Bonfires blazed in every street and, by their red glare, crowds met and exchanged congratulations, amid the wildest enthusiasm; while the beverage dear to the cis-Atlantic heart was poured out in libations wonderful to see!

One-half of the country thought that this victory of a few untrained gunners would prevent further progress of the war; that the Federal Government, seeing how determined was the stand the South had taken—how ready she was to defend her principles—would recede and grant the concessions demanded. The other half felt that, however fair an augury for the future the great and bloodless victory might be—and it will be recollected that the only loss was the death of a few United States soldiers, in the salute Beauregard permitted them to give their flag—the real tug of the struggle was not yet commenced; that the whole power of a government, never yet overstrained, or even fully tested, would be hurled on the new confederation, to crush ere it could concentrate its strength.

The Confederate Government was on the side of this opinion; and now, for the first time, preparations for war began in earnest. Though the people of Montgomery still murmured, as they had done from the beginning, at the influx of corrupting social influences from Sodom on the Potomac, and still held the hordes of unintroduced strangers aloof from their firesides, they continued most strenuous exertions and made most selfless sacrifices to serve the beloved cause. Storehouses were freely offered for the public use; and merchants moved from their places of business, on shortest notice, to turn them over to the Government.

A great, red brick pile, originally built for warehouses and counting-rooms, had early been converted into public offices and popularly named the "Government House." Here the departments were all crowded together; and now, under the pressure of close necessity, the War office was organized into bureaux, at the heads of which were placed the most competent officers of the old service at the disposal of the Executive. Bureaux of Adjutant-General, Ordnance, Engineers and Medicine were soon put in as perfect a state as the condition of the South allowed; and their respective chiefs were tireless in endeavor to collect the very best assistants and material, in their various branches, from every quarter.

Commissioners were sent to all the states that had not already joined the Confederacy, to urge them to speedy action; and the dispatches they sent back were so full of cheer, that day after day a salute of cannon from the street in front of the Government House announced to the roused Montgomerans that another ally had enlisted under the flag; or, that a fresh levy of troops, from some unexpected quarter, had been voted to the cause.

Officers, carefully selected from those who left the United States Army, or who had received military education elsewhere, were promptly sent to all points in the South, to urge and hasten the organization of troops; to forward those already raised to points where they might be most needed; and to establish recruiting stations and camps of instruction. The captured arsenals were put in working order, new ones were started, depots for clothes, ordnance and medicines were prepared; and from one boundary of the Confederacy to the other, the hum of preparation told that the leaders of the nation had at last awakened to its real demands.

The mass of the people—who, from the first, had been willing and anxious, but doubtful what to do—now sprang to their places; moneyed men made large and generous donations of cash; the banks offered loans of any amount, on most liberal terms; planters from every section made proffers of provisions and stock, in any quantities needed; and the managers of all the railroads in the South held a convention at Montgomery and proffered the use of their roads to the Government; volunteering to charge only half-rates, and to receive payment in the bonds of the Confederate States.

Especially did the women go heart and soul into the work; urging the laggards, encouraging the zealous, and laboring with sacrificial zeal upon rough uniforms for the most unprepared of the new troops.

The best blood of the South went cheerfully into the ranks, as the post of honor; and the new regiments endeavored to be perfectly impartial in selecting the best men for their officers, irrespective of any other claim. That they failed signally in their object was the fault, not of their intention, but of human nature in many cases—of circumstance in all.

At this time the plan of filling up the regular army was abandoned. Officers coming from the United States service were, by law, entitled to at least as high rank in it as they had there held; but volunteers were asked for and accepted by companies, or regiments, with the privilege of choosing their own leaders; and these regulars were only given commands where vacancies, or the exigencies of the service, seemed to demand it imperatively.

Every hour of the day could be heard the tap of the drum, as the new troops from depot, or steamer, marched through the town to their camps in the suburbs; or as the better drilled volunteer companies passed through to Pensacola, where Brigadier-General Braxton Bragg already had a considerable force. And toward that point every eye was strained as the next great theater of action.

All day long the churches were open, and crowds of ladies, from town and country, assembled in them and sewed on the tough, ungainly pants and jackets; while their negro maids, collected on the porches, or under the trees, worked as steadily as their mistresses, many a ringing guffaw and not unmusical song rising above them.

Great numbers of the interested and the curious visited the camps, carrying substantial tokens of sympathy for the cause and its defenders in the shape of hams, loaves and sometimes bottles. Nor was such testimony often irrelevant; for as yet the quartermaster and commissary—those much-erring and more-cursed adjuncts to all armies—were not fully aware of what they were to do, or how to do it, even with the means therefor provided. But the South was at last awake! And again the popular voice averred that it was not Congress, or Cabinet; that the President alone was the motive power; that his strong hand had grasped the chaos and reduced it to something like order. Rapidly one needful and pointed law after another emanated from Congress; and what had been a confused mass of weak resolves assumed shape as clear and legible statutes. It was generally said that Mr. Davis had reduced Congress to a pliable texture that his iron fingers could twist at will into any form they pleased. Newspaper correspondents wrote strange stories of the length to which that dignified body allowed him to carry his prerogative. They declared that frequently, the framing of a bill not suiting him, it was simply returned by his private secretary, with verbal instructions as to emendations and corrections, which were obediently carried out.

Some even went to the length of asserting that, before any bill of importance was framed, a rough draft was sent down from the President's office and simply put into form and voted a law by the ductile legislators.

However much of this one may allow for exaggeration of "our correspondent," it is certain that Mr. Davis was the heart and brains of the government; and his popularity with the people was, at this time, unbounded. They were perfectly content to think that the government was in the hollow of his hand; and pronounced any of his measures good before they were tried. His energy, too, was untiring; and it was wonderful to look on the frail body and believe that it endured the terrible physical and mental strain he imposed upon it.

At this time the President and his family, having left their temporary quarters at the hotel, were living at a plain mansion provided for them, but a few steps from the Government House. In the latter building were the executive office and the Cabinet room, connected by an always open door; and in one or the other of these Mr. Davis spent some fifteen hours out of every twenty-four. Here he received the thousands of visitors whom curiosity, or business, brought; consulted with his secretaries, revised bills, or framed new projects for strengthening the defenses of the open and wide frontier. It was said that he managed the War Department, in all its various details, in addition to other manifold labors; finding time not only to give it a general supervision, but to go into all the minutiæ of the working of its bureaux, the choice of all its officers, or agents, and the very disbursement of its appropriations.

His habits were as simple as laborious. He rose early, worked at home until breakfast, then to a long and wearing day at the Government House.   Often, long after midnight, the red glow from his office lamp, shining over the mock-orange hedge in front of his dwelling, told of unremitting strain.   Thus early in the drama, Mr. Benjamin had become one of its leading actors; having more real weight and influence with Mr. Davis than any, or all, of his other advisers. The President did not believe there was "safety in a multitude of counsellors;" and he certainly chose the subtlest, if not the safest, head of the half-dozen to aid him.   With Mr. Mallory, too, he seemed on very friendly and confidential terms.   These two he met as friends and advisers ; but beside them, the Cabinet—as such—had scarcely a practical existence.   Mr. Davis very naturally considered that the War Department had become the government, and he managed it accordingly.   The secretaries were, of course, useful to arrange matters formally in their respective branches; but they had scarcely higher duties left them than those of their clerks; while Congress remained a formal body to pass bills and ratify acts, the inspiration for which it derived from the clearest and coolest brain in the South.

The crisis had called in plain terms that it was time for the leading spirit of the revolution to take its management; and he had risen to the occasion and faced the responsibilities, before which the chosen of the new nation had hitherto cowered.

And naturally, under the iron hand, things began to work more smoothly than they had under the King-Log reign of a few weeks previous; and the country felt the change from the Potomac to the Gulf.   True, politicians still grumbled, but less loudly ; for even they found something to do, where everybody began to be busy.   The great crowd that at first collected had thinned greatly, from assignments to duty in divers quarters ; and that portion of it left in Montgomery began to settle into a regular routine.

The ladies of the executive mansion held occasional receptions, after the Washington custom, at which were collected the most brilliant, the most gallant and most honored of the South.   But the citizens still held aloof from general connection with the alien crowd. They could not get rid of their idea that Sodom had come to be imposed on them; and to their prejudiced nostrils there was an odor of sulphur in everything that savored of Washington society.   And yet, while they grumbled—these older people of Montgomery—they wrought, heart and soul for the cause; yielded their warerooms for government use, contributed freely in money and stores, let their wives and daughters work on the soldiers' clothing like seamstresses, and put their first-born into the ranks, musket on shoulder.

Early on the morning of the 18th of April, a salute of seven guns rang out from the street before the public building. The telegraph had brought the most welcome news that, on the evening before, Virginia had passed the ordinance of secession.

Wild was the rejoicing at the southern Capital that day!

The Old Dominion had long and sedately debated the question; had carefully considered the principles involved and canvassed the pros and cons, heedless alike of jeers from without and hot-headed counsels within her borders.

She had trembled long in the balance so tenderly adjusted, that the straining eyes of the South could form no notion how it would lean; but now she turned deliberately and poured the vast wealth of her influence, of her mineral stores and her stalwart and chivalric sons into the lap of the Confederacy.

The victory of the week before paled before this; and men looked at each other with a hope in their eyes that spoke more than the braying of a thousand bands.

And the triumph was a double one; for great as was the accession to the South in boundary, in men and means, greater far was the blow to the Union, when its eldest and most honored daughter divorced herself from the parent hearth and told the world, that looked on with deep suspense, that the cause of her sisters must in future be her own!

CHAPTER V.

A SOUTHERN RIVER BOAT RACE.

"Hurry, my boy! Pack up your traps and get ready for the boat," cried Styles Staple, bursting into my room in his usual sudden fashion the day we got the news from Virginia. "All's fixed. The colonel, you and I are to have a trip of a week, stop at Mobile and then run down t' Orleans!"

So by sundown we were quietly smoking our cigars on the topmost deck of the "Southern Republic."

Nowhere in the world can be found just such boats as those that navigate our south-western rivers. Great three or four-storied constructions, built upon mere flats of the lightest possible draught, with length and breadth of beam sufficient to allow storage room for an immense number of cotton bales and barrels upon the lowest deck; with their furnaces, boilers and machinery all above the water line, they look like up-country hotels that, having got out of their element, contemplate a down-trip for the benefit of their health—or *cuisine.*

The "Southern Republic" was a new boat, built after the most approved plan, on a scale of size and magnificence unequaled on the river. Sitting flat and square upon the water, her four decks rising one above the other—with the thousand doors and windows of her state-rooms seeming to peer like eyes over the balconies around them—she seemed more like some fabled marine monster than a vessel meant for speed and comfort. Her length was immense, and her draught necessarily very light—not four feet when full loaded; for the Alabama is subject to many vagaries and what was a clear channel yesterday may be only a two-foot shoal to-day. Of course, with solidity and strength sacrificed to this extreme lightness, when the powerful engines are put to any strain, the high, thin fabric thrills from stem to stern with their every puff, like a huge card-house.

The speed of a first-class high-pressure boat is very great in the longer "reaches;" but, the Alabama is a most tortuous stream. Often you stand by the pilot-house and see, right under the quarter, a gleaming streak of water across a neck of land over which you might toss a stone; and yet you may steam on miles around the point that juts ahead, before you get into it.

The "Southern Republic," from her immense size and unusually handsome equipment, was a novelty even to the river people; and each afternoon of her starting, crowds came aboard to bid farewell to friends and roam over the vessel, or collected on the bluffs above to see her swing out to the shrill notes of her "calliope," the best and least discordant on the river. A few evenings before we left, a large party had collected in honor of General Earl Van Dorn. He had recently resigned; and the commission as colonel of the only regiment of regular cavalry in the Confederacy was tendered him. Now, on the eve of departure for his well-known expedition to Texas— then considered a momentous and desperate one—numbers of fair women thronged the bluffs to catch a glimpse of the hero of the hour, while friends gathered round to grasp the hand, than which no firmer ever drew blade!

Few men had started in the war with brighter auspices and more ardent well-wishings—none could have had a sadder ending! I remember well the last sight I ever had of his neat but powerfully-knit figure, as he stood with one hand resting on the rail of the upper deck and the other raising his broad sombrero over the clear, sharp features, with the peaked moustache and beard of the *cuirassier*. A brilliant and handsome staff surrounded him; from the bluffs, the ladies waved their handkerchiefs and the men their hats; the wild notes of the calliope echoed back the "Marseillaise;" but in memory's photograph of the scene, his figure alone—the proud swell of the thin nostril and the deep, smothered flame in the cold gray eye— stands out clear and sharp.

We are aboard the "Southern Republic;" the last bell has sounded, the last belated trunk has been trundled over the plank; and we are off, the calliope screaming "Dixie" like ten thousand devils, the crowds on the bank waving us *bon voyage!*

The main saloon of the boat was a spacious apartment, a hundred feet long by thirty in breadth, gorgeously decorated with modern paint and brilliantly lighted; the galleries leading to the state-rooms rising tier upon tier entirely around it, while above, a skylight of tinted glass shed a soft, warm light.

There were offices, card-rooms, bar-rooms aboard all these boats; and as the down-trip occupies from forty-eight to one hundred hours—according to the stage of the river and the luck in running aground, a performance to be expected once in each trip—we become quite a mutual amusement community by the time it is over.

This trip the boat was very crowded, and at supper the effect of the line of small tables, filled with officers in uniform, ladies tastefully dressed and a sprinkling of homespun coats—all reflected in the long mirror—was very bright and gay. After meals, there is generally a promenade on the upper deck, where people talk, smoke, inspect each other and flirt. They then adjourn to state-room, saloon or card-room, to lounge or read to kill time; for the Alabama is anything but a picturesque stream, with its low, marshy banks only varied by occasional "cotton slides" and "negro quarters."

This night was splendidly clear, the moon bright as day, and Staple and I with our cigars staid on deck to scrape acquaintance with the pilot and the small, seedy Frenchman who officiated at the calliope. He was an original in his way—"the Professor"—his head like a bullet, garnished with hair of the most wiry blackness, cut close as the scissors could hold it, looking like the most uncompromising porcupine. Of course, he was a political refugee.

"*Dixie!* *Aire nationale! pas bonne chose!*" he exclaimed, seating himself at his instrument and twirling a huge moustache. "*Voila le Marseillaise!* Zat make hymn national for you!" And he made the whistle roar and shriek in a way to have sent the red caps into the air a hundred miles away.

"Grand! Splendid!" roared Styles above the steam. "Why, Professor, you're a genius. Come and take some brandy."

The professor banged the lid of his instrument, led the way instanter down to our state-room; and, once there, did take something; then something else and, finally, something more, till he got very thick-tongued and enthusiastic.

"Grand aire of ze Liberte!" he cried at last, mounting again to his perch by the smoke-stack. "Song compose by me for one grand man—ze Van Dorn. I make zees—me, myself—and dedicate to heem!" And he banged at the keys till he tortured the steam into the Liberty duet, from "*Puritani.*"

"How you fine zat, eh? Zat makes ze hymn for ze Souse. Me,

I am républicain! *Voila!* I wear ze moustache of ze *revolutionaire*—my hairs cut themselves *en mécontent!* Were zere colere more red as red, I should be zat!"

The professor was so struck by the brilliancy of this idea, that he played the air again, until it rang like a phantom chorus over the still plantations. At last, overcome by emotion and brandy, he slid from the stool and sat at the foot of the smoke-stack, muttering:

"Zat is ze hymn—*hic*—dedicate to ze general and to ze—*hic*—countree!" Then he slept the sleep of the just conscience.

"Thar's the 'Senator,' and she's gainin' on us," said the pilot, as we walked forward, pointing to a thin column of smoke rising over the trees just abreast of us.

"How far astern?"

"A matter of two mile round that pint."

"Splendid night for a race," muttered Styles. "Will she overtake us, Cap'n?"

"Wail, maibee!" replied the old river dog, while the most professional grin shot over his hard-wooden features. "Specially ef I ease up this 'ar ole gal."

"Ha! Now we'll have it. We won't turn in just now," chuckled Styles, banging me in the back.

Almost imperceptibly our speed slackens, the thin dark column creeps nearer round the trees on the point in our wake; at last the steamer bursts into sight, not a pistol shot astern.

There is a sharp click of our pilot's bell, a gasping throb, as if our boat took a deep, long breath; and just as the "Senator" makes our wheel we dash ahead again, with every stroke of the piston threatening to rack our frail fabric into shreds.

The river here is pretty wide and the channel deep and clear. The "Senator" follows in gallant style, now gaining our quarter, now a boat's length astern—both engines roaring and snorting like angry hippopotami; both vessels rocking and straining till they seem to paw their way through the churned water.

Talk of horse-racing and *rouge-et-noir!* But there is no excitement that can approach boat-racing on a southern river! One by one people pop up the ladders and throng the rails. First come the unemployed deck-hands, then a stray gentleman or two, and finally ladies and children, till the rail is full and every eye is anxiously strained to the opposite boat.

She holds her own wondrous well, considering the reputation of ours. At each burst, when she seems to gain on us, the crowd hold their breath; as she drops off again there is a deep-drawn, gasping sign of relief, like wind in the pines. Even the colonel has roused himself from dreams of turtle at the St. Charles, and red fish at Pensacola; coming on deck in a shooting jacket and glengary cap, that make him look like a jaunty *Fosco.* He leans over the stern rail, smoking his cabana in long, easy whiffs as we gain a length; sending out short, angry puffs at the "Senator" as she creeps up on us.

Foot by foot, we gain steadily until the gap is widened to three or four boat-lengths, though the "Senator" piles her fires till the shores behind her glow from their reflection; and her decks—now black with anxious lookers-on—send up cheer after cheer, as she snorts defiantly after us.

Suddenly the bank seems to spring up right under our port bow! We have cut it too close! Two sharp, vicious clicks of the bell; our helm goes hard down and the engines stop with a sullen jar, as I catch a hissing curse through the set teeth of the pilot.

A yell of wild triumph rises from the rival's deck. On she comes in gallant style, shutting the gap and passing us like a race-horse, before we can swing into the channel and recover headway. It is a splendid sight as the noble boat passes us; her black bulk standing out in the clear moonlight against the dim, gray banks like a living monster; her great chimneys snorting out volumes of massive black smoke that trail out level behind her, from the great speed. Her side toward us is crowded with men, women and children; hats, handkerchiefs and hands are swung madly about to aid the effort of the hundred voices.

Close down to the water's edge—scarce above the line of foam she cuts—her lower deck lies black and undefined in the shadow of the great mass above it. Suddenly it lights up with a lurid flash, as the furnace-doors swing wide open; and in the hot glare the negro stokers—their stalwart forms jetty black, naked to the waist and streaming with exertion that makes the muscles strain out in great cords— show like the distorted imps of some pictured inferno. They, too, have imbibed the excitement. With every gesture of anxious haste and eyeballs starting from their dusky heads, some plunge the long rakes into the red mouths of the furnace, twisting and turning the crackling mass with terrific strength ; others hurl in huge logs of resinous pine, already heated by contact till they burn like pitch. Then the great doors bang to; the *Yo ! Ho !* of the negroes dies away and the whole hull is blacker from the contrast; while the "Senator," puffing denser clouds than ever, swings round the point a hundred yards ahead!

There is dead silence on our boat—silence so deep that the rough whisper of the pilot to the knot around him is heard the whole length of her deck : " Damnation ! but I'll overstep her yit, or——bust !"

" Good, old man !" responds Styles—" Let her out and I'll stand the wine !"

Then the old colonel walks to the wheel; his face purple, his glengary pushed back on his head, his cigar glowing like the " red eye of battle," as he puffs angry wheezes of smoke through his nos-trils.

" Damned hard ! sir—hard ! Egad ! I'd burn the last ham in the locker to overtake her !"—and he hurls the glowing stump after the " Senator," as the Spartan youth hurled their shields into the thick of the battle ere rushing to reclaim them.

On we speed, till the trees on the bank seem to fly back past us ; and round the point to see the " Senator," just turning another curve !

On still, faster than ever, with every glass on board jingling in its frame ; every joint and timber trembling, as though with a congestive chill !

Still the black demons below ply their fires with the fattest logs, and even a few barrels of rosin are slyly slipped in ; the smoke behind us stretched straight and flat from the smoke-stack.

Now we enter a straight, narrow reach with the chase just before us. Faster—faster we go till the boat fairly rocks and swings from side to side, half lifted with every throb of the engine. Closer and closer we creep—harder and harder thump the cylinders—until at last we close ; our bow just lapping her stern ! So we run a few yards.

Little by little—so little that we test it by counting her windows— we reach her wheel—pass it—lock her bow, and run nose and nose for a hundred feet !

The stillness of death is upon both boats; not a sound but the creak and shudder as they struggle on. Suddenly the hard voice of our old pilot crashes through it like a broadaxe:

"Good-bye, Sen'tor! I'll send yer a tug!"—and he gives his bell a merry click.

Our huge boat gives one shuddering throb that racks her from end to end—one plunge—and then she settles into a steady rush and forges rapidly and evenly ahead. Wider and wider grows the gap; and we wind out of sight with the beaten boat five hundred yards behind us.

The cigar I take from my mouth, to make way for the deep, long sigh, is chewed to perfect pulp. A wild, pent-up yell of half-savage triumph goes up from the crowded deck; such as is heard nowhere besides, save where the captured work rewards the bloody and oft-repeated charge. Cheer after cheer follows; and, as we approach the thin column of smoke curling over the trees between us, Styles bestrides the prostrate form of the still sleeping professor and makes the calliope yell and shriek that classic ditty, "Old Gray Horse, come out of the Wilderness!" at the invisible rival.

I doubt if heartier toast was ever drunk than that the colonel gave the group around the wheel-house, when Styles "stood" the wine plighted the pilot. The veteran was beaming, the glengary sat jauntily on one side; and his voice actually gurgled as he said:.

"Egad! I'd miss my dinner for a week for this! Gentlemen, a toast! Here's to the old boat! God bless her —— *soul!*"

CHAPTER VI.

BOAT LIFE AFLOAT AND AGROUND.

The day after the race our trio exhausted all usual resources of boat life. We lounged in the saloon and saw the young ladies manage their beaux and the old ones their children; dropped into the card-rooms and watched the innocent games—some heavy ones of "draw poker" with a "bale better;" some light ones of "all fours," with only an occasional old sinner deep in chess, or solitaire. For cards, conversation, tobacco, yarns and the bar make up boat life; it being rare, indeed, that the *ennui* is attacked from the barricade of a book. Then we roamed below and saw the negroes—our demons of the night before, much modified by sunlight—tend the fires and load cotton. A splendidly developed race are those Africans of the river boats, with shiny, black skins, through which the corded and tense muscles seem to be bursting, even in repose. Their only dress, as a general thing, is a pair of loose pantaloons, to which the more elegant add a fancy colored bandanna knotted about the head, with its wing-like ends flying in the wind; but shirts are a rarity in working hours and their absence shows a breadth of shoulder and depth of chest remarkable, when contrasted with the length and lank power in the nether limbs. They are a perfectly careless and jovial race, with wants confined to the only luxuries they know—plenty to eat, a short pipe and a plug of "nigger-head," with occasional drinks, of any kind and quantity that fall to their lot. Given these, they are as contented as princes; and their great eyes roll like white saucers and their splendid teeth flash in constant merriment.

As we got further down the river, the flats became less frequent and high, steep bluffs took their place; and at every landing along these we laid-by for cotton and took in considerable quantities of "the king."

Some of the bluffs were from sixty to eighty feet in height; and down these, the cotton came on slides. These, in most cases, were

4

at an angle of forty-five degrees, or less; strongly constructed of heavy beams, cross-tied together and firmly pegged into the hard bluff-clay. A small, solid platform at the bottom completed the slide.

Scarcely would the plank be run out when the heavy bales came bounding down the slide, gaining momentum at every yard of descent, till at the bottom they had the velocity of a cannon-ball. The dexterity and strength of the negroes were here wonderfully displayed.

Standing at the edge of the boat—or at the foot of the slide, as the conformation of the landing indicated—heavy cotton-hook in hand, they watch the descending bale, as it bounds fiercely toward them; and just at the right moment two men, with infinite dexterity of hand and certainty of eye, strike their hooks firmly into the bagging—holding on to the plunging mass and going with it halfway across the boat. Full in front of it a third stands, like a *matador* ready for the blow; and striking his hook deep in the end, by a sudden and simultaneous twist the three stand the bale upon end. Once stopped, two or three more jerks of the hooks and it is neatly stowed away alongside, or on top of, its fellows.

One constantly sees huge bales of from five to six hundred pounds bound down a slide eighty feet high—scarcely touching the rail more than three times in their steep descent—looking almost round from the rapidity of their motion. Yet two negroes drive their hooks into, and spin along with them; visibly checking their speed, till the third one "heads up" and stops them still, in half a boat's width.

Sometimes a hook slips, the bagging gives, or the footing yields, when the mixed mass of man and bale rolls across the boat and goes under together. But frightful as it looks to unaccustomed eyes, a more serious accident than a ducking seldom occurs; and at that, the banks resound with the yells of laughter Sambo sends after his brother-in-water.

"We've pretty thoroughly done the boat," said Styles, about midday. "Let's go up to the professor's den and see if his head aches from 'ze Van Dorn.' "

So up we mounted, passing on the way the faro bank, that advertises its neighborhood by most musical jingling of chips and half dollars.

"Hello, Spring Chicken," cried Styles, to a youth in a blue sack with shoulder straps, who sat at the door of a state-room near by. "Look out for the tiger! I hear him about."

"No danger, me boy," responded the youth. "I'm too old a stager for that."

"Aye, aye! we seen that before," put in his companion, a buttoned middie of eighteen, innocent of beard. "A confounded pigeon came by here just now, jingling his halves and pretending he'd won 'em. Wasting time! Wasn't he, Styles? *We're* too old birds to be caught with chaff."

"Look alive, my hearty," answered Staple, "You're pretty near the beast, and mamma doesn't know you're out." With which paternal admonition we ascended.

The professor was still in a deep sleep; having been transferred by the aid of a deck hand, or two, to his bower. This was a box of a state-room six feet by nine, in which was a most dilapidated double-bass, a violin case and a French horn. Over the berth, a cracked guitar hung by a greasy blue ribbon. Staple waked him without ceremony—ordered Congress water, pulled out the instruments; and soon we were in "a concord of sweet sounds," the like of which the mermaids of the Alabama had not heard before.

Suddenly, in the midst of a roaring chorus, there was a short, heavy jar that sent us pellmell across the state-room; then a series of grinding jolts; and, amid the yelling of orders, jangling of bells and backing of the wheels, the boat swung slowly round by the bows. We were hard and fast aground!

Of all the unpleasant episodes of river travel, the worst by far is to be grounded in the daytime. The dreary monotony of bank and stream as you glide by increases ten-fold when lying, hour after hour, with nothing to do but gaze at it. Under this trial the jolliest faces grow long and dismal; quiet men become dreadfully blue and the saturnine look actually suicidal. Even the negro hands talk under their breath, and the broad *Yah! Yah!* comes less frequently from below decks.

Here we lay, two miles above Selma—hard and fast, with engines and anchors equally useless to move us a foot—until midnight. About sundown an up-boat passed just across our bows. Little is the sympathy a grounded boat gets unless actually in danger. Every

soul aboard of her, from captain to cook's boy, seemed to think us
fair game, and chaff of all kinds was hailed from her decks.   But she
threw us a Selma paper of that evening, and a hundred eager hands
were stretched over the side to catch it.

It fell at the feet of a slight, wiry man of about fifty, with twink-
ling gray eyes, prominent features and fierce gray moustache.   There
was something in his manner that kept the more ardent ones from
plucking it out of his fingers, as he stooped quietly to pick it up ; but
few on board ever knew that their quiet fellow-passenger was the
most widely known "rebel of them all."

Many a man has read, with quickening breath, of the bold deeds
of Admiral Raphael Semmes ; and some have traced his blazing track
to the, perhaps, Quixotic joust that ended his wild sea-kingship, never
recalling that impassive fellow-passenger.   Yet it was he who, seated
on the rail of the " Southern Republic," read to the crowd that
evening.

"What's the Washington news ? "—"Anything more from Virginia ! "—" What about Tennessee convention ? "— " Has Bragg commenced business ? "—and a thousand equally eager questions popped
from the impatient crowd.

" There *is* news, indeed ! " answered Captain Semmes.   " Listen,
my friends, for the war has commenced in earnest."

And here, on the quiet southern river, we first heard how Baltimore had risen to drive out the troops ; how there had been wild
work made in spite of the police, and how hot blood of her citizens
had stained the streets of the town.   The account ended with the
city still in frightful commotion, the people arming and companies
assembling at their armories ; and without even hinting the number
of those hurt in the fight.

No more *ennui* on board now.   All was as much excitement as if
we were racing along again ; and, through the buzz and angry excla-
mations of the knots collected on all hands, we could catch the most
varied predictions of the result, and speculations as to President
Lincoln's real policy.

" Maryland must act at once.   Egad, sir, *at once*, if she wants to
come to us, sir," said the colonel, haranguing his group.   " If she
doesn't, egad ! she'll be tied hand and foot in a week ! *Facilis
descensus*, you know ! "

" Pshaw, Baltimore's noted for mobs," said an Alabamian. "This is only a little more than usual. In a week she'll forget all about it."

"This is more than a mob," answered a Virginian quietly. "Blood must come out of it; for the people will all go one way now, or make two strong and bitter parties. For my part, I believe Maryland will be with us before this boat gets off."

Late at night we swung loose and rushed past Selma, with the calliope screaming "Dixie" and "ze Van Dorn;" for the professor was himself again and waxed irate and red-patriotic over the news. We could get no more papers, however; so suspense and speculation continued until we reached Mobile.

There we heard of the quelling of the riot; of the course of the citizens; of Mr. Lincoln's pledges to the Baltimore committee, that no more troops should pass through the town; of his statement that those already passed were only intended for the defense of the Capital.

"Pretty fair pledges, Colonel," said Styles, when we got this last news.

"Fair pledges!" responded the colonel, with serious emphasis, "Egad, sir!—*we've lost a State!*"

CHAPTER VII.

MOBILE, THE GULF CITY.

Mobile was in a state of perfect ferment when we arrived. The news from Maryland had made profound sensation and had dissipated the delusive hopes—indulged there as well as in Montgomery—like mists before the sun.

All now agreed that war must come. Many thought it already upon them. Groups, anxious and steadfast, filled the hotels, the clubs and the post-office; and the sense of all was that Maryland had spoken not one hour too soon; having spoken, the simple duty of the South was to prevent harm to a hair of her head for words said in its defense.

Those who had been the hottest in branding the action of Virginia as laggard, looked to her for the steadiest and most efficient aid, now that the crisis faced them; while all felt she would meet the calls of the hour with never a pause for the result. The sanguine counted on Maryland, bound by every community of interest, every tie of sympathy—as already one of the Confederate States. She was no longer neutral, they said. She had put her lance in rest and rallied to the charge, in the avowed quarrel that the troops attacked were on their way to oppress her next sister. And nothing could follow but Virginia's bright falchion must flash out, and the states must lock shields and press between her and the giant she had roused.

The Gulf City had not been idle. The echo of the first gun at Charleston had roused her people; and with a wonderful accord they had sprung to arms. Law books were thrown aside, merchants locked up their ledgers, even students of theology forgot that they were men of peace—and all enrolled themselves in the " crack " companies. No wonder, when the very best blood of the state ran in the veins of the humblest private; when men of letters and culture and wealth refused any but " the post of honor," with musket on shoulder; when the most delicate fingers of their fairest worked the flags that floated over them, and the softest voices urged them to their *devoir;* no wonder, then, that high on the roll of fame are now written the names of the Mobile Cadets—of the Gulf City Guards—of the Rifles—and enough others to make the list as long as Leporello's. Not one in ten of the best born youth of Mobile remained at home; the mechanics, the stevedores and men of every class flocked to follow their example, so that the city alone gave two full regiments and helped to fill up others. The news from Virginia and Maryland had given but a fresh impetus to these preparations; and, before my return to Montgomery, these regiments had passed through, on their way to the new battle ground on the Potomac frontier.

On the night of our arrival in the Gulf City, that escape valve for all excitement, a dense crowd, collected in front of the Battle House and Colonel John Forsyth addressed them from the balcony. He had just returned from Washington with the southern commissioners and gave, he said, a true narrative of the manner and results of their mission. At this lapse of time it is needless to detail even the substance of his speech; but it made a marked impression on the crowd, as the surging sea of upturned faces plainly told. John Forsyth, already acknowledged one of the ablest of southern leaders, was a veritable Harry Hotspur. His views brooked no delay or temporizing; and, as he spoke, in vein of fiery elegance, shouts and yells of defiant approval rose in full swell of a thousand voices. Once he named a noted Alabamian, whom he seemingly believed to have played a double part in these negotiations; and the excited auditory greeted his name with hisses and execrations. That they did their fellow-citizen injustice the most trying councils of the war proved; for he soon after came South and wrought, with all the grand power in him, during the whole enduring struggle.

Staple was tired of politics, and hated a crowd; so he soon lounged off to the club, an institution gotten up with a delightful regard to the most comfortable arrangement and the most accomplished *chef* in the South. There one met the most cordial hospitality, the neatest entertainment and the very best wines in the Gulf section. The cook was an artist, as our first supper declared; and play could be found, too, as needed; for young Mobile was not slow, and money, in those days, was plenty.

Altogether, the tone of Mobile society was more cosmopolitan than that of any city of the South, save, perhaps, New Orleans. It may be that its commercial connections, reaching largely abroad, produced the effect; or that propinquity to and constant intercourse with its sister city induced freer mode of thought and action. Located at the head of her beautiful bay, with a wide sweep of blue water before her, the cleanly-built, unpaved streets gave Mobile a fresh, cool aspect. The houses were fine and their appointments in good, and sometimes luxurious, taste. The society was a very pleasure-loving organization, enjoying the gifts of situation, of climate and of fortune to their full. *On dit*, it sometimes forgot the Spartan code ; but the stranger was never made aware of that, for it ever sedulously remembered good taste.

Between the drives, dinners and other time-killers, one week slipped around with great rapidity ; and we could hardly realize it when the colonel looked over his newspaper at breakfast and said :

"Last day, boys! Egad! the cooking here *is* a little different from Montgomery—but we must take the ' Cuba ' this evening."

So adieux were spoken, and at dusk we went aboard the snug, neat little Gulf steamer of the New Orleans line. She was a trimmer craft than our floating card-house of river travel, built for a little outside work in case of necessity, or the chances of a norther.

We scudded merrily down the bay toward Fort Morgan, the grim sentinel sitting dark and lonely at the harbor's mouth and showing a row of teeth that might be a warning. The fort was now put in thorough repair and readiness by Colonel Hardee, of the regular army of the Confederate States.

I was following Styles down from the upper deck, when we heard high voices from the end of the boat, and recognized one exclaiming :

"Curse you! I'll cut your ear off!"

Round the open bar we found an excited crowd, in the center of which was our worldly-minded middie of river-boat memory and "Spring Chicken," his colleague; both talking very loud, and the latter exhibiting a bowie-knife half as long as himself. By considerable talk and more elbowing, we made our way to the boys; and, with the aid of a friendly stoker, got them both safely in my state-room.

Once there, the man of the world—who, unlike the needy knife-grinder, had a story—told it. After getting on the boat, Spring Chicken had been taking mint with sugar and something; and he took it once too often. Seeing this, the worldling tried to get him forward to his state-room; but, as we passed the fort, a jolly passenger, who had also taken mint, waved his hat at the fortification and cried out:

"Hurrah for Muggins!"

Spring Chicken stopped, balanced himself on his heels and announced with much dignity——

"Sir, *I* am Muggins!"

"Didn't know you, Muggins," responded the shouter, who fortunately had not taken fighting whisky. "Beg pardon, Muggins! Hurrah for Peacock! *Yah—a-h!*"

"See here, my good fellow, I'm Peacock!" repeated Spring Chicken.

"The thunder you are! You can't be two people!"

"Sir!" responded Spring Chicken, with even greater dignity, "I do not—*hic*—desire to argue with you. I am Peacock!"

The man laughed. "The Peacock I mean is a northern man——"

"*I'm* a northern man," yelled the now irate Spring Chicken. "Curse you, sir! what are my principles to you? I'll cut your ear off!" And it was this peaceful proposition that attracted our attention, in time to prevent any trouble with the ugly knife he drew from his back.

Spring Chicken had remained passive during the recital of the more sober worldling. Sundry muttered oaths had sufficed him until it was over, when he made the lucid explanation:

"Reas'l didl't—*hic*—dam decoy—bet ol red—ev'ry cent—*hic!*"

This the worldling translated and the murder was out. When we lost sight of the boys on the Southern Republic, they had ordered wine. At dinner they had more; and—glowing therewith, as they sat over their cigars on the gallery—did not "stop their ears," but, on the contrary, "listed to the voice of the charmer." When the stool pigeon once more stood in the doorway, rattling his half dollars, they followed him into the den of the tiger.

"Faro" went against them; "odd-and-even" was worse; *rouge-et-noir* worst of all; and at night they were sober and dead broke, an unpleasant but not infrequent phase of boat life.

" Didl't have aly wash to spout," remarked Spring Chicken, with his head under his arm.

"Yes—we owed our wine bill," continued the middie, whose worldliness decreased as he got sober, "and our trunk was in pawn to the nigger we owed a quarter for taking care of it. So as soon as the boat touched, I ran for'ard and jumped off, while he waited to keep the things in sight till I came back."

" So he was in pawn, too, egad !" said the colonel.

" Thasso, ol' cock !" hiccoughed Spring Chicken.

"And when I got the money and we went up town, we met the cussed decoy again, and we were fools enough to go again——"

" Williz molley—damniz—*hic*—eyes !" interpolated the other.

" ——And we got broke again—and this fellow that hollowed Muggins looked like the decoy, but he wasn't. That's the whole truth, Mr. Styles."

" Mussput—*hic*—fi dollus on-jack ?" remarked Spring Chicken. " See yer, Styse—o'boy, damfattolman—Con'l is !" and he curled from the lounge to the floor and slept peacefully.

" My young friend," remarked Styles gravely to the middie, as we tucked the insensible Spring Chicken into his berth—"If you want to gamble, you'll do it—so I don't advise you. But these amphibious beasts are dangerous; so in future play with gentlemen and let them alone."

"And, my boy," said the colonel, enunciating *his* moral lesson— " gambling is bad enough, egad! but any man is lost—yes, sir, lost! —who will drink mint—*after dinner !*"

With which great moral axioms we retired and slept until our steamer reached the " Queen City of the South."

CHAPTER VIII.

NEW ORLEANS, THE CRESCENT CITY.

At a first glimpse, New Orleans of those days was anything but a picturesque city. Built upon marshy flats, below the level of the river and protected from inundation by the Levee, her antique and weathered houses seemed to cower and cluster together as though in fear.

But for a long time, "The Crescent City" had been at the head of commercial importance—and the desideratum of direct trade had been more nearly filled by her enterprising merchants than all others in the South. The very great majority of the wealthy population was either Creole, or French; and their connection with European houses may account in some measure for that fact. The coasting trade at the war was heavy all along the Gulf shore; the trade with the islands a source of large revenue, and there were lines and frequent private enterprises across the ocean.

For many reasons, it was then believed New Orleans could never become a great port. Foremost, the conformation of the Delta, at the mouth of the river, prevented vessels drawing over fifteen feet— at most favorable tides—from crossing either of the three bars; and the most practical and scientific engineers, both of civil life and the army, had long tried in vain to remedy the defect for longer than a few weeks. Numerous causes have been assigned for the rapid reformation of these bars; the chemical action of the salt upon the vegetable matter in the river water; the rapid deposit of alluvium as the current slackens; and a churning effect produced by the meeting of the channel with the waves of the Gulf. They could not be successfully removed, however, and were a great drawback to the trade of the city; which its location at the mouth of the great water avenue of the whole West, makes more advantageous than any other point in the South.

The river business in cotton, sugar and syrup was, at this time,

immense; and the agents of the planters—factor is the generic term
—made large fortunes in buying and selling at a merely nominal rate
of percentage.   The southern planter of *ante-bellum* days was a man
of ease and luxury, careless of business and free to excess with
money; and relations between him and his agent were entirely unique.

He had the same factor for years, drawing when he pleased for
any amount, keeping open books.   When his crop came in, it was
shipped to the factor, the money retained—subject to draft—or invested.   But it was by no means rare, when reckoning day came, for
the advance drafts to have left the planter in debt his whole crop to
the factor.   In that case, it used to cost him a trip to Europe, or
a summer at Saratoga only ; and he stayed on his plantation and did
not cry over the spilt milk, however loudly his ladies may have
wailed for the missing *crême-de-la-crême* of Virginia springs.

The morning after arrival we at last saw "the house;" which, far
from being an imposing edifice, was a dingy, small office, just off the
Levee, with the dingier sign of "Long, Staple & Middling" over
the door.   There were a few stalwart negroes basking in the sun
about the entrance, sleeping comfortably in the white glare, or showing glancing ivories, in broad grins—each one keeping his shining
cotton hook in full view, like a badge of office.   Within was a perfect steam of business, and Staple *père* was studying a huge ledger
through a pair of heavy gold spectacles—popping orders like fire-
crackers, at half a dozen attentive clerks.   Long, the senior partner,
was in Virginia—and Middling, the junior, was hardly more than an
expert foreman of the establishment.

"Happy, indeed, to meet you, sir!—93 of Red River lot, Mr.
Edds—Heard of you frequently—Terribly busy times these, sir, partner away—13,094 middlins, for diamond B at 16⅓, Adams ——.
We dine at seven, you remember, Styles—Don't be in a hurry, sir! —
1,642 A. B., page 684, Carter —— Good day—See you at seven."

And it was only over the perfect claret, at the emphasized hour,
that we discovered Mr. Staple to be a man of fine mind and extensive culture, a hearty sympathizer in the rebellion—into which he
would have thrown his last dollar—and one of the most successful
men on the Levee.   Long, his senior partner, was a western man of
hard, keen business sense, who had come to New Orleans fifty years
before, a barefooted deck-hand on an Ohio schooner.   By shrewd-

ness, dogged industry and some little luck, he made "Long's" the best known and richest house in the South-west, until in the crash of '37 it threatened to topple down forever. Then Mr. Staple came forward with his great credit and large amount of spare capital, saved the house and went into it himself; while Middling, the former clerk of all work, was promoted, for fidelity in the trying times, to a small partnership.

Like all the heavy cotton men of the South, Mr. Staple believed firmly that cotton was king, and that the first steamer into a southern port would bring a French and British minister.

"It's against our interest for the present to do so," he said, confidently; "but my partner and I have advised all our planters to hold their cotton instead of shipping it, that the market may not be glutted when the foreign ships come in. And, yet, sir, it's coming down now faster than ever. Everybody prefers, in the disorganized state of things, to have ready money for cotton, that in three months' time must be worth from twenty to thirty cents!"

"Hard to believe, sir, isn't it? Yet our planters, looking at things from their own contracted standpoint, think the English and French cabinets will defer recognition of our Government. As for 'the house,' sir, it will put all it possesses into the belief that they can not prove so blind!"

Like most of the wealthy men in New Orleans, Mr. Staple had a charmingly located villa a mile from the lake and drove out every evening, after business hours, to pass the night.

"Not that I fear the fever," he explained. "What strangers regard as such certain death is to us scarce more than the agues of a North Carolina flat. 'Yellow Jack' is a terrible scourge, indeed, to the lower classes, and to those not acclimatized. The heavy deposits of vegetable drift from the inundations leave the whole country for miles coated four or five inches deep in creamy loam. This decomposes most rapidly upon the approach of hot weather, and the action of the dews, when they begin to fall upon it, causes the *miasmata* to rise in dense and poisonous mists. Now these, of course, are as bad in country—except in very elevated localities—as in town; but they are only *dangerous* in crowded sections, or to the enervated constitutions that could as ill resist any other disease."

"You astonish me, indeed," I answered. "For I have always

classed yellow fever and cholera as twin destroyers. They must be, from such seasons as you have every few years."

" So all strangers think. But to the resident, who from choice, or business engagements, has passed one summer in the city, 'Jack' loses his terrors. The symptoms are unmistakable. Slight nausea and pain in the back, headache and a *soupçon* of chill. The work-ingman feels these. He can not spare the time or the doctor's bill, perhaps. He poohs the matter—it will pass off—and goes to work. The delay and the sun set the disease; and he is brought home at night—or staggers to the nearest hospital—to die of the black vomit in thirty-six hours. Hence, the great mortality.

" Now, I feel these pains, I at once recognize the fever, go right home, bathe feet and back in hot water, take a strong aperient, put mustard on my stomach and pile on the blankets. In an hour I am bathed in sweat till maybe it drips through the mattress. I put on another blanket, take a hot draught with an opiate, and go to sleep. It is not a pleasant thing, with the thermometer at ninety degrees in the shade; but when I wake in the morning, I have saved an attack of fever."

This regimen was constantly repeated to me. In the district crowded with the poorer classes, who are dependent on their daily labor for their daily bread, the fever stalks gaunt and noisome, mark-ing his victims and seldom in vain. All day long, and far into the night in bad seasons, the low, dull rumble of the dead-cart echoed through the narrow streets; and at the door of every squalid house was the plain pine box that held what was left of some one of its loved inmates. Yet through this carnival of death, steadily and fearlessly, the better class of workers walk; not dreading the contagion and se-cure in their harness of precaution.

To sleep in the infected atmosphere in sickly quarters was thought more dangerous; but any business man considered himself safe, if he only breathed the poisonous air in the daytime. The resident phy-sicians, in their recent treatment, feel the disease quite in their hands, when no other foe than the fever is to be combated. Any preceding excess of diet, drink or excitement is apt to aggravate it; but in ordi-nary cases, where proper remedies are taken in season, nine out of ten patients recover.

Otherwise, this ratio is just reversed; and in the working classes—

especially strangers—to take the fever, in bad years, is to die. The utmost efforts of science, the most potent drugs—even the beautiful and selfless devotion of the "Howard Association" and its like— availed nothing in the wrestle with the grim destroyer, when he had once fairly clutched his hold. And in the crowded quarters, where the air was poison without the malaria, his footing was too sure for mortal to prevail against him.

New Orleans was, at this time, divided into two distinct towns in one corporation—the French and American. In the one, the French language was spoken altogether for social and business purposes, and even in the courts. The theaters were French, the cafés innocent of English, and, as Hood says, the "very children speak it." Many persons grow up in this quarter—or did in years back—who never, to their old age, crossed to the American town or spoke one word of English. In the society of the old town, one found a miniature— exact to the photograph—of Paris. It was jealously exclusive, and even the most petted beaux of the American quarter deemed it privilege to enter it. A stranger must come with letters of the most urgent kind before he could cross its threshold. All the etiquette and form of the *ancien régime* obtained here—the furniture, the dress, the cookery, the dances were all French.

In the American town the likeness to Mobile was very marked, in the manners and style of the people. The young men of the French quarter had sought this society more of late years, finding in it a freedom from restraint, for which their associations with other Americans in business gave them a taste. The character of the society was gay and easy—and it was not hedged in so carefully as that of the old town. Strangers were cordially—if not very care- fully—welcomed into it; and the barriers of reserve, that once pro- tected it, were rapidly breaking down before the inroads of progress and petroleum.

The great hotels—the "St. Charles," "St. Louis" and others— were constantly filled with the families of planters from all points of the river and its branches, and with travelers from the Atlantic border as well. Many of these were people of cultivation and re- finement; but many, alas! the roughest of diamonds with a western freedom of expression and solidity of outline, that is national but not agreeable. In the season these people overflowed the hotels, where they had constant hops with, occasionally, splendid balls and even masques. Many of them were "objects of interest" to the young men about town, by reason of papa's business, or Mademoiselle's proper bank account. So the hotels—though not frequented by the ladies of the city at all—became, each year, more and more thronged by the young men; and consequently, each year, the outsiders gained a very gradual, but more secure, footing near the home society and even began to force their way into it.

It must be confessed that some damsels from Red River wore diamonds at breakfast; and that young ladies from Ohio would drive tandem to the lake! And then their laughs and jokes at a soiree would give a dowager from Frenchtown an apoplexy!

Que voulez vous? Pork is mighty! and cotton was king!

There was much difference of opinion as to the morals of the Crescent City. For my own part, I do not think the men were more dissipated than elsewhere, though infinitely more wedded to enjoyment and fun in every form. There was the French idea prevalent that gambling was no harm; and it was indulged to a degree certainly hurtful to many and ruinous to some. From the climate and the great prevalence of light wines, there was less drunkenness than in most southern towns; and if other vices prevailed to any great extent—they were either gracefully hidden, or so sanctioned by custom as to cause no remark, except by straight-laced strangers.

Oh! the delicious memories of the city of old! The charming cordiality to be found in no colder latitude, the cosy breakfasts that prefaced days of real enjoyment—the midnight revels of the *bal masqué!* And then the carnival!—those wild weeks when the Lord of Misrule wields his motley scepter—leading from one reckless frolic to another till *Mardi Gras* culminates in a giddy whirl of delirious fun on which, at midnight, Lent drops a somber veil!

Sad changes the war has wrought since then!

The merry "Krewe of Comus" has been for a time replaced by the conquering troops of the Union; the *salons* where only the best and brightest had collected have been sullied by a conquering soldiery; and their leader has waged a vulgar warfare on the noble womanhood his currish spirit could not gaze upon without a fruitless effort to degrade.

Of the resident ladies, I can only say that to hear of a fast one—in ordinary acceptation of that term—was, indeed, rare.

The young married woman monopolized more of the society and its beaux than would be very agreeable to New York belles; but, if they borrowed this custom from their French neighbors, I have not heard that they also took the license of the Italian.

Public and open improprieties were at once frowned down, and people of all grades and classes seemed to make their chief study good taste. This is another French graft, on a stem naturally susceptible, of which the consequences can be seen from the hair ribbon of the *bonne* to the decoration of the Cathedral.

The women of New Orleans, as a rule, dress with more taste—more perfect adaptation of form and color to figure and complexion—than any in America. On a dress night at the opera, at church, or at a ball, the *toillettes* are a perfect study in their exquisite fitness—their admirable blending of simplicity and elegance. Nor is this confined to the higher and more wealthy classes. The women of lower conditions are admirably imitative; and on Sunday afternoons, where they crowd to hear the public bands with husbands and children, all in their best, it is the rarest thing to see a badly-trimmed bonnet or an ill-chosen costume. The men, in those days, dressed altogether in the French fashion; and were, consequently, the worst dressed in the world.

The most independent and obtrusively happy people one noticed in New Orleans were the negroes. They have a sleek, shiny blackness here, unknown to higher latitudes; and from its midst the great white eyeballs and large, regular teeth flash with a singular brilliance. Sunday is *their* day peculiarly—and on the warm afternoons, they bask up and down the thoroughfares in the gaudiest of orange and scarlet bandannas. But their day is fast passing away; and in place of the simple, happy creatures of a few years gone, we find the discontented and besotted idler—squalid and dirty.

The cant of to-day—that the race problem, if left alone, will settle itself—may have some possible proof in the distant future; but the few who are ignorant enough to-day to believe the " negro question " already settled may find that they are yet but on the threshold of the " irrepressible conflict " between nature and necessity.

To the natural impressibility of the southron, the Louisianian adds the enthusiasm of the Frenchman. At the first call of the governor for troops, there had been readiest response; and here, as in Ala-

5

bama, the very first young men of the state left office and counting-room and college to take up the musket.   Two regiments of regulars, in the state service, were raised to man the forts—"Jackson" and "St. Philip"—that guarded the passes below the city.   These were composed of the stevedores and workingmen generally, and were officered by such young men as the governor and council deemed best fitted.   The Levee had been scoured and a battalion of "Tigers" formed from the very lowest of the thugs and plugs that infested it, for Major Bob Wheat, the well-known filibuster.

Poor Wheat! His roving spirit still and his jocund voice now mute, he sleeps soundly under the sighing trees of Hollywood—that populous "city of the silent" at Richmond. It was his corps of which such wild and ridiculous stories of bowie-knife prowess were told at the Bull Run fight. They, together with the "Crescent Rifles," "Chasseurs-à-pied" and "Zouaves," were now at Pensacola.

The "Rifles" was a crack corps, composed of some of the best young men in New Orleans; and the whole corps of "Chasseurs" was of the same material. They did yeomen's service in the four years, and the last one saw very few left of what had long since ceased to be a separate organization. But of all the gallant blood that was shed at the call of the state, none was so widely known as the "Washington Artillery." The best men of Louisiana had long upheld and officered this battalion as a holiday pageant; and, when their merry meetings were so suddenly changed to stern alarums, to their honor be it said, not one was laggard.

In the reddest flashings of the fight, on the dreariest march through heaviest snows, or in the cozy camp under the summer pines, the *guidon* of the "W. A." was a welcome sight to the soldier of the South—always indicative of cheer and of duty willingly and thoroughly done.

It was very unwillingly that I left New Orleans on a transport, with a battalion of Chasseurs for Pensacola.   Styles was to stay behind for the present, and then go on some general's staff; so half the amusement of my travel was gone.   "The colonel" was *desolé*.

"*Such* a hotel as the St. Charles!" he exclaimed, with tears in his voice—"such soups. Ah! my boy, after the war I'll come here to live—yes, sir, to live! It's the only place to get a dinner. Egad, sir, out of New Orleans *nobody* cooks!"

I suggested comfort in the idea of red snapper at Pensacola.

"Red fish is good in itself. Egad, I think it *is* good," replied the colonel. "But eaten in camp, with a knife, sir—egad, with a knife—off a tin plate! *Pah!* You've never lived in camp." And in a hollow, oracular whisper, he added: "Wait!"

And they were real models, the New Orleans hotels of those days, and the colonel's commendations were but deserved. In *cuisine*, service and wines, they far surpassed any on this continent; and for variety of patrons they were unequaled anywhere.

Two distinct sets inhabited the larger ones, as antagonistic as oil and water. The *habitués*, easy, critical to a degree, and particular to a year about their wines, lived on comfortably and evenly, enjoying the very best of the luxurious city, and never having a cause for complaint. The up-river people flocked in at certain seasons by the hundred. They crowded the lobbies, filled the spare bed-rooms, and eat what was put before them, with but little knowledge save that it was French. These were the business men, who came down for a new engagement with a factor, or to rest after the summer on the plantation. One-half of them were terribly busy; the other half having nothing to do after the first day—they always stay a week—and assuming an air of high criticism that was as funny to the knowing ones as expensive to them.

At our hotel, one evening, as favored guests, we found ourselves on an exploring tour with mine host. It ended in the wine-room.

The mysteries of that vaulted chamber were seldom opened to the outer world; and passing the *profanum vulgus* in its first bins, we listened with eager ears and watering mouths to recital of the pedigree and history of the dwellers within.

Long rows of graceful necks, golden crowned and tall, peered over dust and cobwebs of near a generation; bottles aldermanic and plethoric seemed bursting with the hoarded fatness of the vine; clear, white glass burned a glowing ruby with the Burgundy; and lean, jaundiced bottles—carefully bedded like rows of invalids—told of rare and priceless Hocks.

From arch to arch our garrulous *cicerone* leads us, with a heightened relish as we get deeper among his treasures and further away from the daylight.

"There!" he exclaims at last with a great gulp of triumph.

"There! that's *Sherry*, the king of wines! Ninety years ago, the Conde Pesara sent that wine in his own ships. Ninety years ago— and for twenty it has lain in my cellar, never touched but by my own hand"—and he holds up the candle to the shelf, inch deep in dust, while the light seems to dart into the very heart of the amber fluid, and sparkle and laugh back again from the fantastic drapery the spiders had festooned around the bottles. "Yes, all the Pesaras are dead years gone; and only this blood of the vine is left of them."

"But you don't sell that wine!" gasps the colonel. "Egad! you *don't* sell it to those—people—up stairs!"

"I did *once*"—and mine host sighs. "A great cotton man came down. He was a king on the river—he wanted the best! Money was nothing to him, so I whispered of this, and said twenty dollars the bottle! And, Colonel, he didn't——*like it!*"

"Merciful heaven!" the colonel waxes wroth.

"So Francois there sent him a bottle of that *Xeres* in the outer bin yonder—we sell it to you for two dollars the bottle—and he said *that* was wine!"

But of the other family—who live in an American hurry and eat by steam—was the goblin diner of whom a friend told me in accents of awe. One day, at the St. Charles, a resident stopped him on the way to their accustomed table:

"Have you seen these people eat?" he asked. "No? Then we'll stop and look. This table is reserved for the up-river men who have little time in the city and make the most of it. While they swallow soup, a nimble waiter piles the nearest dishes around them, without regard to order or quality. They eat fish, roast and fried, on the same plate, swallowing six inches of knife blade at every bolt. Then they draw the nearest pie to them, cut a great segment in it, make three huge arcs therein with as many snaps of their teeth; seize a handful of nuts and raisins and rush away, with jaws still working like a flouring-mill. Ten minutes is their limit for dinner." My friend only smiled. The other adding:

"You doubt it? Here comes a fine specimen; hot, healthy and evidently busy. See, he looks at his watch! I'll bet you a bottle of St. Peray he 'does' his dinner within the ten."

"Done"—and they sat opposite him, watch in hand.

And that wonderful Hoosier dined in seven minutes!

CHAPTER IX.

A CHANGE OF BASE.

Whatever activity and energetic preparation there may have been elsewhere, Pensacola was the first organized camp in the South. General Bragg and his adjutant-general were both old officers, and in the face of the enemy the utmost rigor of discipline prevailed. There had been no active operations on this line, yet; but the Alabama and Louisiana troops collected—to the number of about nine thousand—had already become soldiers, in all the details of camp life; and went through it in as cheerful a spirit as if they had been born there.

In popular view, both Bragg and Beauregard were on probation as yet; and it was thought that upon the management of their respective operations depended their status in the regular army. All was activity, drill and practice in this camp; and if the army of Pensacola was not a perfectly-disciplined one, the fault certainly was not with its general.

The day we reached camp the President and Secretary of the Navy came down from Montgomery on a special train for an inspection. They were accompanied only by one or two officers, and had a long and earnest conference with General Bragg at his headquarters. After that there was a review of the army; and the then novel sight was made peculiarly effective by surroundings.

On the level, white beach, glistening in the afternoon sun, were drawn up the best volunteer organizations of the South—line upon line, as far as eye could reach—their bright uniforms, glancing muskets and waving banners giving color to the view. Far in the rear the fringed woods made dim background; while between, regular rows of white tents—laid out in regiments and company streets—dotted the plain.

Out in the foreground stretched the blue waters of Pensacola harbor—the sun lighting up the occasional foam-crests into evanescent diamonds—the grim fortress frowning darkly on the rebellious display, while a full band on the parapet played the "Star Spangled Banner." Over to the left, half hidden under the rolling sand hills, stood Pensacola, with the navy yard and hospitals; and yellow little Fort McRea, saucy and rebellious, balanced it on the extreme right.

As the President, with the general and his staff, galloped down the line, the band of each regiment struck up; and the wildest huzzas—not even restrained by the presence of their "incarnate discipline"—told how firm a hold Mr. Davis had taken upon the hearts of the army.

By the time the review was over twilight had fallen; and a thousand camp-fires sprang up among the tents, with flickering, uncertain light. In it sat groups preparing their suppers and discussing what the visit and review might mean. Some said it was for the secretary to inspect the navy yard; some to examine into the defenses of the fort; and some said that it meant scaling ladders and a midnight assault.

That night we had a jolly time of it in an Alabama captain's tent—with songs, cards and whisky punch, such as only "Mac" could brew. Even "the colonel" confessed himself beaten at his great trick; and in compliment drank tumbler after tumbler. As we walked over to our tent in the early mist before dawn, he said:

"Egad! there's mischief brewing—mischief, sir! The seat of war's to be removed to Virginia and the capital to Richmond!"

I stopped and looked at the colonel. Was it the punch?

"That's what the council this evening meant?"

"Just so. Bragg remains, but part of his garrison goes to Beauregard, in Virginia. Trains to Montgomery will be jammed now, so we'd better be off. And, egad, sir! I'm to get ready for the field. Yes, sir, for the field!"

Next morning the information that had filtered to me through the colonel's punch was announced in orders, and enthusiastic cheers greeted the news that some of the troops were to go to a field promising active service and speedily at that.

The routine of camp life had already begun to pall upon the better class of men, and all were equally anxious to go where they could prove more clearly how ready they were to do their *devoir.*

Some Alabamians, two Georgia regiments, the *Chasseurs-à-pied*, the "Tigers" and the Zouaves were to go to Virginia; and through the courtesy of the officers of the latter corps, we got seats to Mont-gomery in their car; two days later.

Meantime, all was hum and bustle through the whole camp, and as the limited rolling stock on the still unfinished railroad could only accommodate a regiment at a time, they left at all hours of the day, or night, that the trains arrived. Constantly at midnight the dull tramp of marching men and the slow tap of the drum, passing our quarters, roused us from sleep ; and whatever the hour, the departing troops were escorted to the station by crowds of half-envious com-rades, who " were left out in the cold." And as the trains started—box cars, flats and tenders all crowded, inside and out—yell after yell went up in stentorian chorus, echoing through the still woods, in place of

"That sweet old word, good-bye!"

One gray dawn, six hundred Zouaves filed out of the pines and got aboard our train. They were a splendid set of animals; medium sized, sunburnt, muscular and wiry as Arabs; and a long, swingy gait told of drill and endurance. But the faces were dull and brutish, generally; and some of them would vie, for cunning villainy, with the features of the prettiest Turcos that Algeria could produce.

The uniform was very picturesque and very—dirty. Full, baggy, scarlet trowsers, confined round the waist by the broad, blue band or sash, bearing the bowie-knife and meeting, at mid-leg, the white gaiter; blue shirt cut very low and exhibiting the brawny, sunburnt throat; jacket heavily braided and embroidered, flying loosely off the shoulders, and the jaunty *fez*, surmounting the whole, made a bright *ensemble* that contrasted prettily with the gray and silver of the South Carolinians, or the rusty brown of the Georgians, who came in crowds to see them off.

But the use of these uniforms about the grease and dust of Pensa-cola camp-fires had left marks that these soldiers considered badges of honor, not to be removed.

Nor were they purer morally. Graduates of the slums of New Orleans, their education in villainy was naturally perfect. They had the vaguest ideas of *meum* and *tuum ;* and small personal difficulties were usually settled by the convincing argument of a bowie-knife, or brass knuckle.

Yet they had been brought to a very perfect state of drill and efficiency. All commands were given in French—the native tongue of nearly all the officers and most of the men ; and, in cases of insubordination, the former had no hesitancy in a free use of the revolver. A wonderful peacemaker is your six-shooter.

They might be splendid fellows for a charge on the " Pet Lambs," or on a—pocket ; but, on the whole, were hardly the men one would choose for partners in any business but a garroting firm, or would desire to have sleep in the company bedroom.

Their officers we found of a class entirely above them; active, bright, enthusiastic Frenchmen, with a frank courtesy and soldierly bearing that were very taking. They occupied the rear car of the train, while the men filled the forward ones, making the woods ring with their wild yells, and the roaring chorus of the song of the *Zou-Zou.*

We had crossed the gap at Garland, where the road was yet unfinished, and were soon at the breakfast house, where we mounted the hill in a body; leaving our car perfectly empty, save a couple of buglers who stood on the platform. As I looked back, the elder musician was a most perfect picture of the *Turco.* He had served in Algiers, and after the war in Italy brought a bullet in his leg to New Orleans. He was long past fifty—spare, broad-shouldered and hard as a log of oak. His sharp features were bronzed to the richest mahogany color, and garnished with a moustache and peak of grizzled hair " a cubit and a span "—or nearly—in length. And the short, grizzled hair had been shaved far back from his prominent temples, giving a sinister and grotesque effect to his naturally hard face. Turc was a favorite with the officers, and his dress was rather cleaner than that of the others ; a difference that was hardly an improvement.

We were just seated at breakfast—and having a special train we took our time—when a wild scream of the whistle, succeeded immediately by the heavy rumble of cars, came up the hill. We rushed to the windows, just in time to see a column of smoke disappearing round the curve and the officers' car standing solitary and empty on the road.

The Zouaves had run away with the train !

The language the officers used, as we surrounded the " sole survivors "—the two buglers—was, at least, strong ; and short, hard words not in the church service dropped frequently from their lips.

It was no use ; the train had gone and the men with it, and the best we could do was to speculate on the intention of the runaways, while we waited the result of the telegrams sent to both ends of the line for another engine. At last it came puffing up, and we whirled at its full speed into Montgomery.

Meanwhile the *Zou-Zous* had several hours' start. Led by one ardent spirit—whose motto had been *similia similibus*, until he lost his balance of mind—they had uncoupled the officers' car and forced the engineers to take them on. On arriving at Montgomery, they wandered over the town, "going through" drinking-houses until they became wild with liquor; then bursting open the groceries to get whisky, threatening the citizens and even entering private houses. The alarm became so great, as the Zouaves became more maddened, that the first Georgia regiment was ordered out and stationed by platoons, with loaded muskets and fixed bayonets, across the streets where the rioters were. Serious trouble was beginning, when the car with their officers dashed into the depot.

The charge of the Light Brigade was surpassed by those irate Creoles. With the cars still in rapid motion, they leaped off, revolver in hand; and charged into the quarter where their drunken men were still engaged in every sort of excess. The old bugler still trotted at their head, his black eyes gleaming at the prospect of the row, and his bugle occasionally raised to sound the "rally." Into the midst of the drunken and yelling crowd dashed the officers; crackling French oaths rolling over their tongues with a snapping intonation, and their pistols whirling right and left like slung-shot, and dropping a mutineer at every blow. Habit and the rough usage overcame even the drunken frenzy of the men, and they dropped the plunder from their arms, snatched muskets from the corners they had been whirled into, and rapidly dressed into line in the street.

I saw one beardless boy, slight and small, rush to a huge sergeant and order him into ranks. The soldier, a perfect giant, hesitated to drop the handful of shoes he had seized, only for a second. But that was enough. The youth had to jump from the ground to seize his throat; but, at the same moment, the stock of the heavy revolver crashed over his temple, and he fell like a stricken ox.

"Roll that carrion into the street!" said the lieutenant to another soldier near; and before his order was obeyed the store was empty.

In a half hour from the officers' arrival the battalion was mustered on Main street, and only nine absentees were reported at roll-call; but many a *fez* was drawn far down over a bleeding forehead, and many a villainous countenance was lighted by one eye, while the other was closed and swollen.

The colonel and I had jumped from the car and run on with our French friends; but the colonel was not the son of Atalanta, and by reason of a *soupçon* of gout his feet were not beautiful upon Zion or any other place. Neither could he make them "swift to shed blood."

As we entered the street where the rioters were, I turned and saw him, perfectly breathless, bear his two hundred and fifty pounds avoirdupois against a door. It was not closed, but had only been slammed by the score of *Zou-Zous* enjoying the whisky within; and as I looked I saw a dignified colonel in the C. S. army turn a complete somersault into a group of red-legged devils, who immediately closed around him.

Gabriel Ravel, though a lighter man, never made a cleaner leap through the third story in the side-scene; but there was no time to waste and I went back at speed. I had scarcely turned when I saw the colonel's huge form tower among the red-legs. By the time I reached the door my apparition, revolver in hand, completed what he had begun; and they slipped by and vanished.

Luckily the bar of the door had fallen with him, and the old gymnastics of other days coming back like a flash, he had seized it, made two rapid blows and laid as many of his assailants at his feet; roaring, meanwhile, oaths as thunderous as they were unintelligible.

"*Sacré-é nom!*" he shouted as he saw me; "shoot 'em, me boy! *Poltrons,* egad! Laugh at me! D——n their eyes! *Can-n-naille!*"

There was a wicked light in my fat friend's eye, and he had recovered his second wind; so we sallied out, the colonel still clinging to his weapon of chance.

"Good enough for these dogs!" he roared, wrathfully shaking the bar. "Saves the pistol."

That night at "the Ranche," as later about many a camp-fire, our French visitors declared that the colonel's bar had done more effective service than their revolvers; and, as it stood dented and blood-smeared in the corner of that vine-clad porch, it did not belie their praise.

CHAPTER X.

EN ROUTE FOR THE BORDER.

Very soon after their state went out of the Union, and it became settled that the policy of the central Government was to take possession of the border states by force, the people of Virginia decided that the battle was to be fought on her soil. Her nearness to Washington, the facility of land communication, and the availabilty of her waterways for transportation purposes, all pointed to this; and the southern Government also became aware that the Potomac boundary of the Confederacy was the one to be most jealously guarded. Under these circumstances, when the tender of the use of the state capital at Richmond was made to the Montgomery Government, the advantages of the move were at once apparent, and the proffer was promptly accepted.

When we returned to Montgomery, preparations for removal were in such state of progress that the change would be made in a few days. Archives and public property not in daily use had already been sent on, and some of the force of the executive departments were already in the new capital, preparing for the reception of the remainder. Troops in large bodies had already been forwarded to Virginia from all parts of the South, and all indications were that, before the summer was over, an active campaign on the soil of the Old Dominion would be in progress.

About this time, a telegram from Montgomery appeared in the New York *Tribune*, which created as much comment at the South as at the North. It stated, in so many words, that the whole South was in motion; that a few days would see Mr. Davis in Virginia at the head of thirty thousand men, Beauregard second in command. With the two sections in a state of open hostility, and with armies already in the field and manœuvering for position, it was somewhat singular that the avowed correspondent of a northern journal should be allowed in the southern Capital; but, when his dispatches bore on their face some signs of authoritative sanction, it became stranger still.

The correspondent of the *Tribune* was a well-known lobby member of years standing, but avowedly a southern man. His intercourse with the leaders of the government was, at least, friendly, and his predictions and assertions in the columns of that newspaper were generally borne out in fact. The state of the country was an anomalous one, but this method of waging war was still more so.

The history of the dispatch in question was simply this: There had been much jubilation in Montgomery over the news from Virginia. Serenades had been made, speeches delivered, and the invariable whisky had not been neglected.

Late at night, I was shown a copy of this dispatch, as one about to be sent. On my doubting it, I was credibly informed that it had been shown to at least one cabinet officer, and received his approval. And it went!

When it was finally settled that the Capital was to be moved to Virginia, the city of Montgomery began to wail. It had all along been utterly and most emphatically opposed to the location of the government there. It would ruin the trade, the morals and the reputation of the town. Dowagers had avowed their belief that the continuance of the Congress there for one year would render the city as perfect a Sodom as Washington—would demoralize the society beyond purification.

Men of business had grumbled at being disturbed from their fixed routine of many years. But now that the incubus was to be removed, there was a strong pressure to prevent—and bitter denunciations of—the outrage!

Leaders came out in the papers, advising against the practicability; scathing articles about perfidy sometimes appeared; and it was, on all hands, prophesied that the government would lose caste and dignity, and become a traveling caravan if the change were made. Where will the nations of Europe find it when they send their ministers to recognize the Confederate Government?—was the peroration of these eloquent advocates.

Now, as there was no contract made or implied, in locating the provisional government at Montgomery, that it was to be the permanent Capital; or that the exigencies of the war might not necessitate a change to some point more available, this was at least unnecessary. True, the people had made sacrifices, and had inconvenienced themselves. But what they had done was for the country, and not for the Government; and had, besides, been done equally elsewhere. And the location, even temporarily, of the Government there had aided the town greatly. It had become the converging point of railroad and contract business for the Confederacy; and the depots and storehouses located there would be of course continued, throwing a vast amount of business activity and money into it. So, though the people might be somewhat morbid on the subject, their arguments against the change were, on the whole, if natural, not founded on fact.

But, perfectly regardless of the thunders of the press and the growlings of the people, the preparations for removal and the change of base to Virginia went steadily on, By the 20th of May, everything had been completed—the President and Cabinet left Montgomery—the fact, that had for some time been a real one, was formally consummated; and Montgomery became again the Capital of Alabama.

I had nothing to keep me in town longer, so I started for a leisurely trip to Richmond. But man proposes; and in this instance, the Quartermaster's Department disposed that travel was to be anything but practicable.

Trains, crowded with troops from all directions, met at the junctions, and there had to lay over for hours, or days. Burden trains, with supplies for the army, munitions of war, or government property from Montgomery, blocked the road in all directions; and trains running "not on time" had to proceed much more carefully than ordinarily. In fact, there was not the amount of transportation at the disposal of the roads that the greatly enhanced demands required; and at every station nearer Richmond, the pressure of passengers and freight became greater.

Through Georgia I bore the troubles of the transit like a philosopher; but under three detentions between Augusta and Columbia, of from nine to thirteen hours, patience and endurance both gave way.

South Carolina had gone into the war with her eyes wider open than those of her sisters; and while she had yet time, was straining every nerve to utilize all her available resources and to make new ones. Her factories, tanneries and foundries were all in constant and active operation; she was making bountiful preparation for the future.

Everywhere in the South was earnest endeavor and heartfelt enthusiasm for the cause; but I saw it nowhere directed into such practical and productive channels, thus early, as in South Carolina. Charleston, Pensacola and Virginia had drained her of younger and more active men; but the older ones and her vast resources of slave labor made up for the loss, and neither time nor energy seemed to be misapplied.

After a rest, I found a freight train with a philanthropic conductor, and started for Kingsville. *Væ Victis!*

I reached that station—what a misnomer!—in a driving mist and a very bad humor. Neither was a fine preparation for the news that a train had smashed seventeen miles above, tearing up the track and effectually blocking the road. The down train, with which we were to connect, could not come through; not a car was visible; no one knew when we could get off, and the engine we had left was just disappearing around a curve—Charlestonward.

One hopeful individual ventured a mild suggestion that we should have to stay all night. He weighed a hundred and eighty pounds, at least—not a fraction less—so I remained passive; but ten pounds subtracted from his avoirdupois would have brought him a black eye. Stay all night! The idea was an ague!

Kingsville was a splendid aggregation of one house and a long platform. The town—*i. e.*, the house—had, even in palmy days, been remarkable on the road for great dirt, wretched breakfasts and worse whisky. You entered at one door, grabbed a biscuit and a piece of bacon and rushed out at the other; or you got an awful decoction of brown sugar and turpentine in a green tumbler. Constant travel and crowds of passing soldiers had not improved it in any particular. The very looks of the place were repugnant enough in the daytime, but

> " Bold was he who hither came
> At midnight—man or boy!"

I felt that a night in the rain under the pines, with my bag for a pillow, would be endurable; but no mortal with a white skin could dare those bloated and odorous feather-beds, where other things—in the shape of mordants, vivacious, active and gigantic—besides

> " Wicked dreams abuse the curtained sleeper."

To mend matters, Gartrell's regiment of Georgians, eight hundred and fifty *strong*, and three other companies of Georgians from Pen-sacola, had been left here to meet a way-train, which failing, they bivouacked by the roadside. In all there were over eleven hundred tobacco-and-gin redolences, remarkably quiet for them; shooting at a mark, going through squad drill, drinking bad liquor by the canteen and swearing in a way that would have made the "Army in Flanders" sick with envy.

In the latter amusement I joined internally; and it did me so much good that I bought the anti-administration newspaper of Charleston and, getting out of bullet range, put my back against a tree and tried to read. *Mercury* was ever a blithe and sportive god, and his gam-bols on Mount Olympus were noted in days of yore; but the modern namesake—or else my present position—had soporific tendencies; and fear of the target shooters growing dimmer and dimmer, I lost myself in sleep.

It was near sundown when I was awakened by the snort of a loco-motive, and a freight train hove in sight. The drums rolled, the troops formed in line, each one packing his household on his back as he trotted along; and, as the cars backed up, the men broke ranks and jumped aboard, filling every crack and corner, and seeming to pile on top of each other.

A berth there was utterly impracticable to any man with any of his senses in active operation. That squirming, dense mass of humanity was more than the oldest traveler could stand, and I gave up my place in the rush. Luckily, there was an express car along, and I found the agent. He was very busy; and eloquence worthy of Gough, or Cicero, or Charles Sumner got no satisfaction. Desperation suggested a masonic signal, with the neck of a black bottle protrud-ing from my bag. The man of parcels melted and invoked terrible torments on the immortal part of him if he didn't let me " g'long wi' the 'spress," as he styled that means of locomotion.

The accommodation was not princely—six feet by ten, cumbered with packages of all shapes and sizes and strongly flavored with bacon and pipe. Yet, "not for gold or precious stones" would I have exchanged that redolent corner. The agent waxed more and more polite as the bottle emptied. regretted the want of room, regaled himself with frequent "nips," and me with anecdotes of a professional nature.

From him was learned that he was with the train that had carried my old friends, the Zouaves, to their fresh fields of glory in Virginia. They retained a lively recollection of their lesson at Montgomery, and had kept rather quiet till reaching Columbia. There the devil again got unchained among them, and they broke out in a style to make up for their enforced good behavior.

" Sich a shooting of cattle and poultry, sich a yelling and singing of ther darned frenchy stuff—sich a rolling of drums and a damning of officers, I ain't hear yit "—said the agent. "And they *does* ride more on the outside of the cars than the inside, anyhow."

Beyond Weldon a knot were balancing themselves on the connecting beams of the box-cars. Warned by their officers, they laughed ; begged by the conductors, they swore. Suddenly there was a jolt, the headway of the cars jammed them together, and three red-legged gentlemen were mashed between them—flat as Ravel in the pantomime.

"And I'm jest a-thinkin'," was his peroration, " ef this yere reegement don't stop a-fightin' together, being shot by the Georgians and beat by their officers—not to mention a jammin' up on railroads— they're gwine to do darned leetle sarvice a-fightin' of Yanks! "

After this period the agent talked, first to himself and then to the black bottle ; while I, seated on a box of cartridges, lit my pipe and went into a reverie as to the treatment the surgeons would use in the pneumonia sure to result from the leaks in the car.

In the midst of an active course of turpentine and stimulants, I was brought to myself by a jolt and dead halt in mid-road. The engine had blown off a nut, and here we were, dead lame, six miles from a station and no chance of getting on.

My Express friend advised very quietly to " quit this and walk onter Florence."

" 'Taint but a small tramp after all," he said. "And ye'll jest catch the A. M. up train and miss the sojers. Jest hand this yere to the A. & Co.'s agent, and he'll help yer ef she's crowded. Here's luck ! " and he took a long pull at the bottle and handed it back— rather regretfully—with a dingy note on the back of an Express receipt.

For the benefit of literature in ages yet unborn, I give a careful transcription of this document :

"Deer bil this gentilman Is a verry peerticular frend of mine—also My brother-en-law. And you must give him sum Help ef he needs any cos Our engen she's run of the track And I won't be long afore to morrer.
"Yours trewly, GRIMES."

Thus armed, I shouldered my bag and started on my tramp over the wet and slippery track, reaching Florence at gray dawn. As I came in sight, there stood the train, the engines cold and fires unlit. I had full time, but my good luck—the first since I started—put me in a glow, and I stepped out in a juvenile pace that would have done credit to "the Boy" in training days. As I came nearer, my mercury went rapidly down to zero. Every car was jammed, aisles packed and box-cars crowded even on top. The doorways and platforms were filled with long rows of gray blankets that smelt suggestively human! Crowds of detained passengers and three companies of the "Crescent Guard" had taken their places at midnight, and slept with a peacefulness perfectly aggravating. As I walked ruefully by the windows, there was no hope! Every seat was filled, and every passenger slept the sleep of the just; and their mixed and volleyed snoring came through,

> " Keeping time, time, time,
> In a sort of Runic rhyme."

There was no sort of use. I'd have to try the Express, and deep was my chuckle as I reread my friend Grimes' remarkable production. It would be an oasis in this desert—that Express car; but lo! when I went to look for it there was none on the train!

Dead beat I sat on the platform and awaited day. When a fireman began operations on the engine, I meekly queried where the Express was.

" Be n't none," was the surly rejoinder.

I was wet and tired and generally bewildered. Was it a wonder that I then and there swore at that fireman, as only meek and long-suffering men, when aroused, can swear? The volley was effective, however, and he very politely told me the agent would "be roun'" before the train started. Presently he pointed out the desired individual, to whom I hastened to hand my note. Now the terrible denunciations my former friend had made on his own soul were as nothing to what the present representative of Adams & Co. called down upon his own and everybody else's immortal function.

"Well, I hope to be eternally —— —— by ——! But it ain't no use! —— —— my —— soul, ef yer shan't ride somehow!" remarked this profane expressman. "Yer be Hector Grimes' brother, and by ——! go yer shell! Yer married his sister Cynthy—the one as squints? Why —— —— me! I knowed her when she wasn't knee high—and yer done —— —— well, by ——! Here, Potty!" and he addressed a greasy man just mounting the mail car—"Here be Grimes' brother, as *must* git to Weldon, by —— ——! So hist him along, will yer?"

"O. K. Jump in, Mr. Grimes," agreed the mail agent; and by this time I was so wet and disgusted I didn't care who I was. So in I went, playing *Grimes* "for this night only."

"Here's luck, Potty! may —— —— me, but I'm glad I met yer, Grimes," remarked my profane friend, taking a long pull at the bottle I handed him in my gratitude. "Here's to your wife, Grimes!" and the cars starting just then, "deer bil" took another pull and, with great absence of mind, put the bottle in his pocket and waved us adieu.

The Mail car, like the Express, was a box ten feet by six—one-half the space filled with counter and pigeon-holes, and the other half with mail-bags. Into the remainder were crammed the agent—specific gravity equal to that of two hundred and ninety pounds of feathers—a friend of his and myself. The friend I soon found was what is known as "a good traveling companion;" *i. e.*, a man who keeps himself primed with broad stories and bad whisky, and who doesn't object to a song in which the air always runs away with the harmony. After we started I tried to sleep. It was no use. Lying on one mail-bag with another for a pillow, that is liable to be jerked out at any station to the near dislocation of your neck, with a funny man sitting nearly on you, are not sedatives. My bottle was gone, so I drank gin out of the funny man's. I hate gin—but that night I hated everything and tried the *similia similibus* rule.

We missed connection at Weldon. Did anybody ever make connection there? We were four hours late, and with much reason had, therefore, to wait five hours more. If Kingsville is cheap and nasty, Weldon is dear and nastier. Such a supper! It was inedible even to a man who had tasted nothing but whisky, gin and peanuts for forty-eight hours. Then the landlord—whose hospitality was only equaled by his patriotism—refused to open his house at train time. We must either stay all night, or not at all—for the house would shut at ten o'clock—just after supper. So a deputation of the Crescents and I waited on him, and after a plain talk concluded to " cuss and quit." So we clambered into some platform cars that were to go with the train, and, after a sumptuous supper of dried-apple pies and peanuts, slept the sleep of the weary.

CHAPTER XI.

"ON TO RICHMOND!"

Of course, Petersburg was reached two hours after the train for Richmond had left, but in full time to get half a cold breakfast, at double price. For, about the first development one noted in the South was the growth of an inordinate greed in the class who had anything to sell, or to do, that was supposed to be indispensable. The small hotels and taverns along the railways peculiarly evidenced this; for, demands of passengers must be supplied, and this was the moment for harvest full and fat. Disgust, wetting, gin and detention had made me feel wolfish; but I wanted none of *that* breakfast. Still, I gave the baldheaded man, with nose like a vulture—collecting nimbly the dollars of the soldiers—a very decided expression of my opinion. He seemed deeply pained thereat; but no one ever mentioned that he had put down the price.

At the depot was Frank C., an old chum of Washington "germans," in the new dress of first sergeant of a Georgia battery. He was rushing a carload of company property to Richmond, and was as eager as I and the Crescents to get to that goal. So, between us, the railroad superintendent was badgered into an extra engine; and, mounting Frank's triumphal car, we bumped away from fellow travelers, wandering dolefully through the mud in vain attempt at time-killing until the evening train. That freight-car—piled as it was with ammunition, wheels and harness—was a Godsend, after the past three days. Cicero, Frank's ancient and black Man Friday, dispensed hot coffee and huge hunks of bread and ham; and a violin and two good voices among the Crescents made the time skim along far faster than since starting.

"How is it you haven't your commission?" one of the Creoles asked the Georgian. "When we parted at Montgomery it was promised you."

"Pledges are not commissions, though," was the careless reply. "I got tired of waiting the Secretary's caprices, when there was real work to be done; so one day I went to the War Department and demanded either my sheepskin, or a positive refusal. I got only more promises; so I told the Sec. I needed no charity from the government, but would present it with a company! Then, to be as good as my word, I sold some cotton and some stock, equipped this company and —*voila tout!*"

"But you are not commanding your company?"

"Couldn't do it, you see. Wouldn't let the boys elect me an officer and have the Sec. think I had *bought* my commission! But, old fellow, I'll win it before the month is out; and, if God spares me, mother shall call her boy Colonel Frank, before Christmas!"

Poor Frank! Before the hoped-for day his bones were bleaching in front of Fort Magruder. One morning the retreat from York-town—a pitiful roadside skirmish—a bullet in his brain—and the tramp of McClellan's advancing hosts packed the fresh sods over his grave, *herois monumentum!* He was one of many, but no truer heart or readier hand were stilled in all the war.

Passing out of the cut through the high bluff, just across the "Jeems" river bridge, Richmond burst beautifully into view; spreading panorama-like over her swelling hills, with the evening sun gilding simple houses and towering spires alike into a glory. The city follows the curve of the river, seated on amphitheatric hills, retreating from its banks; fringes of dense woods shading their slopes, or making blue background against the sky. No city of the South has grander or more picturesque approach; and now—as the slant rays of the sun kissed her a loving good-night—nothing in the view hinted of war to come, but all of holy peace.

Just here the James narrows its bed between high banks, and for some three miles—from Hollywood cemetery down to "Rockett's" landing—the shallow current dashes over its rocky bed with the force and chafe of a mountain torrent; now swirling, churned into foamy rapids, again gliding swiftly smooth around larger patches of islands that dot its surface. On the right hand hills, behind us, rises the suburb village of Manchester, already of considerable importance as a milling town; and the whole *coup d'œil*—from the shining heights of Chimborazo to the green slopes of the city of the silent, the grim, gray old capitol as a centerpiece—makes a Claud landscape that admits no thought of the bloody future!

The railroad bridge—then a frail, giddy structure, wide enough, for a track and footway—spans near a mile across the boiling current. From the car-platform, the treetops far below and the rugged, foam-crowned rocks look inhospitably distant. I have whirled round the high trestles on the Baltimore & Ohio when the work swayed and rattled under the heavy train, threatening each moment to hurl us down the precipitous mountain into the black, rocky bed of the Cheat, hundreds of feet below; have dashed at speed round steep grades hewn in the solid rock, where the sharp, jagged peaks rose a thousand feet beneath us; and I have raced in pitchy nights on the western rivers in tinder-box boats, that seemed shaking to pieces away from their red-hot furnaces; but I do not recall any piece of travel that gave the same sense of the instability of railroad affairs as that James river bridge.

The city was thoroughly jammed—its ordinary population of forty thousand swelled to three times that number by the sudden pressure. Of course, all the Government, with its thousand employés, had come on; and in addition, all the loose population along the railroad over which it had passed seemed to have clung to and been rolled into Richmond with it. Not only did this mania seize the wealthier and well-to-do classes, but the queerest costumes of the inland corners of Georgia and Tennessee disported themselves with perfect composure at hotels and on the streets. Besides, from ten to fifteen thousand troops were always collected, as a general rendezvous, before assignment to one of the important points—Norfolk, the Peninsula, or the Potomac lines. Although these were in camp out of town, their officers and men thronged the streets from daylight to dark, on business or pleasure bent; and the variety of uniforms—from the butternut of the Georgia private to the three stars of the flash colonel—broke the monotony of the streets pleasingly to the eye.

Hotel accommodations in Richmond were always small and plain, and now they were all overflowing. The Spotswood, Exchange and American held beds at a high premium in the parlors, halls and even on the billiard-tables. All the lesser houses were equally packed, and crowds of guests stood hungrily round the dining-room doors at meal-times, watching and scrambling for vacated seats. It was a clear case of "devil take the hindmost," for their *cuisine* decreased in quantity and quality in exact ratio to augmentation of their custom. The Richmond hotels, always mediocre, were now wretched. Such a thing as a clean room, a hot steak, or an answered bell were not to be bought by flagrant bribery. I would fain believe that all concerned did their best; but rapid influx absolutely overwhelmed them; and resources of the neighboring country—ample to support one-third the numbers now collected—were quickly exhausted under suddenly tripled demand. No transportation for private supplies was available in the overtaxed condition of the railroads; so the strangers, perforce, had to "grin and bear it," dry soever as the grin might be. Private boarding-houses sprang up like mushrooms on every block; bereaved relicts and ambitious spinsterhood equally clutching the chance to turn an honest penny. And naturally, ordinary trials of boarding-house life were aggravated by circumstance. Discomfort of the hotels was great enough; but, dessicated into the boarding-house can, it became simply unendurable. In this strait many private families were induced to open their doors to the better class of strangers; and gradually the whole dense population settled down, wedged into comparative quiet. Happily, my lines fell in these pleasanter places; and, whatever the unavoidable trials, it were base ingratitude in an experimental pilgrim among the mail-bags to indite a new Jeremiad thereon.

Suites of rooms had been reserved at the Spotswood hotel for the President and some of his Cabinet; so that house naturally became headquarters. Mr. Davis' office, the "Cabinet-room" with the State and Treasury Departments were located in the custom-house; and the other bureaux of the Government were relegated to the "Mechanics' Institute," an ungainly pile of bricks, formerly used as library and lecture-rooms.

The State of Virginia, though not at all on pleasure bent in inviting the Government to her capital, had yet been of frugal enough mind not to commence preparations in advance of acceptance; and the hejira followed so swiftly upon it that we plumped down into their very midst. Miss Bremer—who declared Alexandria entirely finished because she never heard the sound of a hammer—would have been more than amused at Richmond. The great halls of the Institute were cutting up into offices, with deafening clatter, day and night; and one of the Cabinet secretaries—who did not exhibit, if indeed he possessed, that aspiration ascribed to the devil when ill—swore himself almost to a shadow.

Both these public offices faced upon Capitol Square; a large, iron-fenced space, beautifully undulating and with walks winding under grand old trees. On the central hill stood the old State Capitol, picturesque from the river, but grimly dirty on close inspection. It is a plain, quadrangular construction, with Grecian pediment and columns on its south front and broad flights of steps leading to its side porticoes. Below were the halls of the legislature, now turned over to the Confederate States Congress; and in the small rotunda connecting them stood Houdon's celebrated statue of Washington—a simple but majestic figure in marble, ordered by Dr. Franklin from the French sculptor in 1785—of which Virginians are justly proud. In the cool, vaulted basement were the State officials; and above the halls the offices of the governor and the State library. That collection, while lacking many modern works, held some rare and valuable editions. It was presided over by the gentlest and most courteous *littérateur* of the South. Many a bedeviled and ambitious public man may still recall his quiet, modest aid, in strong contrast to the *brusquerie* and "insolence of office," too much the general rule; and his touching, heart-born poems were familiar at every southern hearth and camp-fireside. Soon after, the familiar voice of friendship was dulled to him—*exul patriæ*—by the boom of the broad Atlantic; and now his bones rest far away from those alcoves and their classic dust.

John R. Thompson, the editor of the famous "Southern Literary Messenger," went to London to edit "The Index," established in the never-relinquished hope of influencing European opinion. On reaching New York, when the cause he loved was lost, the staunch friendship of Richard Henry Stoddard and the appreciation of William Cullen Bryant found him congenial work on "The Post." But the sensitive spirit was broken; a few brief years saw the end, and only a green memory is left to those who loved, even without knowing, the purest southern poet.

From the roof of the Capitol is had the finest view of Richmond, the surrounding country lying like a map for a radius of twenty miles. Only from this bird's-eye view can a perfect idea be gained of the elevation of the city, perched above a rolling country—its stretches of meadowland below cut by the valley of the James; the river stealing in sluggish, molten silver through it, or heaving up inland into bold, tree-bearded hills, high enough to take the light from the clouds on their tops, as a halo. Far northward alternate swells of light and depressions of shadow among the hills; the far-off horizon making a girdle of purple light, blended into the blue of undefined woods. On clear days, a splendid ozone fills the air at that high perch, the picture having, as far as the eye can travel, stereoscopic clearness.

Immediately beneath lies the Square; its winding walks, rare old trees and rich sweep of sod filled with children, so full of enjoyment that one is half-minded to drop down and roll over the grass with them. On the central walk, midway between the Capitol and St. Paul's church, stands Crawford's equestrian Washington in bronze, resting upon a circular base and pedestal of plain granite, in which are bases for statues of the mighty Virginians of the past. Only the three southern ones were now occupied; but those figures—Jefferson, Mason and Henry—were accepted as surpassing in merit the central work. The Washington is imposing in size and position, but its art is open to criticism. The horse is exaggeration of pose. and muscle; being equally strained, though not rampant, as that inopportune charger on which Clark Mills perched General Jackson, at the national Capital. Nor is this " first in peace " by any means " the first " on horseback; the figure being theatric rather than dignified, and the extended arm more gymnastic than statuesque.

An irate senator once told the august body he addressed that it was a warning to them—"pointing straight to the penitentiary!" So, as a whole, the group, if not thoroughly classic, may be admirably useful.

From Capitol Square, open, wide streets—neatly built up and meeting each other at right angles—stretch away on all sides; an occasional spire or dome, and frequent houses larger than the rest, breaking the monotony. Below, toward the river, lie the basins, docks and rows of warehouses; and further still is the landing, "Rockett's," the head of river navigation, above which no vessels of any size can come. Just under the Capitol—to the East—stands the governor's house, a plain, substantial mansion of the olden time, embosomed in trees and flower-beds. Further off, in the same line, rise the red and ragged slopes of Church Hill. It takes its name from the old church in which Patrick Henry made his celebrated speech—a structure still in pretty good preservation. And still further away—opposite the vanishing point of the water view—are seen the green tops of Chimborazo Heights and Howard's Grove—hospital sites, whose names have been graven upon the hearts of all southern people by the mordant of sorrow!

Just across the river, to the South, the white and scattered village of Manchester is prettily relieved against the green slopes on which it sits. There the bridge cuts the shining chafe of the river like a black wire; and just under it, the wind sighs softly in the treetops of Belle Isle, afterward to become so famous in the newspaper annals of the North, as a prison for the Union soldiers captured in the long struggle for the city.

Far to the west, higher shafts of Hollywood Cemetery gleam among the trees; and the rapids, dancing down in the sunlight, break away into a broader sheet of foam around its point. Except, perhaps, " Bonnie Venture " (*Buona Ventura*), at Savannah, there is no site for a cemetery in the South, naturally so picturesque and at the same time solemn, as this. Rising from comparatively level ground in the rear, it swells and undulates in a series of gentle hills to the river, that embraces it on three sides. Rows of magnificent old trees in many places arch quite across the walk—giving, even at midday, a half-twilight—and the sigh of the river breeze in their tops, mingling with the constant roar of the rapids, seems to sing a *Te Deum* for the dead. The graves are simple and unpretending—only an occasional column of any prominence rearing itself above the humbler surroundings.

On a hill—just behind the point where the river curves round the extreme point—rest the ashes of Monroe, enclosed in a large and ornate mausoleum, where they were laid when escorted south by the New York Seventh Regiment. That escort was treated with all the generous hospitality Virginia can so well use; and numerous and deep were the oaths of amity between the citizen-soldiers. Though the Seventh were not notoriously deadly, in the war that followed, only the shortest of memories—or, indeed, the most glowing of patriotism—could have erased the brother-love, then and there bumpered down!

Under the hills of the cemetery—the dirty, dull canal creeping between them—stand the buildings, dam and powerful pumps of the water service; ordinarily more than adequate for all uses. Usually, the water was pure and clear; but when heavy rains washed the river lands, the "noble Jeems" rushed by with an unsavory and dingy current, that might have shamed the yellow Tiber and rivaled the Nile itself. Sometimes the weary and worn patriot took his whisky and mud, thick enough to demand a fork; and for days

> "The water is muddy and dank
> As ever a company pumped."

The outskirts of Richmond are belted by bold crests, near enough together to form a chain of natural forts. These were now fortifying; the son of wealth, the son of Erin and the son of Ham laboring in perspiration and in peace side by side. Later these forts did good turn, during cavalry raids, when the city was uncovered and the garrison but nominal.

Gamble's hill, a pretty but steep slope, cuts the river west of the bridge. Rising above its curves, from the Capitol view-point, are the slate-roofed Tredegar Works; their tall chimneys puffing endless black smoke against the sunshine, which reflects it, a livid green, upon the white foam of the rapids. So potent a factor in the aggressive power of the Confederacy was this foundry that it overtopped the regular government agencies. When the war began, this was the only rolling-mill of great capacity, of which the South could boast; the only one, indeed, capable of casting heavy guns. Almost the first decisive act of Virginia was to prevent, by seizure, the delivery to United States officers of some guns cast for them by the Tredegar Works; and, from that day, there were no more earnest and energetic workers for the cause of southern independence than the firm of Jos. R. Anderson & Co. It was said, at this time, that the firm was in financial straits. But it thrived so well on government patronage—spite of sundry boards to consider if army and navy work was not paid for at ruinously low rates—that it greatly increased in size; added to its utility by importations of costly machinery, through the blockade; stood loss of one-third of its buildings, by fire; used a ship of its own for importation; and, at the close of the struggle, was in better condition than at the commencement. The senior partner was, for a time, in the field at head of his brigade; but affairs were so well managed, in the interval, by the Messrs. Tanner—father and son, who were partners with General Anderson—that his absence was not appreciable in the work.

It was at the Tredegar Works that the famous " Brooke gun "—a rifled 7-inch—was cast, tested and perfected. Here the plates for the iron-clads, in almost all southern waters, were rolled or made ready for use. Here heavy ordnance for the forts was cast, together with shells and shot; and here the torpedoes—sometimes so effective, and usually so useless—were contrived and made. Indeed, the Tredegar Works so greatly aided the Confederacy, that the lengthening of the war may be, in large measure, attributed to their capacity, and to the able zeal with which they were managed.

So great and effective an agent could not fail to receive, from the Richmond government, every aid in obtainance of supplies, labor and transportation. "The Works" had mines, mills and pork-packeries in various sections of the South; thus obtaining coal and metals, as well as food—at reduced rates, within reach of their wages—for an army of employés. So great was the necessary number of these—whites, skilled in labor—that even closest conscription left the junior of the firm a full battalion of infantry. This, drilled and equipped from his own shops, Major Tanner led in person, when raids or other straits made their soldiering paramount to other occupation. And—even when greatest scarcity of provisions came—the agents of " the Works " proceeded with those of the commissary of the Confederacy, *pari passu.*

An odd incident, coming to mind just here, will point the general estimate of the importance of the Tredegar Works. A special train was crossing the bridge, en route for Petersburg, at a time when transportation was rare. A huge negro, blacker than the soot upon his face, sat placidly on the platform of the rear car.

" What are you doing here ? " was asked by the officer in charge.

" Rid'n' t' Petesbug," was the placid reply.

" Have you paid your fare ? "

" Don' got nun t' pay, boss. Rides onner pass, I does ! "

" Work for the government ? "—this rather impatiently.

Ebo rolled his eyes, with expression of deep disgust, as he reponded, grandly :

" No—*sah!* Fur t'uther consarn ! "

CHAPTER XII.

Notwithstanding the haste of removal from Montgomery, the vast amount of work to be reduced to regular order, and the apparent confusion of the executive departments, affairs rapidly shaped themselves into working form soon after the arrival in Richmond.

That city, as the terminus of railway travel from the South and West, was naturally the rendezvous for all troops coming from the various quarters of the Confederacy; and, at the date of the change of government, some fifteen thousand were already collected in the camps about the town. These comprised levies from every section of the ten states that had adhered to the southern government—regulars, volunteers and militia and of all arms.

South Carolina and Louisiana had immediately on their secession organized regular armies, on a more perfect and permanent basis than their sister states, and had garrisoned their forts—and points then supposed most vulnerable—with them. The call of the Confederate Government for more troops had not interfered with these organizations, but had brought into the field new material in the shape of volunteer regiments and battalions of cavalry, artillery and infantry.

While, as a general thing, the rank and file of the state regulars were composed of the laboring classes, foreigners and the usual useless and floating portion of their populations, officered by gentlemen of better position and education, appointed by the governors, the volunteers had in their ranks men of all conditions, from the humblest laborer to the scholar, the banker and the priest.

They were commanded by men they themselves elected, as being the most competent and acceptable, either by reason of greater ability, or military education.

Upon the action of her convention, Virginia was found to have been in nowise behind the other states in her preparations. In fact, she had anticipated its somewhat tardy movement and had marshaled into order an array of her stout yeomanry that was in itself no contemptible army. When she joined the Confederacy, she offered to its acceptance over twenty full regiments, and parts of others sufficient to make eight or ten more.

Almost all the officers of the United States Army and Navy, from her borders, had promptly resigned and tendered their swords and services to her governor. Robert E. Lee—with his great family influence and connection—Joseph E. Johnston, Magruder, Stuart, and a host of others whose names shine bright in the annals of war, had even anticipated the formal act of secession; and its passage found them busily working, with any rank and in any way that could best conduce to the good of the state. With their aid, Virginia, too, had organized a regular army; and, feeling the necessity for prompt action to be imminent, had armed, drilled and equipped it to the limit of her straightened means; and had already begun to put her frontiers into a state of defense.

General Lee was made commander-in-chief, and the flower of Virginia, from the old army, were made generals and subordinate officers under him.

The gentlemen of the Old Dominion were not slow to show a good example to the lower classes. Crack companies that had been unused to any more dreadful war than the blank cartridge of a holiday pageant, went in to a man; whole battalions were formed from which no drop of blood might be spilled, that did not flow straight from one of the known and honored of her history.

Who has not heard of the First Virginia? a name that brings back the grand old days of chivalric devotion and doughty deed! Who in the South does not honor it? though scarce a dozen of the noble hearts that first flocked to its proud banner can now gather round the grim and shattered old lion, who bought with many a wound in front the right to lead it to the fray. And "Co. F," in whose ranks were the brilliant advocate, the skillful surgeon, the man of letters and the smooth-faced pet of the Mayday gathering—all that made the pride, the boast and the love of Richmond!

The beacon had been lighted on the mountain top, and had gleamed by her river sides! The sturdy hunter from the West, and the dashing horseman from the East; the merchant at his till, and the farmer, with hard hand on the plough-handle—all heard the voice of the bugle and answered with a shout!

Men of all classes—from the highest-born and richest to the humblest and poorest—from the grandsire with his flint-lock to the sunny-haired stripling scarcely in his teens—with one accord

"———Came forth at the call
With the rush of their rivers when tempests appall,
And the torrents their sources unseal!"

Thus, when the Government first felt that Virginia was to be the battle-ground and decided to lash its fortunes to hers amid the black billows that were surging around it, an army was already in the field; partially armed, already somewhat proficient in drill and learning, by the discipline of camp and bivouac, to prepare for the stern realities of war.

In many instances, the posting of their regulars by the respective state governments had been considered so judicious, that the War Department made no change; as, for instance, in garrisoning the forts in Charleston harbor by the South Carolina Regular Artillery, and those at New Orleans by the 1st and 2d Louisiana Regulars. But after the necessary garrison had been left in the most exposed points, every available man was ordered to Virginia. Here the work of organization went on with a smoothness and regularity scarcely to have been looked for. Occasionally a hitch occurred that threatened to get the threads of preparation into an ugly knot; but it was ever unraveled without the Gordian treatment.

Fresh troops from every quarter were collecting rapidly. First came Gregg's regiment of South Carolinians; and they were met with open arms by the Virginians, soldiery and citizens. They received the first gush of the new brotherhood of defiance and of danger; and their camp—constantly visited by the ladies and even children of Richmond—had more the air of a picnic than of a bivouac. Many of the men and most of the officers in the First Carolina bore

"Names,
Familiar in their mouths as household words."

They were descendants from that other revolution, the political celebrities, or the watering-place beaux; and the houses of Richmond were opened to them at once. Dinners, parties and rides were improvised, and the first comers were voted, especially by the ladies, a "joy forever." Gradually, as regiment after regiment marched in and the city filled to overflowing with the still welcome strangers, the novelty wore off; and, though the feeling of fellowship and kindliness was just as strong, the citizens found that their hearts were larger than their houses, and that even Virginia hospitality must have a limit. Varied, indeed, were the forms one met on every street and road about Richmond. Here the long-haired Texan, sitting his horse like a centaur, with high-peaked saddle and jingling spurs, dashed by—a pictured *guacho*. There the western mountaineer, with bearskin shirt, fringed leggings, and the long, deadly rifle, carried one back to the days of Boone and the " dark and bloody ground." The dirty gray and tarnished silver of the muddy-complexioned Carolinian ; the dingy butternut of the lank, muscular Georgian, with its green trimming and full skirts ; and the Alabamians from the coast, nearly all in blue of a cleaner hue and neater cut ; while the Louisiana troops were, as a general thing, better equipped and more regularly uniformed than any others in the motley throng.

But the most remarked dress that flashed among these varied uniforms was the blue-and-orange of the Maryland Zouaves. At the time of the riot of the 19th of April, there had just been perfected a splendid organization of the younger gentlemen of the Monumental City—a veritable *corps d' élite*—known as the " Maryland Guard." It was as remarkable for excellence of discipline and perfection of equipment, as for containing the very best blood of the city ; and, though taking no part—as an organization—in the riot, it was immediately afterward put by its officers at the disposal of the Baltimore authorities.

When it became apparent that Maryland could take no active part in the struggle, many members of this corps promptly left the luxuries of their homes, their early associations, and even the very means of livelihood, to go south and battle for the principles they held. They unhesitatingly expatriated themselves, and gave up all they held dear—except honor—to range themselves under that flag for which they had declared. Many of them had been born and reared southerners—many had only the chivalric intention to fight for the cause they felt right. Their sympathies all went with the South, and their blood leaped to help her in this her hour of sore trial.

Was it strange that the generous Virginian should have opened his arms to give these men the embrace of fellowship and brotherhood ; that they should have been honored guests at every hospitable board ; that bright eyes should have glanced brighter at a glimpse of the orange and blue ?

Much has been said and much written of the Marylanders in the South; of their demoralized condition, their speculative tendencies, and their wild dissipations. Not a few of them came for plunder—some left their country for their country's good:—but in the veins of such only a muddy current ran! Where the Maryland gentleman was found on the stranger soil, it was musket in hand, battling for it; and so well was his *devoir* done, that he rapidly changed the bayonet for the sword ; and more than one general, whose name will live in the South, came from their number.

Almost all the soldiery wore the broad, soft *slouch*, in place of the more military, but less comfortable, *kepi*. There was something about it characteristic of the race—it seemed to suit exactly the free, care-less port of the men—and it was equally useful as a protection from the fierce June sun, or beating rain, and as a night-cap.

Arms, too, were as varied as the uniforms. Many whole regi-ments were armed with the Belgian or Springfield musket—light, and carrying a large ball an immense distance; others had only the Mis-sissippi rifle; while some again sported a mixture of rifles, muskets and shot-guns. The greatest variety was in the cavalry—if such it could be called. Men accustomed from infancy to the saddle and the rifle had seized whatever weapon they were possessed of; and more at home on horseback than on foot, they were, no doubt, ugly enemies in a bush fight, or an ambuscade. Many whole companies had no sabers but those their officers carried, and the very individ-uality and self-reliance of the men acted as an invincible opponent to drill and discipline. Mounted on horses of all sizes and colors; equipped with all varieties of trappings; and carrying slung at their backs every known game-killer—from rifle to duck gun—they would have been a strange picture to the European officer to which their splendid horsemanship and lithe, agile figures could have added no varnish to make him believe them cavalry.

But every man you met, mounted or footman, carried in his belt the broad, straight, double-edged bowie-knife, useful alike for war-like, or culinary purposes; and few, indeed, did not balance it with the revolver. In some of the crack corps this was strictly prohib-ited ; for the difficulty has ever been in armies to teach the men to use efficiently the *one* weapon belonging to them ; and that there is no safety in a multitude.

7

Long before the first scene of the bloody drama was done—and stern realities had taken the gilt from the pomp and circumstance of war—the actors had cast aside all the "properties" they did not absolutely need. The exhaustion of their first few battles, or a couple of Jackson's marches, taught them that in this race for life and limb, there was no need to carry extra weight. I constantly had brought to mind the anecdote of the Crimean Zouaves, about to charge a redan, who answered their officer's query as to the number of cartridges they had by tapping their saber bayonets.

The arriving regiments were inspected, mustered into the Confederate service and drilled by competent officers; vacancies were filled; and such wanting equipments, as could be supplied, bestowed upon them. They were then brigaded, and after time enough to become accustomed to their commanders and to each other, were forwarded to points where, at the moment, troops appeared most needed.

The three points in Virginia, considered as vital, were the Peninsula, formed by the James and York rivers, Norfolk, and the open country around and about Orange Courthouse to the Potomac. Fortress Monroe impregnable to assault, by the land side, and so easily provisioned and garrisoned by sea, was looked upon as the most dangerous neighbor. From its walls, the legions of the North might, at any moment, swoop down upon the unprotected country around it and establish a foothold, from which it would be hard to dislodge them, as at Newport's News. Its propinquity to Norfolk, together with the vast preponderance of the United States in naval power, made an attack upon that place the most reasonable supposition. The State of Virginia had already put it in as good defense as the time permitted. General Huger, a distinguished officer of Ordnance from the U. S. service, had at once been sent there; and his preparations had been such that an unfinished earth work, at Sewell's Point, stood for four hours, on the 19th of May, the bombardment of the U. S. ships "Minnesota" and "Monticello."

The Confederate War Department felt such confidence in the engineering and administrative ability of General Huger, that it endorsed the action of Virginia by giving him a brigadier's commission and instructions to put Norfolk and the avenues of its approach in complete state of defense. A sufficient garrison of picked troops—among them the Third Alabama and some of the best Richmond companies—was given him; and Norfolk was soon declared securely fortified.

The Peninsula was even more exposed to land attack from Fortress Monroe; and General John B. Magruder had been sent there with a part of the Virginia army, with headquarters at Yorktown. General Magruder had long been a well-known officer of the U. S. Army, where his personal popularity and a certain magnificence of manner had gained him the sobriquet of "Prince John." He possessed energy and dash in no mean degree; and on arriving at his sphere of duty, strained every nerve to put the Peninsula in a state of defense. His work, too, was approved by the Confederate War Department; the commission of brigadier conferred upon him, and re-enforcements —sufficient in its judgment, though not in his—were sent at once to his command.

While Fortress Monroe threatened the safety of Norfolk, and, by the Peninsula of the lower approaches to Richmond, Alexandria could hold a formidable army, ready at any moment to swoop down by the upper and more accessible approaches around Orange Courthouse. The occupation of Alexandria by the Union forces on the 24th of May was looked upon by Confederate leaders as the most decided act of war yet ventured upon by their wary adversary. Whatever may have been done within the *non-seceded* states, the South deluded herself that it was simply an exposition of the power of the government—a sort of Chinese warfare of gongs and tom-toms. The passage of the Potomac and seizure of a city under the ægis of the Confederate Government was actually crossing the Rubicon and carrying the war directly into the southern territory. Fortress Monroe and other fortified points still held by the United States, in the South, were conceded to be in a measure hers, at least by the right of possession; but Alexandria was considered part and parcel of the Confederacy, and as such sacred from invasion. Hence no means were taken to prevent its occupation. On Virginia soil—many of its citizens already in the rebel ranks, and its houses a rendezvous for the cavalry of the Virginia army, its seizure was construed to mean real invasion.

The possession of this key to the land approaches of Richmond; its great facilities of re-enforcement and supply by propinquity to the depots at Washington and elsewhere; and the determined intention of the Federals to hold and use it, could not be misunderstood.

And while the Southern Government felt the advantages its posses-

sion gave the Union troops for concentrating and advancing, the people were aroused to a pitch of high indignation by the choice of the
troops sent to first invade their soil.

The war, too, was yet young enough to leave all the romance
about it; scenes of violence were as yet rare; and the death of Jackson, with the circumstances attending it, caused a deep and general
feeling of bitterness. While the southern public opened its arms and
took to its sympathy and protection the widow and orphans of the
first Virginian whose blood was shed in her cause, many and bitter
were the vows made around the bivouac to avenge his untimely end.
The men who made the grim vow were of the stuff to keep it; the
name of "Jackson, the Martyr," became a war-cry, and the bloody
tracks of Manassas

" How that oath was kept can tell! "

On the 23d of May, Joseph E. Johnston received his commission
as General in the Regular Army, and went to Harper's Ferry in
command of all troops in that region—known as the Army of the
Shenandoah. Beauregard, with the same grade, was recalled on his
way to the West, and sent to command at Manassas.

From the great ease of putting troops across the fords of the Potomac into Virginia, it was considered necessary to concentrate, at
points from which they could be easily shifted, a sufficient reliable
force to meet any such movement; and the two officers in whom the
government had greatest confidence as tacticians, were sent to watch
for and checkmate it.

Meanwhile, Missouri had risen, the governor had declared the
rights of the State infringed; and the movements of Generals Lyon
and Blair—culminating in the St. Louis riots between the citizens and
the Dutch soldiery—had put an end to all semblance of neutrality.
Governor Jackson moved the state archives, and transferred the capital from Jefferson City to Boonesville. On the 13th of June he issued
a proclamation calling for fifty thousand volunteers to defend the
State of Missouri from Federal invasion; and appointed Sterling Price
a major-general, with nine brigadiers, among whom were Jeff
Thompson, Clark and Parsons. Perhaps no state went into open resistance of the United States authority as unprepared in every way as
Missouri. Her population was scattered; one-half Union, and utterly
ignorant of drill, discipline, or any of the arts of war. They were,

besides, perfectly unarmed, except with their hunting pieces, and the state Capital, the arsenals and all the larger towns were in possession of the Union troops. These laughed at the attempt of Missouri to shake off the grasp of the government, and their generals boldly proclaimed that "she was under the paws of the lion, and her first movement would cause them to close and crush her life out."

Still, Price, seconded by his brigadiers, went to work with great activity to collect their scattered adherents and put them into form. In a country held by superior forces, with communications cut up and no means of information, the task was Herculean, indeed. Yet they endeavored by zeal and energy to make amends for these deficiencies and for the want of supplies. Price's name was a tower of strength in itself; his hardy compatriots flocked around him, and nearly every day there were collisions between them and the United States troops. These skirmishes, though unimportant in themselves, gave the new soldiers lessons in war; and not infrequently added to their scanty stock of arms and equipments. They were but the first dashes in the grand tableaux of war that Price was yet to hew, with the bold hand of a master, from the crude mass of material alone in his power to use.

CHAPTER XIII.

THE LEADERS AND THE LED.

Thus much of detail arranged, General Lee was, for the present, detained in Richmond by the President, as consulting and organizing officer; and to aid the Adjutant-General—Samuel Cooper, senior general of the five—in the location of armies, distribution of troops, and assignment of officers. General Lee's perfect knowledge of the *materiel* of the Virginia army and of the topographical features of the state, peculiarly fitted him for this work; but every step was taken subject to the decision of Mr. Davis himself. The appointments of officers, the distribution of troops—in fact, the minutiæ of the War Department—were managed by him in person.

He seemed fully alive to the vital importance of making the groundwork of the military system solid and smooth. Real preparations had begun so late that only the strong hand could now avail; and though Mr. Walker still held the empty portfolio of the secretaryship, he, and the army, and the country knew who, in fact, did the work. But to do Mr. Davis justice, he did not make his *fantoccini* suffer if he pulled the wires the wrong way. He was not only President and secretary of five departments—which naturally caused some errors; but that spice of the dictator in him made him quite willing to shoulder the responsibilities of all the positions.

Now, as in Montgomery, I wondered that the frail body—that could not bend—did not break beneath the load of anxiety and bodily labor he imposed upon it. His energy and industry were untiring; and every afternoon the declining sun found him in the saddle, inspecting and reviewing the troops, at one of the many camps near town. Sometimes the hard, stolid face of the Postmaster-General appeared at his side; again Senator Wigfall galloped along, with his pants stuck in his boots and seeming to enjoy the saddle much more than the curule chair; and often "Little Jeff"—the Benjamin of Mr. Davis' household—trotted at his side. But there was never a suite, seldom a courier; and wherever he went, plain, stirring syllables of cheer—and strong, grave words of incentive—dropped from his lips among the soldiery. They were treasured as the truth, too, by that rough auditory; for as yet, Mr. Davis was in the zenith of his popularity—a perfect idol with army and people. The first sight of the tall, erect figure, swaying so easily to the action of the powerful gray, was a signal for the wildest cheers from the camps; and the people in the streets raised their hats and stood uncovered while the representative man passed.

Cavil, jealousy and partisan intrigue, in which he and the cause finally went down together, had not yet done their work. There were many murmurers at real, many growlers at supposed, errors; but no opposition party—truer to itself and its interests than to the cause —had yet been organized on a basis strong enough to defy and thwart "the man."

Every one connected with the government remarked the vast difference of its reception by the Richmond and Montgomery people. The Alabamians came forward with decision and alacrity to offer their lives and fortunes to the cause. They made any sacrifices to the government, as such; but, privately, they regarded the individuals connected with it as social brigands come to rob their society of all that was good and pure in it.

Richmond, on the contrary, having given the invitation, made the best of it when accepted. The people united in sincere effort to show a whole-souled hospitality to all strangers deserving of it. Gentlemen in the government were received with frank and free-handed kindness; and even a wretch, who had wintered in the shade of the Washington upas, was allowed to flutter about and not be gunned for by the double-barreled spectacles of every respectable dowager!

Richmond was always a great place for excitements; but with the great addition of inflammable material recently, it required but a very small spark to raise a roaring, if not dangerous, flame. On a bright Sunday in April, when

> "The beams of God's own hallowed day
> Had painted every spire with gold,
> And, calling sinful men to pray,
> Long, loud and deep the bell had tolled"—

the citizens were worshipping quietly and a peaceful stillness reigned everywhere. Suddenly, as if a rocket had gone up, the rumor flew from mouth to mouth that the "Pawnee" was steaming up the river to shell the city. The congregations, not waiting to be dismissed, rushed from the churches with a single impulse; the alarm bell in the Square pealed out with a frightened chime. For once, even the women of Richmond were alarmed. The whole population flocked toward "Rocketts"—every eye strained to catch a first glimpse of the terrible monster approaching so rapidly. Old and young men, in Sunday attire, hastened along with rusty muskets and neat "Mantons" on their shoulders; groups of bareheaded ladies were at the corners, asking the news and repeating every fear-invented tale; and more than one of the "solid men" was seen with hand-baskets, loaded with rock, to dam the river! Late in the evening, the veterans of six hours were dismissed, it turning out that there was no cause whatever for the alarm ; and when after events showed them that vessel —so battered and badgered by the river batteries— "Pawnee Sunday" became a by-word among the citizens.

Richmond was not cosmopolitan in her habits or ideas, and there was, in some quarters, a vague, lingering suspicion as to the result of the experiment ; but the society felt that the government was its guest, and as such was to be honored. The city itself was a small one, the society was general and provincial; and there was in it a sort of brotherly-love tone that struck a stranger, at first, as very curious. This was, in a great measure, attributable to the fact that the social circle had been for years a constant quantity, and everybody in it had known everybody else since childhood.

The men, as a general thing, were very cordial to the strangers, and some very delightful and some very odd acquaintances were made among them. Chief among the latter was one, whom we may call— as he would say "for euphony"—Will Wyatt; the most perfect specimen of the genus man-about-town in the city. He was very young, with wealth, a pleasing exterior, and an absolute greed for society. His naturally good mind had been very prettily cultivated—by himself rather than his masters—and he had traveled just enough to understand, without despising, the weaknesses of his compatriots. He and the omniscient Styles were fast friends, and a card to Wyatt, signed "Fondly thine own, S. S.," had done the business for me. His house, horses and friends were all at my service; and in the few intervals that anxiety and duty left for ennui, he effectually drove the monster off.

"I'm devilish sorry, old man," he said, one day, after we got well acquainted, "that there's nothing going on in the social line. Drop in on me at six, to dinner; and I'll show you a clever fellow or two, and maybe have some music. You understand, my dear boy, we don't entertain now. After all, it's so late in the season there'd be little doing in peace times; but this infernal war has smashed us up completely. Getting your nose red taking leave of your tender family is the only style they vote at all nobby now—*À diner!*"

The dinner and music at Wyatt's were not warlike—and particularly was the wine not of that description; but the men were. Over cigars, the conversation turned upon the organization of the army; and, accustomed as I was to seeing "the best men in the ranks," the way these young bloods talked rather astounded me.

"Private in 'Co. F,'" answered John C. to my query—he represented one of the finest estates on the river—"You've heard of 'F,' of course. We hang by the old company. Wyatt has just refused a captaincy of engineers to stick as third corporal."

"Neat that, in John," put in Wyatt, "when he was offered the majority of a regiment of cavalry and refused it to stay in."

"And why not?" said George H. shortly. "Pass the Madeira, Will. I would'nt give my place in 'F' for the best majority going. As far as that goes it's a mere matter of taste, I know. But the fact is, if we of the old organizations dodge our duty now by hunting commissions, how can we hope that the people will come to time promptly?" George H. had a quarter of a million to his credit, and was an only son—"Now, I think Bev did a foolish thing not to take his regiment when Uncle Jeff offered him the commission.

"I don't see it," responded Beverly I. in an aggrieved tone. "You fellows in 'F' were down on your captain when he took his colonelcy; and I'm as proud of my junior lieutenancy in the old First, as if I commanded 'F' company itself!"

"But is it usual," I queried, "for you gentlemen to refuse promotion when offered—I don't mean to not seek it—to remain with your old companies? Would you stay in the ranks as a private when as a captain or major you might do better service?"

"*Peutêtre* for the present," responded Wyatt—"Don't misunderstand us; we're not riding at windmills, and I sincerely hope you'll see us all with wreaths on our collars yet. But there's a tacit agreement that just now we can do more good in the ranks than anywhere else. For myself, I don't delight in drill and dirt, and don't endorse that sentimental bosh about the ' post of honor.' But our duty is where we can do most good, and our example will decide many doubtful ones and shame the laggard."

"And we'll all go out after a few fights, if we don't get popped off," put in George H., "and then we'll feel we've won our spurs!"

"Well, I'm not too modest to say that I think we *are* pretty expensive food for powder," said John C., "but then we're not worth more than the 'Crescents,' the 'Cadets,' or 'Hampton's Legion.' The colonel's sons are both in the ranks of the Legion, and refused commissions. Why should the best blood of Carolina do more than the best blood of Virginia?"

"And see those Baltimore boys," said Adjutant Y., of a Georgia legion. "They've given up home, friends and wealth to come and fight for us and the cause. They don't go round begging for commissions! If my colonel didn't insist I was more useful where I am, I'd drop the bar and take a musket among them. That sort of stock I like!" But if Lieutenant Y. *had* taken the musket, a stray bullet might have spoiled a most dashing major-general of cavalry.

"I fear very much," I answered, "that the war will be long enough for all the really good material to come to the surface. The preparations at the North are on a scale we never before dreamed of, and her government seems determined to enforce obedience."

"God forbid!" and Wyatt spoke more solemnly than I ever heard him before. "But I begin to believe as you do. I'd sooner risk my wreath than that 'the good material' you speak of should have the 'chance to come to the surface.' Think how many a good fellow would be under the surface by that time!"

"It sometimes sickens me on parade," said George H., "when I look down the line and think what a gap in our old set a volley will make! I think we *are* pretty expensive food for powder, John. Miniés are no respecters of persons, old fellow; and there'll be many a black dress in Richmond after the first bulletin."

"God send we may all meet here after the war, and drink to the New Nation in Wyatt's sherry!" said Lieutenant Y. "It's better than the water at Howard's Grove. But the mare 'll have hot work to get the adjutant into camp before taps. So, here's how!" and he filled his glass and tossed it off, as we broke up.

I have recorded the spirit of a private, every-day conversation, just as I heard it over a dinner-table, from a party of giddy young men. But I thought over it long that night; and many times afterward when the sickening bulletins were posted after the battles.

Here were as gay and reckless a set of youths as wealth, position and everything to make life dear to them could produce, going into a desperate war—with a perfect sense of its perils, its probable duration and its rewards—yet refusing promotion offered, that their example might be more beneficial in calling out volunteers.

And there was no Quixotism. It was the result of reason and a conviction that they were only doing their duty; for, I believe every man of those I had just left perfectly appreciated the trials and discomforts he was preparing for himself, and felt the advantages that a commission, this early in the war, would give him!

It may be that this "romance of war" was not of long duration; and that after the first campaign the better class of men anxiously sought promotion. This was natural enough. They had won the right to it; and the sacrifice of their good example had not been without effect. But I do think it was much less natural that they should have so acted in the first place.

Industry and bustle were still the order of the day in camp; and, in town, the activity increased rather than abated. There were few idlers about Richmond, even chronic "do-nothings" becoming impressed with the idea that in the universal work they must do something.

The name of Henry A. Wise was relied upon by the Government as a great power to draw volunteers from the people he had so frequently represented in various capacities. The commission of brigadier-general was given him, with authority to raise a brigade to be called the "Wise Legion," to operate in Western Virginia. Though there was no reason to think Wise would make a great soldier, his personal popularity was supposed to be sufficient to counterbalance that objection; for it was of the first importance to the Government that the western half of the State should be saved to the Confederate cause. In the first place, the active and hardy population was splendid material for soldiers, and it was believed at Richmond that, with proper pressure applied, they would take up arms for the South in great numbers; otherwise, when the Federal troops advanced into

their country, they might go to the other side. Again, the products
of the rich western region were almost essential to the support of the
troops in Virginia, in view of contracted facilities for transportation; and the product of the Kanawha Salines alone—the only regular and very extensive salt works in the country—were worth a
strenuous effort. This portion of Virginia, too, was a great military
highway for United States troops, *en route* to the West; and once
securely lodged in its almost impregnable fastnesses, their ejection
would be practically impossible.

General Garnett—an old army officer of reputation and promise—
was already in that field, with a handful of troops from the Virginia
army; among them a regiment from about Richmond, commanded by
Lieutenant Colonel Pegram. The Federals, grasping at once the full
importance of this position, had sent to meet this demonstration an
army under General McClellan, with Rosecrans commanding the
advance. There had been no collision, but its approach could not
be long delayed; and the South wanted men.

In this posture of affairs, General Wise received his commission
and orders. The old politician donned his uniform with great alacrity; called about him a few of the best companies of Richmond,
as a nucleus; and went to work with all the vim and activity expected by those who knew him best. The "Richmond Light Infantry Blues"—the oldest company in Richmond, commanded by his
son—was foremost among them. "Co. F" was to go West, too; and
though its members, one and all, would have preferred a more promising sphere of duty, at Yorktown, or on the Potomac, every man
acquiesced with cheerful spirit.

"Sair was the weeping" of the matrons and maidens of Richmond, when told their darlings were to go; but their sorrow did
not prevent the most active demonstrations toward the comfort of
the outer and inner man.

"Not a pleasant summer jaunt we're to have, old man," Wyatt
said when he bade me good-bye. "I've been to that country hunting and found it devilish fine; but 'tisn't so fine by half when you're
hunting a Yank, who has a long-range rifle and is likewise hunting for
you. Then I've an idea of perpetual snow—glaciers—and all that
sort of thing. I feel like the new John Franklin. But I'll write a
book—'Trapping the Yank in the Ice-fields of the South.' Taking

title, eh? But seriously, I know we can't all go to Beauregard; and there'll be fighting enough all round before it 'holds up.' God bless you! We'll meet somewhere; if not before, when I come down in the fall to show you the new stars on my collar!"

Thus " Co. F" went into the campaign. Its record there is history. So is that of many another like it.

As I have tried to show, this spirit pervaded the whole South to an almost universal extent. Companies like these, scattered among the grosser material of the army, must have been the alloy that gave to the whole mass that true ring which will sound down all history! The coarse natures around could but be shamed into imitation, when they saw the delicately nurtured darlings of society toiling through mud knee deep, or sleeping in stiffening blankets, without a murmur! And many a charge has been saved because a regiment like the First Virginia or the Alabama Third walked straight into the iron hail, as though it had been a carnival pelting!

The man who tells us that blood has little effect must have read history to very little purpose; or have looked very carelessly into the glass that Nature hourly holds up to his view.

Wyatt was right when he said "there was nothing doing" socially. But there was much doing otherwise. The war was young yet, and each household had its engrossing excitement in getting its loved ones ready for the field. The pets of the ball-room were to lay aside broadcloth and kids; and the pump-soled boots of the "german" were to be changed for the brogan of the camp.

The women of the city were too busy now to care for society and its frippery; the new objects of life filled every hour. The anxieties of the war were not yet a twice-told tale, and no artificial excitements were needed to drive them away. The women of Virginia, like her men, were animated with a spirit of devotion and self-sacrifice. Mothers sent their youngest born to the front, and bade them bear their shields, or be found under them; and the damsel who did not bid her lover "God speed and go!" would have been a finger point and a scoff. And the flags for their pet regiments—though many a bitter tear was broidered into their folds—were always given with the brave injunction to bear them worthily, even to the death!

The spirit upon the people—one and all—was " The cause—not

us!" and under the rough gray, hearts beat with as high a chivalry
as- –

> " In the brave, good days of old,
>   When men for virtue and honor fought
>   In serried ranks, 'neath their banners bright,
>   By the fairy hands of beauty wrought,
>   And broidered with 'God and Right!'"

CHAPTER XIV.

THE BAPTISM OF BLOOD.

On the afternoon of June 10, 1861, Richmond was thrown into a commotion—though of a different nature—hardly exceeded by that exciting Sabbath, "Pawnee Sunday." Jubilant, but agitated crowds collected at the telegraph offices, the hotels and the doors of the War Department, to get the news of the first fight on Virginia soil.

That morning the enemy had pressed boldly forward, in three heavy columns, against Magruder's lines at Big Bethel Church. He had been sharply repulsed in several distinct charges, with heavy loss, by D. H. Hill's regiment—the first North Carolina, and two guns of the Richmond Howitzers, commanded by Major John W. Randolph—afterward Secretary of War.

Naturally there was great and deep rejoicing over this news in all quarters and from all classes. None had expected a different general result; for the confidence in Magruder's ability at that time, and in the pluck of his troops, was perfect; but the ease and dash with which the victory had been achieved was looked upon as the sure presage of great success elsewhere.

Although the conduct of the fight had been in the hands of Colonel D. H. Hill—afterward so well known as a staunch and hard fighting officer—and his North Carolinians had illustrated it by more than one act of personal daring; still the cannon had done the main work and it was taken as a Richmond victory.

The small loss, too, where the home people had been so deeply interested, added a cheering glow to the news that nothing else could have given. Bowed and venerable men, little girls and tremulous old women spoke of the fight "we won." And why not? Were not their sons, and husbands, and brothers, really a part of them?

It was curious to see how prone the women were to attribute the result to a special interposition of Divine aid, and to share the laurels, gathered that bright June day, with a higher Power than rested in a Springfield rifle, or a 12-pr. howitzer.

"Don't you tell me one word, cap'n!" I heard an old lady exclaim in great ire, at the door of the War Department, "Provi-*dence* is a-fightin' our battles for us! The Lord *is* with us, and thar's his hand-writin'—*jest as plain!*"

"Don't say nothin' agin' that, marm," answered the western captain, with Cromwellian sagacity; "but ef we don't help Providence powerful hard we ain't agoin' ter win!"

There was a perfect atmosphere of triumph all over the state. Troops lying in camp began to get restless and eager to go at once—even half-prepared as many of them were—to the front. Perfect confidence in the ability of the South to beat back any advance had been before the too prevalent idea of army and people; and the ease of the victory added to this conviction a glow of exultation over the invincibility of the southern soldier.

But the confidence begotten by the result had, as yet, a beneficial rather than a bad effect. Enlistments were stimulated and camps of instruction vied with each other in energy of preparation and close attention to drill. Every soldier felt that the struggle might be fierce, but would certainly be short; and the meanest private panted to have his share in the triumphant work while there was yet a chance. The women worked harder than ever; and at every sewing-circle the story of the fight was retold with many a glowing touch added by skillful narration. And while soft eyes flashed and delicate cheeks glowed at the music of the recital, needles glanced quicker still through the tough fabric for those "dear boys!"

Along the other army lines, the news from Magruder's inspired the men with a wild desire to dash forward and have their turn, before the whole crop of early laurels was gathered. An aide on General Beauregard's staff came down from Manassas a few days after Bethel, in charge of prisoners; and he told me that the men had been in a state of nervous excitement for an advance before, but now were so wild over the news, it was hard to restrain them from advancing of their own accord.

The clear-headed generals in command, however, looked over the flash and glitter of the first success, to the sterner realities beyond; and they drew the bands of discipline only tighter—and administered the wholesome tonic of regular drill—the nearer they saw the approach of real work.

The Government, too, hailed the success at Bethel as an omen of the future; but rather that it tested the spirit of the troops and their ability to stand fire, than from any solid fruits of the fight. They understood that it was scarcely a check to the great advance to be made; and though perhaps not "only a reconnaissance that accomplished its intention," as the Federal officers declared, it was yet only the result of such a movement. True, eighteen hundred raw troops, never under fire, had met more than double their number and fought steadily and well from nine o'clock till two; and had, besides, accomplished this with the insignificant loss of *one* killed and seven wounded!

But this was not yet the test that was to try how fit they were to fight for the principles for which they had so promptly flown to arms. The great shock was to come in far different form; and every nerve was strained to meet the issue when made.

The Ordnance Department had been organized, and already brought to a point of efficiency, by Major Gorgas—a resigned officer of the United States Artillery; and it was ably seconded by the Tredegar Works. All night long the dwellers on Gamble's Hill saw their furnaces shine with a steady glow, and the tall chimneys belch out clouds of dense, luminous smoke into the night. At almost any hour of the day, Mr. Tanner's well-known black horses could be seen at the door of the War Department, or dashing thence to the foundry, or one of the depots. As consequence of this energy and industry, huge trains of heavy guns, and improved ordnance of every kind, were shipped off to the threatened points, almost daily, to the full capacity of limited rolling stock on the roads. The new regiments were rapidly armed; their old-style muskets exchanged for better ones, to be in their turn put through the improving Tredegar process. Battery equipments, harness works, forges—in fact, all requirements for the service—were at once put in operation under the working order and system introduced into the bureaux. The efficiency of the southern artillery—until paralyzed by the breaking down of its horses —is sufficient proof how this branch was conducted.

The Medical Department—to play so important and needful a part in the coming days of blood—was now thoroughly reorganized and placed on really efficient footing. Surgeons of all ages—some of first force and of highest reputation in the South—left home and

8

practice, to seek and receive positions under it.   These, on passing examination and receiving commission, were sent to points where most needed, with full instructions to prepare to the utmost for the comfort of the sick and wounded.   Medicines, instruments, stretchers and supplies of all sorts were freely sent to the purveyors in the field—where possible, appointed from experienced surgeons of the old service ; while the principal hospitals and depots in Richmond were put in perfect order to receive their expected tenants, under the personal supervision of the Surgeon-General.

The Quartermaster's Department, both for railroad transportation and field service, underwent a radical change, as experience of the early campaign pointed out its imperfections.   This department is the life of the army—the supplies of every description must be received through its hands.   Efficiently directed, it can contribute to the most brilliant results, and badly handled, can thwart the most perfectly matured plans of genius, or generalship.

Colonel A. C. Myers, who was early made Acting Quartermaster-General, had the benefit of the assistance and advice of an able corps of subordinates—both from the old service and from the active business men of the South; and, whatever may have been its later abuses, at this time the bureau was managed with an efficiency and vigor that could scarcely have been looked for in so new an organization.

The Commissariat alone was badly managed from its very inception.   Murmurs loud and deep arose from every quarter against its numerous errors and abuses; and the sagacity of Mr. Davis—so entirely approved elsewhere—was in this case more than doubted. Colonel Northrop had been an officer of cavalry, but for many years had been on a quasi sick-leave, away from all connection with any branch of the army—save, perhaps, the paymaster's office.   The reason for his appointment to, perhaps, the most responsible bureau of the War Department was a mystery to people everywhere.

Suddenly the news from Rich Mountain came.   It fell like a thunderbolt from the summer sky, that the people deluded themselves was to sail over them with never a cloud!   The flood-tide of success, upon which they had been floating so gaily, was suddenly dammed and flowed back upon them in surges of sullen gloom.

The southern masses are essentially mercurial and are more given to sudden extremes of hope and despondency than any people in the world—except, perhaps, the French. Any event in which they are interested can, by a partial success, carry them up to a glowing enthusiasm, or depress them to zero by its approach to failure. The buzz and stir of preparation, the constant exertion attending it and their absorbing interest in the cause, had all prepared the people, more than ordinarily even, for one of these barometric shiftings. The news from Bethel had made them almost wild with joy and caused an excessive elation that could ill bear a shock. The misfortune at Rich Mountain threw a corresponding gloom over the whole face of affairs; and, as the success at Bethel had been overrated from the Potomac to the Gulf, so this defeat was deemed of more serious importance than it really was.

This feeling in Richmond was much aggravated by her own peculiar loss. Some of her best men had been in the fight, and all that could be learned of them was that they were scattered, or shot. Garnett was dead; the gallant DeLagnel was shot down fighting to the last; and Pegram was a prisoner—the gallant regiment he led cut up and dispersed!

Only a few days before, a crowd of the fairest and most honored that Richmond could boast had assembled at the depot to bid them God speed! Crowds of fellow soldiers had clustered round them, hard hands had clasped theirs—while bright smiles of cheer broke through the tears on softest cheeks; and, as the train whirled off and the banner that tender hands had worked—with a feeling " passing the love of woman "—waved over them, wreathed with flowers, not a heart was in the throng but beat high with anticipation of brave deed and brilliant victory following its folds.

Scarcely had these flowers withered when the regiment—shattered and beaten—was borne down by numbers, and the flag itself sullied and torn by the tramp of its conquerors. And the shame of defeat was much heightened to these good people, by the agonies of suspense as to the fate of their loved ones. It was three days after the news of the disaster reached the War Department before the death of Garnett was a certainty; and longer time still elapsed ere the minor casualties were known. When they did come, weeping sounded through many a Virginia home for its stay, or its darling, stark on the distant battle-field, or carried into captivity.

The details of the fight were generally and warmly discussed, but with much more of feeling than of knowledge of their real bearings. Public opinion fixed the result decidedly as the consequence of want of skill and judgment, in dividing the brigade at a critical moment. There was a balm in the reflection, however, that though broken and beaten, the men had fought well in the face of heavy odds; and that their officers had striven by every effort of manhood to hold them to their duty. General Garnett had exposed himself constantly, and was killed by a sharp-shooter at Carrock's Ford—over which he had brought the remnant of his army by a masterly retreat—while holding the stream at the head of a small squad. Pegram fought with gallantry and determination. He felt the position untenable and had remonstrated against holding it; yet the admirable disposition of his few troops, and the skill and courage with which he had managed them, had cost the enemy many a man before the mountain was won. Captured and bruised by the fall of his horse, he refused to surrender his sword until an officer, his equal in rank, should demand it. De Lagnel cheered his men till they fell between the guns they could no longer work; then seized the rammer himself and loaded the piece till he, too, was shot down. Wounded, he still fought with his pistol, till a bayonet thrust stretched him senseless.

These brilliant episodes illustrated the gloomy story of the defeat; but it still caused very deep and general depression. This was only partly relieved by the news that followed so closely upon it, of the brilliant success of General Price's army at Carthage. Missouri was so far away that the loudest shouts of victory there could echo but dimly in the ears at Richmond, already dulled by Rich Mountain. Still, it checked the blue mood of the public to some extent; and the Government saw in it much more encouragement than the people.

There had been much doubt among the southern leaders as to the *materiel* of the western armies, on both sides. Old and tried officers felt secure, *ceteris paribus*, of success against the northern troops of the coast, or Middle States; but the hardy hunters from the West and North-west were men of a very different stamp. The resources of the whole country had been strained to send into Virginia such an army in numbers and equipment as the preparation for invasion of her borders seemed to warrant. This had left the South and South-west rather more thinly garrisoned than all deemed prudent. The grounds for security in Virginia were that the mass of the southern troops were thoroughly accustomed to the use of arms and perfectly at home on horseback; and no doubts were felt that the men of the North-eastern States, there opposed to them, were far below them in both requirements. The superior excellence of the latter in arms, equipment, and perhaps discipline, was more than compensated to the former by their greater familiarity with the arms they carried and their superiority of physique and endurance. Any advantage of numbers, it was argued, was made up by the fact of the invading army being forced to fight on the ground chosen by the invaded; and in the excellence of her tacticians, rather more than in any expected equality of numbers, the main reliance of the southern government was placed. Hence it was full of confidence as to the result in the East.

In the West, it was far different. There the armies of the United States were recruited from the hardy trappers and frontiersmen of the border; from the sturdy yeomen of the inland farms; and, in many instances, whole districts had separated, and men from adjoining farms had gone to join in a deadly fight, in opposing ranks. Though the partisan spirit with these was stronger than with other southern troops—for they added the bitterness of personal hate to the sectional feeling—yet thinking people felt that the men themselves were more equally matched in courage, endurance and the knowledge of arms.

It is an old axiom in war, that when the *personnel* of armies is equal, victory is apt to rest with numbers. In the West, the United States not only had the numbers in their favor, but they were better equipped in every way; and the only hope of the South was in the superiority of its generals in strategic ability.

Thus, the fight at Carthage was viewed by the Government as a test question of deep meaning; and Sterling Price began at once to rank as a rising man. The general gloom through the country began to wear off, but that feeling of overweening confidence, in which the people had so universally indulged, was much shaken; and it was with some misgivings as to the perfect certainty of success that they began to look upon the tremendous preparations for the Virginia campaign, to which the North was bending its every effort, under the personal supervision of General Scott. The bitterness that the mass of the people of the South—especially in Virginia—felt against that officer did not affect their exalted opinion of his vast grasp of mind and great military science. The people, as a body, seldom reason deeply upon such points; and it would probably have been hard to find out why it was so; but the majority of his fellow-statesmen certainly feared and hated "the general" in about an equal degree. It was a good thing for the South that this was the case; and that the mighty "On to Richmond!"—the clang of which was resounding to the farthest limits of the North and sending its threatening echoes over the Potomac—was recognized by them as a serious and determined attempt upon the new Capital.

Every fresh mail, through "the blockade," brought more and more astounding intelligence of these vast preparations. Every fresh cap that was exploded, every new flag that was broidered, was duly chronicled by the rabid press. The editors of the North seemed to have gone military mad; and when they did not dictate plans of battles, lecture their government and bully its generals, they told wondrous stories of an army that Xerxes might have gaped to see.

All the newspaper bombast could easily be sifted, however; and private letters from reliable sources of intelligence over the Potomac all agreed as to the vast scale and perfection of arrangement of the onward movement. The public pulse in the South had settled again to a steady and regular beat; but it visibly quickened as the time of trial approached.

And that time could not be long delayed!

The army of Virginia was in great spirits. Each change of position—every fresh disposition of troops—told them that their leaders expected a fight at any moment; and they panted for it and chafed under the necessary restraints of discipline, like hounds in the leash.

When General Johnston took command of the "Army of the Shenandoah" at Harper's Ferry, he at once saw that with the small force at his command the position was untenable. To hold it, the heights on both sides of the river commanding it would have to be fortified, and a clear line of communication maintained with his base.

General McClellan, with a force equal to his, was hovering about Romney and the upper Valley, ready at any moment to swoop down upon his flank and make a junction with Patterson, who was in his front, thus crushing him between them. Patterson was threatening

Winchester, at which point he would be able to cut Johnston's supplies and at the same time effect his desired junction with McClellan.

To prevent this, about the middle of June, General Johnston evacuated Harper's Ferry, destroying the magazines and a vast amount of property, and fell back to Winchester. Then, for one month, Patterson and he played at military chess, on a field ranging from Winchester to Martinsburg, without advantage on either side. At the end of that time—on the 15th of July—the former made his grand feint of an advance, which Colonel Jeb Stuart—who was scouting in his front—declared to be a real movement; warning General Johnston that the blow was at last to fall in earnest. This warning the clear-headed and subtle tactician took in such part, that he at once prepared to dispatch his whole force to Manassas to join Beauregard. Well did General Scott say, "Beware of Johnston's retreats;" for—whatever the country may have thought of it at the time—the retreat from Harper's Ferry culminated in the battle of Manassas!

Meanwhile, in Richmond the excitement steadily rose, but the work of strengthening the defenses went steadily on. Fresh troops arrived daily—from the South by cars—from the West by railroad and canal; and from the country around Richmond they marched in. Rumors of the wildest and most varied sort could be heard at any hour. Now Magruder had gained a terrible victory at Big Bethel, and had strewn the ground for miles with the slain and spoils! Then Johnston had met the enemy at Winchester and, after oceans of blood, had driven him from the field in utter rout! Again Beauregard had cut McDowell to pieces and planted the stars-and-bars over Alexandria and Arlington Heights! Such was the morbid state of the public mind that any rumor, however fanciful, received some credit.

Each night some regiments broke camp noiselessly and filed through the streets like the army of specters that

"Beleaguered the walls of Prague,"

to fill a train on the Central, or Fredericksburg road, *en route* for Manassas. Constantly, at gray dawn the dull, rumbling sound, cut sharply by the clear note of the bugle, told of moving batteries; and the tramp of cavalry became so accustomed a sound, that people scarcely left their work even to cheer the wild and rugged-looking horsemen passing by.

Then it began to be understood, all over the country, that the great advance would be over the Potomac; that the first decisive battle would be joined by the Army of the Shenandoah, or that of Manassas.

A hushed, feverish suspense—like the sultry stillness before the burst of the storm—brooded over the land, shared alike by the people and government.

My old friend—the colonel of the "Ranche" and "Zouave" memory—was stationed at Richmond headquarters. Many were the tribulations that sorely beset the soul of that old soldier and clubman. He had served so long with regulars that he could not get accustomed to the irregularities of the "mustangs," as he called the volunteers; many were the culinary grievances of which he relieved his rotund breast to me; and numerous were the early bits of news he confidentially dropped into my ear, before they were known elsewhere.

The evening of the 18th of July—hot, sultry and threatening rain—had been more quiet than usual. Not a rumor had been set afloat; and the monotony was only broken by a group of officers about the "Spotswood" discussing Bethel, Rich Mountain and the chances of the next fight. One of them, with three stars on his collar, had just declared his conviction :

"It's only a feint, major! McDowell is too old a soldier to risk a fight on the Potomac line—too far from his base, sir! He'll amuse Beauregard and Johnston while they sweep down on Magruder. I want *my* orders for Yorktown. Mark my words! What is it, adjutant?" The colonel talked on as he opened and read a paper the lieutenant handed him—"Hello! Adjutant, read that! Boys, I'm off for Manassas to-night. Turning my back on a fight, by——!"

Just then I felt a hand on my shoulder; and turning, saw my colonel with his round face—graver than usual—near mine. The thought of some devilish invention in the pudding line flashed across me, but his first word put cooks and dinners out of my mind.

"The ball's open, egad!" he said seriously. "We whipped McDowell's advance at Bull Run to-day, sir! Drove 'em back, sir! Did you hear that *mustang* colonel? Turning his back on a fight! Egad, he'll turn his stomach on it before the week's out!"

It was true. How McDowell's right had essayed to cross at

Blackburn's Ford; how Longstreet's Virginians and the Washington Artillery met them; and how, after a sharp fight, they retired and gave up the ford is too well known history to be repeated here.

In an hour the news was public in Richmond and—though received with a deep, grave joy—braced every nerve and steadied every pulse in it. There was no distaste to face the *real* danger when it showed itself; it was only the sickening suspense that was unbearable. No one in the city had really doubted the result, from the first; and the news from the prelude to the terrible and decisive fight, yet to come, but braced the people, as a stimulant may the fevered patient.

The heavy pattering of the first drops had come, and the strained hush was broken.

Beauregard telegraphed that the success of Bull Run was complete; that his men had borne their baptism of fire, with the steadiness of veterans; and that a few days—hours, perhaps—must bring the general assault upon his lines.

He urged that every available man should be sent him; and within twenty-four hours from the receipt of his despatch, there was not a company left in Richmond that had arms to carry him.

Surgeons were sent up; volunteer doctors applied by dozens for permission to go; ambulance trains were put upon the road, in readiness at a moment's warning. Baskets of delicacies and rare old wines and pure liquors; great bundles of bandages and lint, prepared by the daintiest fingers in the "Old Dominion;" cots, mattresses and pillows—all crowded in at the medical purveyor's. Then Richmond, having done all she could for the present, drew a deep breath and waited.

But she waited not unhopefully!

Every eye was strained to Manassas plains; every heart throbbed stronger at the mention of that name. All knew that there the giants were soon to clinch in deadly wrestle for the mastery; that the struggle was now at hand, when the flag of the South would be carried high in triumph or trampled in the dust!

But no one doubted the true hearts and firm hands that had gathered there to uphold that banner!

No one doubted that, though the best blood of the South might redden its folds, it would still float proudly over the field—consecrated, but unstained!

CHAPTER XV.

AFTER MANASSAS.

By noon on the 21st of July the quidnuncs found out that the President had left that morning, on a special train and with a volunteer staff, for Manassas.   This set the whole tribe agog, and wonderful were the speculations and rumors that flew about.   By night, certain news came that the battle had raged fiercely all day, and the sun had gone down on a complete, but bloody, victory.   One universal thrill of joy went through the city, quickly stilled and followed by the gasp of agonized suspense.   The dense crowds, collected about all probable points of information, were silent after the great roar of triumph went up at the first announcement.   The mixed pressure of grave, voiceless thankfulness and strained anxiety, was too deep for words; and they stood still—expectant.

By midnight the main result of the day's fight was known beyond a doubt; how the enemy, in heavy masses, had attacked the Confederate left, and hurled it back and around, entirely flanking it; how the raw troops had contested every inch of ground with stubborn valor, but still gave way until the change of front *had made itself;* how the supports brought up from the right and center—where a force had to be maintained to face the masses threatening them—came only to meet fresh masses that they could only check, not break; how the battle was at one time really lost!

When science had done all it could to retrieve the day, but the most obstinate even of the southern troops—after doing more than desperate courage and determined pluck could warrant—were breaking and giving way, then the wild yell of Elzey's brigade broke through the pines like a clarion!   On came that devoted band, breathless and worn with their run from the railroad; eight hundred Marylanders—and only two companies of these with bayonets—leading the charge!   On they came, their yells piercing the woods before they are yet visible; and, as if by magic, the tide of battle turned! The tired, worn ranks, all day battered by the ceaseless hail of death, catch that shout, and answering it, breast the storm again; regiment after regiment hears the yell, and echoes it with a wild swelling chorus! And ever on rush the fresh troops—past their weary brothers, into the hottest of the deadly rain of fire—wherever the blue coats are thickest! Their front lines waver—General Smith falls, but Elzey gains the crest of the plateau—like a fire in the prairie spreads the contagion of fear—line after line melts before the hot blast of that charge—a moment more and the "Grand Army" is mixed in a straining, struggling, chaotic mass in the race for life—the battle is won!

I have heard the fight discussed by actors in it on both sides; have read accounts from northern penny a-liners, and English correspondents whose pay depended upon their neutrality; and all agree that the battle was saved by the advent of Kirby Smith, just at that critical moment when the numbers of the North were sweeping resistlessly over the broken and worn troops of the South. Elzey's brigade no doubt saved the day, for they created the panic.

"But I look upon it as a most causeless one," once said an Austrian officer to me, "for had the Federals stood but half an hour longer—which, with their position and supports, there was no earthly reason for their not doing—there could have been but one result. Smith's forces could not have held their own that much longer against overwhelming numbers; and the weary troops who had been fighting all day could not even have supported them in a heavy fight. Had Smith reached the scene of action at morning instead of noon, he, too, might have shared the general fate, and a far different page of history been written. Coming as he did, I doubt not the battle turned upon his advent. The main difference I see," he added, "is that the Confederates were whipped for several hours and didn't know it; but just as the Federals found it out and were about to close their hands upon the victory already in their grasp, they were struck with a panic and ran away from it!"

By midnight the anxious crowds in Richmond streets knew that the fight was over,

"And the red field was won!"

But the first arrivals were ominous ones—splashed and muddy hospital stewards and quartermaster's men, who wanted more stretchers and instruments, more tourniquets and stimulants; and their stories threw a deeper gloom over the crowds that—collected at departments, hotels and depots—spoke in hushed whispers their words of solemn triumph, of hope, or of suspense.   They told that almost every regiment had been badly cut up—that the slaughter of the best and bravest had been terrible—that the "Hampton Legion" was annihilated— Hampton himself killed—Beauregard was wounded—Kirby Smith killed—the first Virginia was cut to pieces and the Alabama troops swept from the face of the earth.   These were some of the wild rumors they spread; eagerly caught up and echoed from mouth to mouth with a reliance on their truth to be expected from the morbid anxiety. No one reflected that these men must have left Manassas before the fighting was even hotly joined; and could only have gained their diluted intelligence from the rumors at way-stations.   As yet the cant of camp followers was new to the people, who listened as though these terrible things must be true to be related.

There was no sleep in Richmond that night.   Men and women gathered in knots and huddled into groups on the corners and door-steps, and the black shadow of some dreadful calamity seemed brooding over every rooftree.   Each splashed and weary-looking man was stopped and surrounded by crowds, who poured varied and anxious questioning upon him.   The weak treble of gray-haired old men besought news of son, or grandson; and on the edge of every group, pale, beseeching faces mutely pleaded with sad, tearless eyes, for tidings of brother, husband, or lover.

But there was no despairing weakness, and every one went sadly but steadily to work to give what aid they might.   Rare stores of old wines were freely given; baskets of cordials and rolls of lint were brought; and often that night, as the women leaned over the baskets they so carefully packed, bitter tears rolled from their pale cheeks and fell noiselessly on bandage and lint.   For who could tell but that very piece of linen might bind the sore wound of one far dearer than life.

Slowly the night wore on, trains coming in occasionally only to disappoint the crowds that rushed to surround them.   No one came who had *seen* the battle—all had *heard* what they related.   And though no man was base enough to play upon feelings such as theirs, the love of common natures for being oracles carried them away; and they repeated far more even than that.   Next day the news was more

full, and the details of the fight came in with some lists of the wounded. The victory was dearly bought. Bee, Bartow, Johnson, and
others equally valuable, were dead. Some of the best and bravest
from every state had sealed their devotion to the flag with their blood.
Still, so immense were the consequences of the victory now judged to
be, that even the wildest rumors of the day before had not told one
half.

At night the President returned; and on the train with him were
the bodies of the dead generals, with their *garde d'honneur.* These
proceeded to the Capitol, while Mr. Davis went to the Spotswood
and addressed a vast crowd that had collected before it. He told
them in simple, but glowing, language that the first blow for liberty
had been struck and struck home; that the hosts of the North had
been scattered like chaff before southern might and southern right;
that the cause was just and must prevail. Then he spoke words of
consolation to the stricken city. Many of her noblest were spared;
the wounded had reaped a glory far beyond the scars they bore; the
dead were honored far beyond the living, and future generations
should twine the laurel for their crown.

The great crowd listened with breathless interest to his lightest
word. Old men, resting on their staves, erected themselves; reckless boys were quiet and still; and the pale faces of the women, furrowed with tears, looked up at him till the color came back to their
cheeks and their eyes dried. Of a truth, he was still their idol. As
yet they hung upon his lightest word, and believed that what he did
was best.

Then the crowd dispersed, many mournfully wending their way
to the Capitol where the dead officers lay in state, wrapped in the
flag of the new victory. An hour after, the rain descending in torrents, the first ambulance train arrived.

First came forth the slightly wounded, with bandaged heads, arms
in slings, or with painful limp.

Then came ugly, narrow boxes of rough plank. These were tenderly handled, and the soldiers who bore them upon their shoulders
carried sad faces, too; for happily as yet the death of friends in the
South was not made, by familiarity, a thing of course. And lastly—
lifted so gently, and suffering so patiently—came the ghastly burdens of
the stretchers. Strong men, maimed and torn, their muscular hands

straining the handles of the litter with the bitter effort to repress complaint, the horrid crimson ooze marking the rough cloths thrown over them; delicate, fair-browed boys, who had gone forth a few days back so full of life and hope, now gory and livid, with clenched teeth and matted hair, and eyeballs straining for the loved faces that must be there to wait them.

It was a strange crowd that stood there in the driving storm, lit up by the fitful flashes of the moving lanterns.

The whole city was there—the rich merchant—the rough laborer —the heavy features of the sturdy serving-woman—the dusky, but loving face of the negro—the delicate profile of the petted belle—all strained forward in the same intent gaze, as car after car was emptied of its ghastly freight. There, under the pitiless storm, they stood silent and still, careless of its fury—not a sound breaking the perfect hush, in which the measured tramp of the carriers, or the half-repressed groan of the wounded, sounded painfully distinct.

Now and then, as a limping soldier was recognized, would come a rush and a cry of joy—strong arms were given to support him—tender hands were laid upon his hair—and warm lips were pressed to his blanched cheek, drenched with the storm.

Here some wife, or sister, dropped bitter tears on the unconscious face of the household darling, as she walked by the stretcher where he writhed in fevered agony. There

"The shrill-edged shriek of the mother divided the shuddering night,"

as she threw herself prone on the rough pine box; or the wild, wordless wail of sudden widowhood was torn from the inmost heart of some stricken creature who had hoped in vain!

There was a vague, unconscious feeling of joy in those who had found their darlings—even shattered and maimed; an unbearable and leaden weight of agonizing suspense and dread hung over those who could hear nothing. Many wandered restlessly about the Capitol, ever and anon questioning the guard around the dead generals; but the sturdy men of the Legion could only give kindly and vague answers that but heightened the feverish anxiety.

Day after day the ambulance trains came in bearing their sad burdens, and the same scene was ever enacted. Strangers, miles from home, met the same care as the brothers and husbands of Richmond; and the meanest private was as much a hero as the tinseled officer.

It is strange how soon even the gentlest natures gain a familiarity with suffering and death. The awfulness and solemnity of the unaccustomed sight loses rapidly by daily contact with it; even though the sentiments of sympathy and pity may not grow callous as well. But, as yet, Richmond was new to such scenes; and a shudder went through the whole social fabric at the shattering and tearing of the fair forms so well known and so dear.

Gradually—very gradually—the echoes of the fight rolled into distance; the wildest wailing settled to the steady sob of suffering, and Richmond went her way, with only here and there a wreck of manhood, or pale-faced woman in deepest mourning, to recall the fever of that fearful night.

Though the after effect of Manassas proved undoubtedly bad, the immediate fruits of the victory were of incalculable value. Panic-struck, the Federals had thrown away everything that could impede their flight. Besides fifty-four pieces of artillery of all kinds, horses and mules in large numbers, ammunition, medical stores and miles of wagon and ambulance trains, near six thousand stand of small arms, of the newest pattern and in best condition, fell into the hands of the half-armed rebels.

These last were the real prize of the victors, putting a dozen new regiments waiting only for arms, at once on an effective war-footing. Blankets, tents and clothing were captured in bulk; nor were they to be despised by soldiers who had left home with knapsacks as empty as those of Falstaff's heroes.

But the moral effect of the victory was to elate the tone of the army far above any previous act of the war. Already prepared not to undervalue their own prowess, its ease and completeness left a universal sense of their invincibility, till the feeling became common in the ranks—and spread thence to the people—that one southern man was worth a dozen Yankees; and that if they did not come in numbers greater than five to one, the result of any conflict was assured.

Everything was going smoothly. The first rough outlines had been laid in, with bold effectiveness, a rosy cloud floated over the grim distance of the war; and in the foreground—only brilliant and victorious action.

The Confederate loss, too, was much smaller than at first supposed,

not exceeding eighteen hundred; and many of the slightly wounded
began already to hobble about again, petted by the communities
and justly proud of their crutches and scars.   The Federal loss was
harder to estimate.   Many of their wounded had been borne away
by the rush of the retreat; the Government, naturally anxious to calm
the public mind of the North, made incomplete returns;. while large
numbers of uncounted dead had been buried on the field and along
the line of retreat, both by the victorious army and country people.
From the best data obtainable, their loss could not have been much
short, if at all short, of five thousand.   The army was satisfied, the
country was satisfied, and, unfortunately, the Government was satisfied.

Among the people there was a universal belief in an immediate
advance.   The army that had been the main bulwark of the National
Capital was rushing—a panic-stricken herd—into and beyond it; the
fortifications were perfectly uncovered and their small garrisons utterly demoralized by the woe-begone and terrified fugitives constantly
streaming by them.   The triumphant legions of the South were almost near enough for their battle-cry to be heard in the Cabinet;
and the southern people could not believe that the bright victory that
had perched upon their banners would be allowed to fold her wings
before another and bloodier flight, that would leave the North prostrate at her feet.   Day after day they waited and—the wish being
father to the thought—day after day the sun rose on fresh stories of an
advance—a bloody fight—a splendid victory—or the capture of
Washington.   But the sun always set on an authoritative contradiction of them; and at last the excitement was forced to settle down
on the news that General Johnston had extended his pickets as far as
Mason's and Munson's hills, and the army had gone into camp on
the field it had so bloodily won the week before.

CHAPTER XVI.

THE SPAWN OF LETHARGY.

Considering the surroundings, it seems inevitable that the lull after the first great victory should have been followed by reaction, all over the South; and that reasons—as ridiculous as they were numerous—should have been assigned for inaction that appeared so unwarranted.

Discontent—at first whispered, and coming as the wind cometh—gradually took tongue; and discussion of the situation grew loud and varied. One side declared that the orders for a general advance had been already given, when the President countermanded them upon the field, and sent orders by General Bonham to withdraw the pursuit. Another version of this reason was that there had been a council of the generals and Mr. Davis, at which it was agreed that the North must now be convinced of the utter futility of persisting in invasion; and that in the reaction her conservative men would make themselves heard; whereas the occupation of Washington would inflame the North and cause the people to rise as one man for the defense of their capital. An even wilder theory found believers; that the war in the South was simply one of defense, and crossing the Potomac would be *invasion*, the effect of which would retard recognition from abroad. Another again declared that there was a jealousy between Generals Johnston and Beauregard, and between each of them and the President, that prevented concert of action.

The people of the South were eminently democratic and had their own views—which they expressed with energy and vim—on all subjects during the war; so these theories, to account for the paralysis after Manassas, were each in turn discussed, and each found warm defenders. But gradually it came to be generally conceded that none of them could be the true one. The President took no command on his visit to Manassas, for he reached the field only after the battle had been won and the flight commenced. Any suggestions that occurred to him were naturally made to General Johnston. There is good authority for stating that he did not make any criticism on one

9

material point, stating to both generals that the whole plan, conduct and result of the battle met his fullest approval; and on reflection the whole people felt that their chief was too much a soldier to have committed the gross breach of discipline indicated. The story of the council came to be regarded as a silly fabrication. The fear of inflaming the North, coming on the heels of a complete and bloody victory, was about as funny as for a pugilist whose antagonist's head was "in chancery" to cease striking lest he should anger him; and events immediately following Manassas showed there could be little jealousy or pique between the generals, or between them and the President. General Johnston, with the magnanimity of the true knight his whole career has shown him to be, declared that the credit of the plan and choice of the field of battle was due to General Beauregard; and Mr. Davis' proclamation on the success was couched in language that breathed only the most honest commendation of both generals and of their strategy. The fear of invasion prejudicing opinion abroad was as little believed as the other stories, for—outside of a small clique—there grew up at this time all over the South such a perfect confidence in its strength and its perfect ability to work its own oracle, that very little care was felt for the action of Europe. In fact, the people were just now quite willing to wait for recognition of their independence by European powers, until it was already achieved. So, gradually the public mind settled down to the true reasons that mainly prevented the *immediate* following up of the victory.

A battle under all circumstances is a great confusion. With raw troops, who had never before been under fire, and who had been all day fiercely contending, until broken and disordered, the confusion must necessarily have been universal. As they broke, or fell back, brigade overlapped brigade, company mixed with company, and officers lost their regiments. The face of the country, covered with thick underbrush, added to this result; so that when the enemy broke and the rout commenced, it was hard to tell whether pursuers or pursued were the most disorganized mass. The army of Manassas was almost entirely undisciplined, and had never before felt the intoxication of battle. On that terrible day it had fought with tenacity and pluck that belonged to the race; but it had largely been on the principle prevalent at weddings in the "ould country"—when you see a head, hit it! The few officers who desired a disciplined resistance soon saw the futility of obtaining it, and felt that as the men, individually, were fighting bravely and stubbornly, it were better only to hold them to that. When the pursuit came, the men were utterly worn and exhausted; but, burning with the glow of battle, they followed the flying masses fast and far —each one led by his own instincts and rarely twenty of a company together.

A major-general, who left his leg on a later field, carried his company into this fight. During the pursuit he led it through a by-path to intercept a battery spurring down the road at full speed. They overtook it, mastered the gunners and turned the horses out of the press. In the deepening twilight, he turned to thank the company, and found it composed of three of his own men, two " Tiger Rifles," a Washington artilleryman, three dismounted cavalry of the " Legion," a doctor, a quartermaster's clerk, and the Rev. Chaplain of the First —— !

This was but a specimen of the style of the pursuit. There was but little cavalry—one regiment under Lieutenant-Colonel Stuart and a few single companies. No one brigade could be collected in anything like order; night was deepening and the enemy's flight was approaching what was reasonably supposed to be his reserve. Under these circumstances it was apparent that prudence, if not necessity, dictated calling in the pursuit by the disordered troops. General Bonham—the ranking officer in front—saw this plainly; and on his own authority gave the order that appeared most proper to him. I never heard that, *at this time*, it was objected to by his superior officers.

Moreover, it was not only the demoralization caused by the pursuit that was sufficient reason for not following up Manassas. The army, ordinarily, was not in a condition to advance into an enemy's country, away from its regular communications. In the first place, there was no transportation, and the arms were bad. It was a work of time to utilize the spoils; to distribute arms where most needed; to put the captured batteries in condition for use; and to replace with the splendid ambulances and army wagons, that had been prepared for the holiday march to Richmond, the hastily and clumsily-constructed ones already in use; and to so give out the captured horses as best to utilize them. This latter was of the utmost moment before an advance could be attempted. The Confederates were shorter of transportation—even of defective character—than of anything else ; and for days after the fight the flood-gates of heaven seemed to stand open, to deluge the country around Manassas until it became a perfect lake of mud.   Roads already bad were washed into gullies; holes generally knee-deep became impassable.   It is perfectly easy, therefore, to understand why, for a week after the battle, delay was necessary; but as week after week passed, and there was still no forward movement, it ceased to be strange that the people should murmur, and ask why it was the army was satisfied with laurels easily won when fresh ones were within its grasp.   All felt that veteran officers handling raw troops had to be more careful in their management, and to count more closely before putting them into the new and dangerous position of an invading army, than would meet with the concurrence of a populace naturally ardent and doubly heated by triumph.

But it is equally true that for ten days after the battle, Washington lay perfectly at the mercy of the South ; and by that time the army of Manassas was in better condition than could be expected later; and it was anxious to move forward.

But the auspicious moment was not seized; time was given for the broken fragments of the Union army to be patched again into something like organization.   Fresh forts and earthworks were hastily thrown up; a perfect chain of defenses formed around Washington, and strongly garrisoned.   The pickets of the opposing armies were near enough to exchange constant shots, and even occasional "chaff."

Still there was no movement; the summer wore away in utter inactivity.   The camp at Orange Courthouse began to be looked upon as a stationary affair; while the usual difficulties of camp life—aggravated by the newness of the troops and the natural indisposition of the southron to receive discipline—began to show themselves.   The army at this time was principally composed of the better educated and better conditioned class, who were the first to volunteer ; and as I have already said, many of the privates were men of high position, culture and wealth.   Thus composed, it was equal to great deeds of gallantry and dash.   *Elan* was its characteristic—but it was hard to reduce to the stratified regularity of an army.   Napier has laid down as an axiom that no man is a good soldier until he has become a perfect machine.   He must neither reason nor think—only obey.   Critics, perhaps equally competent, in reviewing the Crimean war, differ from this and declare the main advantage of the French troops over the Russian was a certain individuality—a pride in themselves and their army that had been entirely drilled out of their stolid adversaries. Be this as it may, the *esprit de corps* of the Frenchman was in his corps only as such; and he would no more have discussed the wisdom, or prudence of any order—even in his own mind—than he would have thought of disobeying it.

The steady-going professional men who sprung to arms throughout the South could face a deadly fire, without blenching, for hours; but they could not help reasoning, with nothing to do for twenty hours out of every twenty-four.

The gay young graduates of the promenade and ball-room could march steadily, even gaily, into the fiery belching of a battery, but they could not learn the practice of unreasoning blindness; and the staunch, hard-fisted countryman felt there was no use in it—the thing was over if the fighting was done—and this was a waste of time. *Nostalgia*—that scourge of camps—began to creep among the latter class; discontent grew apace among the former. Still the camp was the great object of interest for miles around; there were reviews, parades and division dinners; ladies visited and inspected it, and some even lived within its lines; but the tone of the army went down gradually, but steadily. During the summer more than one of Beauregard's companies—though of the best material and with a brilliant record—had to be mustered out as " useless and insubordinate." Excellence in drill and attention to duty both decreased ; and it was felt by competent judges that rust was gradually eating away the fabric of the army. This was certainly the fault to a great extent of the officers, though it may, in part, have been due to the men themselves. In the beginning these had tried honestly to choose those among them best fitted for command; but like all volunteers, they fell into the grave error of choosing the most popular. Almost all candidates for office were equally eligible and equally untried; so personal considerations naturally came into play. Once elected, they did their duty faithfully, in the field; but were either too weak, or too inexperienced, to keep the strict rules of discipline applied during the trying inactivity of camp; and they were too conscious of the social and mental equality of their men to enforce the distinction between officer and private, without which the command loses half its weight. In some instances, too, the desire for popularity and for future advancement at the hands of friends and neighbors introduced a spirit of demagogism hurtful in the extreme.

For these combined reasons the army of Manassas, which a few weeks before had gone so gaily "into the jaws of death," began rapidly to mildew through warp and woof; and the whole texture seemed on the point of giving way.

Thoughtful men—who had waited calmy and coolly when the first burst of impatience had gone up—began now to ask why and how long this lethargy was to continue. They saw its bad effects, but believed that at the next blast of the bugle every man would shake off the incubus and rise in his might a patriot soldier; they saw the steady stream of men from North and West pouring into Washington, to be at once bound and held with iron bands of discipline—the vast preparation in men, equipments, supplies and science that the North was using the precious days granted her to get in readiness for the next shock. But they felt confident that the southern army—if not allowed to rust too long—would again vindicate the name it had won at Manassas.

These thinkers saw that some branches of the Government still kept up its preparations. Throughout the length of the land foundries were going up, and every improvement that science or experience could suggest was making in the construction of arms and ammunition; water-power, everywhere off the line of attack, was utilized for powder-mills and rope-walks; every cloth factory in the country was subsidized; and machinery of great variety and power was being imported on Government account. Over Richmond constantly hung a dense cloud of coal smoke; and the incessant buzz of machinery from factories, foundries and lathes, told of increased rather than abated effort in that branch of the Government. Then, too, the most perfect confidence was felt in the great strategic ability of General Johnston—who had already found that high level in the opinion of his countrymen, from which neither the frowns of government, the combination of cliques, nor the tongues of slanderers could afterward remove him.

They believed, too, in the pluck and dash of Beauregard; and, combining this with the outside activity, evident in every direction, felt there must be good and sufficient reason for the—to them—inexplicable quiet about the Potomac.

But perhaps the very worst feature was the effect of the victory upon the tone of the people at large. The very tongues that had wagged most impatiently at the first delay—that had set in motion the wild stories by which to account for it—had been the first to become blatant that the North was conquered. The minutest details of the fight were carried over the land, repeated at country courts and amplified at bar-room assemblages, until the common slang was everywhere heard that one Southron was equal to a dozen Yanks. Instead of using the time, so strangely given by the Government, in making earnest and steady strides toward increasing the army, improving its *morale* and adding to its supplies, the masses of the country were upon a rampage of boastfulness, and the notes of an inflated triumph rang from the Potomac to the Gulf.

In this regard the effect of the victory was most injurious; and had it not been for the crushing results—from a strategic point of view—that would have followed it, partial defeat might have proved a blessing in its place.

The one, while it threw a gloom over the country, would have nerved the people to renewed exertion and made them look steadily and unwaveringly at the true dangers that threatened them. The other gave them time to fold their hands and indulge in a complacency, ridiculous as it was enervating.

They ceased to realize the vast resources of the Union in men, money and supplies; and more than all, they underrated the dogged perseverance of Yankee character. It was as though a young boxer, in a deadly conflict with a giant, had dealt a staggering blow; and while the Titan braced his every muscle for a deadlier gripe, the weaker antagonist wasted his time lauding his strength and feeling his biceps.

Meantime, the keen, hard sense of the Washington Government wasted no time in utilizing the reaction on its people. The press and the public clamored for a victim, and General Scott was thrown into its maw unhesitatingly. The old hero was replaced by the new, and General McClellan—whose untried and inexperienced talent could hardly have augured his becoming, as he did, the best general of the northern army—was elevated to his place to please the "dear public."

The rabid crowds of men and men-women—whose prurient curiosity had driven them to follow the great on-to-Richmond, with hopes of a first view of the triumphant entry of the Grand Army—soon forgot their uncomfortable and terrified scramble to the rear. They easily changed their whine of terror to a song of triumph; and New England Judiths, burning to grasp the hair of the Holofernes over the Potomac, pricked the flagging zeal of their male companions.

The peculiar error that they were fighting for the Union and the flag—so cruelly dissipated of late—threw thousands into the ranks; heavy bounties and hopes of plunder drew many more; and the still frequent interstices were filled with many an Irish-German amalgam, that was supposed to be peculiarly good food for powder.

And so the summer wore on, the demoralizing influence of the inaction in the camps of the South increasing toward its close. The affair at Leesburg, occurring on the 20th of October, was another brilliant success, but equally barren of results. It showed that the men would still fight as readily and as fiercely, and that their officers would lead them as gallantly, as before; it put a few hundred of the enemy *hors de combat* and maintained "the right of way" by the river to the South. But it was the occasion for another shout of triumph—perfectly incommensurate with its importance—to go up from the people; and it taught them still more to despise and underrate the power of the government they had so far successfully and brilliantly defied.

Elsewhere than on the Potomac line, the case had been a little different. Magruder, on the Peninsula, had gained no success of note. A few unimportant skirmishes had taken place and the Confederate lines had been contracted—more from choice than necessity. But the combatants were near enough—and respected each other enough—for constant watchfulness to be considered necessary; and, though the *personnel* of the army was, perhaps, not as good as that of the Potomac, in the main its condition was better.

At Norfolk nothing had been done but to strengthen the defenses. General Huger had striven to keep his men employed; and they, at least, did not despise the enemy that frowned at them from Fort Monroe, and frequently sent messages of compliment into their camps from the lips of the "Sawyer gun." The echo of the pæans from Manassas came back to them, but softened by distance and tempered by their own experience—or want of it.

In Western Virginia there had been a dull, eventless campaign, of strategy rather than action. General Wise had taken command on the first of June, and early in August had been followed by General John B. Floyd—the ex-U. S. Secretary of War.

These two commanders unfortunately disagreed as to means and conduct of the campaign; and General R. E. Lee was sent to take general command on this—his first theater of active service. His management of the campaign was much criticised in many quarters; and the public verdict seemed to be that, though he had an army of twenty thousand men, tolerably equipped and familiar with the country, Rosecrans out-manœuvered him and accomplished his object in amusing so considerable a Confederate force. Certain it is that, after fronting Lee at Big Sewell for ten or twelve days, he suddenly withdrew in the night, without giving the former even a chance for a fight.

The dissatisfaction was universal and outspoken; nor was it relieved by the several brilliant episodes of Gauley and Cotton Hill, that General Floyd managed to throw into his dark surroundings.

It is hard to tell how much foundation the press and the public had for this opinion. There had been no decisive disaster, if there had been no actual gain; and the main result had been to maim men and show that both sides would fight well enough to leave all collisions matters of doubt.

It may not here be out of place to correct a false impression that has crept into the history of the times regarding General Floyd. The courteous press of the North—and not a few political enemies who felt safety in their distance from him—constantly branded him as "traitor" and "thief." They averred that he had misused his position and betrayed the confidence reposed in him as U. S. Secretary of War, to send government arms into the South in view of the approaching need for them. Even General Scott—whose position must have given him the means of knowing better—reiterates these calumnies, the falsity of which the least investigation exposed at once.

Mr. Buchanan, in his late book, completely exonerates General Floyd from this charge; and the committee to whom it was referred reported that of 10,151 rifles distributed by him in 1860, the Southern and South-Western states received only 2,849!

Followed by the hate of one government to receive the coldness of the other, John B. Floyd still strove with all his strength for the cause he loved.

"After life's fitful fever he sleeps well"

in his dear Virginia soil; and whatever his faults—whatever his errors —no honest man, North or South, but must rejoice that his enemies even acquitted him of this one.

Then the results elsewhere had not been very encouraging when compared with the eastern campaign; though Sterling Price had managed to more than hold his own against all obstacles, and Jeff Thompson had been doing great things with little means in south-western Missouri.

Still, since Rich Mountain, no serious disaster had befallen Confederate arms, and the people were fain to be satisfied.

CHAPTER XVII.

FROM COURT TO CAMP.

The winter of '61–2 set in early, with heavy and continued rains. By Christmas the whole surface of the country had been more than once wrapped in heavy snow, leaving lakes of mud over which no wheeled thing could work its way.

Active operations—along the whole northern frontier at least—were certainly suspended until spring; and both armies had gone into winter quarters. Military men agree that a winter in camp is the most demoralizing influence to which any troops can be subjected. To the new soldiers of the South it was a terrible ordeal—not so much from the actual privations they were called upon to endure as from other and more subtle difficulties, against the imperceptible approaches of which they could not guard. The Government had used every effort to make the men comfortable, and to supply them with all necessaries at its disposal; but still there were numerous articles it could not command.

The good caterers at home spared no pains, no exercise of ingenuity, and no pinching from fireside supplies, to make the loved ones in camp comfortable. The country had not begun to feel the effects of actual want in any quarter; but increased demand had lessened supplies on hand and somewhat enhanced prices; so the men were comfortably clothed, fed with plain, but plentiful and wholesome food, and supplied with all the absolute necessaries of camp life. In addition to these, boxes of all sizes, shapes and contents came into the camps in a continuous stream; and the thousand nameless trifles—so precious because bearing the impress of home—were received daily in every mess from the Rio Grande to the Potomac. Still, as the winter wore on, news from the armies became gloomier and gloomier, and each successive bulletin bore more dispiriting accounts of discontent and privation, sickness and death. Men who had gone into their first fight freely and gaily; who had heard the whistling of bullets as if it had been accustomed music, gave way utterly before the unseen foes of "winter quarters."

Here and there, a disciplinarian of the better sort—who combined philosophy with strictness—kept his men in rather better condition by constant watching, frequent and regular drills, rapid
marches for exercise, and occasional change of camp. But this
was the exception, and the general tone was miserable and gloomy.
This could in part be accounted for by the inexperience of the
men, and of their immediate commanders—the company officers—
in whose hands their health and spirits were in no small degree reposed. They could not be brought to the use of those little appliances of comfort that camp life, even in the most unfavorable circumstances, can afford—strict attention to the utmost cleanliness in
their persons and huts; care in the preparation of their food, and in
its cookery; and careful adherence to the simple hygienic rules laid
down in constant circulars from the medical and other departments. Where men live and sleep in semi-frozen mud, and breathe
an atmosphere of mist and brush smoke—and every one knows the
wonderfully penetrating power of camp-fire smoke—it is not to be
expected that their comfort is enviably great; especially where
they have left comfortable homes, and changed their well-prepared,
if simple, food for the hard and innutritious army ration. But such
creatures of habit are we that, after a little, we manage by proper
care to make even that endurable.

Soldiers are like children, and require careful watching and constant reminding that these small matters—which certainly make up the
sum of camp life—should be carefully attended to for their own good.
Rigid discipline in their enforcement is necessary in the beginning
to get novices properly started in the grooves. Once set going, they
soon become matters of course. But once let soldiers get accustomed
to careless and slovenly habits, and no amount of orders, or punishment, can undo the mischief. Unfortunately, the armies of the South
began wrong this first winter, and the descent was easy; and they
made the new road upon which they had entered far harder than
necessary, by neglecting landmarks so plainly written that he who runs
may read. *Nostalgia*—that scourge of camps—appeared in stubborn
and alarming form; and no exertion of surgeon, or general, served to
check or decrease it. Men, collected from cities, accustomed to
stated hours of business and recreation, and whose minds were accustomed to some exercise and excitement, naturally drooped in the

monotony of a camp knee in mire, where the only change from the camp-fire —with stew-pan simmering on it and long yarns spinning around it—was heavy sleep in a damp hut, or close tent, wrapped in a musty blanket and lulled by the snoring of half a dozen comrades.

Hale, sturdy countrymen, accustomed to regular exercise and hard work, with nothing to do all day but sun themselves and polish their bayonets, naturally moped and pined for the homes that were missing them so sorely. They, too, found the smoky blaze of the camp-fire but a sorry substitute for the cheerful hearth, where memory pictured the comely wife and the sturdy little ones. The hardy mountaineer, pent and confined to a mud-bound acre, naturally molded and panted for the fresh breezes and rough tramps of his far-away "roost."

The general morality of the camps was good, but praying is a sorry substitute for dry homes and good food; and, though chaplains were earnest and zealous, the men gradually found cards more exciting than exhortations. They turned from the "wine of life" to the canteen of "new dip" with a spiteful thirst. There were attempts by the higher officers—which proved abortive—to discountenance gambling; and the most stringent efforts of provost-marshals to prevent the introduction of liquor to camp reduced the quantity somewhat, but brought down the quality to the grade of a not very slow poison.

Being much in the numerous camps that winter, I was struck with the universal slouch and depression in ranks where the custom had been quick energy and cheerful faces. Through the whole army was that enervating moldiness, lightened only by an occasional gleam from those "crack companies" so much doubted in the beginning of the war.

It had been thought that the gay young men of cities, used to the sedentary life of profession, or counting-room—and perhaps to the irregularities of the midnight dinner and next-morning ball—that these men, steady and unflinching as they might be under fire—and willing as they seemed to undertake "what man dare" in danger or privation, would certainly break down under the fatigues of the first campaign.

They had, on the contrary, in every instance that came under my ken, gone through that campaign most honorably; had borne the marches, the most trying weather and the greatest straits of hunger, with an elasticity of mind and muscle that had long since astounded and silenced their most active scoffers. Now, in the bitter depths of winter, they went through the dull routine of camp, cheerful and buoyant, at all times ready for their duty, and never grumbling at the wearing strain they felt to be necessity. When I say that in every Confederate camp *the best* soldiers of that winter were "crack companies" of the gay youths of the cities, I only echo the verdict of old and tried officers. Where all did their duty nobly, comparison were invidious; but the names of "Company F," the Mobile Cadets, the Richmond Blues, and Washington Artillery, stand on the record of those dark days as proof of the statement. Many men from the ranks of these companies had already been promoted to high positions, but they had not yet lost their distinctive characteristics as *corps d' élite;* and admission to their ranks was as eagerly sought as ever. A strange fact of these companies was frequently stated by surgeons of perfect reliability: their sick reports were much smaller than those of the hardiest mountain organizations. This they attributed to two causes: greater attention to personal cleanliness and to all hygienic precautions; and the exercise of better trained minds and wills keeping them free from the deadly " blue devils." Numbers of them, of course, broke down at once. Many a poor fellow who would have achieved a brilliant future perished mid the mud of Manassas, or slept under the snowy slopes of the western mountains. The practice was kill or cure, but it was in a vast majority of cases, the latter; and men who stood the hardship thrived upon it.

The Marylanders, too, were a marvel of patience. Self-made exiles, not only from the accustomed comforts of home, but cut off from communication with their absent ones and harrowed by vague stories of wrong and violence about them—it would have been natural had they yielded to the combined strain on mind and matter. At midwinter I had occasion to visit Evansport and Acquia creek. It had been bitter cold; a sudden thaw had made the air raw and keen, while my horse went to his girths at every plunge. More than once I had to dismount in mire girth-deep to help him on. Suddenly I came upon a Maryland camp—supports to a battery. Some of the soldiers I had known as the gayest and most petted of ball-room and club; and now they were cutting wood and frying bacon, as if they had never done anything else. Hands that never before felt an ax-helve plied it now as if for life; eyes that were accustomed to look softly into

"The sweetest eyes that ever were,"

in the pauses of a waltz, now peered curiously in the reeking stewpan. Many of their names recalled the history of days long gone, for their father's fathers had moved in stately pageant down its brightest pages; and blood flowed in their veins blue as the proudest of earth's nobility. They had left affluence, luxury, the caresses of home—and, harder than all, the habits of society—for what?

Was it thoughtlessly to rush foremost in the delirious shock of battle; to carelessly stand unflinchingly where the wing of death flapped darkest over the glare of the fight; to stand knee-deep in Virginia mud, with high boots and rough shirts, and fry moldy bacon over fires of wet brush? Or was it that the old current in their veins bounded hotly when they believed a wrong was doing; that all else—home—luxury—love—life!—faded away before the might of principle?

It was an odd meeting with the crowd that collected about me and anxiously asked the news from Richmond, from abroad, but above all, from home. Bronzed and bearded, their huge boots caked with Potomac mud and rough shirts open at their sunburnt throats; chapped hands and faces grimy with smoke and work, there was yet something about these men that spoke them, at a glance, raised above the herd. John Leech, who so reveled in the "Camps at Cobham," would here have found a companion-piece for the opposition of the picture.

"Hello, old boy! any news from home?" yelled a whiskered sergeant, jumping from a log where he was mending a rent in his pants, and giving me a hand the color of his favorite tan gloves in days lang syne—"Pretty tight work up here, you see, but we manage to keep comfortable!"—God save the mark!

"What do you think Bendann would give for a negative of me?" asked a splendid fellow leaning on an ax, the rapid strokes of which he stilled at my approach—"Not a half bad thing for a fancy ball, eh?" Charles street had no nattier man than the speaker in days gone; and the tailors had found him their pearl beyond price. But Hilberg's best was now replaced by a flannel shirt with many a rent, army pants and a jacket that had been gray, before mud and smoke had brought it near the unity of Joseph's best garment.

"I'd show well at the club—portrait of a gentleman?" he added lightly.

"Pshaw! Look at *me!* There's a boot for a junior assembly! Wouldn't that make a show on a waxed floor?" and little Charley H. grinned all the way across his fresh, fair face, as he extended a foot protruding from what had been a boot.

"D—l take your dress! Peel those onions, Charley!" cried a baldheaded man from the fire —"Don't your heart rise at the scent of this *olla*, my boy? Don't it bring back our dinners at the Spanish legation? Stay and dine with us—if Charley ever has those onions done—and you'll feast like a lord-mayor! By the way, last letters from home tell me that Miss Belle's engaged to John Smith. You remember her that night at Mrs. R.'s fancy ball?"

"Wouldn't mind having a bottle of Mrs. R.'s sherry now to tone up these onions," Charley said ruefully. "It *would* go well with that stew, taken out of a tin cup—eh, cookey?"

"We had lots better at the club," the cook said, thoughtfully stirring the mess on the fire—"It was laid in before you were born, Charley. Those were days, boys—but we'll drink many a bottle of it yet under the stars and bars!"

"That we will, old man! and I'll carry these boots to a junior assembly yet. But I *would* like a bottle of old Mrs. R.'s to drink now, *faute de mieux*, to the health of the Baltimore girls—God bless 'em!"

"That I would, too," said the sergeant. "But that's the hard part of it!"—and he stuck his needle viciously through the pants—"I always get savage when I think of our dear women left unpro—"

"No particular one, sergeant? You don't mean Miss Mamie on Charles street, do you? Insatiate archer!" cried Charley.

"Do your cooking, you imp! I mean my dear old mother and my sick sister. D—n this smoke! It will get in a fellow's eyes!"

When Miss Todd gave her picnic in the valley of Jehoshaphat and talked London gossip under the olives, it was an odd picture; it is strange to see the irrepressible English riding hurdles in the Campagna, and talking of ratting in the shadow of the Parthenon, as though within the beloved chimes of Bow; but it was stranger still to see those roughened, grimed men, with soleless boots and pants tattered "as if an imp had worn them," rolling out town-talk and well-known names in such perfectly natural manner.

And this was only a slice from any camp in the service. The gentlemen troops stood hardships better, and bore their troubles and difficulties with lighter hearts, than any of the mixed corps. It is true that few of them were left as organizations at the end of the war.

As the army increased, men of ability and education naturally sifted to higher place; but they wore their spurs after they had won them. They got their commissions when they had been through the baptism of blood and fire, and of mud and drudgery as well. They never flinched. The dreariest march—the shortest rations—the deepest snow and the midnight " long roll "—found them ready and willing. History furnishes no parallel. The bloods of the cavalier wars rode hard and fought long. They went to the battle with the jest upon their lips, and walked gaily to the scaffold if need be. But they not only died as gentlemen—they lived as they died. Their perfumed locks were never draggled in the mire of the camp, and their silken hose never smirched but in the fray. Light songs from dainty lips and brimming goblets from choice *flacons* were theirs; and they could be merry to-night if they died to-morrow.

The long rapiers of the Regency flashed as keen in the smoke of the fight as the jest had lately rung in the mistress' bower; and how the *blasé* club man and the lisping dandy of Rotten Row could change to the avenging war god, the annals of the "Light Brigade" can tell.

But these lived as gentlemen. In the blackest hour, when none believed "the king should have his own again;" in the deadliest fray and in the snow-bound trench, *they* waved the sword of command, and the only equality they had with their men was who should fight the furthest.

But here were gentlemen born—men of worth and wealth, education and fashion—delving side by side with the veriest drudge; fighting as only gentlemen can fight, and then working as gentlemen never worked before!

Delicately bred youths who had never known rougher work than the *deux temps*, now trudged through blinding snows on post, or slept in blankets stiff with freezing mud; hands that had felt nothing harder than billiard-cue or cricket-bat now wielded ax and shovel as men never wielded them for wages; the epicure of the club mixed a steaming stew of rank bacon and moldy hard-tack and then—ate it!

10

And all this they did without a murmur, showing an example of steadfast resolution and unyielding pluck to the hardier and tougher soldiers by them; writing on the darkest page of history the clear axiom: *Bon sang ne peut mentir!*

CHAPTER XVIII.

SOCIETY AT THE CAPITAL.

But while everything was dull and lifeless in the camps of the South, a far different aspect was presented by its Capital. There was a stir and bustle new to quiet Richmond. Congress had brought crowds of attachés and hangers-on; and every department had its scores of dependents. Officers from all quarters came in crowds to spend a short furlough, or to attend to some points of interest to their commands before the bureaux of the War Department. The full hotels showed activity and life unknown to them. Business houses, attracted by the increased demands of trade and the new channels opened by Government necessities, sprang up on all sides; and the stores—though cramped by the blockade—began to brush off their dust and show their best for the new customers. Every branch of industry seemed to receive fresh impetus; and houses that had for years plodded on in moldy obscurity shot, with the rapidity of Jonah's gourd, up to first-class business.

The streets presented a scene of unwonted activity; and Franklin street—the promenade *par excellence,* vied with "the avenue" in the character and variety of the crowds that thronged its pavement. The majority of the promenaders were officers, their uniforms contrasting brightly with the more quiet dresses around. While many of them were strangers, and the peculiarities of every State showed in the faces that passed in rapid panorama, yet numbers of "Richmond boys" came back for a short holiday; almost every one bringing his laurels and his commission.

My friend, Wyatt, had kept his laughing promise, and showed me a captain's bars. General Breckinridge had found him hiding in the ranks, and had added A. A. G. to his title.

"Knew it, old man!" was his comment—"Virtue must be rewarded—merit, like water, will find its level. Captain Wyatt, A. A. G.—demnition neat, eh? Now, I'll be here a month, and we must do something in the social line. I find the women still industry mad; but the sewing-circles get up small *dullabilities*—'danceable teas,' as papa Dodd abroad calls them. They're not splendid to a used-up man, like you—not Paris nor yet Washington, but they'll show you our people."

And Wyatt was right. The people of Richmond had at first held up their hands in holy horror at the mere mention of amusement! What! with a war in the land must people enjoy themselves? Never! it would be heartless!

But human nature in Virginia is pretty much like human nature everywhere else; and bad as the war was, people gradually got used to "the situation." They had lost friends—a relation or two was pretty badly marked perhaps—but what glory the tens and hundreds left had gained! There was no fighting now; and the poor fellows in camp would be only too glad to know that their brothers-in-arms were being paid for their toils by the smiles of the fair. The great majority of the strangers, too, were young men who had been recommended to the mercy of the society by these very sufferers in camp.

Gradually these influences worked—the younger and gayer people indulged in the "danceable teas," Wyatt spoke of, after their sewing-circles. Imperceptibly the sewing was left for other times; and by Christmas there was a more constant—if less formal and general—round of gaiety than had been known for years. This brought the citizens and strangers more together, and naturally the result was a long season of more regular parties and unprecedented gaiety. Many still frowned at this, and, as usual, made unhappy Washington the scapegoat—averring that her pernicious example of heartlessness and frivolity had worked the evil.

These rigid Romans staid at home and worked on zealously in their manufacture of warm clothing, deformed socks and impossible gloves for the soldier boys. All honor to them for their constancy, if they thought they were right, and the harmless gaiety wrong; and they fought the good fight, from behind their *abatis* of knitting needles, only with the innocent weapons of tongue and precept. But human nature and inclination still held their own; and there were many defections from the ranks of the elect, to those of the more practical— and probably equally well-intentioned—pleasure-seekers.

But parties were by no means the only resource for pleasure-lovers. Anything that combined amusement and put dollars in the treasuries of charitable societies became the rage ; and here the rigidly virtuous and the non-elect met on neutral ground. Among the amateurs of the city were some who would have taken high rank in any musical circle, and these gave a series of concerts for the benefit of distressed families of the soldiers. The performers were the most fashionable of the society ; and, of course, the judgment of their friends—who crowded to overflowing the churches where the concerts were held—was not to be relied on. But critics from New Orleans and all parts of the South declared the performances creditable to any city. After them the audience broke up into little cliques and had the jolliest little suppers the winter produced, with the inevitable "lancers" until the smallest of small hours.

Then, there were charades and tableaux parties ; while a few—more ambitious of histrionic fame—got up private theatricals. Altogether, in the gay set, the first winter of the war was one to be written in red letters, for old Richmond rang with a chime of merry laughter that for the time drowned the echo of the summer's fights and the groans of the wayside hospitals.

One unique point in the society of Richmond struck me with a constantly recurring surprise. I could not get accustomed to the undisputed supremacy of the unmarried element that almost entirely composed it. It constantly seemed to me that the young people had seized the society while their elders' heads were turned, and had run away with it for a brief space ; and I always looked to see older people come in, with reproof upon their brows, and take charge of it again. But I looked in vain. One day at a dinner, I remarked this to my next neighbor; suggesting that it was only because of the war. She was one of the most charming women the society could boast—scarcely more than a bride, just out of her teens, beautiful, accomplished and very gay.

"Strangers always remark this," she answered; "but it is not the result of the war, or of the influx of strangers, as you suppose. Since I can remember, only unmarried people have been allowed to go to parties by the tyrants of seventeen who control them. We married folks do the requisite amount of visiting and teaing-out; and sometimes even rise in our wrath and come out to dinner. But as for

a party—no!   As soon as a girl is married, she must make up her
mind to pay her bridal visits, dance a few weeks upon sufferance and
then fold up her party dresses.   No matter how young, how pretty, or
how pleasant she may be, the Nemesis pursues her and she must
succumb.   The pleasant Indian idea of taking old people to the river
bank and leaving them for the tide, is overstrictly carried out by our
celibate Brahmins.   Marriage is our Ganges.   Don't you wonder how
we ever dare to declare ourselves old enough ?"

I did wonder; for it had always been a hobby of mine that a
certain amount of the married leaven was necessary in every society
to give it tone and stamina.   Though the French principle of exclud-
ing young ladies from all social intercourse, and giving the patent of
society to *Madame*, may be productive of more harm than good, the
converse seems equally objectionable.   I can recollect no society in
which some of the most pleasant memories do not center around the
intercourse with its married portion.   Richmond is no exception to
the rule.   In the South, women marry younger than in the colder
states; and it often happens that the very brightest and most attractive points of character do not mature until an age when they have
gotten their establishment.   The education of the Virginia girl is so
very different in all essential points from that of the northerner of the
same station, that she is far behind her in self-reliance and *aplomb*.
There is, doubtless, much in native character, but more in early
surroundings and the habit of education.   The southerner, more
lanquid and emotional, but less self-dependent—even if equally "up
in" showier accomplishments—is not formed to shine most at an
early stage of her social career.   Firmer foothold and more intimate
knowledge of its intricacies are necessary to her, before she takes her
place as a woman of the world.

Hence, I was much puzzled to account for the patent fact that the
better matured of its flowers should be so entirely suppressed, in the
Richmond bouquet, by the half-opened buds.   These latter, doubtless, gave a charming promise of bloom and fragrance when they
came to their full; but too early they left an effect of immaturity and
crudity upon the sense of the unaccustomed.   Yet Richmond had
written over the portals of its society: Who enters here no spouse
must leave behind!   and the law was of the Medan.   A stranger
within their gates had no right to cavil at a time-honored custom;

but not one could spend a winter week in the good old town, and fail to have this sense of unfinishedness in her society fabric.

The fair daughters of the Capital are second to none in beauty, grace and the higher charm of pure womanhood. Any assembly showed fresh, bright and gentle faces, with constant pretty ones, and an occasional marked beauty. There is a peculiar, lithe grace, normal to the South, that is hard to describe; and, on the whole, even when not beautiful, there is a *je ne sais quoi* that renders her women very attractive.

The male element at parties ranged from the *passé* beau to the boy with the down still on his cheek—ancient bachelors and young husbands alike had the open sesame. But if a married lady, however young in years or wifehood, passed the forbidden limits by accident—*Væ victis!*

She was soon made to feel that the sphere of the mated was pantry or nursery—not the ball-room. To stranger dames—if young and lively—justice a little less stern was meted; but even they, after a few offenses, were made to feel how hard is the way of the transgressor.

In a community like Richmond, where every one in the circle had played together in childhood, or was equally intimate, such a state of things might readily obtain. In a larger city, never. It spoke volumes for the purity and simplicity of the society that for years it had gone on thus, and no necessity for any matronage had been felt. But now the case was different—a large promiscuous element of military guests was thrown into it; and it struck all that society must change its primitive habit.

The village custom still prevailed in this—a gentleman could call for a lady—take her in his charge alone and without any chaperone—to a party and bring her back at the "we sma' hours." This was not only well, as long as the "Jeanette and Jenot" state of society prevailed, but it told convincingly the whole story of the honest truth of men and women. But with the sudden influx—when a wolf might so readily have imitated the guise of the lamb—a slight hedge of form could in no manner have intimated a necessity for it. Yet Richmond, in the proud consciousness of her simple purity, disdained all such precautions; and the informalities of the country town obtained in the salons of the nation's Capital.

But parties were not the only hospitalities the wanderers received at the hands of the Virginians. In no state in the country one becomes domesticated so soon as in the Old Dominion. You may come to any of its towns a perfect stranger, but with a name known to one prominent citizen, or fortified with a few letters from the right source, and in a time astonishingly short you find yourself at home. This has been time out of mind Virginian custom; and as Richmond is but a condensation of all that is Virginian, it prevailed here as well. If the stranger did not give himself up to the whirl and yield himself, "rescue or no rescue," to the lance of the unmarried, he could find, behind the *chevaux de frise* of clashing knitting-needles, the most genial welcome and most whole-souled hospitality.

"Stupid party last night—too full," criticised Wyatt, as he lounged in my room one morning. "You seemed bored, old man, though I saw you with Nell H. Desperate flirt—pretty, too! But take my advice; let her alone. It don't pay to flirt."—The ten years between the captain and myself were to *my* credit on Time's ledger—"It's all very well to stick up your pennon and ride gaily into the lists to break a lance with all comers. Society cries *laissez aller!* and her old dowagers shower *largesse*. Presto! my boy, and you find your back on the grass and your heels in the air. But I've some steady-going cousins I want to introduce you to. Suit you exactly."

Confound the boy! Where did he get that idea? But I was introduced to the "steady-going cousins" and to me now the Richmond of memory begins and ends in their circle. The jovial, pleasant family dinner around the old-time board; the consciousness of ready welcome to the social fireside, or partake of the muffin at eight, or the punch—brewed very near Father Tom's receipt—at midnight. Then the never-to-be-forgotten coterie of the brightest women of the day under the shaded droplight, in the long winter evenings! And none were excluded by the "steady goers" because they had committed matrimony. They did quantities of work that season; baskets of socks, bales of shirts and boxes of gloves, in numbers marvelous to see, went from that quiet circle to warm the frozen hands and feet, keeping watch and ward for them. And the simple words of cheer and love that went with them must have warmed hearts far colder than beat under the rough shirts they sent.

And never did the genial current of talk—sometimes chatty, sometimes brilliant—flag for a moment. The foremost men of government and army were admitted, and I doubt if ever the most ardent of the unmarried—wilting in the lancers, or deliquescing in the *deux temps*—found very much more genuine enjoyment than the " easy goers," over their distorted socks and impracticable gloves.

They talked of books, events and people, and no doubt gossiped hugely; but though some of the *habituès* were on the shady side of thirty and were sedately walking in the quiet parts of spinsterhood, I never heard one bitter—far less one scandalous, word!

Ferat qui meruit palmam! Let the green leaves adorn those wonderful women!

But the novelty most remarked in the society of this winter was the household of President Davis. Soon after the Government was firmly established in Richmond, the State of Virginia placed at his disposal a plain but comfortable house; and here—with only the ladies of his family and his private secretary—he lived with the quiet simplicity of a private citizen.

It will hardly be invading her *sacra privata* to say that the President's lady did everything to remove false ideas that sprung up regarding the social atmosphere of the "Executive Mansion." She was "at home" every evening; and, collecting round her a staff that numbered some of the most noted men and brilliant women both of the stranger and resident society, assured all her varied guests a warm welcome and a pleasant visit. In this circle Mr. Davis would, after the trying business of the day, give himself an hour's relaxation before entering on labors that went far into the night; and favored friends and chance visitors alike here met the man, where they expected the official.

Austere and thoughtful at all times, rarely unbending to show the vein of humor hidden deep under his stern exterior, and having besides "the divinity that doth hedge" even a republican president, Mr. Davis was never calculated for personal popularity. Even in the early days of his career he forced by his higher qualities—rather than sought by the arts of a trickster—the suffrages of his people; and they continued to cast their shells for him, even while they clamored that he was "the Just."

Whatever grave errors reflecting criticisms may lay at his door; whatever share in the ruin of the South, the future historians may

ascribe to his unswerving self-will and unvarying faith in his own
power—no one who traces his career from West Point to the New
Saint Helena—will call them failings of the demagogue.

In these informal receptions of his lady, Mr. Davis said little;
listening to the varied flow of talk that showed her equally cogni-
zant and appreciative of social, literary and sterner topics. For the
edification of the gayer visitor, she related odd experiences of her
public life, with rare power of description and admirable flashes of
humor. She discussed the latest book with some of the small *littér-
ateurs* with whom she was infested; or talked knowingly of the last
picture, or the newest opera, faint echoes from which might elude
the grim blockaders on the coast.

Mr. Davis spoke little, seeming to find a refreshing element in
her talk, that—as she pithily said of some one else—was like tea,
that cheers but not inebriates. Occasionally he clinched an argument, or gave a keener point to an idea by a short, strong sentence.

After all had partaken of the cup of tea handed round informally,
Mr. Davis retired to his study and once more donned his armor for
battle with the giants without and the dwarfs within his territory.

These informal " evenings " began to grow popular with the better class of Virginians, and tended to a much more cordial tone
between the citizens and their chief. They were broken by bi-
monthly "levees," at which Mr. and Mrs. Davis received "the
world and his wife."

But the formal "levee" was a Washington custom and smacked
too much of the "old concern" to become very popular, although
curiosity to see the man of the hour and to assist at an undress review
of the celebrities of the new nation, thronged the parlors each fort-
night. A military band was always in attendance; the chiefs of
cabinet and bureaux moved about the crowd; and generals—who
had already won names to live forever—passed, with small hands
resting lightly on their chevrons, and bright eyes speaking most eloquently that old truism about who best deserve the fair.

More than once that winter General Johnston moved through the
rooms—followed by all eyes and calling up memories of subtle strategy and hard-won victory. Sometimes the burly form of Longstreet
appeared, ever surrounded by those "little people" in whom he delighted; and the blonde beard of Hood—whose name already began

to shine with promise of its future brilliance—towered over the throng of leading editors, "senior wranglers" from both houses of Congress, and dancing men wasting their time in the vain effort to talk.

But not only the chosen ten thousand were called. Sturdy artisans, with their best coats and hands scrubbed to the proper point of cleanliness for shaking the President's, were always there. Moneyed men came, with speculation in their eyes, and lobby members trying to throw dust therein; while country visitors—having screwed their courage up to the desperate point of being presented—always dropped Mr. Davis' hand as if its not over-cordial grasp burned them.

But the "levees" on the whole, if odd exhibitions, were at least useful in letting the "dear public" have a little glimpse of the inner workings of the great machine of government. And they proved, even more than the social evenings, the ease of right with which Varina Howell Davis wore her title of "the first lady in the land."

The men of Richmond have spoken for themselves. They wrote the history of their class when they came forward—one and all, to sacrifice ease—affluence—life for the cause they felt to be just. There were some, as I shall hereafter endeavor to show, who were dwellers with them, but were not of them. These did nothing and gave nothing willingly for a cause in which they saw only a speculation. This is not the place to speak of such. They belong not to the goodly company of those who—whatever their weaknesses, or even their errors—proclaimed themselves honest men and chivalric gentlemen.

The young men of the whole South are off-hand and impulsive; either naturally careless in pecuniary matters, or made so by habit. Sowing wild oats is an almost universal piece of farming; and the crop is as luxuriant in the mountains of Virginia as in the overflowed lands of Louisiana.

Perhaps in Richmond they were not now seen from the most advantageous point of view. They were generally young planters from the country, reckless, jovial and prone to the lighter dissipations; or the young business and professional men, who rebounded from the routine of their former lives into a little extra rapidity. One and all —for the eyes they sought would not have looked upon them else— they had gone into the army; had fought and wrought well; and now with little to do, boon companionship and any amount of

petting, they were paying for it. The constant strain of excitement
produced much dissipation certainly—but it seldom took the repre-
hensible form of rowdyism and debauch. Some men drank deeply—
at dinners, at balls and at bar-rooms; some gambled, as Virginians
always had gambled—gaily, recklessly and for ruinous stakes. But
find them where you would, there was about the men a careless pervading *bonhomie* and a natural high tone resistlessly attractive, yet
speaking them worthy descendants of the "Golden Horse Shoe
Knights."

As yet the influence of the Government was little felt socially.
The presence of a large congregation of army men from the various
camps had given an impetus to gaiety it would not otherwise have
known; but this was all. There was little change in the habits and
tone of social intercourse. The black shadow of Washington had
not yet begun to spread itself, and its corrupt breath had not yet
polluted the atmosphere of the good old town.

The presence of Congress, with its ten thousand followers, would
hardly be considered as elevating anywhere. There is an odor of tobacco—of rum—of discredit—of anything but sanctity about the
American politician that makes his vicinage unpleasant and unprofit-
able.

Congress had met in the quiet halls of the Virginia legislature.
At first all Richmond flocked thither, crowding galleries and lobbies
to see the might and intellect of the new nation in its most august
aspect; to be refreshed and strengthened by the full streams that
flowed from that powerful but pure and placid fountain; to hear
words that would animate the faint and urge the ready to braver and
higher deeds.

Perhaps they did not hear all this; for after a little they stopped
going, and the might and majesty of the new giant's intellect was
left severely to itself. Of the herd of camp-followers who overflowed the hotels and filled the streets, little note was taken. An
occasional curious stare—a semi-occasional inquiry as to who they
were—and they passed even up Franklin street without more remark.
To the really worthy in government or army, the cordial hand of
honest welcome was extended.

The society unvaryingly showed its appreciation of excellence of
intellect or character, and such as were known, or found to possess it,

were at once received on the footing of old friends. But on the whole, the sentiment of the city was not in favor of the run of the new comers. The leaders of society kept somewhat aloof, and the general population gave them the sidewalk. It was as though a stately and venerable charger, accustomed for years to graze in a comfortable pasture, were suddenly intruded on by an unsteady and vicious drove of bad manners and low degree. The thoroughbred can only condescend to turn away.

Willing as they were to undergo anything for the cause, the Virginians could not have relished the savor of the new importations; nor can one who knows the least of the very unclean nature of our national politics for a moment wonder.

Montgomery had been a condensed and desiccated preparation of the Washington stew, highly flavored with the raciest vices. Richmond enjoyed the same mess, with perhaps an additional kernel or two of that garlic.

CHAPTER XIX.

DAYS OF DEPRESSION.

The proverb that misfortunes never come singly soon became a painful verity in the South; and a terrible reaction began to still the high-beating pulses of her triumph.

The merry echoes of the winter had not yet died away, when it became oppressingly apparent that proper methods had not been taken to meet the steady and persevering preparations of the North. Disaster after disaster followed the arms of the South in close succession; and the spirits of all classes fell to a depth the more profound, from their elevation of previous joyance.

As early as the 29th of the previous August, a naval expedition under Commodore Stringham had, after a short bombardment, reduced the forts at Hatteras Inlet. In the stream of gratulation following Manassas, this small event had been carried out of sight; and even the conquest of Port Royal, South Carolina, by Admiral Dupont's fleet, on the 7th of November, had been looked upon as one of those little mischances that only serve to shade all pictures of general victory.

They were not taken for what they really were—proofs of the entirely defenseless condition of an immense sweep of coast, in the face of the heavy and increasing naval armament of the United States. They were considered reverses merely; inquiry went but little deeper and the lesson they should have taught was lost; while the inexplicable tardiness of the War Department left still more important points equally defenseless.

But the news of General Crittenden's utter defeat at Mill Springs, on the 17th of January —of the disastrous results of his miscalculation, or misguided impetuosity, and of the death of Zollicoffer— came with stunning effect; opening wide the eyes of the whole country to the condition in which apathy, or mismanagement, had left it.

As usual, too, in the popular estimate of a success, or a reverse, the public laid much stress on the death of Zollicoffer, who was a favorite both with them and the army. He was declared uselessly sacrificed, and his commanding general and the Government came in for an equal share of popular condemnation.

Mr. Davis soon afterward relieved Secretary Walker from the duties of the War Office; putting Mr. Benjamin in his seat as temporary incumbent. The latter, as before stated, was known as a shrewd lawyer, of great quickness of perception, high cultivation, and some grasp of mind; but there was little belief among the people that he was fit to control a department demanding decision and independence, combined with intimate knowledge of military matters. Besides Mr. Benjamin personally had become exceedingly unpopular with the masses. Whether this arose from the unaccountable influence he—and he alone—had with his chief, or whether the busy tongues of his private enemies received too ready credence, is hard to say. But so the fact was; and his elevation gave rise to scurrilous attacks, as well as grave forebodings. Both served equally to fix Mr. Davis in the reasons he had believed good enough for his selection.

Suddenly, on the 7th of February, Roanoke Island fell!

Constant as had been the warnings of the press, unremittingly as General Wise had besieged the War Department, and blue as was the mood of the public—the blow still fell like a thunder-clap and shook to the winds the few remaining shreds of hope. General Wise was ill in bed; and the defense—conducted by a militia colonel with less than one thousand raw troops—was but child's play to the immense armada with heaviest metal that Burnside brought against the place.

Roanoke Island was the key to General Huger's position at Norfolk. Its fall opened the Sounds to the enemy and, besides paralyzing Huger's rear communications, cut off more than half his supplies. The defeat was illustrated by great, if unavailing, valor on the part of the untrained garrison; by a plucky and determined fight of the little squadron under Commodore Lynch; and by the brilliant courage and death of Captain O. Jennings Wise—a gallant soldier and noble gentleman, whose popularity was deservedly great.

But, the people felt that a period must be put to these mistakes; and so great was their clamor that a congressional committee investigated the matter; and their report declared that the disaster lay at the door of the War Department. The almost universal unpopularity of the Secretary made this a most acceptable view, even while an effort was made to shift part of the blame to General Huger's shoulders. But wherever the fault, the country could not shake off the gloom that such a succession of misfortunes threw over it.

This feeling was, if possible, increased, and the greatest uneasiness caused in all quarters, by Burnside's capture of Newbern, North Carolina, on the 4th of March. Its defenses had just been completed at heavy cost; but General Branch, with a garrison of some 5,000 men, made a defense that resulted only in complete defeat and the capture of even his field artillery. Here was another point, commanding another supply country of great value to the commissariat, lost to the South. But worse still, its occupation gave the Federals an easy base for striking at the Weldon railroad.

Nowhere was the weakness of the South throughout the war shown more fully than in her utterly inefficient transportation. Here were the demands of the army of Virginia and of a greatly-increased population in and around Richmond, supplied by one artery of communication! Seemingly every energy of the Government should have been turned to utilizing some other channel; but, though the Danville branch to Greensboro'—of only forty miles in length—had been projected more than a year, at this time not one rail had been laid.

It is almost incredible, when we look back, that the Government should have allowed its very existence to depend upon this one line—the Weldon road; running so near a coast in possession of the enemy, and thus liable at any moment to be cut by a raiding party. Yet so it was. The country was kept in a state of feverish anxiety for the safety of this road; and a large body of troops diverted for its defense, that elsewhere might have decided many a doubtful battle-field. Their presence was absolutely necessary; for, had they been withdrawn and the road tapped above Weldon, the Virginia army could not have been supplied ten days through other channels, and would have been obliged to abandon its lines and leave Richmond an easy prey.

Meanwhile the North had collected large and splendidly-equipped armies of western men in Kentucky and Tennessee, under command of Generals Grant and Buell. The new Federal patent, "the

Cordon," was about to be applied in earnest. Its coils had already been unpleasantly felt on the Atlantic seaboard; General Butler had " flashed his battle blade "—that was to gleam, afterward, so bright at Fort Fisher and Dutch Gap—and had prepared an invincible armada for the capture of New Orleans; and simultaneously the armies under Buell were to penetrate into Tennessee and divide the systems of communication between Richmond and the South and West.

General Albert Sidney Johnston was sent to meet these preparations, with all the men that could be spared from Western Virginia and the points adjacent to his line of operations. Still his force was very inadequate in numbers and appointment; while to every application for more men, the War Department replied that none could be spared him.

The Federal plan was to advance their armies along the water-courses, simultaneously with their gunboats—light draught constructions prepared expressly for such service; and, penetrating to any possible point, there form depots with water communication to their base. The Tennessee and Cumberland rivers were plainly their highways. The only defenses of these streams were Forts Henry and Donelson—weak works inefficiently garrisoned; for the half million appropriated by Congress for their defense at the eleventh hour could not have been used in time, even had the money been forthcoming from the treasury.

With scarcely a check to their progress, the Federals reduced and passed Fort Henry on the 4th of February, pressing on to Donelson, into and supporting which work, General Johnston had thrown General J. B. Floyd with some ten thousand troops under Pillow and Buckner. After three days' hard fighting, Floyd found the position untenable and further resistance impossible. He, therefore, turned over the command to Buckner—who refused to abandon the part of the garrison that could not escape—and, with General Pillow and some five thousand men, withdrew in the night and made good his escape.

During the siege of Donelson, Johnston evacuated Bowling Green and awaited its issue opposite Nashville. The result being known, it naturally followed that this city—undefended by works of any description and with an army inadequate to its protection—had to be abandoned. The retreat was at once commenced; and it was on that

gloomy march that Forrest first made the name that now stands with
so few rivals among the cavalry leaders of the world. Commanding
a regiment of cavalry from his own section, he seemed as ubiquitous
as untiring. Keeping a constant front to the enemy—now here, now
there, and ever cool, dauntless and unflinching—he gave invaluable
aid in covering the rear of that retreat. About this time, also, John
H. Morgan began to make his name known as a partisan chief; and
no more thrilling and romantic pages show in the history of the times,
than those retailing how he harassed and hurt the Federals while in
Nashville.

During the progress of these events on the Tennessee and Cumberland, Richmond had been shaken by alternate spasms of suspense
and premature exultation.

Her citizens could scarcely yet realize that the hitherto despised
Yankees had been able to march, almost unchecked, into the heart
of a territory protected by southern forts, southern troops, and the
noblest names in all her bright array. Feeling thus, they still placed
some credence in any rumors that came.

One morning, news reached Richmond of a brilliant victory at
Donelson, and it was received with wild rejoicing. Next night the
War Department issued the stunning bulletin of the fall of Nashville! When this was generally believed, a gloom settled over the
Capital, such as no event of the war had yet produced. The revulsion was too sudden and complete to be met by reason, or argument; the depression was too hopeless and despairing to be removed
by any declaration of the valor of the defense, of the orderly character of the retreat, or of the far stronger position Johnston had
gained by a concentration of his force on a ground of his own choice.

The very name of gunboat began to have a shuddering significance to the popular mind. A vague, shadowy power of evil far
beyond that of any floating thing, ancient or modern, was ascribed
to it; and the wild panic constantly created in the Federal mind the
year before by the dreaded name of "Black Horse," or the mere
mention of masked battery—was re-enacted by the South in defer-
ential awe of those floating terrors.

Under this morbid state of gloom, the Government fell into greater
and greater disfavor. Without much analytical reasoning, the people
felt there must have been a misuse of resources, at least great enough

to have prevented such wholesale disaster. Especial odium fell upon the War Department and reacted upon the President for retaining incapable—or, what was the same to them, unpopular—ministers in his council at such vital moment. The press—in many instances filled with gloomy forebodings and learned disquisitions on the I-told-you-so principle, fanned the flame of discontent. Mr. Davis soon found himself, from being the idol of the people, with nearly half the country in open opposition to his views.

At this moment, perhaps, no one act could have encouraged this feeling more than his relieving Floyd and Pillow from command, for abandoning their posts and leaving a junior officer to capitulate in their stead. Certainly the action of these generals at Donelson was somewhat irregular in a strictly military view. But the people argued that they had done all that in them lay; that they had fought nobly until convinced that it was futile; that they had brought off five thousand effective men, who, but for that very irregularity, would have been lost to the army of the West; and, finally, that General Johnston had approved, if not that one act, at least their tried courage and devotion.

Still, Mr. Davis remained firm, and—as was his invariable custom in such cases—took not the least note of the popular discontent. And still the people murmured more loudly, and declared him an autocrat, and his cabinet a bench of imbeciles.

Thus, in a season of gloom pierced by no ray of light; with the enemy, elated by victory, pressing upon contracting frontiers; with discontent and division gnawing at the heart of the cause—the "Permanent Government" was ushered in.

The 22d of February looked dark and dismal enough to depress still more the morbid sensibilities of the people. A deluge of rain flooded the city, rushed through the gutters in small rivers, and drenched the crowds assembled in Capitol Square to witness the inauguration.

In the heaviest burst of the storm, Mr. Davis took the oath of office at the base of the Washington statue; and there was something in his mien—something solemn in the surroundings and the associations of his high place and his past endeavor—that, for the moment, raised him in the eyes of the people, high above party spite and personal prejudice.

An involuntary murmur of admiration, not loud but heart-deep, broke from the crowds who thronged the drenched walks; and every foot of space on the roof, windows and steps of the Capitol. As it died, Mr. Davis spoke to the people.

He told them that the fortunes of the South, clouded and dim as they looked to-day, must yet rise from the might of her united people, to shine out as bright and glorious as to-morrow's sun.

It was singularly characteristic of the man, that even then he made no explanation of the course he had seen fit to take—no excuses for seeming harshness—no pledge of future yielding to any will but his own. The simple words he spoke were wholly impersonal; firm declaration that he would bend the future to his purpose; calm and solemn iteration of abiding faith that a united South, led by him, must be unconquerable.

There was a depth in the hearts of his hearers that discontent could not touch:—that even discontent had not yet chilled. They saw in him the representative man of their choice—headstrong certainly, erring possibly. But they saw also the staunch, inflexible champion of the South, with iron will, active intellect, and honest heart bent steadily and unweariingly to one purpose; and that purpose the meanest one among them clasped to his heart of hearts!

Then, through the swooping blasts of the storm, came a low, wordless shout, wrenched from their inmost natures, that told, if not of renewed faith in his means, at least of dogged resolution to stand by him, heart and hand, to achieve the common end.

It was a solemn sight, that inauguration.

Men and women left the square with solemn brows and serious voices. There was none of the bustle and pride of a holiday pageant; but there was undoubtedly a genuine resolve to toil on in the hard road and reach the end, or fall by the wayside in the effort.

Having laid out a fixed line of policy, Mr. Davis in no way deviated from it. There were no changes of government measures and no changes of government men, except the elevation of General George W. Randolph to the Secretaryship of War. This gentleman —a clear-headed lawyer, a tried patriot and soldier by education and some experience—was personally very popular with all classes. He was known to possess decision of character and a will as firm as the President's own; and the auguries therefrom were, that in future the

chief of the War Office would also be its head. His advent, therefore, was hailed as a new era in military matters.

But Mr. Benjamin, who became daily more unpopular, had been
removed from the War Department only to be returned to the portfolio of State, which had been kept open during his incumbency of
the former. This promotion was accepted by the Secretary's enemies
as at once a reproof to them, and a blow aimed at the popular foreign
policy. They boldly averred that, though the foreign affairs of the
Government might not call for very decided measures, Mr. Benjamin
would not scruple—now that he more than ever had the ear of his
chief—to go beyond his own into every branch of the Government,
and to insert his own peculiar and subtle sophisms into every recess
of the Cabinet.

To do the Secretary justice, he bore the universal attack with most
admirable good nature and *sang froid.* To all appearance, equally
secure in his own views and indifferent to public odium, he passed
from reverse to reverse with perfectly bland manner and unwearying
courtesy; and his rosy, smiling visage impressed all who approached
him with vague belief that he had just heard good news, which would
be immediately promulgated for public delectation.

The other members of the Cabinet, though not equally unpopular,
still failed fully to satisfy the great demands of the people. Two of
them were daily arraigned before the tribunal of the press—with what
reason, I shall endeavor, hereafter, to show.

Mr. Reagan's administration of the Post-office, while very bad,
was possibly as good as any one else could have inaugurated, with
the short rolling-stock and cut roads of ill-managed, or unmanaged systems; and the Attorney-General was of so little importance for the
moment as to create but little comment.

Thus the permanent government of the struggling South was inaugurated amid low-lowering clouds. Every wind from the North
and West threatened to burst them into overwhelming flood; while,
within the borders of the nascent Nation, no ray of sunshine yet
reflected from behind their somber curtain.

And through the gloom—with no groping hand and with unfaltering tread;—straight to the fixed purport of its own unalterable purpose, strode the great, incarnate Will that could as little bend to
clamor, as break under adversity!

CHAPTER XX.

FROM SHILOH TO NEW ORLEANS.

Within two weeks of his inauguration, the strongly hopeful words of President Davis seemed to approach fulfillment, through the crushing victory of the "Merrimac" in Hampton Roads, on the 8th March. There was no doubt of the great success of her first experiment; and the people augured from it a series of brilliant and successful essays upon the water. The late bugbear—gunboats—began to pale before the terrible strength of this modern war-engine; and hopes were cherished that the supremacy afloat—which had been the foundation of the claim of Federal victory—was at an end.

On the 23d of the same month, Jackson—who was steadily working his way to the foremost place in the mighty group of heroes—struck the enemy a heavy blow at Kernstown. His success, if not of great material benefit, was at least cheering from its brilliance and dash.

But the scale, that trembled and seemed about to turn in favor of the South, again went back on receipt of the news of Van Dorn's defeat, on the 7th March, in the trans-Mississippi. Price and his veterans—the pride of the whole people, and the great dependence in the West—had been defeated at Elk Horn. And again the calamity assumed unwonted proportions in the eyes of the people from the death of Generals Ben McCollough and McIntosh—the former a great favorite with Government, army and public.

This news overshadowed the transient gleam from Hampton Roads and Kernstown; plunging the public mind into a slough of despond, in which it was to be sunk deeper and deeper with each successive despatch.

After Nashville, Island No. 10—a small marsh-surrounded knob in the Mississippi river—had been selected by General Beauregard, and fortified with all the appliances of his great engineering skill, until deemed well-nigh impregnable. It was looked upon as the key to the defenses of the river, and of the line of railroad communication between New Orleans and the West with the Capital. In the middle of March the Federal flotilla commenced a furious bombardment of that station; and though a stubborn defense was conducted by its garrison, some boats succeeded in running its batteries on the 6th April. It was then deemed necessary at once to abandon the post, which was done with such precipitate haste that over seventy valuable guns—many of them perfectly uninjured; large amounts of stores, and all of the sick and wounded, fell into the hands of the captors.

On the same day was joined the hardest and bloodiest battle that had to this time drenched the land with the best blood in it.

General Grant, with an army of not less than 45,000 fresh and well-equipped soldiers, had been facing General A. S. Johnston, seeking to amuse him until a junction with Buell could surely crush his small force—not aggregating 30,000 effective men. To frustrate this intent, Johnston advanced to the attack on the plains of Shiloh, depending upon the material of his army, and his disposition of it, to equalize the difference of numbers.

At early dawn on Sunday, the 6th April, General Hardee, commanding the advance of the little army, opened the attack. Though surprised—in many instances unarmed and preparing their morning meal—the Federals flew to arms and made a brave resistance, that failed to stop the onward rush of the southern troops. They were driven from their camp; and the Confederates—flushed with victory, led by Hardee, Bragg and Polk, and animated by the dash and ubiquity of Johnston and Beauregard—followed with a resistless sweep that hurled them, broken and routed, from three successive lines of entrenchments. The Federals fought with courage and tenacity. Broken, they again rallied; and forming into squads in the woods, made desperate bush-fighting.

But the wild rush of the victorious army could not be stopped! On its front line swept!—On, like the crest of an angry billow, crushing resistance from its path and leaving a ghastly wreck under and behind it!

While leading a charge early in the afternoon, General Johnston received a Minié-ball in his leg. Believing it but a flesh wound, he refused to leave the ground; and his falling from his horse, faint with the loss of blood, was the first intimation the staff had of its serious nature; or that his death, which followed almost immediately, could result from so slight a wound.

The loss of their leader was hidden from the men; and they drove the enemy steadily before them, until sunset found his broken and demoralized masses huddled on the river bank, under cover of the gunboats.

Here Grant waited the onset, with almost the certainty of annihilation. But the onset never came; that night Buell crossed upward of 20,000 fresh troops; the broken army of Grant was reformed; Wallace's division of it joined the main body; and next day, after a terrible and disastrous fight, the southrons slowly and sullenly retired from the field they had so nobly won the day before.

A horrid scene that field presented, as foot by foot the fresh thousands of the Federals wrenched it from the shattered and decimated Confederates; the ground furrowed by cannon, strewn with abandoned arms, broken gun-carriages, horses plunging in agony, and the dead and dying in every frightful attitude of torture!

The battle of Shiloh was the bloodiest of the war. The little army of the South had lost near one-third of its whole number; while the Federals had bought back their camp with the loss of not less than 16,000 men.

And, while the bloodiest field, none had so splendidly illustrated the stubborn valor of the men and the brilliant courage of their leaders. Gladden had fallen in the thickest of the fight—the circumstances of his death sending a freshened glow over the bright record he had written at Contreras and Molino del Rey. The names of Bragg, Hardee and Breckinridge were in the mouths of men, who had been held to their bloody work by these bright exemplars. Wherever the bullets were thickest, there the generals were found—forgetful of safety, and ever crying—"Come!"

Governor Harris had done good service as volunteer aid to General Johnston; and Governor George M. Johnson, of Kentucky, had gone into the battle as a private and had sealed his devotion to the cause with his blood. Cheatham and Bushrod Johnson bore bloody marks of the part they took; while Breckinridge, who had already won undying fame, added to his reputation for coolness, daring, and tenacity, by the excellence with which he covered the rear of the army on its retreat to Corinth.

The results of the battle of Shiloh—while they gave fresh cause for national pride—were dispiriting and saddening. It seemed as though the most strenuous efforts to marshal fine armies—and the evacuation of city after city to concentrate troops—were only to result in an indiscriminate killing, and no more ; as if the fairest opportunities for a crushing blow to the enemy were ever to be lost by error, or delay.

The death of General Johnston, too—seemingly so unnecessary from the nature of his wound—caused a still deeper depression ; and the public voice, which had not hesitated to murmur against him during the eventful weeks before the battle, now rose with universal acclaim to canonize him when dead. It cried out loudly that, had he lived through the day of Shiloh, the result would have been different.

It must be the duty of impartial history to give unbiased judgment on these mooted points ; but the popular verdict, at the time, was that Beauregard had wasted the precious moment for giving the *coup-de-grace.* The pursuit of the Federals stopped at six o'clock ; and if, said people and press, he had pushed on for the hour of daylight still left him, nothing could possibly have followed but the annihilation, or capitulation, of Grant's army.

On the other hand, Beauregard's defenders replied that the army was so reduced by the terrible struggle of twelve hours—and more by straggling after the rich spoils of the captured camp—as to render further advance madness. And in addition to this, it was claimed that he relied on the information of a most trusty scout—none other than Colonel John Morgan—that Buell's advance could not possibly reach the river within twenty-four hours. Of course, in that event, it was far better generalship to rest and collect his shattered brigades, and leave the final blow until daylight.

An erroneous impression prevailed in regard to this fight, that Johnston had been goaded into a precipitate and ill-judged attack by the adverse criticisms of a portion of the press. No one who knew aught of that chivalric and true soldier would for an instant have believed he could lend an ear to such considerations, with so vast a stake in view ; and the more reasonable theory came to be accepted—that he desired to strike Grant before the heavy columns that Buell was pouring down could join him.

At all events, the sad waste of position and opportunity, and the heavy loss in brilliant effort and valuable lives, caused equal dissatisfaction and gloom. Beauregard's new strategic point commanded a valuable sweep of producing territory, protected the communications, and covered Memphis. Still people were not satisfied; and tongues and pens were busy with the subject, until an event occurred that wrapped the whole country in wondering and paralyzing grief.

On the 26th April New Orleans surrendered to Admiral Farragut!

The Federal fleet had long been hovering about the twin forts at the mouth of the river; and daily telegrams of the progress of the bombardment and of their impregnability had schooled the country into the belief that the city was perfectly secure. Day after day the wires repeated the same story of thousands of shell and nobody hurt, until inquiry ceased to be even anxious; and the people were ready to despise this impotent attempt upon the most important point of the far South.

So secure had the Government been in her defenses, that regiment after regiment had been withdrawn from New Orleans and sent to Corinth, until General Lovell found his command reduced to less than three thousand effective men—and more than half of these local militia and volunteer organizations.

Suddenly came the despatch that the fleet had passed the forts at dawn on the 24th! All was consternation in the city. The confidence had been so great that daily avocations went on as usual; and the news found every one as unprepared for it, as though·no enemy had been near.

Confusion ruled the hour. General Lovell reached the city from below; and, feeling that his handful of men could effect nothing and might only offer an excuse for bombardment, he yielded to the desire of the city authorities and withdrew to Camp Moore. He carried with him all the munitions and supplies that were capable of transportation; and held himself ready to return at a moment's notice from the Council.

Meanwhile, the Federal fleet had engaged the Confederate flotilla —consisting of an incomplete iron-clad, a plated tow-boat ram, and eight or ten useless wooden shells—and after a desperate fight had driven them off only to be blown up, one by one, by their own commanders.

The water-batteries then offered no effective resistance. The obstructions had been opened to remove accumulated raft, and could not be closed; and the fleet moved slowly up to seize the rich prize that lay entirely within its grasp.

On the 26th April, the "Hartford" leading the van, it anchored off the city to find it hushed as death and wrapped in the eddying smoke-clouds from fifteen thousand burning bales of cotton. After the first burst of consternation, the people took heart; and even at the sight of the enemy's shipping did not lose all hope. There were no soldiers aboard; Butler's army could not dare the passage of the forts in the shells of transports that contained it; the fleet, cut off as it was from all re-enforcement and supply, could, at worst, only shell the city and retire—again running the gauntlets of the two forts; and then the only loss to the city—for the flotilla in its incomplete state could not have been made effective as a defense—would have been the cotton and the trifling damage done by the shells.

So the people hoped on. A long correspondence, coupled with reiterated threats of bombardment, ensued between Mayor Monroe and Admiral Farragut, relative to the State flag that still floated over the Custom House. Still the city was not in Federal power and there might yet be a chance.

But on the 28th, the news of the fall of the forts in consequence of the surrender of their garrisons—took the last support from the most hopeful. The city yielded utterly; the marines of the "Hartford" landed, took formal possession, raised the stars and stripes over the City Hall; and the emblem of Louisiana's sovereignty went down forever!

Three days after, General Butler landed and took command of the city, for which he had not struck a blow. He stationed his garrison in the public buildings, the hotels, and even in private houses; and then commenced a system of oppression and extortion, that—while it made the blood boil in the veins of every southron—has sent his name to the honest thinkers of the future linked with a notoriety which all history proves to be unique.

The annals of the war are not free from small pilferers and vicious imbeciles; but high above the tableau they form, this warrior has perched himself upon a pinnacle—let us hope—unattainable again!

It is hard to overrate the consequences of the fall of New Orleans. The commercial city and port of the whole South-west—its depot and granary—the key to communication with the trans-Mississippi, and

the sentinel over vast tracts of rich and productive territory—her loss
was the most stunning blow that had yet been dealt the cause of the
South.

It opened the whole length of the Mississippi as a new base for
operations against the interior; and gave opportunities for establishing a series of depots, from which the Federal armies—if ever beaten
and shattered—could be rapidly and effectively recruited.

Not the least disastrous effect of this blow was its reception by the
people. After the first bitter wail went up over the land, inquiry
came from every quarter how long this state of things could last.
Position after position—fortress after fortress—city after city—declared impregnable by the Government up to the very last moment,
fell suddenly and mysteriously; only to expose, when too late, the
chain of grievous errors that inseparably linked the catastrophe with
the Government.

The public demanded at least an explanation of these things—a
candid exposé of the condition to which they were reduced. If told
they were battling hopelessly for their frontiers; that the enemy was
too strong and the extent of territory too large for sure defense; if
told, even, there were grave reason to doubt the ultimate issue—they
were yet willing to battle for the hope, and to go uncomplainingly to
the front and face the gloomy truth.

But to be buoyed day by day with high-sounding protestations
of invincibility, only to see their strongest points dropping, one by
one, into the lap of the enemy; to be lulled into security to find, too
late, that the Government had deceived them, while it deceived itself;
and thus to imbibe a deep distrust of the hands in which their hopes
and the future were placed—this was more than they could bear; and
"a thick darkness that could be felt" brooded over the land.

But as yet this feeling had not begun in any way to react upon the
army. The hardy soldiers had enough to do to keep them busy;
and besides had laid up a stock of glorious reminiscences, upon which
to fall back when bad news reached them. Only the bare facts of
these rapid and terrible blows reached the camps; and stubborn,
hard-fisted "Johnny Reb," looked upon them smilingly as reverses to
be made up to-morrow, or the next time he caught "Mr. Yank."

To the Louisiana soldiers, the news of the fall of their beautiful city
had a far deeper and more bitter import. Some of the business men
of New Orleans, who remained in the city, yielded to the prompt-

ings of interest and fell to worshipping the brazen calf, the Washington high priest had set up for them. Some refused to degrade themselves and remained to be taught that might is right; and that handcuffs are for the conquered. Others collected what little they could and fled to Europe; while nobler spirits eluded the vigilance of their captors and came by scores into the Confederate camps.

But the women of New Orleans were left behind. They could not come; and against them the Pontiff of Brutality fulminated that bull, which extorted even from the calm and imperturbable British Premier the exclamation—" Infamous!"

The intended insult fell dead before the purity of southern womanhood; but the malignancy that prompted it seared deep into their hearts. Though their defenders were away, the women of New Orleans rose in their majesty of sex; and, "clothed on with chastity," defied the oppressor and called on manhood everywhere to judge between him and them. As

" When the face of Sextus was seen amid the foes " —

in those earlier days when Roman womanhood was roused to defy that elder traducer—

" No women on the housetops
But spat toward him and hiss'd;
No child but scream'd out curses
And shook its little fist!"

And the cry echoed in the hearts of the Louisianians in the battle's front. It mattered not so much to them if the defenses had been neglected; if the proper precautions had not been taken, and their firesides and families sacrificed, while they were battling so nobly far away. They only felt that those dear homes—their wives, and sisters, and sweethearts—were now in the relentless grasp of a hero who burned to war against women.

And deep in their souls they swore a bitter oath to fight in the future, not only for the cause they loved, but for themselves; to strike each blow, nerved by the thought that it was for the redemption of their homes and their loved ones; or, if not for this—for vengeance!

Gradually this spirit inoculated their fellow-soldiers. The bitter feelings of the struggle, strong enough before, became intensified; and in every Confederate camp was brewing a sullen and somber war-cloud, the sudden flashes from which were to strike terror to the heart of the North before that summer was done.

CHAPTER XXI.

THE CONSCRIPTION AND ITS CONSEQUENCES.

In the midst of the gloom, weighing upon the country about the days of Shiloh, the Confederate Congress moved on a point of vital import to its cause. Weak and vacillating as that body had proved; lacking as it was in decision, to force its views on the executive, or to resist popular clamor, backed by *brutum fulmen* of the press—a moment had come when even the blindest of legislators could not fail to see.

More men, was the cry from every general in the field. With more men, the army of Manassas could have carried the war over the Potomac frontier; perhaps have ended it there. With more men, Nashville would have been saved and Shiloh won. With more men, the enemy, pouring over the daily contracting frontiers, if not checked in their advance, might be restrained from, or chastised for, the brutal and uncivilized warfare that now began to wage, away from all great army centers.

Great as was the need for new blood and new brains, in the council of the nation—still more dire was the need for fresh muscle in its armies. Levies must be raised, or all was lost; and the glories that had wreathed the southern flag, even when it drooped lowest—price-less blood that had been poured as a sacrament to consecrate it—would all be set at naught by the imbecility of the chosen lawgivers of the people. Thus, after a pressure of months from cooler heads in government, the more thoughtful of the people, and the most far-sighted of the press, the few live men in Congress wrung from it the "Conscription Act" on the 16th day of April.

The reader may have gained some faint idea of the alacrity with which men of all classes rushed into the ranks; of the steady endeavor and unmurmuring patience with which they bore the toils and dangers of their chosen position; of their unwavering determination to fight the good fight to the end. That the same spirit as genuinely pervaded the masses of the army now, there is little doubt; but the South—instead of husbanding her resources, had slept during these precious months the North utilized to bring a half million of men against her.

Now, when she woke to the plain fact that her existence depended —not only on keeping in the ranks every man already there, but of adding largely to their numbers—it was but natural that the Government's torpor had, in a slight degree, reacted upon its soldiers.

When the Government had assumed more form and regularity with increased proportions and the conviction, forced upon the most ob- tuse mind, that a struggle was at hand demanding most perfect organ- ization, the looseness of a divided system had become apparent. The laws against any State maintaining a standing army were put into ef- fect; and the combined military power was formally turned over, as a whole, to the Confederate authorities. This change simply meant that complete organizations were accepted as they stood, as soldiers of the Confederacy instead of soldiers of the states; the men were mustered into the Confederate service and the officers had their state commissions replaced by those from the Confederate War Depart- ment. From that date, the troops were to look to the central Gov- ernment for their pay, subsistence, and supplies.

In mustering in, all troops—with only exceptions where their con- tracts with state governments demanded—were received "for three years of the war." At Montgomery, many admirable organizations had been tendered to the Government for one year; and much discussion had ensued on the subject of their reception. It was then generally believed, even by the longest heads in the Cabinet, that the war would be *only a campaign.* I have elsewhere alluded to the te- nacity with which its supporters clung to this idea; and Mr. Davis was almost alone in his persistent refusal to accept the troops for less than three years, or the war. To the one campaign people he said, very justly, that if the troops were taken for twelve months, and the war were really over in six, here was the Government saddled with the incubus at a standing army, infinitely greater than its needs; and here large bodies of men who might be of incalculable service elsewhere, tied to the vitiating and worse than useless influences of a peace camp. On the other hand, should the war last longer, in its very climax a large body of educated soldiers, just trained to a point of usefulness, would have the right to demand their discharge, when their places would be difficult to fill even with raw levies. There was much dissatisfaction among the one campaign people; but their own argument—that, if received for the war, the troops would get home before their proposed twelve months expired—was unanswerable. Now, when the same arguments were used to enforce the passage of the Conscription Act, the enemies that Mr. Davis had by this time gathered around him, little recked that in their wisdom, they were quoting him.

This transfer to the Confederate Government covered *all* the troops of the several states, except the militia. This, of course, remained under the authority of their respective governors.

Naturally, with the addition to the force originally contemplated by "the assembled wisdom of the land," the five brigadier-generals allowed by Congress proved totally inadequate. A law had subsequently been forced from them, granting the appointment of five *generals* —a rank paramount to that of field-marshal in European armies—of the regular army, who were to command volunteers; and allowing the President to appoint such number of brigadiers of volunteers as the necessities of the service demanded.

There had been little hesitancy in the selection of the generals—all of them men who had served with distinction in the army of the United States; and who had promptly left it to cast their lot with the new Government. So little difference could be found in their claims for precedence, that the dates of their old commissions decided it. They were Samuel Cooper, Albert Sidney Johnston, Robert E. Lee, Joseph E. Johnston and Pierre G. T. Beauregard.

These nominations had been received with unanimity by the Senate, and with profound satisfaction by the people. Had fitness and right been consulted equally in other appointments, much priceless blood might have been saved to the South.

Still, at the time, it was believed that the commissions of brigadier of volunteers were conferred upon the most meritorious of the resigned officers; or, where there was reason to hope good results to the service—upon the best of those men the troops had chosen as commanders. Strong pressure was, of course, brought to bear upon the President, regarding these appointments; but the verdict of army and people was that *these first* selections were made with as much judgment and impartiality as the untried state of the army permitted.

But fifteen months' quiet endurance of hardship, danger and doubt; the universal wail from homes that had never before known a dark hour, but where unaccustomed toil now fought vainly against misery and disease; a pervading sense of insecurity for any point, and that those homes—broken and saddened as they were—might meet a yet worse fate—all these causes had done their work. Undaunted and unconquered as the men were, the bravest and most steadfast still longed for a sight of the dear faces far away.

The term of service of more than a hundred regiments would expire soon; enlistments had become slow and were not to be stimulated by any inducements legislation could offer. The very danger that had been pointed out in refusing more "twelve months' men" became too imminent to evade.

The soldiers of the South were more anxious than ever to meet the foe. Added to their love for the cause, many now felt bitter personal incentive to fight; and every blow was now struck alike for country and for self. But while panting for the opportunity, they had a vague feeling that they must fight nearer home and—forgetting that the sole protection to their loved ones lay in a union, closer and more organized than ever—each yearned for the hour when he would be free to go and strike for the defense of his own hearthstone.

The intent of the conscription was to put every man in the country, between the ages of eighteen and thirty-five, into the army; restricting "details" from the field within the narrowest limits of absolute necessity. It retained, of course, every man already in the field; and, had its spirit been vigorously carried out, would have more than doubled the army by midsummer.

It provided for the separate enrollment of each state under a "Commandant of Conscripts;" and for collecting new levies at proper points in "Camps of Instruction," under competent officers, that recruits might go to the army prepared in drill and knowledge of camp life for immediate service.

But, the Conscription Act, like all other congressional measures, was saddled with a companion, "Bill of Exemptions." This—while so loosely constructed as almost to nullify all good effect of the law—opened the door to constant clashing of personal and public interests, and to great abuses of the privilege.

12

It would, of course, have been folly to draw every able-bodied male from districts already so drained of effective population as to have become almost non-producing. Such a course would have put thousands of additional mouths into the ranks, and still further have reduced the straitened means for feeding them. And it would have been equally suicidal to draw from forge and from lathe, those skilled artisans who were day and night laboring to put weapons in the hands of those sent to wield them.

But the "Bill of Exemptions" left possible both of these things, at the same time that it failed to restrain abuses of privileges in certain high quarters. The matter of "details" was, of course, essential; and it was only to be supposed that generals in the field could best judge the value of a man in another position than the front.

But the most objectionable feature to the army was the "Substitute Law," which allowed any one able to buy a man, not subject to the action of conscription, to send him to be shot at in his place. Soldiers who had endured all perils and trials of the war, naturally felt that if they were retained in positions they objected to, those who had been comfortably at home—and in many instances coining that very necessity into fortunes—should be forced at the eleventh hour to come and defend themselves and their possessions. Besides, the class of men who were willing to sell themselves as substitutes were of the very lowest order. All citizens of the South were liable to conscription; and the "exempts" open to purchase, were either strange adventurers, or men over and under age, who—argued the soldiers—if fit for service should come of their own free will.

Veteran troops had a low enough opinion of the "conscript" as a genus; but they failed not to evince, by means more prompt than courteous, their thorough contempt for the "substitute."

These causes produced much discontent, where men would cheerfully have acquiesced in a law essential to the preservation of the fabric they had reared and cemented with their blood. To quell this feeling, a reorganization of the army was effected. A certain time was allowed for any liable man to volunteer and choose his branch of the service and, if practicable, his regiment; and so great was the dread of incurring the odium of conscription, that the skeleton veteran regiments rapidly filled up to a point of efficiency. They were then allowed to choose their own officers by election; and, though this lost to the service many valuable men who had become unpopular, still the army was better satisfied within itself.

The refilled regiments were re-brigaded by states when practicable, a general from a different state being sometimes placed in command; and the whole army was divided into corps, of three divisions each, commanded by a lieutenant-general.

Whatever the weakness of its construction—and the abuses of the exemption and detail power in carrying it out—there can be little doubt that the conscription at this time saved the country from speedy and certain conquest; and credit should be given to the few active workers in the congressional hive who shamed the drones into its passage.

Had the men whose term expired been once permitted to go home, they could never again have been collected; the army would have dwindled into a corporal's guard here and there; the masses the North was pouring down on all sides would have swept the futile resistance before it; and the contest, if kept up at all, would have degenerated into a guerrilla warfare of personal hatred and vengeance, without a semblance of confederation, or nationality.

Once passed, the people of the whole country aquiesced in and approved the conscription, and gave all the aid of their influence to its progress. Here and there a loud-mouthed demagogue would attempt to prejudice the masses against the measure; but scarcely a community failed to frown down such an effort, in the great extremity of the country, as vicious and traitorous. The opposition that the project had met in the administration—from doubt as to its availability—was removed by its very first working. What had been in its inception an unpopular measure, received now the approbation of all classes; and the governors of every state—save one—went to work with hearty good will to aid its carrying out.

This exception was Governor Joseph E. Brown, of Georgia, who entered into a long wrangle with the administration on the constitutional points involved. He denied the right of Congress to pass such an act, and of the Executive to carry it out within the limits of a sovereign state; averred—with much circumlocution and turgid bombast—that such attempt would be an infringement of the State Rights of Georgia, which he could not permit.

Mr. Davis replied in a tone so reasonable, decorous and temperate as to wring unwilling admiration even from his opponents. He pointed out briefly the weak points that rendered the governor's position utterly untenable, ignored the implied warning of resistance to the law; and succinctly stated that he relied upon the patriotism of Georgians to grasp the full meaning of the crisis their executive failed to comprehend; and he closed by stating that the conscription must go on.

Governor Brown found no supporters for his extreme views, even in the anti-administration party. The people felt the imminence of the danger; and here, as in all matters of deep import, they placed the conservation of the cause high above partisan prejudices, or jealousies of cliques. Utterly silenced by the calm dignity and incisive logic of Mr. Davis, and abandoned by the few supporters his defiance of the administration had at first collected around him, Governor Brown was forced to yield; achieving only the conviction that he had the general condemnation of the popular voice.

Once set in motion, the machinery of conscription worked rapidly and somewhat smoothly. The Camps of Instruction in all states not possessed by the enemy filled rapidly, and the class of conscripts on the whole was fairly good. By early summer they began to arrive in Richmond and " Camp Lee "—the station where they were collected —became a point equally of curiosity to the exempt and of dread to the liable.

It was curious to note the prevalence of the various state-traits, showing in the squads of conscripts from time to time passing through the city. The sturdy farmers from the interior, especially those from Virginia, Georgia and Alabama, though lacking the ease and careless carriage of the veteran soldier, had a determined port that spoke for their future usefulness. They were not merry naturally. Called from accustomed avocations and leaving behind them families defenseless and without means of support, they could scarcely have marched gaily, even when willingly, into the Carnival of Death. But they were resolute men, earnest in their love for the South and honest in their wish to serve her—with the musket, if that were better than the plough.

Tall and lank, but long-limbed and muscular, the Georgians had a swinging stride of their own; and, even when the peculiar dialect did not ring out over their ranks, something in their general style gave the idea that these were the men who would one day be fellow-soldiers of the famous " fighting Third."

Ever and anon came a dejected, weary squad with slouching gait and clayey complexions. Speaking little and then with a flat, unintoned drawl that told of the vicinage of "salt marsh;" bearing the seeds of rice-field fevers still in them, and weakly wondering at the novel sights so far from home, the South Carolina conscripts were not a hopeful set of soldiers. As soon as the tread of hostile battalions had echoed on her soil, the sons of the Palmetto State flew to their posts. State regulars went to the coast, picked volunteer corps came to Virginia. None stayed behind but those really needed there by the Government, or that refuse class which had determined to dodge duty, but now failed to dodge " the conscript man." The former were, of course, as much needed now as ever ; the latter did not ride into the battle with defiance on their brows, but, on the contrary, seemed looking over their shoulders to find a hole in the mesh that implacable conscription had drawn about them.

Their next neighbors of the Old North State were hardly better in the main, but some men among them seemed not unlike the militia that had fought so well at Roanoke Island. Green and awkward; shrinking away from the chaff of passing regulars; looking a little sheepish for being conscripts, "Zeb Vance's boys" yet proved not unworthy the companionship of the men of Bethel, of Manassas and of Richmond.

At first the border states, or those overrun by the enemy, gave few additions to the conscript camps.

Kentucky, on whose adherence and solid aid to the cause such reliance had been placed in the beginning, had sadly failed to meet it. With the reminiscences of her early chivalry, her romantic warfare of the " Dark and Bloody Ground," and the warlike habits of her men, mingled considerations of the usefulness of her vast resources and her natural points for defense, lying so near the Federal territory. But as the war wore on and the state still wavered, the bent of her people seemed strangely to incline to the northern side. Seeking a neutrality that was clearly impossible, the division in her councils admitted the Federals within her borders. Then, when it was hopeless to do more, the noblest and most honored of her sons left Kentucky and ranged themselves under that banner they had in vain sought to unfurl over her.

Like Maryland, Kentucky had early formed a *corps d' élite*, called the "State Guard," which numbered many of the best-born and most cultured young men of the state, with headquarters at Louisville. This was commanded by General S. B. Buckner and under the general control of Governor Magoffin. This corps was supposed to represent the feelings of all better citizens in its opposition to the Union cause.

But when the action of political schemers—aided by the designs of a money-loving and interested populace—laid Kentucky, like Maryland, bound hand and foot at the feet of the Federal government; when the Union council of the state strove to disarm or put them in the Union ranks, the soldiers of the "State Guard" left unhesitatingly and joined the army of the South in large numbers.

Late in November, 1861, a convention had met; and, declaring all bonds with the Union dissolved, passed a formal Ordinance of Secession and sent delegates to ask admission from the Richmond Congress. A month later Kentucky was formally declared a member of the Confederacy; but before that time Buckner and Breckinridge had received the commissions, with which they were to win names as proud as any in the bright array of the South; a Kentucky brigade—whose endurance and valiant deeds were to shed a luster on her name that even the acts of her recreant sons could not dim—were in General Johnston's van; some of her ablest and most venerable statesmen had given up honors and home for the privilege of being freemen! All the South knew that the admission of the state was but an empty form—powerless alike to aid their cause, or to wrest her from the firm grasp the Federal government had set upon her.

At the time of the first conscription the few men left in Kentucky, who had the will, could not make their way into Confederate camps; far less could the unwilling be forced to come.

Tennessee, also, had been a source of uneasiness to the Richmond Government from the spread of Union tendencies among a portion of her inhabitants. Though she had been a member of the Confederacy near a year, still the half civilized and mountainous portions of her territory, known as East Tennessee, had done little but annoy the army near it, by petty hostilities and even by a concerted plan for burning all the railroad bridges in that section and thus crippling communications.

Fortunately this scheme had been frustrated, and the half-savage population—for the better class of Tennesseans were almost unanimous in expression of loyalty to the South—kept in subjection.

But now with her soil overrun by Federal soldiers, and with a Federal fleet in every river, the state could not respond to the call of the South; and, of course, the soldiers she yielded the conscription were from the narrow tracts in Confederate possession only.

One hears much of the "Union feeling" in the South during the war. Immediately on its close, a rank crop of "southern loyalists" had sprung up in many quarters; basking in the rays of the Freedmen's Bureau and plentifully manured with promises and brotherly love by the open-mouthed and close-fisted philanthropy of New England. But like all dunghill products, the life of these was ephemeral. Its root struck no deeper than the refuse the war had left; and during its continuance the genus was so little known that a Carlyle, or a Brownlow, was looked upon with the same curiosity and disgust as a very rare, but a very filthy, exotic.

With the exceptions of portions of Kentucky and Tennessee, no parts of the South were untrue to the government they had accepted.

Florida was called "loyal" and General Finnegan proved with what truth. "Loyal" Missouri has written her record in the blood of Price's ragged heroes. Louisiana, crushed by the iron heel of military power, spoiled of her household gods and insulted in her women's name, still bowed not her proud head to the flag that had thus become hostile.

And the Valley of Virginia! Ploughed by the tramp of invading squadrons—her fair fields laid waste and the sanctity of her every household invaded—alternately the battle-ground of friend and foe—where was her "loyalty?"

Pinched for her daily food, subsidized to-day by the enemy and freely giving to-morrow to their own people—with farming utensils destroyed and barns bursting with grain burned in wanton deviltry—the people of the Valley still held to the allegiance to the flag they loved; and the last note of the southern bugle found as ready echo in their hearts as in the first days of the invasion—

> " Their foes had found enchanted ground—
> But not a knight asleep ! "

In possibly one or two instances, the official reports of invading generals may have been in some slight degree erroneous; newspaper correspondents are not in every instance absolutely infallible; and perhaps it was more grateful to the tender sensibilities of the war party at the North to feel that there were hearts of brothers beating for them in the glare of burning rooftrees, or swelling with still more loyal fervor to the cry of the insulted wife !

But at this day—when the clap-trap of war has died away with the roll of its drums; when reason may in some sort take the place of partisan rage—not one honest and informed thinker in the North believes that " loyal " feeling ever had deep root anywhere among the southern masses; or that " loyal citizens " were as one in ten thousand !

Whole communities may have murmured; there may have been " schism in the council and robbery in the mart ; " demagogues may have used wild comparisons and terrible threats about the Government; staunch and fearless newspapers may have boldly exposed its errors and mercilessly lashed its weak or unworthy members; some men may have skulked and dodged from their rightful places in the battle's front !

But, however misplaced the world's verdict may declare their zeal—however great the error for which they fought and suffered and died—no man to-day dare refuse to the southern people the meed of their unparalleled constancy !

Even conquered—manacled and gagged by the blind and blood-thirsty faction in power—the southern people held to the small fragments of rights left them, with brave tenacity. Willing to accept that arbitration to which they had submitted their cause, and ready to take the hand of fellowship if offered, they still preferred to suffer with the bright memories of their past, rather than to efface them by signing their own degradation.

They were conquered and bound in the flesh, but there was enough of manhood left in the spirit to say—

> " Though ye conquer us, men of the North, know ye not
> What fierce, sullen hatred lurks under the scar ?
> How loyal to Hapsburg is Venice, I wot !
> How dearly the Pole loves ' his father '—the Czar ! "

No more singular sight was presented by all the war than the conscript depot at Richmond. The men from the "camps of instruction" in the several states—after a short sojourn to learn the simplest routine of the camp, and often thoroughly untaught in the manual even—were sent here to be in greater readiness when wanted. Such officers as could be spared were put in charge of them, and the cadets of the Virginia Military Institute were employed as drill officers.

Citizens of various states—young, old, honest and vicious alike—the conscripts were crowded together in camp, left to their own devices enough to make them learn to live as soldiers; and put through constant drill and parade to accustom them to the use of arms.

Almost every variety of costume obtained among them. The butternut jacket with blue pants of the Federal soldier, the homespun shirt with the cast-off pants of some lucky officer; and the black broadcloth frock and jauntily-cut pants that some friendly lady had ransacked her absent one's stores to give, all appeared on dress parade; surmounted by every variety of head gear, from the straw hat of many seasons to the woolen night-cap the good "marm" had knitted.

Notwithstanding much work, there was still too much leisure time; and "apple jack" filtered its way through provost guards, and cards, the greasiest and most bethumbed, wiled many an hour for the unwary and verdant.

The lower class of conscripts were almost invariably from the cities—the refuse population of the wharf, bar-room and hotel. Unwilling to volunteer, these gentry skulked behind every excuse to avoid conscription; but when forced off at last, they and the substitutes banded in an unholy brotherhood to make the best of their position.

Ringleaders in every insubordination and every vice they assumed a *degagé* air of superiority, and fleeced their verdant companions of the very clothes they wore; while they made the impure air of the camps more foul with ribald jest and profane song.

A single glance segregated this element from the quiet country conscripts. The latter were generally gloomy, thinking of the field untilled and the wife and little ones, perhaps, unfed. When they drank "new dip" it was to drown thought, for the fumes of every stew-pan brought back shadowy memories of home and comfort; and when they slept on the damp ground—wrapped in the chance rug, or worn scrap of carpet charity had bestowed—a sad procession marched through their dreams, and sorrowful and starving figures beckoned them from mountain side and hamlet.

Great misery and destitution followed the conscription. Large numbers of men, called from their fields just as they were most needed, cut down greatly the supplies of grain. Almost all who remained at home bought their exemption by giving so large a portion of their product to Government as to reduce civil supplies still more; and these two facts so enhanced the price of food—and so reduced the value of money—that the poorer classes rapidly became destitute of all but the barest means of life. Whether this was the result of inevitable circumstance, or the offspring of mismanagement, in no way affects the fact. Food became very hard to procure even at high prices; and the money to get it was daily more and more monopolized by a grasping few.

The Confederate soldier now had a double share of toil and torture. When the smoke of the fight rolled away, and with it the sustaining glow of battle, thought bore him but grim companionship at the camp fireside; for he saw famine stalk gaunt and pale through what had been his home.

When tidings of want and misery came, he strove to bear them. When he heard of burning and outrage—where naught was left to plunder—who may wonder that he sometimes fled from duty to his country, to that duty more sacred to him of saving his wife and children!

Who does not wonder, rather, in reading the history of those frightful days, that desertions were so few—that untutored human nature could hide in its depths such constancy and devotion to principle!

But, great as were the privation and the suffering caused by the first conscription, they were still to be increased. Through those twin abortions of legislation, the substitute and exemption bills, the results of the first law proved inadequate to fill the gaps of the fatal fights of the summer.

Detail and substitute had done their work, as thoroughly as had the shells of Malvern Hill, the bullets of Sharpsburg, or the raw corn of the retreat to the river.

More men were wanted! At whatever cost in territory, or in suffering, more men must be had. And on the 27th September, Congress passed an act extending the age of conscription from 18 to 45 years. But the exemption and substitute laws remained as effective as ever. True, some feeble moves were made toward narrowing the limits of the former; but while it stood a law in any form, enough could be found to read it in any way. The extension law, while it still further drained the almost exhausted country—and left in its track deeper suffering and destitution, that brought famine from a comparative term into an actual verity—still left in the cities an able-bodied and numerous class; who, if not actually useless, were far more so than the food-producing countrymen sent to the front to take their places.

Yet so blind was the Congress—so impervious to the sharpest teachings of necessity and so deaf to the voice of common sense and reason, that unceasingly upbraided it—that this state of things continued more than a year from the passage of the extension act.

Then, when it was almost too late for human aid to save the cause —when the enemy had not only surrounded the contracted territory on every side, but had penetrated into its very heart—the substitute bill was repealed, and every man in the land between the ages of 18 and 45, declared a Confederate soldier subject to service. Then, too, the abuses of exemption and detail, so often and so clearly pointed out, were looked into and measurably corrected.

Further than this, all boys from 16 to 18, and older men, from 45 to 60, though not conscripted, were formed into reserve "home guards;" and then General Grant wrote to Washington that the cause was won when the Rebels "robbed the cradle and the grave."

But the infantile and the moribund murmured not; and more than once a raid was turned and a sharp skirmish won, when the withered cheek of the octogenarian was next the rosy face of the beardless stripling!

Only one complaint came, and that was heard with grim amusement alike by veteran, by conscript, and by substitute.

The substitute buyers now loudly raised a wail of anguish. Plethoric ledger and overflowing till, alas! must be left; the auctioneer's hammer and the peaceful shears must alike be thrown aside, and the rusty musket grasped instead; soft beds and sweet dreams of to-morrow's profit must be replaced by red mud and the midnight long roll!

It was very bitter; and rising in their wrath, a few of these railed at the perfidy of the Government in breaking a contract; and even employed counsel to prove that in effect they were already in the field.

One ardent speculator even sought the War Department and logically proved that, having sent a substitute, who was virtually himself, and that substitute having been killed, he himself was a dead man, from whom the law could claim no service!

But the Department was now as deaf as the adder of Scripture; and the counsel, let us hope, pleaded not very earnestly.   So the substitute buyers—except in the few cases where the long finger of influential patronage could even now intervene—went, as their ill-gotten dollars had gone before.

It is plainly impossible, in limits of a desultory sketch, to give even a faint outline of the conscription.   Its ramifications were so great— the stress that caused it so dire, and the weaknesses and abuses that grew out of it so numerous, that a history of them were but a history of the war.

Faithfully and stringently carried out, it might have saved the South.   Loosely constructed and open to abuse, it was still the most potent engine the Government had used; and while it failed of its intent, it still for the first time caused the invader to be met by anything approaching the whole strength of the country.

Under its later workings, every man in the South was a soldier; but that consummation, which earlier might have been salvation—came only when the throes of death had already begun to seize her vitals.

CHAPTER XXII.

WAITING FOR THE ORDEAL BY COMBAT.

If any good fruits were to grow from the conscription, the seed had not been planted a moment too soon.

The whole power of the Union was now to be exerted against the South; and the Washington idea plainly was to lay the ax at the very root of the rebellion.

Desultory movement had already begun in the Valley and along the river; but it masked in nowise plain indication of the massing of troops for another, and a greater, "On to Richmond!"

The separate corps of Banks, Fremont and Shields were hovering about the flanks of the devoted Army of Manassas; and the decisive blow was evidently to be aimed at that point. But the clear-sighted and cool-headed tactician at the head of the bulwark of Virginia saw far beyond the blundering war-chess of his antagonist. He prepared to checkmate McClellan's whole combination; and suddenly—after weeks of quiet preparation, of which the country knew no more than the enemy—Manassas was evacuated!

To effect this movement, it was necessary to abandon all the heavy river batteries, guarding the Potomac, at immense loss in guns and material; and to destroy large quantities of commissary stores, for which there was no transportation. But, "Joe Johnston" held the movement to be necessary; and, by this time the South had learned to accept that what he thought must be correct. The great disparity in numbers, and the evident purpose of the Federals to make Richmond the focal point of attack, spoke plainly to that perfect soldier the necessity—*coute que coute*—of bringing his army within easy striking distance of the Capital.

Stonewall Jackson—with Ewell's and Early's divisions of less than ten thousand men of all arms—was detached to watch the enemy; and the retrograde movement was completed so successfully that McClellan never suspected the evacuation. Two days later, his grand array—"an army with banners," bands braying and new arms glinting in the sun—moved down to the attack; and then, doubtless to his infinite digust, he found only the smoking and deserted *débris* of the Confederate camp. The army he had hoped to annihilate was on its steady and orderly march for Richmond.

Immediately, the baffled Federal embarked his entire force and landed it on the Peninsula—formed by the junction of the York and James rivers—in front of Magruder's fortifications. Failing at the front door, McClellan again read Cæsar, and essayed the back entrance.

Magruder's line of defense—a long one, reaching entirely across the Federal advance—was held by a nominal force, not exceeding 7,500 effective men. Had this fact been known to its commander, the "grand army" might easily have swept this handful before it and marched, unopposed, into the Southern Capital. But "Prince John" was a wily and bold soldier; and, while he sent to the rear most urgent statements of his dire need and pressed the government for re-enforcement, he kept his front covered by ceaseless vigilance, constant shifting of his thinned battalions and continued active advance skirmishing. So effective was this as entirely to deceive the enemy. McClellan sat down before him and began to fortify!

Amid the anxiety of that moment and the rapid rush of grave events that followed immediately upon it, the great importance of Magruder's tactics on the Peninsula has largely been lost sight of. That they were simply not to be overestimated, it is tardy justice to state. For, there were scores of occasions in those grim four years, when the cant went out—"We might have ended the war right here!" It was ever coupled with—and nullified by—a large and sonorous "if;" but there is no question but that—had Magruder permitted the tactician in his front to estimate his weakness—the "Seven days' fights" would never have been won, for Richmond would have been lost!

It were impossible to describe accurately the state of public feeling, which now prevailed in the Southern Capital. Absolutely in the dark as to the actual movement and its consequences; knowing only that their cherished stronghold, Manassas, was deserted and its splendid system of river batteries left a spoil; hearing only the

gloomiest echoes from the Peninsular advance and ignorant of Johnston's plans—or even of his whereabouts—it was but natural that a
gloomy sense of insecurity should have settled down upon the masses,
as a pall. A dread oppressed them that the recent dramas of Nashville and New Orleans were to be re-enacted on their own central
theater; and, ever barometric, the people let the mercury drop to
zero, as they read the indications in one another's faces. Social
pleasures lately so frequent—social intercourse almost—were now
known no more. The music one heard was the quick tap of the
timing drum; the only step thought of, the double quick to the front.

But gradually, the army that had been manœuvering about the
Rappahannock began to arrive; and day and night the endless
stream of muddy men poured down Main street, in steady tramp for
the Peninsula. Grim and bronzed they were, those veterans of
Manassas; smeared with the clay of their camp, unwashed, unkempt,
unfed; many ragged and some shoeless. But they tramped through
Richmond—after their forced march—with cheery aspect that put to
flight the doubts and fears of her people. Their bearing electrified
the citizens; and for the moment, the rosy clouds of hope again
floated above the horizon.

Even the scanty ration the soldiers had become inured to had been
reduced by necessities of their rapid march; and that knowledge
caused every corps that passed through to receive substantial tokens
of the sympathy and good will of the townspeople. Ladies and
children thronged the sidewalks, pressing on their defenders everything which the scanty Confederate larder could supply; while, from
many of the houses, gloves, socks and comforters rained down upon
the worst clad of the companies.

"Johnny Reb" was ever a cheerful animal, with a general spice
of sardonic humor. Thus refreshed, inwardly and outwardly, the
men would march down the street; answering the waving handkerchiefs at every window with wild cheers, swelling sometimes into the
indescribable "rebel yell!" Nor did they spare any amount of
good-natured chaff to those luckless stay-at-homes encountered on
the streets.

"Come out'r that black coat! I see yer in it!"—"I know ye're a
conscrip'. Don't yer want 'er go for a sojer?"—"Yere's yer chance
ter git yer substertoot!"—and like shouts, leveled at the head of some

unlucky wight, constantly brought roars of laughter from the soldiers and from his not sympathetic friends. Passing one house, a pale, boyish-looking youth was noted at a window with a lady. Both waved handkerchiefs energetically; and the men answered with a yell. But the opportunity was too good to lose.

" Come right along, sonny! The lady 'll spare yer! Here's a little muskit fur ye' !"

"All right, boys !" cheerily responded the youth, rising from his seat—" Have you got a leg for me, too?" And Colonel F. stuck the shortest of stumps on the window-sill.

With one impulse the battalion halted; faced to the window, and spontaneously came to " Present!" as the ringing rebel yell rattled the windows of that block. The chord had been touched that the roughest soldier ever felt!

Then came the calm; when the last straggler had marched through to the front and Johnston's junction with Magruder was accomplished. The rosy clouds faded into gray again; and, though the fluttering pulse of Richmond beat a little more steadily, it was not entirely normal. Rumors came from Yorktown of suffering and discontent. Coupled with exaggerations of the really overwhelming force the enemy had massed before it, they proved anything but encouraging. Still, there was no hopelessness; and the preparations, that had by this time become a matter of certainty—stretchers—bandages—lint and coarse, narrow sheets—went steadily on.

The brave women of the city were a constant reproach, in their quiet, unmurmuring industry, to the not infrequently faint-hearted and despondent men. Constantly they worked on, and tried to look cheerfully on the future by the light of the past. No one among them but knew that real and serious danger threatened; no one among them but believed that it would be met as it had been met before—boldly without doubt; triumphantly if God willed!

No need for Virginia's sons to read of the Gracchi, with a thousand Cornelias working cheerily and faithfully on the hard, tough fabrics for them. One day an order came for thirty thousand sand-bags. Never before did needles fly so fast, for who could tell but what that very bag might stand between death and a heart dearer far than aught else on earth. Thirty hours after the order came, the women of Richmond had sent the bags to Yorktown!

At length, after three weeks of trying suspense, filled with every fantastic shape of doubt and dread, came news of the evacuation of Norfolk, the destruction of the iron-clad "Virginia," and of the retreat from the Peninsula. Not appreciating the strategical reasons for these movements, Richmond lost her temporary quiet and again fell to lamenting the dark prospects for the city.

On the 4th of May, the last of the Confederate forces evacuated Yorktown; reluctantly turning their backs on the enemy, to take up the line of march for Richmond.

Next day McClellan's advance pressed on; and overtaking their rear, under Longstreet, began heavy skirmishing to harass it, near Williamsburg. Seeing the necessity of checking too vigorous pursuit, and of teaching the Federals a lesson, Longstreet made a stand; and, after a severe conflict—in which he inflicted much heavier loss than he sustained, besides capturing several field pieces and colors—again took up his march unmolested.

The battle of Williamsburg was the one brilliant episode of that gloomy retreat. Although the main army could not be checked to give him re-enforcement, and his wounded had to be left in the hands of the enemy, Longstreet had gained a decided and effective success. But this one misfortune for the moment dimmed the luster of his achievement in the eyes of the Richmond people; and, perhaps, prevented much of the good effect its decisive character might otherwise have had.

The appearance of the army, after the retreat from Williamsburg, did not tend to cheer the inexpert. First came squads of convalescent sick, barely able to march, who had been sent ahead to save the ambulances for those worse than they. It was a black Sunday afternoon, when those wan and hollow-eyed men limped painfully through the streets on their weary way to Camp Winder Hospital. Weak—mud-encrusted and utterly emaciated—many of them fell by the roadside ; while others thankfully accepted the rough transportation of any chance wagon, or cart, that could carry them to the rest they yearned for.

But willing and energetic workers were at hand. Orders were obtained ; and carriages returning from church, hotel omnibuses—every wheeled thing upon the streets were impressed for the service of mercy. By late afternoon the wards of Winder Hospital were over-

13

flowing; but negligent, or overworked, commissaries had neglected to provide food, and many of the men—in their exhausted condition —were reported dying of starvation! Few women in Richmond dined that Sabbath. Whole neighborhoods brought their untasted dinners to the chief worker among them; and carriages and carts— loaded with baskets and hampers and bearing a precious freight of loving womanhood—wended their way to the hospital. By night hundreds of poor fellows had eaten such food as they had not dreamed of for months; gentle hands had smoothed their pillows and proffered needed stimulants; and sympathizing voices had bid them be of good cheer, for to-morrow would dawn bright for all.

But were these worn and wretched men a fair sample of the army that was to battle for their dear city against the fresh thousands of McClellan? Oh, God! Had toil and privation done its work so thoroughly; and were these the proud array that had marched to Manassas—the hardened, but gallant host that had gone gaily to Yorktown? Were these the only dependence of their hopes and their cause?

Sad and troubled were the hearts that beat that day, around the wretched cots of the sufferers. But never a hand trembled—never a voice faltered, as those grand women wrought on at their mission of mercy.

After these came a few stragglers and camp followers in hardly better plight; then the wagon trains; and, finally, the army.

The roads were in wretched condition. Spring rains and constant use had churned them into liquid red mud. Hungry and worn, the men struggled through it day after day—bearing their all on their backs, unable to halt for cooking; and frequently stopped to labor on a broken-down battery, or a mired wagon. Discipline naturally relaxed. It was impossible to keep the weary and half-starved men to regular routine. They straggled into Richmond muddy—dispirited —exhausted; and, throwing themselves on cellar doors and sidewalks, slept heavily, regardless of curious starers that collected around every group.

Never had the Southern army appeared half so demoralized; half so unfit to cope with the triumphant and well-appointed brigades pressing close upon it. Had McClellan been at hand, there is little doubt as to what the result would have been; but a few days sufficed to change the appearance of the whole army fabric.

Renewed discipline—that magnetic " touch of the elbow "—attention to the commissariat and the healthy location of their new camping grounds brought the men back to good condition in a time wonderfully short to the lookers-on in the city.

But they were to have little rest. McClellan advanced to the Chickahominy and strongly fortified his position. Johnston fronted him; and though too weak to attack at this moment, it became apparent that the first move in the game for the great stake must be made in a few days. And it was equally plain that it was to be made under the loving eyes of those all fought best for; within hearing of the Cabinet itself!

The details of the campaign of this eventful summer are too well known—and have been too minutely and eloquently described, even were there space—for me to attempt their repetition here.

For a week the armies faced each other, plainly in sight; the shrill notes of " Dixie " mingling with the brazen strains from the Federal bands; and yet no movement was made. Once more Richmond assumed her old activity and became a vast camp. Busy looking officers hastened from point to point; regiments shifting position passed through town every hour; mounted orderlies dashed in all directions and batteries, wagon trains and ambulances rumbled in and out of town by every road. The reflection of the activity around them, and the improved condition of the army—in physique and morale—inspired the people; and they once more began to feel hopeful, if not overconfident.

Still the river was undefended. There was no fort. Only a few water batteries—out of which the men could easily be shelled—and a few useless wooden gunboats protected the water approach to the Capital. Up this the heavy fleet of Federal iron-clads was even now carefully sounding its way. Every means had been taken to wake the Government to the necessity of obstructing the river; but either carelessness, or the confusion consequent on the retreat, had rendered them unavailing. Now at the last moment, every nerve was strained to block the river and to mount a few guns on Drewry's Bluff—a promontory eighty feet high, overhanging a narrow channel some nine miles below the city.

On the 15th of May, the iron-clads approached the still unfinished obstructions. There was just time to sink the "Jamestown"—one of the wooden shells that had done such good work under the gallant Barney—in the gap; to send her crew and those of the "Virginia" and "Patrick Henry" to man the three guns mounted on the hill above—when the iron-clads opened fire.

Their cannonade was terrific. It cut through the trees and landed the missiles a mile inland. The roar of the heavy guns, pent and echoed between the high banks, was like continuous thunder, lit by lurid flashes as they belched out 13-inch Shrapnel and scattered ounce balls like hail among the steadfast gunners on the bluff.

But the terrible plunging fire of Captain Farrand's sea-dogs damaged the plating of the armored vessels and kept the wooden ones out of range; while the galling sharp-shooting of Taylor Wood's men, on the banks below, cleared their decks and silenced their guns. Once more the wager of battle was decided for the South; and the iron-clads retired badly damaged.

This result was most cheering; but, unlike the early success of the war, it was received with a solemn, wordless thankfulness. Then, when the imminent danger was passed, the Government went rapidly to work to improve the obstruction and strengthen the battery at Drewry's Bluff. This became a permanent fort, admirably planned and armed with navy guns, worked by the seamen of the disused vessels. The Federals stuck to the name they first gave it—Fort Darling—for no reason, perhaps, but because of the tender reminiscences clinging around it.

Then came another season of stillness on the Chickahominy lines, which General McClellan improved to protect his rear communications; and to throw up strong embrasured fortifications along his whole front—indicating his intention to sit down before the city in regular siege; or to fight behind his works.

Meantime, the course of the Government would have inspired anything but confidence, had not the people placed the deepest and most abiding faith in the mettle and truth of their soldiers.

Congress, after weak and more than useless debates on the propriety of the step, precipitately adjourned and ran away from the threatened danger. These wise legislators had read history. They felt that the cackling which saved Rome was but one of the miracles of that philosophic Muse who teaches by experience: and that—as they could not save their city—they had better save themselves.

The Departments were packed in case of necessity for flight; and some of the archives were even put on board canal boats and towed beyond the city. This may have been only a just precaution; but the citizens of Richmond—looking upon its defense as the key to all further resistance—saw in it only acceptance of the worst results; and, when the families of the principal officials and officers fled from the Capital and sought safer homes in North Carolina and Georgia, her people would not accept as the real reason the averred necessity for saving the very small amount of provision they consumed.

But the Legislature of Virginia and the City Council of Richmond met and resolved that they were willing to stand any loss of property and life—even the destruction of the city—before giving it up to the enemy. They waited upon the President and so explained to him. Mr. Davis solemnly announced his resolution to defend the position while a man remained; and to cast his fate with that of a people who could act so bravely.

Still, so doubtful was the issue of the contest held by the lukewarm, or cowardly, few that they hesitated not to express their belief that the war was done; and they stored in secret places quantities of tobacco to be used as currency when the invaders came in!

When the *dies iræ* really came; and burning Richmond sent similarly hidden store,

" With the smoke of its ashes to poison the gale "—

little was the sympathy borne on the breeze for them, who—living early enough—had shamed the money-changers scourged from the Temple!

CHAPTER XXIII.

AROUND RICHMOND.

In the dead stillness of the afternoon of May 30th, the dull thunder of artillery and the crackling roll of musketry were distinctly heard in every house in Richmond.

Deep and painful suspense filled all hearts; until at night it was known that the enemy had been driven back and badly punished.

The history of "Seven Pines" is familiar to all. Some days previous, General Keyes' division had been thrown across the Chickahominy, for the purpose of feeling the Confederate lines and throwing up works that would secure the Federals that stream. The river, swelled by recent rains, rose so suddenly as to endanger Keyes' communications with his rear; and Johnston determined to attack, while he could thus strike in detail. The miscarriage of part of his plan—by which Huger's troops did not join the attack—and his own wound, by a piece of shell, late in the afternoon, alone prevented Johnston's utter destruction of this Federal corps. As it was, the enemy was driven two miles back of his camp. Heavily re-enforced next day, he resisted and drove back a desperate attack about Fair Oaks.

Now, for the first time, the people of Richmond began to see the realities of war. When the firing began, many ladies were at work for the soldiers in the churches. These flocked to the doors, pale and anxious, but with a steady determination in their faces, vainly looked for in many of the men. Gradually wagons and ambulances began to come in; slowly at first, toward nightfall more rapidly—each one bearing some faint and suffering form. Then, and not till then, those women left their other work and tended the wounded men; giving "the little cup of water" so precious to them, speaking brave words of cheer while their very souls grew sick at the unwonted sight of blood and suffering.

One poor old man, dirty and ragged, lay in a rough, springless cart; his hard, shoeless feet dropping out at its back, and his long, gray beard drenched in the blood that welled from his chest at every jolt. By his side, in the gathering twilight, walked one of Richmond's fairest daughters; her gentle voice smoothing the rough way to the hospital, and her soft hand wiping the damps from his forehead.

And there was no romance in it. *He* could not be conjured into a fair young knight—old, dirty, vulgar as he was. But he had fought for her—for the fair city she loved better than life—and the gayest rider in all that band were not more a hero to her!

Next morning the usual stillness of Sunday was broken by the renewed rattle of musketry—though farther off and less continuous than the day before; and by the more constant and nearer rumble of ambulance and dead cart. At dawn many of the townspeople had gone in buggies, wagons, and even the huge vans of the express companies, taking with them food and stimulants, to aid the very limited ambulance corps of the army.

All day long the sad procession came in. Here a van with four or five desperately wounded stretched on its floor; now a buggy with a faint and bandaged form resting on the driver; again the jolting coal cart with the still, stiff figure, covered by the blanket and not needing the rigid upturned feet to tell the story. The hospitals were soon overcrowded; huge tobacco warehouses had been hastily fitted up and as hastily filled; while dozens of surgeons, bare-armed and bloody, flitted through them, doing what man might to relieve the fearful havoc man had made.

Women of all ranks and of all ages crowded to them, too; some wan and haggard, seeking with tearless suspense the dear one they knew to have been stricken down; some bearing baskets of stimulants and nourishing food; but one and all eager and willing

> "To do for those dear ones what woman
> Alone in her pity can do."

The struggle had been brief but bitter. Most of the wounds were above the waist, for the fighting had been among undergrowth and partly against *abatis;* but the short-range volleys had mowed the men down by ranks. More warerooms and even stores on Main street were opened, fitted with bunks, and filled with the maimed and suffering.

At all hours, day and night, the passer down Main street would see through the open doors long, even rows of white bunks, each one bearing some form distorted with agony, or calmly passing away; while the tireless surgeon moved from cot to cot. And at the head of each a still, patient form, almost motionless, waved the ceaseless fan or breathed the low promise of the Living Word, to one who trembled on the verge of the Valley of the Shadow of Death.

The war was at the very gates now. These palpable witnesses were too numerous to doubt. But the lips of every gaping wound spoke an eloquent pledge that, while such as these kept watch and ward, the city was safe.

Little by little the hospitals thinned; the slightly wounded went back to duty and the badly hurt began to hobble about. But on every hand were the gaunt, sad forms stretched on the narrow cots over which Life and Death wrestled for the mastery. And still the tireless love of woman watched by them—and still unworded prayers went up that the Destroyer might not prevail.

The stillness that followed "Seven Pines" was not unbroken. The armies were so near together that the least movement of either brought on a collision, and constant skirmishing went on. Not a day but had its miniature battle; and scarce an hour but added to the occupants of the hospitals. As these conflicts most frequently resulted in a Confederate success, they only served to encourage the people, and to bring them to the high pitch necessary for the prolonged note of war that was soon to sound so near them.

Just a month after the repulse of the iron-clads from Drewry's Bluff, the bold and daring "Pamunkey Raid" still further aided in this effect. General J. E. B. Stuart had by his successful conduct of the cavalry, no less than by his personal gallantry, worked his way from the colonelcy he held at Manassas to a major-generalcy of all that arm of the Virginia army. He had gained the confidence of General Lee and the greatest popularity in and out of the army; and, ably seconded by his brigadiers, "Jeb Stuart" was expected to do great deeds in the coming campaign.

Information being desired of the enemy on certain points, he volunteered to obtain it. With the advice and direction of the commanding-general, Stuart started from Richmond; made his reconnaissance; penetrated to the White House on the Pamunkey and burned the depot there; whipped the enemy's cavalry wherever he met them; and, making a complete circuit of the Federal rear, with all his captured men and horses, rode back into the city in triumph.

Whatever may be said of raids in the abstract, this was certainly a most dashing one ; and was received with loud acclamation by army and people. The latter were by this time in better spirit to receive encouragement; and, dazzled by its brilliance, rather than weighing its solid advantages, placed this achievement perhaps above the more useful success at Williamsburg.

Then came the news from the Valley.

That wonderful campaign—which far exceeds in strategic power, brilliant dash and great results any other combination of the war— had been fought and won! It has been justly compared, by a competent and eloquent critic, to Napoleon's campaign in Italy ; and—paling all his other deeds—it clearly spoke Stonewall Jackson the Napoleon of the South.

Coolly looking back at its details, the thinker even now is struck with respectful wonder.

Hurling his little force against Front Royal; flashing to Winchester and routing Banks; slipping between the close converging lines of Fremont and Shields—just in time to avoid being crushed between them—and bearing with him miles of wagon train and spoils; turning on the pursuing columns of Fremont, driving him back, and then sweeping Shields from his path like chaff—Jackson clears his way and marches on for Richmond!

Still onward, scarcely halting for food or rest—ever on to strike new terror when thought far away ; weary, footsore—with scarcely one-half its former number, but flushed with victory and panting for further fame—the little band toils on, passes around Richmond and, just as the opposing cannon begin their last grim argument for her possession, hurl themselves like an Alpine torrent on the flank of the enemy!

The loss in this wonderful campaign was comparatively small, when we consider the rapidity of the movements; the terrible marches and the stubborn fighting against overwhelming numbers.

But there was one place vacant that none could fill. There was one name that brought the cloud to the brow of the giddiest youth, or the tear to the eye of the toughest veteran in those sturdy ranks ; one name that stilled the song on the march and hushed the rough gossip of the bivouac to a saddened whisper. Turner Ashby was dead!

True knight—doughty leader—high-hearted gentleman—he had fallen when the fighting was well-nigh over—his *devoir* nobly done and his name as stainless as the bright blade he ever flashed foremost in the fight!

Chivalric—lion-hearted—strong armed—

> " Well they learned, whose hands have slain him,
>   Braver, knightlier foe
>   Never fought 'gainst Moor or Paynim—
>   Rode at Templestowe ! "

All the country missed Ashby. But Virginia mourned him most; and among her stricken sons, those hard-handed, ragged heroes of Jackson's *Old Guard*—who had marched the furthest and fought the hardest following him—were the chiefest mourners. Jackson had reared a noble monument, to be viewed from all the dimmest vistas of the future. But the fair column was shattered near its top ; and the laurel leaves that twined it were mingled with evergreen cypress.

Then the strained suspense was broken. On the 26th of June began that memorable series of fights that northern and southern history—voluminous reports of generals and detailed accounts of newspapers, have made familiar to all who care to read of battles.

A. P. Hill's steady attack at Mechanicsville, though at great cost, drove the enemy's right wing back; to be struck next morning on the flank by Jackson and sent, after a sullen and bloody resistance, to the works near Gaines' Mill. Still on the barefooted boys press with resistless rush, leaving dead or mangled brothers and writhing foemen in their gory track ! Never pausing to look back, but each successive day driving the enemy at the bayonet's point from works frowning with cannon.

Cold Harbor has told its brilliant story. Frasier's Farm is fought and won !

With ranks fearfully thinned, scant of food and pausing not to rest, the struggling men press on—ever on ! Weary and faltering on the march, the first sharp crack of the rifle lights a new fire in every eye ; and drinking the hot breath of the battle,

> "Stalwart, they court like Anak's sons
>   The rapture of the fight !"

The tide of the battle swung round and the retreating army of McClellan—fighting steadily by day and retreating noiselessly in the night—fronted from the city which now lay on its left flank.

The Federals were neither demoralized, nor panic struck, as has been sometimes believed; and such an error, while it has bloody refutation in the nameless graves that make the track of these fights precious to the southron—does less than justice to the constancy and enduring valor of the little army that wrung the victory from them at such fearful cost.

Their retreat was orderly and steady. Driven each day from works on which they relied—marking their path with untold destruction of munitions, supplies and even of food on which they depended —the soldiers of the North were well held together; never refusing to turn and face the resistless foe that hurled itself against them, careless alike of cannon and steel, weariness and death!

There can be little doubt now of the consummate tact of McClellan's retreat. It is *the* bright page in the northern annals of strategy. Beaten each day and driven from his well-chosen strongholds—clearly chosen with a view to such necessities—he still held his army thoroughly in his grasp and carried it off in such order as no Federal force had yet preserved in the face of retreat. Only the resistless impetuosity of the southern troops drove all before them; and though careful analysis may prove in theory that, but for the blunder of a subordinate, Lee could one day have utterly destroyed him, this fact should not detract, in the impartial mind, from the great ability of McClellan which really prevented it.

Still, up to the last bloody day at Malvern Hill, the city lay open to the Federal general had he known the truth. Between him and the coveted prize was a mere handful of men, who could have offered but slight resistance to his overwhelming numbers; the main army of defense was in his front, further away than many points of his retreat; and, had he fully understood the position, a bold and dashing stroke of generalship might have turned the scale, spite of all the red successes of southern arms. More than once in the "Seven Days" a rapid march by the flank would have put McClellan in possession of the Capital and secured him in its strong defenses; from which the wearied troops of Lee could scarcely have ejected him.

But it was not to be. When the shattered and torn Confederates drew off, like lions at bay, from the horrid slopes of Malvern Hill— leaving them drenched with priceless blood and piled thick with near one-third their number—McClellan declined further battle and withdrew his beaten army to the fleet.

He had made a great retreat. But he had lost his great stake.

When the armies lay at Mechanicsville, both were plainly visible from many points in the city. From the Capitol, miles of encampment could be seen, spreading out like a map; and in the dusk the red flash of each gun and the fiery trail of its fatal messenger were painfully distinct. The evening before Hill's advance, the poet-librarian of the Capitol was pointing out the localities to a company of officers and ladies. Among them was a lady who had suffered much in the flesh and been driven from her home for brave exertions in that cause, which was in the end to leave her widowed spirit with no hope on this side of the narrow house. A terrific thunder-storm had just passed over the hostile hosts; but the dense masses of cloud had rolled away to the river, leaving it in deep shadow, while a bright reflection from the sunset wrapped both camps in a veil of mellow light. Not a shot disturbed the still peacefulness of the scene, to give token of the wild work already shaped out for the next week. Suddenly a glorious rainbow shaped itself in the transparent mist over the Confederate camp, spanning it from end' to end. The lady pointed it to the poet.

"I hail the omen!" she said. "It is a token of God's promise that yonder flood will not overwhelm us! That His hand will be raised as of old, to hurl it back from His chosen people!"

And when the omen was accomplished and Richmond was safe, the poet sent the lady those classic lines so well-known in the South —"The Battle Rainbow."

Next afternoon the great fight began. The sharp, quick rattle of small arms, and the dull incessant boom of artillery told of hot work even nearer than "Seven Pines." So sharp and clear were the reports that it seemed the fight must be on the very edge of town; and the windows rattled at every discharge.

Almost every man, worthy of the name, was at the front; but the brave and steadfast women of Richmond collected in groups and— while they listened with blanched faces and throbbing hearts—still tried to cheer and comfort each other.

They spoke of the past; of their faith in the flower of the South at that moment battling for them; and they heard the sound of the cannon growing farther and fainter, only to feel more loving trust in those who, under God, had saved them from that chiefest of ills!

Day by day, as the tide of battle surged farther off, it sent into Richmond cheering news that nerved afresh these brave hearts for the horror to come. Gaines' Mill, Cold Harbor and Frasier's Farm rolled back their echoes of triumph; news came of the strait into which McClellan was driven and that one day more must see him a prisoner in the city he had dared—his splendid host swept away and destroyed. Finally the news of Malvern Hill—the wild shout of battle scarce drowning the death-cry—sent a thrill of mingled agony and pride to their very heart's core.

But day by day, as the red tide rolled back, it swept into Richmond terrible fragments of the wreck it had made. Every conveyance that could follow the army, or could be pressed from the almost stripped country around it, bore in from the River Road its load of misery. Manassas had hinted the slaughter of a great fight; Seven Pines had sketched all the hard outlines of the picture; but the Seven Days put in the dismal shadows, with every variation of grotesque horror.

In the dearth of transportation and the hurry of onward movement, many had been left for days with stiffening wounds on the field, or roadside. Others had undergone the loss of limbs at field hospitals; some were bent and distorted in their agony; and again the stiff, set jaw and wide, glassy eye, told that the journey was over before the end was reached.

The chain of regular hospitals and even the temporary one—nearly emptied since Seven Pines—now rapidly filled and overflowed. Private houses swung wide their doors and took in wounded men—brothers alike if gentle-blooded Louisianian, or hard-handed mountainmen—and the women, one and all, wrought as if their energies had never before been taxed or even tested.

But a black shadow had come and broc___d deep over Richmond. Half the gentle forms gliding noiselessly among the suffering were draped in black; and many a pale face was saddened with an anguish deeper than furrowed those resting on the coarse pillows around.

The fight was won. The enemy that had for months flaunted his victorious flag in full sight of the Capitol was baffled and beaten. New glories had clustered round the flag of the South; new quarrels and doubts had been sent to the North. Lee, Jackson, Longstreet, the Hills and Hood had added fresh laurels to brows believed to have room for no leaf more. Almost every officer had proved himself worthy of the prayers of such women as the South owned—of that even higher glory of leading such troops as fought to defend them.

But at what awful cost had all this been bought! The slaughter of their nearest and dearest had been terrific: women, the highest and lowliest, met by the cot of the sufferer; and, in the free masonry of love, tended the living and comforted each other for their dead.

But through the brave endeavor of their sacred office, these noble sisters of mercy showed no yielding to the claims of self. Over their own sorrows they rose triumphant—tended the faint—cheered the despondent—filling the place of wife and mother to those who should nevermore see home—even while

> " The air is filled with farewells to the dying
>   And wailings for the dead ;
>   The voice of Rachel for her children crying
>   Can not be comforted."

CHAPTER XXIV.

ECHO OF SEVEN DAYS, NORTH AND SOUTH.

The result of the "Seven Days" was to produce a profound joyousness in the South, which lightened even those deep shadows from the sorrows that had fallen upon individuals; to raise the spirits of the whole people and to send into every heart that loved the cause a glow of confident pride in the southern soldier—chastened somewhat by present sorrow and tempered, perhaps, by the lessons of the past—that nothing in their after misfortunes could quench.

But while it taught the people this, the victory taught the Government that no energy could be too great—no watchfulness misplaced, in preparing for the heavy blows of the northern government at all times, and at any point, to carry out its pet scheme of reducing the southern Capital.

The blatant triumph that had followed other victories and the secure apathy of the southern government, had alike been swept away by that terrific surge of battle, rolled back harmlessly, only when on the point of overwhelming us; and in their stead came the deep-seated resolve to *act* in the present, even while they *dreamed* in the future.

In the North, a hoarse roar of rage went up. The good behavior of their troops and the great ability of their general—unquestioned even by the men who had steadily fought and doggedly driven him before them—were both lost sight of in the wild wail that went up over—the cost!

Millions upon millions had been spent in equipping the grand army—all wasted now in that futile effort to conquer the Rebel Capital —offered as a burnt offering to the avenging War God; and only the blood of its thousands to manure the fields in front of the coveted city!

There was a howl of malediction against the only general so far tried—who had proved himself a tactician in anything but name; and as part of its policy the northern government shamelessly sacrificed McClellan, while it could not but unhesitatingly acknowledge his merit.

Unlike the South, the North throughout the whole war bent its every energy toward concentrating the most useful elements among its many parties. Seeming to bend to the will of each; propitiating all popular elements and utilizing all able ones; listening patiently to the mouthing of demagogues and the vituperation of the press; distributing its contracts so as to make every dollar of patronage tell; and handling the great engine, Wall street, in masterly style—the Washington government simply collected and sifted the varied mass of opinion and material—to form from it a composite amalgam-policy that proved its only salvation. Through every change in that policy—through every gradation of animus that affected the complexion of the war—the masses of the North really believed they were fighting for the Constitution—for the flag, and for the Union!

Whether they were so tightly blindfolded as not yet to see their error, is no question to be discussed here.

No sooner had the howl gone up through the North, against the General who—spite of refused re-enforcements, jealousy and intrigue behind his back, and the terrible enemy before him—had saved his army, than the Government responded to it. Large numbers of men were sent from Harrison's Landing to Acquia Creek; the Federal forces at Warrenton, Alexandria and Fredericksburg were mobilized and strengthened; and the baton of command was wrenched from the hand of McClellan to be placed in that of Major-General John Pope!

The history of this new popular hero, to this time, may be summed up by saying that he had been captain of Topographical Engineers; and that the books of that bureau showed he had prosecuted his labors with perhaps less economy than efficiency.

Rapidly promoted for unknown reasons in the western armies, the public hit upon him as the right man at last; and the complaisant Government said: "Lo! the man is here!" and made him general-in-chief of the Army of Virginia.

From the command of Pope dates a new era in the war. No longer a temperate struggle for authority, it became one for conquest and annihilation. He boldly threw off the mask that had hitherto

concealed its uglier features, and commenced a systematic course of pillage and petty plundering—backed by a series of curiously bombastic and windy orders.

Calmly to read these wonderful effusions—dated from "Headquarters in the saddle"—by the light of his real deeds, one could only conceive that General Pope coveted that niche in history filled by Thackeray's *O'Grady Gahagan;* and that much of his reading had been confined to the pleasant rambles of Gulliver and the doughty deeds of Trenck and Munchausen.

To sober second thought, the sole reason for his advancement might seem his wonderful power as a braggart. He blustered and bragged until the North was bullied into admiration; and his sounding boasts that he had "only seen the backs of his enemies," and that he had "gone to look for the rebel, Jackson"—were really taken to mean what they said. When Pope did at last "find the rebel, Jackson," the hopeful public over the Potomac began to believe that their truculent pet might have simply paraphrased Falstaff, and cried—

"Lying and thieving have blown me up like a bladder!"

For Jackson gave the bladder a single prick, and lo! it collapsed.

Resting his wearied and shattered troops only long enough to get them again into fighting trim, General Lee prepared to check the third great advance upon Manassas. Working on the inner line and being thus better able to concentrate his strength, he left only enough troops around Richmond to delay any advance of McClellan from the Peninsula; and, before the end of July, sent Stonewall Jackson—with Ewell's, A. P. Hill's, and his own old division under General Charles S. Winder, in all about 10,000 men—to frustrate the flatulent designs of the gong-sounding commander, whose Chinese warfare was echoing so loudly from the frontier.

Cautious, rapid and tireless as ever, Jackson advanced into Culpeper county; and on the 9th of August gave the gong-sounder his first lesson on the field of Cedar Mountain. Throwing a portion of his force under Early on the enemy's flank and bringing Ewell and, later, Winder against his front, Jackson forced him from his position after a bloody fight, which the advance of A. P. Hill turned into a complete victory.

Cedar Mountain was a sharp and well-contested fight; but the

14

Confederates inflicted a loss five times their own, held the field, and captured a number of prisoners and guns. General Winder led his troops gallantly to the charge, but just at the moment of collision he was struck and mortally wounded by a shell. And the unstained spirit of the gallant son of Maryland winged its flight, ere the shouts of victory could cheer it on its way!

The Washington government at once ordered the remains of Mc-Clellan's army to General Pope; and massing with them Burnside's army at Fredericksburg and the vicinity, strained every nerve to aid his successful advance.

But here we may digress for the moment, to take a bird's-eye view of matters of grave moment passing in distant quarters of the Confederacy.

While victory had perched upon Confederate banners in Virginia, a heavy cloud was gathering over the West; threatening to burst and sweep ruin and destruction over the whole trans-Alleghany region. Not dispirited by the reverses in Virginia, the northern government remitted nothing of its designs upon the West, but rather pushed them toward more rapid completion. These designs were to hold the State of Kentucky by the army under Buell, wrest from the South the possession of Tennessee and Alabama—as a base for attack upon Georgia and cutting through to the seaboard; and to push the army under Grant down through Mississippi to the Gulf. These movements would not only weaken the Confederacy, by diverting so many men, ill to be spared, to watch the various columns; but would, moreover, wrest from it the great grain-producing and cattle-grazing sections from which the armies were mainly fed. Simultaneously with these a heavy force was to be massed under McClernand in Ohio, to sweep down the Mississippi; while the weak show of Confederate force in the states west of the river was to be crushed before it could make head.

Such was the Federal programme; well conceived and backed by every appliance of means, men and material. To meet it we had but a small numerical force to defend an extensive and varied tract; and at the Capital grave fears began to prevail that the overpowering numbers and points of attack would crush the little armies we could muster there.

Nor was the feeling of the people rendered more easy by their

confidence in the general to whom the defense of this invaluable section was entrusted. General Braxton Bragg—however causeless and
unjust their dictum may have been—had never been popular with the
southern masses. They regarded him as a bloodthirsty martinet, and
listened too credulously to all silly stories of his weakness and severity
that were current, in the army and out. Influenced rather by prejudice than by any real knowledge of the man, they believed him vain,
arrogant and weak; denying him credit for whatever real administrative ability that he possessed. The painful result of his command
was later emphasized by the pessimists, to justify their incredulity as
to his executive powers.

Besides, many people believed that General Bragg was a pet—if
not a creature of Mr. Davis; and that he was thrust into a position
that others deserved far more, when he succeeded Beauregard in command of the army of the West.

The latter officer had, after the evacuation of Corinth, been compelled to retire by ill health; and Bragg was soon sent to take his
place, with the understanding in the minds of the people that Kentucky was to be the theater of active operations, and that a programme of aggression—rather than of defense—was to be carried
out, as suggested by Beauregard.

General Bragg entered upon his command with a show of great
vigor—falling into General Beauregard's views that a diversion toward Ohio, threatening Cincinnati, would leave the main army free
to march upon Louisville before re-enforcements could reach Buell.
With this view General Kirby Smith, with all the troops that could be
spared—ill clad, badly equipped, and with no commissariat—was
pushed forward toward the Ohio. On the 29th of August—while
our victorious cannon were still echoing over the field of the second
Manassas—he met and defeated the enemy at Richmond; pressed on
to Lexington, and thence to a point in easy reach of Cincinnati—at
that moment not only the great granary and storehouse of the Federal
armies of the West, but their depot and arsenal as well; her wharves
crowded with transports, quartermasters' steamers and unfinished
gunboats, and her warehouses bursting with commissary and ordnance stores.

When the news of Smith's triumphant march to the very gates of
Cincinnati reached Richmond, it was universally believed that the

city would be captured, or laid in ashes; and thinking men saw great results in the delay such destruction would cause to the advance of the enemy into the heart of their territory.

Meantime, General Bragg had entered Kentucky from Chattanooga, with an army re-enforced and better equipped than had been seen in that section since the war began. Once more cheering reports came to Richmond that the Confederates were in full march for the enemy; that any moment might bring news of the crushing of Buell before re-enforcements, or fresh supplies, could reach him. Great was the disappointment, therefore, when news really came of the withdrawal of southern troops from before Cincinnati; and that all action of Bragg's forces would be postponed until Smith's junction with him.

Intense anxiety reigned at the Capital, enlivened only by the fitful report of the fight at Munfordville—inflicting heavy loss upon both sides, but not productive of any result; for, after the victory, Bragg allowed Buell to escape from his front and retire at his will toward the Ohio. That a Confederate army, at least equal in all respects, save perhaps numbers, to that of the enemy, should thus allow him to escape was then inexplicable to the people; and, as far as I have learned, it is so still.

There is no critic so censorious as the self-appointed one; no god so inexorable as the people's voice. General Bragg's last hold upon the southern masses—military and civil—was lost now.

The fight at Munfordville occurred on the 17th of September, but it was not until the 4th of the next month that the junction with Smith was effected at Frankfort. Then followed a Federal advance upon that town, which proved a mere diversion; but it produced the effect of deceiving General Bragg and of causing him to divide his forces. Hardee's and Buckner's divisions were sent to Perryville; and they with Cheatham's—who joined them by a forced march—bore the brunt of the battle of Perryville on the 8th of October. Notwithstanding the great disparity of numbers, the vim of the "barefooted boys" prevailed against the veterans of Buell's army, under General G. W. Thomas. They gained a decided advantage over three times their number, but once again what was a mere success might have been a crushing defeat, had Bragg's whole army been massed at Perryville.

It is neither within the scope nor the purpose of this chapter to give more than a bare skeleton of events, or to discuss the delicate points of strategy; but it was a great dash to the hopes of the entire people that what might have been a crushing blow to Buell—freeing three states from Federal occupation—resulted only in the retreat of the Confederates from Kentucky.

For, whatever may have been the cause, or the necessity for the movement, the army was hastily withdrawn. Supplies were burned; disabled carriages and abandoned arms marked the retreat; and the terror-stricken people who had, a few weeks before, dismissed the southern banners with vivas and blessings to certain victory, now saw that same army, to their dismay and sorrow, filing sadly and wearily toward the border.

Almost equally as astonished as their retreating enemy, the Federals pressed on in pursuit, hot and close; and it was only the ability and dash with which General Wheeler covered the retreat of the army—laden as it was with captured arms and munitions, and encumbered with crowds of women and children, who dared not stay behind—that saved it from destruction on that disastrous road from Perryville to Cumberland Gap.

Loud, deep and bitter were the comments of the people when the full news of the Kentucky campaign reached them. Unpopular as the name of Bragg had been before, it was now mentioned often with execration; and the reverses of his universally-condemned favorite reacted upon the popularity of Mr. Davis as well. Without understanding the details of the campaign, and with no patience to listen to the excuses of his few defenders, the public voice was unanimous in denunciation of the plan and conduct of the whole movement; and it arraigned the President for the fault of his inferior, calling him to trial before a jury that daily was becoming more biased and more bitter against him.

Like all the gloomy pages of Confederate history, the Kentucky campaign was illumined by flashes of brilliance, dash and enduring courage, surpassed by no theater of the war. Disastrous as it was in result, it fixed more firmly than ever the high reputation of Kirby Smith; it wreathed the names of Buckner, Hardee, Cheatham and Adams with fresh bays; and it gave to Joseph Wheeler a record that the people of that country will long remember.

In the events first preceding the disaster, too, as well as in his independent raid during July, John H. Morgan had added additional luster to his rising star, that was only to culminate in his exploits of the next year. These were the brighter gleams; but the whole picture was, indeed, a somber one; and there can be no wonder at the people's anger and distrust when they looked upon it. For it showed a vast and rich territory, teeming with those supplies needed most, yielded up to the full uses of the enemy; a people one with the South at heart given over to oppression of an alien soldiery and unable to co-operate with their own long days to come; and across the face of the somber picture was drawn the track of the blood of hundreds of brave men; sacrificed needlessly, the people said—and in a manner stupid, if not barbarous.

A grave injustice had been done the people of Kentucky, because of their conduct during the retreat. Baseless charges of their cowardice and treachery had been bandied about in the mouths of the unreflecting; the many had been made to suffer for the baseness of the few; and the shield of the state had been tarnished because of an inaction her people could not avoid.

Crushed, bound and deserted, as they were—with their only reliance fading away from their eyes, and a bitter and triumphant enemy in hot pursuit at their very doors—it would have been worse than folly—it would have been suicide! had the people on the line of that retreat offered a blatant sympathy. Utterly useless to others it must have been—and even more ruinous to themselves!

And this is the verdict of that Justice who, though slow of foot, fails not to overtake Truth, in her own good time.

CHAPTER XXV.

THE WAR IN THE WEST.

And misfortunes did not come singly, but in battalions.

The trans-Mississippi was so far distant that only broken echoes of its troubles could penetrate the web of hostile armies between it and the Capital. But those echoes were all of gloom. Desultory warfare —with but little real result to either side, and only a steady drain on Confederate resources and men—had waged constantly. A trifling success had been gained at Lone Jack, but it was more than done away with by aggregate losses in bloody guerrilla fighting. Spies, too, had been shot on both sides; but the act that came home to every southern heart was the wanton murder of ten Confederates at Palmyra, by the order of General McNeil, on the flimsy pretext of retaliation. The act, and its attendant cruelties, gained for him in the South the name of "The Butcher;" and its recital found grim response in every southern camp—as each hard hand clasped tighter round the hard musket stock—and there was an answering throb to the cry of Thompson's prompt war song:

> " Let this be the watchword of one and of all—
> Remember the Butcher, McNeil!"

Meantime, Mississippi had been the scene of new disasters. Vicksburg, the "Queen of the West," still sat unhurt upon her bluffs, smiling defiance to the storm of hostile shot and shell; teaching a lesson of spirit and endurance to which the whole country looked with admiration and emulation. On the 15th of August the iron-clad ram, "Arkansas," had escaped out of the Yazoo river; run the gauntlet of the Federal fleet at Vicksburg and made safe harbor under the town, to aid in its heroic defense.

Twenty days thereafter, General Breckinridge made a most chivalrous and dashing, but equally useless and disastrous, attack upon Baton Rouge. His small force was greatly outnumbered by the garrison, behind heavy works and aided by a heavy fleet of gunboats:

and after a splendidly gallant fight, that had but one serious result—
he was forced to withdraw. That result was the loss of the ram
Arkansas—which went down to co-operate with this movement. Her
machinery became deranged, and there was only the choice of sur-
rendering her to the enemy, or of sending her the road that every
Confederate iron-clad went sooner, or later—and she was blown up.

But the gloom was only to grow deeper and deeper, with thickening
clouds and fewer gleams of light.

After the fight at Iuka, in which that popular darling had been
defeated and forced to fall back before superior numbers, Price had
combined his army with that of Van Dorn; and on the 3d of October,
the latter led them to another wild and Quixotic slaughtering—standing out among the deeds even of that stirring time, in bold relief for
brilliant, terrible daring, and fearful slaughter—but hideous in its
waste of life for reckless and ill-considered objects. The forces of
the enemy at Corinth were in almost impregnable works; and Van
Dorn—after worsting them in a hot fight on the 3d, and driving them
into these lines, next day attacked the defenses themselves and was
driven back. Officers and men behaved with a cool and brilliant
daring that savored more of romance than of real war; deeds of personal prowess beyond precedent were done; and the army of Mississippi added another noble page to its record—but written deep and
crimson in its best blood.

And another piteous cry was wrung from the hearts of the people
to know how long, O, Lord! were these terrible scenes—*killings*,
not battles; and with no result but blood and disaster!—to be re-
enacted.

After its retreat from Kentucky, Bragg's army rested for over a
month at Murfreesboro, the men recruiting from the fatigues of that
exhausting campaign; and enjoying themselves with every species of
amusement the town and its kindhearted inhabitants offered—in that
careless reaction from disaster that ever characterized "Johnny Reb."
There was no fresh defeat to discourage the anxious watchers at a
distance; while the lightning dashes of John Morgan, wherever there
was an enemy's railroad or wagon train; and the flail-like blows of
Forrest, gave both the army and the people breathing space.

But fresh masses of Federals were hovering upon the track of the
ill-starred Bragg, threatening to pounce down upon and destroy

him—even while he believed so much in their inaction as to think of forcing them into an advance. The Federals now held West and Middle Tennessee, and they only needed control of East Tennessee to have a solid base of operations against Northern Georgia. Once firmly established there, they could either force their way across the state and connect with their Atlantic seaboard fleets; or could cut the sole and long line of railroad winding through the Confederate territory; thus crippling the whole body by tapping its main vital artery, and causing death by depletion. Rosecrans, with an army of between forty and fifty thousand men, was lying in Nashville, watching and waiting the moment for his telling blow.

This was the posture on Christmas, 1862. Three days after the enemy struck—heavily and unexpectedly.

The first intimation General Bragg had of the movement was cavalry skirmishes with his advance. These continued daily, increasing in frequency and severity until the 30th of December, when the contending armies were near enough for General Polk to have a heavy fight with the Federal right.

Next day, the weather being bitter and the driving sleet filling the atmosphere, the general battle was joined. McCowan and Cleburne, under Hardee, charged the Federal's right through a deadly hail of artillery and small arms, that darkened the air as thickly as the sleet—driving him back at the bayonet's point and swinging his front round from his center. The fierce valor of the southern troops and the brilliant dash of their leaders was resistless; and evening fell upon a field, wet with the blood of the South, but clearly a field of victory. Though the Federals fought with desperation, they were so badly hurt that Bragg believed they would fall back that night, in such confusion as to leave them his easy prey.

Morning of the New Year dawned cold, dark and stormy; but the enemy was still in sight, having only taken up a stronger position on a hill and posted his artillery most advantageously. It began to look as if General Bragg's telegram to Richmond of the victory he had gained, might require a postscript; but all that long New Year's day he allowed the enemy time to recuperate and strengthen his position.

It seemed as though another Shiloh was to be re-enacted; a victory wrenched from heavy odds by valor and skill was to be nullified by delay in crushing the enemy, while yet demoralized.

Next day came; and then Breckinridge was sent through a terrific storm of balls and shell, that cut down his gallant boys like grass before the scythe. On, into the Valley of the Shadow they strode; thinned, reeling, broken under that terrible hail—but never blenching. And the crest was won! but the best blood of Kentucky, Louisiana, Tennessee, Florida, Alabama and North Carolina was flooding that horrid field! Over two thousand noble fellows lay stiff, or writhing with fearful wounds—thick upon the path behind the victorious column.

And then—with that fatality that seemed ever to follow the fortunes of the unfortunate general in command—the army fell back!

Broken was the goblet of victory; wasted the wine of life! And it was accepted as but small consolation, by the people who hoped and expected so much—small surcease to the sob of the widow and the moan of the orphan! that "the retreat to Tullahoma was conducted in good order."

And again the public voice rose loud and hoarse and threatening against the general and the President, whose favorite he was declared to be.

But amid the darkening clouds that frowned close and threatening upon him—fearless of the future and heedless of the ominous roar of dissatisfaction far and near—sat the ruling spirit of the storm he had raised. Grim, steady and purposeful, Jefferson Davis worked his busy brain and frail body almost past belief, to redeem the errors of his chosen instruments—seeking no counsel, asking no aid—and day by day losing the confidence of the sand-shifting populace, who had once made him their God! And one act of his now did more than all besides to reassure the public mind.

Joseph E. Johnston was sent to command the armies of the West! Since his wound at " Seven Pines," the Government—from causes unknown to the people—had allowed this brilliant soldier to rust in inactivity; and now, when all of evil that ill-fortune and want of combination could accomplish had been done in the West, he was singled out, and sent forth to reap the harvest so bitterly sown. He was told, in effect, to take the frayed and scattered ends of armies and campaigns and bind them into a firm and resisting chain of strategy; or—to bear the sins of others upon his shoulders and have the finger of History point to him as the man who lost the West!

But patriot soldier and true knight as he was—little resentful of the coldness of Government as he was doubtful of his own ability— " Joe Johnston " accepted the test cheerily and went forth to do, or die.

> " For the Johnstons have ever borne wings on their spurs,
> And their motto a noble distinction confers——
> '*Ever ready !* ' for friend, or for foe ! "

And this worthy son of noble sires went to clear the Augean Stables of the West; and the God-speed of his own state—swelled into a hearty chorus by the voice of the country—followed him on his knightly errand !

Meantime, Lincoln's famous Proclamation of Emancipation had been promulgated. It made little difference to the people of the South ; for it was at that time looked upon as a vaunt as idle as if he had declared the throne of England vacant. Secure in their belief in their right doing, and in the trusty arms and deadly rifles that defended it, the southern masses never dreamed the day would come when that proclamation would be more than the paper upon which it was engrossed. Still, in the general gloom upon them, it was taken as but another augury of the bitter spirit animating their enemies ; and of the extent to which it would dr've them in this war for the Union and flag.

And so the close of '62 fell dark and dismal upon the distracted country; enlivened only by the sole gleam in Virginia—the repulse of Burnside from Fredericksburg. But even the joy for this triumph was dashed by the precious blood spilled to purchase it ; another vent for that steady drain of men, material and endurance—already almost past bearing.

But there was no weak yielding in Government, or in people. Men looked at each other through the gloom, and even as they asked —" Brother, what of the night ? "—struck hands in a clasp that meant renewed faith in the cause and renewed determination to prove its right.

Early in the New Year, news reached Richmond of Magruder's amphibious victory, the recapture of Galveston ; which town had fallen a prey to the enemy's naval power early in October. On the last night of '62—while the wearied troops of Bragg were sleeping on the bloody field of Murfreesboro—General Magruder, with a mixed command of three regiments of raw infantry, some nineteen pieces of field artillery, and a boarding fleet of four unarmed boats, came down silently to Galveston. The Federal fleet—consisting of the Harriet Lane, the Clifton, the Westfield and the Ossawa—were lying just off the town; covering it with their broadsides and supported by a force of infantry.

Coming suddenly upon them, like shadows through the darkness, Magruder's land force opened a hot fire with field artillery—and aided by the daring boarding of the Lane by Colonel Leon Smith's co-operating water party—captured the former steamer, burned one other, and drove the remaining ones, with their tenders, to sea; where it was impossible to follow them.

This gallant and comparatively bloodless raising of the Galveston blockade was a gleam of hopeful light; especially as it was almost coincident with the first approach to a naval success, by the force of Commodore Ingraham in Charleston Harbor on the 30th of January. The vessels under his command were ill-built, awkward tubs—as will hereafter be seen; but the terrible Brooke gun did its work at long range, and drove the wooden blockading fleet from the harbor for the moment.

This victory, unimportant as it was—for the blockade it claimed to raise was renewed and strengthened within a few days—was cheering; for, said the people, if the Confederates can succeed on the water, surely the star of the South is not really on the wane.

But there was, after the New Year, a sudden stoppage of active movements on both sides. The terrific crash of hostile cannon—the continuous roar of opposing small arms—and the groan of the Federal mixed with the death-cry of the Confederate, were all suddenly stilled. The fearful tornado of war that had swept for many months the once-smiling Southland—-leaving its wake only the blackened track of ruin piled thick with stiffened corpses! was suddenly hushed; as though the evil powers that had raised it must pause to gather fresh strength, before once more driving it in a fiercer and deadlier blast.

In the West, we had lost in the early year the strong position of Arkansas Post with its large accumulation of stores and its garrison of over 3,000 men; but the Queen City still sat defiant and unharmed, the hostile fleet and army having left its fruitless task; and the twin stronghold of Port Hudson showed another row of ugly teeth, into range of which no Federal force seemed yet ready to venture.

On the Atlantic seaboard, too, the prospects, at this time, appeared more cheering. Girt as it was, with one unbroken line of watchful cruisers, with every port apparently sealed by blockade—southern ingenuity and pluck still defied them and ran in precious stores of arms, clothing and medicines. General Beauregard had taken active command of South Carolina and Georgia; and had put the defenses of both coasts—especially of Charleston and Savannah—into such a state of fitness as quite satisfied the Government and made the people of those states calm and confident in his ability to protect them and theirs. General Gustavus W. Smith—the friend and comrade of General Joe Johnston—had, like him, been rewarded for his sacrifices in coming South, and his able exertions afterward, by the coldness and neglect of the Government. But like him, too, he forgot personal wrongs; and, when ordered to North Carolina, threw his whole energy and skill into the works of defense for the coast and for that vital artery of railroad, on which the life of the South depended.

Butler still waged his peculiar warfare upon unarmed men and weak women in the soft nest he had made himself, at New Orleans; but Mobile reared her defiant crest and took into her bosom peaceful vessels laden with stores of priceless utility, only to send them out again—bristling with rifled cannon, fleet-winged and agile, ready to pounce upon the Federal shipping.

In the Middle West, Johnston's presence had acted like oil upon the darkening waters of trouble and despair. There had been no record of fresh disaster, or fresh mismanagement; the troops were recruiting, resting and increasing in numbers and efficiency; the cavalry, mobilized under Van Dorn—at last placed in his proper sphere—had done efficient and harassing, if desultory warfare, upon the enemy's small posts and communications. Pegram—by his effective raid through Kentucky—had shown that her people there were not forgotten by their brothers beyond; and his skillful retreat—laden with heavy droves of cattle and in the face of a superior force—gained him high praise from his superior officers.

And so the people watched and waited—hopeless no longer, but quite recovered from the prostration of the rapid, heavy and continuous blows of the previous autumn. Steadfast and buoyant, as they were ever, the masses of the South once more turned their backs upon past disaster, looking eagerly through the dark cloud for the silver lining they felt must be beyond.

And again, as ever, they turned their eyes toward Virginia—stately and calm amid the shock of battle. And they hoped not in vain; for over her blackened fields—furrowed by shot and shell, drenched with blood of best and bravest, but only more sacred for the precious libation—was again to ring the clarion shout of victory that ever swelled from the lines of Stonewall Jackson!

CHAPTER XXVI.

THE FAILURE IN FINANCE.

When the competent historian shall at last undertake a thoughtful work upon our great struggle, there can be little doubt that he will rank among the primary causes of the Confederacy's dissolution the grave errors of its financial system.

These errors he will find not only in the theory and framework of that system—founded upon a fallacy, but also in the detailed workings of its daily management; and in persistent adherence to a line of policy, each day proved more fatal.

In a previous chapter, allusion has been made to the feeling of conscious superiority, pervading all classes of government and people at the inception of the struggle, at Montgomery. This extended to all classes of the people; and the universal belief in the great dogma of secession—"Cotton is king!"—was doubtless the foundation of that cardboard structure of Confederate finance, which the first rude shock toppled to pieces, and the inexorable breath of demand shriveled into nothingness.

At Montgomery, the promises of ease in money matters were all that could have been asked. The people, everywhere, had come forward with frank, unanimous selfishness. They had faith in the cause—faith in the Government—faith in themselves; and they proved it by their works, giving with lavish hand from their substance. It was felt that the great prosperity of the North had, in a great measure, come from the South; that the looms of New England were fed with southern cotton; that the New York custom house was mainly busied over southern exports; that the soil of the South was, by the alchemy of trade, transmuted annually into three-fifths of the gold in the Federal treasury.

"Egad, sir!—money is our last trouble, sir!" my old friend, the colonel, had cried with enthusiasm. "The country teems with riches—actually teems, sir! with gold. We have only to stretch out our

hands to gather it in—more than we want, egad! *Men* we need, sir!
—but *money*, never!"

And the colonel was right in theory. But that very overweening
confidence in her strength proved the South's greatest weakness; and
where was needed the strong, nervous grasp of a practical and practiced hand, to seize at once the threads of gold, and weave them into
a solid cord of system—weak and shifting fingers were allowed to
tangle and confuse them, till each in turn was snapped and rendered
worse than worthless. Mr. C. G. Memminger, whom the President
elevated to the Treasury Department, was untried and unknown out
of his own State; but so great was the confidence of the people in
their financial power—so simple did the problem of its development
seem to them—that they were trustful and satisfied, until the stern
grasp of necessity roughly shook them from their golden dream.
And they awoke, like the sleeper of German legend, to find their
hands filled with worthless yellow leaves and grains of chaff, where
they had dreamed of treasure beyond compare.

Immediately upon his appointment, thoughtful men—who could
look a little beyond the rose-colored clouds of the present—had
pressed upon Secretary Memminger the necessity for establishing
heavy foreign credits, to draw against in case of future need. The
currency of the southern banks was comparatively nothing, in view
of increased expenditures. The cotton which was gold—food—
clothing—everything to the South, with the open ports of the North,
would be more worthless than the wampum of the Indians, so soon
as the threatened blockade might seal up her ports and exclude the
European purchaser. But, on the contrary, if that cotton were
bought on the faith of the Government—and planters would willingly
have sold their last pound for Confederate bonds; if it were shipped
to Europe at once and sold in her market, as circumstances might
warrant, the Confederacy would, in effect, have a Treasury Department abroad, with a constantly accruing gold balance. Then it
could have paid—without agencies and middlemen beyond number,
who were a constant moth in the Treasury—in cash and at reduced
prices, for all foreign supplies; those supplies could have been purchased promptly and honestly, and sent in before the blockade
demanded a toll of one-half; but above all, the interest and principal
of such bonds to the planters could have been paid in coin, and a

specie circulation thus been made, instead of the fatal and endless paper issues that rendered Confederate credit a scoff, and weakened the confidence of the southern people in the ability and integrity of that department.

In this sense—and this sense alone—*Cotton was king!* But the hands that could have lifted him safely upon a throne and made every fiber a golden sinew of war, weakly wrested the scepter from his grasp, and hid him away from the sight and from the very memory of nations.

It was as though the youngest of the nations aped the legendary traditions of the oldest. After the potent and vigorous King Cotton was killed by starvation, Confederate finance treated him as Jewish myth declares dead King Solomon was treated. In his million-acred temple, he stood—cold, white and useless—leaning upon his broken staff; while timorous leadership gaped at his still majesty—

> " Awed by the face, and the fear, and the fame
> Of the dead king standing there ;
> For his beard was so white and his eyes so cold,
> They left him alone with his crown of gold! "

Had the Government bought—as was urged upon it in the fall of '61—all the cotton in the country, at the then prices, and paid for it in Confederate bonds at six per cent., that cotton—according to calculations of the best cotton men of the South—would have produced in Liverpool, during the next three years, at rapidly-increasing prices, *over one thousand millions of dollars in gold!* Granting this erroneous, even by one-half, it follows that the immense specie balance thus held, would—after paying all accruing interest—have left such a surplus as to have kept the currency issue of Confederate States' notes merely nominal, and even then have held them at a par valuation.

The soldier, who freely bared his breast to the shock of a hundred battles for his country, his fireside and his little ones, could then have sent his pittance of eleven dollars a month to that fireside, with the consciousness it might buy those dear ones bread at least. But long before the darkest days fell upon the South, his whole month's pay would not buy them *one pound of bacon!*

Secretary Memminger would seem to have had some theory, or reasons of his own, for refusing to listen to the plain common sense

15

in these suggestions from practical sources. With a strictly agricultural population to supply, he insisted on the issue of Confederate notes in such volume that the supply far exceeded the demand. For, had there been a large manufacturing population actively employed in the South, as there was in the North, the inflation of currency might have been temporarily concealed by its rapid passage from hand to hand. But with no such demand—with only the daily necessities of the household and of the person to relieve—the plethora of these promises to pay naturally resulted, first in sluggishness, then in a complete break-down of the whole system.

Still, from the joyous days of Montgomery, and the triumphant ones after Manassas—through the doubtful pauses of the next winter and the dark days of New Orleans—on to the very *Dies iræ*—there pervaded government and people a secure belief that the finances of the North would break down, and the war collapse for want of money!

And so tenacious were people and rulers of this ingrained belief, that they cherished it, even while they saw the greenbacks of the Federal Government stand at 25 to 30 per cent. depreciation, while their own Treasury notes dropped rapidly from *one hundred* to *one thousand!*

Let us pause for one moment to examine upon what basis this dream was founded, before going into the sad picture of want—demoralization—ruin! into which the errors of its Treasury plunged the southern people.

Accepting the delusive estimate that all the property of the United States, in 1861, represented but one-fifth more than that of the Confederate States; and that over three-fifths of the gold duties were from cotton and cotton fabrics, and products of the South alone, it was easy for the southern eye to see a future of trial, if not of ruin, for the North. Then, too, at the beginning of the war it was reasoned that the northern army of invasion, working on exterior lines, must necessarily be greater far in numbers and in cost, than the army of defense, working on interior lines. Moreover, the vast-proposed blockade, by increasing to a point of anything like efficiency the vessels, armament, and personnel of the United States navy, would cost many millions. Thus, in short, the southern thinker could very readily persuade himself that the annual expenditures of the Federal

Government must—even with the strictest economy and best management—run to unprecedented and undreamed-of sums.

The demand for increased appropriations with the very first call of Mr. Lincoln for troops, justified this belief; the budget of '62 to the United States Congress went far beyond all expectation; and the wild waste, extravagance, and robbery that swelled each succeeding estimate, were but more and more proof to the southern thinker, that he must be right. But he had made one grave miscalculation.

Into the woof of delusion which he continued to weave, for enwrapping his own judgment, such reasoner omitted wholly to cross the warp of combined result. He neglected that vastly-important filament—proper and value-enhancing handling of his valuable production; the reality that southern cotton, sugar and rice had become so great a factor in national wealth, mainly through manipulation by northern hands. He did not stop to calculate that—those hands removed and, in addition, the ports of the South herself hermetically sealed—all product, not consumable, must become as valueless as the leaves and dross of the German's dreamer!

The expenses of the North have ever been paid by the South, he reasoned. This sum now withdrawn, it follows that not only will the increased expenses of the North not be paid; but the heavy balance will be efficient in the southern Treasury, to meet our far smaller expenses.

With equal ability in management, this result *might* have happened; for there is no sort of doubt that depreciation in southern money was, in some regards, reason for appreciation in northern. But while the policy of the southern Treasury was weak, vacillating and destructive, that of the northern was strong, bold and cautious. While Mr. Memminger—instead of utilizing those products which had heretofore been the life-blood of northern finance—allowed the precious moments to pass; and flooded the country with paper, with only future, instead of present and actual, basis of redemption, the northern Secretary struck boldly at the very root of the matter and made each successive disaster to northern arms another link in the strengthening chain of northern credit.

The Union finances did indeed appear desperate. The stoppage of a sure and heavy means of revenue, at the same moment that the spindles of New England stood still for want of food; the increased demand for fabrics and supplies, that had now to be imported; and the vast increase of expenditure, coincident with decrease in revenue, left but had one door open to escape. The North was flooded with greenback promises to pay, issued with one sole basis of redemption —the chance of absolute conquest of a people roused, warlike, and determined to yield nothing save their lives.

To meet this issue and the interest of the vast debt incurred, taxation in the North rapidly increased, until the oppressive burden represented, in one or another shape, *near* 20 *per cent.* of the real property of the people!

Besides, the North, unlike ourselves—argued the hopeful southern financier—does not go into the war as a unit. New York, the great money center, is entirely opposed to the war; New England is discontented at the stoppage of her factories and the loss imposed upon her people; and the great West, ever more bound to the South than to the East, by community of interest and of pursuit, must soon see that her only road to salvation is down the great river that has heretofore been the one lung that gave her the breath of life! Will the cute Yankee of New England submit to be ruined, and starved, and taxed in addition? Will the great commercial metropolis let the grass grow in her streets and the vessels rot at her wharves, that once laughed with southern cotton? Will the granary and meat-house of the Union yield all her produce for baseless paper promises and, in addition pay heavy tax to carry on a war, suicidal as she must see it?

Such were the delusions of the South—based, it may be, upon reason, and only delusions because underestimating and despising the great ingenuity of the enemy, and the vast cohesive power of *interest!*

If the Washington government could not make the war popular, it could at least make it a great money job. If it could not bring it at once to the hearts of its people, it could at least force it directly upon their pockets.

The vast increase in army and navy gave sudden and excitingly novel employment to thousands of men then out of situations; the unprecedented demand for materials of war—arms—munitions—clothing—supplies—turned the North and East into one vast armory and quartermaster's store; while the West was a huge commissary department. Then the Government paid well and promptly, if it did pay in greenbacks. These daily changed hands and nobody stopped to inquire on what the promise to pay was based.

Great contracts were let out to shrewd and skillful moneyed men; these again subdivided became the means of employing thousands of idle hands—while each sub-contractor became a missionary to the mob to preach the gospel of the greenback!

But above all was the shrewdness and finesse with which the bonds were manipulated. The suction once applied, the great engine, Wall street, was pumped dry; and self-preservation made every bondholder a *de facto* emissary of the Treasury Department.

Banker and baker, soldier and seamstress, were equally interested in the currency. It became greenback or nothing, and the United States used the theory of self-preservation on which to build a substantial edifice of public credit.

These were the hard, real reasons that dissipated at last the dream of the South; that kept the greenback promise of the manufacturing North at little below gold, while the grayback of the producing South went down—down—from two—to ten—twenty—at last, to one thousand dollars for one.

CHAPTER XXVII.

DOLLARS, CENTS, AND LESS.

And now, looking back to the struggling and suffering South, one asks with wonder how these results could have transpired.

Unlike the North, the South went into the struggle with her whole soul and her whole strength. Every man came forward with one accord, willing to work in the way he best might for the cause he held sacred; ready to give his arm, his life, and all he had beside, for the general good. Whole regiments were put into service, armed, uniformed and equipped, without costing the central government one dollar; and in some instances—as of that spotless knight, true gentleman and pure patriot, Wade Hampton—raised by the energy, paid for by the generosity, and led to death itself by the valor of one man!

Corporations came into this general feeling. Railroads put their rolling-stock and their power in the hands of the Government; agreeing, as early as the origin of the Montgomery government, to take their pay *at half rates* and in government bonds. Banks put their facilities and their circulation, manufacturers their machinery and foundries their material, at public disposition, for the bare cost of existence. Farmers and graziers cheerfully yielded all demanded of them! And how the women wrought—how soft hands that had never worked before plied the ceaseless needle through the tough fabric—how taper fingers packed the boxes for camp, full from self-denial at home—shall shine down all history as the brightest page in story of noble selflessness.

In the deadly hail of hostile batteries; in the sweltering harvest-field of August, and at the saddened and desolate fireside of December, the southern people wrought on—hoped on!

And the result of all this willing sacrifice was greatly to reduce the burdens on the treasury. For reasons before stated the southern army was smaller, and its transportation cost far less, than that of the enemy. Its equipment was far cheaper, and its subsistence for every reason infinitely smaller.

Still, with an outlay per diem scarcely more than one-tenth that of the North—which amounted to near $4,000,000 ! daily; with the teeming fields and bursting warehouses filled with cotton—a year back, auriferous in every fiber—worthless now; and with a people thus united to act and to aid it, the Southern Treasury continued to flood the country with paper issues, based only on the silver lining of the cloud that hung darker and ever darker over the South.

With *one-tenth* the population in the field and the rest working for them, there was no real demand for this inordinate issue. One-tenth the volume of currency properly distributed, with a coincident issue of bonds, would have relieved the actual necessities of buyer and seller. But still the wheels worked on—still Treasury notes fluttered out, until every bank and store and till was glutted with them.

Then the results of the inflation came with relentless and rapid pace. With the people still convinced of the inevitable outcome of their united efforts; with the thinkers of the South still evolving their theories of the philosopher's stone to change all this mass of paper into gold; and with the press of the country blatant about the speedy and certain collapse of northern credit; above all, with millions of pounds of cotton rotting in our warehouses—Confederate money, little by little, bought less and less of the necessaries of life.

At first the change was very gradual. In the summer of 1861, persons coming to Richmond from Europe and the North spent their gold as freely as the Treasury notes. Then gold rose to five, ten, fifteen, and finally to forty per cent. premium. There it stuck for a time. But the issues increased in volume, the blockade grew more effective, and misgivings about the Treasury management crept into the minds of the people. Gold went up again, ten per cent. at a jump, until it touched a hundred—then rapidly to a hundred and fifty.

" The whole system looks devilish blue," said Styles Staple, who was curing an ugly wound in his thigh. " I've been writing 'the house' about it, and the Gov. thinks the hour has passed for utilizing the cotton. If that can't be impressed by the Government, the whole bottom will fall out of this thing before many months."

" If it ever passes the two hundred," solemnly quoth the colonel in answer, " egad, sir! 'twill go up like a rocket! Up, sir! egad! clean out of sight!"

I candidly answered that I could not see the end of the inflation.
"I do," Styles growled—"Repudiation!"

"Well, that's no end of a nobby thing!" cried Will Wyatt, who was always bored about anything more serious than the last book, or charging a battery. "Cheerful that, for a fellow's little pile to go up like a rocket, and he not even to get the stick."

"He can have the smoke, however," answered Styles more cheerily, as he hobbled over and gave a $5 note for a dozen cigars.

And this began rapidly to be the tone, everywhere out of trade. A vague feeling of insecurity about the power of the Government to check the onward flood of issue prevailed in all classes. This produced a reckless expenditure for anything tangible and portable. And at last the colonel's prediction was verified; for money touched the two hundred per cent., and went up—up—by the one hundred; until in a time incredibly short—and with such a suddenness that people had no time to be surprised—the Confederate treasury note stood still for a moment, worth *twenty to one* for *gold!*

This may be accounted for, in small part, by the scarcity of supplies and the increasing efficiency of the blockade. But it must be remembered that the value of gold remained a constant quantity and the gold dollar in Richmond, note-flooded and blockade-bound, *bought more* of almost any article than it ever had before.

With a string of active vessels watching every port and cove, to snap up the daring ventures between the island ports and the coast; with a powerful enemy thundering at every point of entrance to southern territory, still the fortunate man who had gold, or who could draw upon Europe, or the North, actually lived much cheaper than in any place beyond the lines! Singular as this statement may appear, it is actual fact. At this moment—before the depreciation of currency became such as to give it no value whatever—board at the best hotels in Richmond was $20 per day—equivalent to $1 in gold, while it was $3 in New York, or Washington; a suit of clothes could be had for $600 or $30 in gold, while in New York it cost from $60 to $80; the best whisky was $25 per gallon—$1.25 in gold, while in the North it was more than double.

Rapidly gold rose in the market, and in the absence of stocks became the only vehicle for financial gambling. From time to time, as a brilliant success would grace Confederate arms, the fall of

Treasury credit would be checked. But it was only for the moment —and it went down steadily, rapidly, fatally. And as steadily, as rapidly and as fatally did the Treasury shuttles fly; spinning out the notes, like a whirlwind in autumn. And tighter grew the blockade, and fewer the means of supply. Stocks on hand were long since gone; little came to replace them, and the rich were driven to great straits to live, while the poor almost starved.

Away from the army lines and great centers of cities, the suffering was dreadful; impressments stripped the impoverished people; conscription turned smiling fields into desert wastes; fire and sword ravaged many districts; and the few who could raise the great bundle of paper necessary to buy a meal, scarce knew where to turn in the general desolation, to procure it even then. In the cities, it was a little better; but when beef, pork and butter in Richmond reached $35 per pound; when common cloth was $60 per yard, shoes $200 to $800 per pair, and a barrel of flour worth $1,400, it became a difficult problem to fill one's stomach at any outlay.

And all this time the soldiers and Government employés were being paid on a gold basis. The private received *eleven* (afterward twenty-one) dollars per month—amounting at the end of 1863 to just *fifty-five cents in coin!* At the last payments, before the final actions at Petersburg, the pay of a private for one month was *thirty-three cents!*

Nor were officers of the army and navy better paid. With their rank in the old service guaranteed them, they also received about the same pay, when gold and paper money were of equal value. Later Congress believed it would be a derogation from its dignity to "practically reduce the value of its issues," as one member said, "by raising officers' pay." Thus a lieutenant in the navy, probably of twenty years' experience, and with a family dependent upon him, though debarred from all other labor, received $1,500 per year— equal in gold to the sum of $4.25 per month; while a brigadier, or other higher general, received nearly $8 per month.

These things would provoke a smile, did they not bring with them the memory of the anguished struggle to fight off want that the wives and children of the soldier martyrs made. I have gone into detail further than space, or the reader's patience may warrant; and still, "Behold, the half is not told!"

I would not, if I could, record the bitter miseries of the last dreadful winter—paint the gaunt and ugly outlines of womanhood, squalid, famished, dying—but triumphant still. One case only will tell the tale for all the rest. A poor, fragile creature, still girlish and refined under the pinched and pallid features of starvation, tottered to me one day to beg work.

"It is life or death for me and four young children," she said. "We have eaten nothing to-day; and all last week we lived on *three pints of rice !*"

Will Wyatt, who was near, made a generous offer of relief. Tears sprang into the woman's eyes as she answered, "You mean kindness, major; but I have never asked charity yet. My husband is at the front; and I only ask a right—to be allowed to work for my children!"

Such were the sufferings, such the spirit of southern women!

When it was too late—when the headlong road to ruin had been more than half-way run—some feeble attempts were made to stay the downward rush. Of course, they were useless—worse than useless, in that they made widespread a feeling of distrust, already deep-seated with reflecting men. The volume of currency had reached such expansion that its value was merely nominal for purposes of subsistence, when the devices of Mr. Memminger to lessen it began to be pressed in earnest.

The people had now begun to see that the whole theory of the Treasury was false; that the moment for utilizing the cotton supply had indeed been lost; and they murmured loud and deep against the Secretary and the President; whom they believed not only retained him in office, but endorsed his destructive policy. Mr. Davis, the people said, was autocratic with his Cabinet, and would have displaced Mr. Memminger summarily, had he not favored that peculiar financial system. Mr. Davis, too, was known to have been hostile to the absorption and exportation by the Government of all the cotton. He had, moreover, recommended against any legislation by Congress to contract the currency and stop the issues. Now, therefore, the inflation and utter inadequacy of the paper money was laid at his door, as well as Mr. Memminger's; and the people, feeling there was no safety for them, began to distrust the good faith of such reckless issue. A system of barter was inaugurated among the country people; and they traded off things only needful for others absolutely essential.

They began to feel a dread of taking the notes of the Government, and in many instances refused them utterly. And yet these very people yielded cheerfully to the constantly insolent, and not infrequently illegal, demands of the impressment officers.

In the cities, too, a point had been reached where the promise of the Government to pay was looked upon as a bitter joke. Bonds were constantly refused in business transactions, and only Treasury notes—as a medium of temporary exchange—were accepted.

Then, as a necessary measure, came the imperative order for funding the currency. All the millions of old issues were to be turned into the treasury, by a certain date, and exchanged for bonds. If the unlucky holder could not, or would not, deposit or exchange, he lost thirty-three per cent. of the value of the Government pledge he held. The old issues went rapidly out of sight; but the measure did not appreciably lessen the current medium, while it *did* very appreciably lessen the confidence in the integrity of the Department.

It is but the first step in repudiation, thought the people. If Government will on any pretext ignore one-third of its obligation, what guarantee have we for the other two? And so, justly or unjustly, the country lost all faith in the money. Men became reckless and paid any price for any article that would keep. Tobacco—as being the most compact and portable—was the favorite investment; but cotton, real estate, merchandise—anything but the paper money, was grasped at with avidity.

It has often been charged that speculators ruined the currency. But, to give the children of the devil their due—we can scarcely think but that the currency made the speculators.

Had the plain system been adopted, by which the currency dollar could have ever approximated to coin, it would have been simply impossible for the holders of supplies to have run prices up to extortionate figures. Not that I would for one instant excuse, or ask any mercy for, those unclean vultures who preyed upon the dead credit of their Government; who grew fat and loathsome while they battened on the miseries of the brave, true men who battled for them in the front ranks of the fight. But while the fault and the shame is theirs, it may not be disguised that the door was not only left open for their base plundering, but in many cases they were urged toward it by the very hands that should have slammed it in their faces.

When we come to consider the question of the blockade, we may, perhaps, see this more clearly. Meantime, in glancing down the past by the light of experience, one can not but marvel at the rapid, yet almost imperceptible, epidemic that fastened incurably upon the people, spreading to all classes and sapping the very foundations of their strength.

In the beginning, as vast crowds poured into Richmond—each man with a little money and anxious to use it to some advantage—trade put on a new and holiday dress. Old shops were spruced up; old stocks, by aid of brushing and additions, were made to appear quite salable and rapidly ran off. The demand made the meat it fed upon, until stores, shops and booths sprang up in all parts of the city and on all the roads leading into it from the camps. Gradually—from causes already noted—supplies became more scarce as money became more plenty. The pinch began to be felt by many who had never known it before; and almost every one, who had any surplus portables, was willing to turn them into money. In this way, those who had anything to sell, for the time, managed to live. But the unfortunates who had only what they needed absolutely, or who were forced to live upon a fixed stipend, that did not increase in any ratio to the decrease of money, suffered terribly.

These were only too ready to take the fever of speculation; and to buy any small lots of anything whatever that might sell again at a profit. This was the class from which the main body of amateur speculators was recruited. One successful venture led to another and gave added means for it. The clerk, or the soldier, who yesterday cleared his hundred on a little turn in whisky, to-morrow might hope to double it—then reinvest his principal and his profits. It was marvelous how values rose over night. One might buy anything, a lot of flour—a line of fruits—a hogshead of molasses, or a case of boots to-day, with almost a certainty of nearly doubling his outlay to-day week.

The ordinary channels of trade became clogged and blocked by its constant increase. Auction houses became the means of brokerage; and their number increased to such an extent that half a dozen red flags at last dotted every block on Main street. And incongruous, indeed, were the mixtures exposed at these sales, as well as in the windows of the smallest shops in Richmond. In the latter, bonnets rested on the sturdy legs of cavalry boots; rolls of ribbon were festooned along the crossed barrel of a rifle and the dingy cotton umbrella; while cartridges, loaves of bread, packages of groceries, gloves, letter paper, packs of cards, prayer-books and canteens, jostled each other in admirable confusion.

At these auctions there was utter want of system. Hogsheads of prime rum would be put up after kegs of spikes; a case of organdies would follow a good cavalry horse; and then might come four second-hand feather-beds and a hundred boarding cutlasses.

But everything soever found a purchaser; some because they were absolutely needed and the buyer dreaded waiting the next week's rise; the majority to sell again in this insane game of money-making.

But varied as were the motives for speculation, the principal ones were breadstuffs and absolute necessities of life; and while the minor speculators—the amateurs—purchased for *quick* profits—the professional vultures bought for *great* ones and could afford to wait.

The first class reached into every rank of society; the second were principally Yankee residents—caught in Richmond by the war, or remaining for the sole purpose of making it pay—and a smaller class of the lowest Polish Jews. Ishmaels both, owning no kinship and no country, their sole hope was gain—gain at the cost of reputation and credit themselves—gain even at the cost of torture and starvation to the whole South beside. These it was who could afford to buy in bulk; then aid the rise they knew must come inexorably, by hoarding up great quantities of flour, bacon, beef and salt.

It mattered not for themselves who suffered—who starved. It mattered not if the noble fellows at the front lived on a scant handful of cornmeal per day—if starving men died before the works they were too weak to mount—if ghastly objects in hospital and trench literally perished, while their storehouses burst with food—waiting for a rise!

It is too ugly a picture to dwell upon. Suffice it that the human hyenas of speculation did prey upon the dying South; that they locked up her salt while the men in the trenches perished for it; that thrice they stored the flour the people felt was theirs, in such quantities and for so long, that before their maw for gain was glutted, serious riots of the starving called for the strong hand to interfere. And to the credit of Government and southern soldier, be it said—even in that dark hour, with craving stomach and sickening soul—"Johnny Reb" obeyed his orders and guarded the den of the hyena—from his own hungering children, perhaps!

No weak words of mine may paint the baseness and infamy of the vultures of the market. Only a Doré, with a picture like his Frozen Hell, or Ugolino—might give it faint ideal.

And with the feeling how valueless was the money, came another epidemic—not so widespread, perhaps, as the speculation fever; but equally fatal to those who caught it—the rage for gambling!

Impulsive by nature, living in an atmosphere of constant and increasing artificial excitement, feeling that the money worth little to-day, perhaps, would be worth nothing to-morrow—the men of the South gambled heavily, recklessly and openly. There was no shame —little concealment about it. The money was theirs, they argued, and mighty hardly earned, too. They were cut off from home ties and home amusements; led the life of dumb beasts in camp; and, when they came to town—ho! for "the tiger."

Whether these reasons be valid or not, such they were. And really to the camp-wearied and battle-worn officer, the saloon of the fashionable Richmond "hell" was a thing of beauty. Its luxurious furniture, soft lights, obsequious servants and lavish store of such wines and liquors and cigars as could be had nowhere else in Dixie— these were only part of the inducement. Excitement did the rest, leaving out utterly the vulgar one of possible gain, so rarely did that obtain. But in these faro-banks collected the leading men, resident and alien, of the Capital. Senators, soldiers and the learned professions sat elbow to elbow, round the generous table that offered choicest viands money could procure. In the handsome rooms above they puffed fragrant and real Havanas, while the latest developments of news, strategy and policy were discussed; sometimes ably, sometimes flippantly, but always freshly. Here men who had been riding raids in the mountains of the West; had lain shut up in the water batteries of the Mississippi; or had faced the advance of the many " On-to-Richmonds "—met after long separation. Here the wondering young cadet would look first upon some noted raider, or some gallant brigadier—cool and invincible amid the rattle of Minié-balls, as reckless but conquerable amid the rattle of ivory chips.

So the faro-banks flourished and the gamblers waxed fat like

Jeshurun, the ass, and kicked never so boldly at the conscript man. Nor were they all of ignoble memory. There is more than one "sport" in the South to-day, who made warm and real friends of high position from his acts of real generosity then.

Whatever may be the vices of gamblers as a class, many a soldier-boy will bear witness to the exception that proves the rule. One of the "hells" at least was a *home* for the refugee; and whether the Maryland soldier came dirty, and hungry and ragged from camp, with never a "stamp" in his pocket; whether he came wearied and worn, but "full of greenbacks," from a trip across the lines—the post of honor at the table, the most cordial welcome and most generous glass of wine were ever his.

However the holy may be horrified—however the princely speculator may turn up his keen-scented nose, I here record that, during the four years of dark and bloody war—of pinching want and bitter trial, there was no more generous, free-hearted and delicate aid given to the suffering soldier-boy, than came from the hand of the Baltimore faro-banker.

So in Richmond high and low gambled—some lightly for excitement's sake—some dashingly and brilliantly—a few sullenly and doggedly going in to gain. Few got badly hurt, getting more in equivalent of wines, cigars and jolly dinners than they gave. They looked upon the "hell" as a club—and as such used it freely, spending what they had and whistling over their losses. When they had money to spare they played; when they had no money to spare—or otherwise —they smoked their cigars, drank their toddies and met their friends in chaff and gossip, with no more idea that there was a moral or social wrong than if they had been at the "Manhattan" or the "Pickwick" of to-day.

I do not pretend to defend the habit; but such it was, and such all the men who remember the Capital will recognize it.

Of that other class, who "went in for blood"—some got badly hurt in reputation and in pocket. But the dead cause has buried its dead; and their errors—the result of an overstrained state of society and indubitably of a false money-system—hurt no one but themselves.

And so, with the enemy thundering at the gates; with the echoed *whoo!* of the great shells almost sounding in the streets; and with the ill-provided army staggering under the burthen of defense—almost too heavy for it to bear—the finances of the Confederacy went from bad to worse—to nothing!

The cotton that the alchemy of genius, or even of business tact—might have transmuted into gold, rotted useless; or worse, as a bait for the raider. The notes, that might have been a worthy pledge of governmental faith, bore no meaning now upon their face; and the soldier in the trench and the family at the desolate fireside—who might have been comfortably fed and clad—were gnawed with very hunger! And when the people murmured too loudly, a change was made in men, if not in policy.

Even if Mr. Trenholm had the ability, he had no opportunity to prove it. The evil seed had been sown and the bitter fruit had grown apace. Confederate credit was dead!

Even its own people had no more faith in the issues of their government; and they hesitated not—even while they groped on, ever on to the darkness coming faster and faster down upon them—to declare that the cause of their trouble was Mr. Memminger; with the President behind him.

But, though the people saw the mismanagement and felt its cause —though they suffered from it as never nation suffered before— though they spoke always bitterly and often hotly of it; still, in their greatest straits and in their darkest hours, no southern man ever deemed it but mismanagement.

The wildest and most reckless slanderer could never hint that one shred of all the flood of paper was ever diverted from its proper channel by the Secretary; or that he had not worked brain and body to the utmost, in the unequal struggle to subdue the monster he had created.

CHAPTER XXVIII.

Of such vast import to the southern cause was Lee's first aggressive campaign in Maryland; so vital was its need believed to be, by the people of the South; so varied and warm was their discussion of it that it may seem proper to give that advance more detailed consideration.

Imperfect and inadequate as such a sketch must be, to the soldier, it may still convey in some sort, the ideas of the southern people upon a momentous question.

Coincident with the evacuation of the Peninsula by the Federals was General Lee's movement, to throw beyond the Rapidan a force sufficient to prevent Pope's passage of that river. After Cedar Mountain, Jackson had disappeared as if the earth had swallowed him up. It was believed in the North that the advance of Pope's masses had cut him off from the main army and locked him up in the Shenandoah Valley; while the South—equally ignorant of his designs and confident of their success—rested on the rumor that he had said:

"Send me more men and no orders!"

Suddenly a beacon flashed into the sky, telling in the flames from the depots at Manassas and Bristow Stations that the famous passage of Thoroughfare Gap had been made—millions of property, stores and rolling-stock given to feed the flames. Jackson was in Pope's rear!

This Confederate corps now fronted toward the main army of Lee, and the bragging Federal found himself between the upper and nether millstones. Still he had little doubt that he could turn upon the small force of Jackson and crush it before Lee could advance to his rescue. Following this plan, and depending also upon the heavy masses Burnside was bringing down to him from Fredericksburg, Pope attacked Jackson in detail at Bristow and at Manassas, with no other effect than to be repulsed heavily in both instances.

16

The attack, however, warned Jackson of the enemy's purpose and of his own critical position; and, on the night of August 28th, he made a masterly flank movement that put him in possession of the old battle-field of Manassas plains; at the same time opening his communications with Lee's advance.

In all this, General Stuart gave most efficient aid both in beating back heavy attacks of the enemy's cavalry, and in keeping Jackson advised of the course of Pope's retreat—or advance, as it might be called—from Warrenton to Manassas.

By the 29th of August, Longstreet's corps had effected the passage of Thoroughfare Gap and united with Jackson; and on that day these corps engaged with Pope's advance in a terrific fight, lasting from midday till dark—the prelude to the great drama that was next day to deluge the field of Manassas a second time with the blood of friend and foe.

Before daylight next morning, the cannon again woke the wearied and battle-worn ranks, sleeping on their arms on the field they had won; and sent a fresh impulse to the hearts of their brothers, toiling steadily on to join them in the great fight to come. Heavy firing and sharp skirmishing for position filled the forenoon; but then the masses of hostile infantry joined in the shock of battle, more terrible than the one of the year before. The men were more disciplined and hardened on both sides; and the Federal leaders, feeling that their only hope lay in victory now, hurled brigade after brigade against the now vindictive and battle-thirsty Confederates.

Line after line emerges from enveloping clouds of smoke, charging the fronts that Longstreet and Jackson steadily oppose to them. Line after line melts before that inevitable hail, rolling back scattered and impotent as the spume the angry ocean throws against a granite headland!

Broken again and again, the Federals, with desperate gallantry, hurl against the unflinching crescent that pours its ceaseless rain of fire through them; while the great guns behind its center thunder and roll

" In the very glee of war,"

sending death-winged bolts tearing and crushing through them.

Through the carnival of death Hood has sent his **Texans and** Georgians at a run—their wild yells rending the dull roar of the fight;

their bayonets flashing in a jagged line of light like hungry teeth! Jackson has swung gradually round the enemy's right; and Stephen Lee's artillery has advanced from the center—ever tearing and crashing through the Federal ranks, scattering terror and death in its unswerving path!

The slaughter has been terrific. Federal and Southron have fought well and long. Piles of mangled and gory dead lie so mingled that gray and blue are undistinguished. But the wild impetuosity of the "ragged rebels"—nerved by the memories of this field's old glories —toned up by the Seven Days, and delirious with the glow of present victory—sweeps the Federal back and doubles his line. It breaks— fresh regiments pour in with deadly shot and fearful yell; the Federal line melts into confusion—rout! and the Second Manassas is won.

The victory was as complete as that of the year before; an absolute rout was only saved the Federals by falling back to the reserve under Franklin, when the retreat became more orderly, as there was no pursuit.

The solid fruits of the victory were the annihilation of all the plans of the gong-sounder, and the complete destruction of the new "On-to-Richmond;" the capture of over 7,000 prisoners—paroled on the field—and his admitted total loss of 28,000 men.

New glories, too, shone around the names of Lee, Jackson, Longstreet, Hood, Kemper and Jenkins; and the efficient aid and splendid fighting of the cavalry of Stuart, Hampton and Bev Robinson, here proved that arm to have reached its point of highest efficiency.

The heart of the South, still throbbing with triumph after the Seven Days and their bright corollary of Cedar Mountain, went up in one wild throb of joyous thanksgiving. So satisfied were the people of the sagacity of their leaders and the invincible valor of their troops; so carried away were they by the splendid reflection from the glory over Manassas plain—that this time they never even stopped to question why there had been no pursuit; why the broken enemy had not been completely crushed. All they felt was that Virginia was free from the invader. For General Loring, in the Kanawha, had driven the enemy before him and entirely cleared that portion of the state; while on this line he was hastening rapidly back to Washington to meet the expected advance of Lee toward the Capital.

Without resting his army, the latter divided it into three corps, under command of Jackson, Longstreet and A. P. Hill; and moved rapidly toward the accomplishment of that cherished hope of the southern people—an offensive campaign on the enemy's soil.

Jackson passed with his accustomed swiftness to the occupation of the heights commanding Harper's Ferry and to the investment of that position; while the other corps moved to the river at different points, to cut off the re-enforcements the alarmed Federals might send to its rescue. Great was the alarm and intense the excitement at Washington. The sudden turn of the tables—the cold dash to hopes that the bragging of their new hero had raised to fever heat, and the transformation of the crushed rebel into an avenging invader, created equal surprise as panic. Pope summarily dropped from the pinnacle of public favor into disgrace; and McClellan was the only mainstay the Federal Government could fall back on, to check the victorious Lee.

Meanwhile, equal excitement reigned in the Rebel Capital, but it was joyous and triumphant. The people had long panted to see the theater of blood and strife transferred to the prosperous and peaceful fields of their enemy. They had a secure feeling that when these were torn with shell and drenched with carnage; when barns were rifled and crops trampled by hostile feet, the northern people would begin to appreciate the realities of a war they had so far only seen by the roseate light of a partial press. Secure and confident in the army that was to work their oracle, the hope of the South already drew triumphant pictures of defeated armies, harassed states, and a peace dictated from the Federal Capital.

On the 14th of September, D. H. Hill, of Longstreet's corps—stationed at Boonesboro to protect Jackson's flank—was attacked by a heavy force. Heavily outnumbered, Hill fought a dogged and obstinate battle—giving and taking terrific blows, only ceasing when night stopped the fight. It was hard to tell which side had the best of the actual fighting; but the great object was gained and the next day Harper's Ferry, with its heavy garrison and immense supply of arms, stores and munitions, was surrendered to Jackson.

Great was the joy in Richmond when the news of the brilliant fight at Boonesboro—the first passage of arms on Maryland soil—and of the capture of the great arsenal of the North reached her anx-

ious people. It was, they felt, but the presage of the great and substantial triumphs that Lee and his veterans *must* win. Higher rose
their confidence and more secure became their calculations; and the
vivid contrast between the ragged, shoeless and incongruous army of
the South with the sleek, spruce garrison surrendered to them, only-
heightened the zest of the victory and the anticipation of those to
follow.

But a sudden check was to come to this mid-career of anticipation,
and a pall of doubt and dismay was to drape the fair form of Hope,
even in her infancy.

Two days after the fall of Harper's Ferry—on the 17th of September—Lee had massed some 35,000 men on the banks of the Antietam, near Sharpsburg—a village ten miles north-east of Harper's
Ferry. McClellan, pressing him hard with an army four times his
own numbers—composed in part of raw levies and hastily-massed
militia, and in part of the veterans of the armies of the Potomac—
seemed determined on battle. Trusting in the valor and reliability
of his troops, and feeling the weakness of being pressed by an enemy
he might chastise, the southern chief calmly awaited the attack—sending couriers to hasten the advance of A. P. Hill, Walker and McLaws,
whose divisions had not yet come up.

Ushered in by a heavy attack the evening before—which was
heavily repulsed—the morning of the 17th saw one of the bloodiest
and most desperate fights in all the horrid records of that war. Hurling his immense masses against the rapidly dwindling Confederate
line; only to see them reel back shattered and broken—McClellan
strove to crush his adversary by sheer strength. No sooner would
one attacking column waver, break, retreat—leaving a writhing and
ghastly wake behind it—than a fresh host would hurl against the ada-
mantine line that sunk and shriveled under the resistless fire, but
never wavered. In all the fearful carnage of the war—whether resulting in gloom, like that of Corinth, or purchasing brilliant victory
with precious blood—men never fought better than did that battle-
torn, service-worn handful that had just saved Richmond—broken
the glittering, brazen vessel of destruction; and now sent its defiant
yell through hostile mountains.

All that valor and endurance could do had been done; and at
mid-afternoon the battle seemed well-nigh lost. Just then the missing

divisions—some 12,000 men—reached the field. Wearied, unfed and
footsore, they were; but the scent of battle rested and refreshed
them as they went into the thickest of the fight. But even they
could not save the day. Outnumbered and shattered, but unconquered still, the Confederates could not advance from the field they
had held at such bitter cost. And when night stopped the aimless
carnage, each army, too crippled to renew the fight, withdrew toward its base. McClellan could not pursue; and the Confederates
fell back doggedly, sullenly, and recrossed into Virginia.

As usual in the North, a wild howl went up against McClellan.
In response to this *brutum fulmen*, he was promptly removed by Hal-
leck, for not conquering an army that had proved itself invincible!

Bitter indeed was the hour that brought to Richmond the story of
Sharpsburg. Flushed with hope, undoubting of triumph, her citizens
only listened for the wild cheer that would echo back from conquered
Washington. But the sound that reached their ears was the menacing roar from retreating ranks that left near one-third their number
stark and ghastly on that grim field, where the Death Angel has so
darkly flapped his wings.

Thus ended the first Maryland campaign.

It had given the people their wish; it had carried the gray jackets
over the border and stricken the enemy sorely on his own soil. But
it had left that soil drenched with the blood of some of the bravest
and best; the noble Branch and chivalric Starke had both fallen where
their men lay thickest—torn and ghastly on that terrible field.

The details of that field which the Richmond people gathered
from the northern papers, deepened their gloom. And through it
rose a hoarse whisper, swelling at last into angry query, why had the
campaign miscarried? If the army was inadequate in numbers, why
had General Lee carried it over that river he had never crossed before, when his own army was better and the enemy less prepared?
And if, as stated, the men were ill-provided in munitions and transportation—as they were known to be with clothes and rations—why
had Government forced its only bulwark well-nigh to annihilation?

It mattered little, the people said, that the results had been far
more disastrous to the North than to the South—both in prestige and
loss. The North could far better afford it. What was the killing of
a few thousand raw troops, or the destruction of a few thousand stand

of arms, compared to the precious cost of holding the field at Sharps-burg?

And gradually these complaints, as in all such cases, answered themselves; and then the vials of southern wrath began to empty over the unfortunate Marylanders, who had not risen to aid their brothers in their sore need. How unjust were these charges will soon be shown.

And so the people murmured to relieve their overfull hearts, until the calm and steady course of the general they had never doubted, quieted them once more.

The outcry in the North resulted in the choice of General A. E. Burnside to command the new invasion; and he was of course hailed as the augur, who was surely this time to read the oracle. Watchful, calm, and steadfast, the Confederate waited, through the months of preparation, to meet the new advance—so disposing part of his force about Winchester as to prevent the favorite Valley-road On-to-Rich-mond. With a renewed, and splendidly appointed, army, Burnside moved in November toward Fredericksburg; thinking that this time he had really gotten between Lee and Richmond.

What was his disgust to find, when he reached the Rappahannock, that the Confederate army was not all at Winchester, but was before him to dispute his crossing. After some unavailing manœuvers for position, the Federals sat down on the heights of Stafford, opposite Fredericksburg; made works at their leisure; and spread a perfect city of tents and booths over a line of some five miles. Outnumbered as he was, General Lee could do nothing but watch and wait for the crossing that must come, sooner or later; and meantime he chose his line of battle.

Just back of Fredericksburg, stretching some two miles south-ward, is a semi-circular plain bordered by a range of hills. These stretch from Hamilton's crossing beyond Mayre's Hill on the left; and are covered with dense oak growth and a straggling fringe of pines. On these hills, Lee massed his artillery, to sweep the whole plain where the enemy must form, after his crossing; and arranged his line of battle with A. P. Hill holding the right and Longstreet the left. On the night of December 10th, Stafford Heights opened a furious bombardment of the town, tearing great gaps through the thickest populated quarters.

Into the bitter winter night tender women and young children were driven, shivering with fright and cold, half clad; seeking safety from the screaming shells that chased them everywhere. Under this bombardment, the pioneers commenced their pontoons at three points. The storm of grape and canister was too great to contest the landing, which was effected next day.

As the heavy fog that had obscured the sun cleared away, the regular lines of the Federals advanced to the attack, raked and torn by batteries. Broken, they were formed again, only to be mowed down afresh; while the scream of a thousand shells from Stafford filled the air with a continuous *whoo*, amid which the rattle of southern musketry sang ever fiercer and swifter. Then dark masses of blue came out of the town and formed for the charge, under a terrific fire from the Washington Artillery on Mayre's Hill. Steadily and fearlessly did Meagher's First Brigade move to the attack. Crowded into the narrow road, swept by the accurate fire of the Louisianians and McLaws' veterans—the head of the column went down, only to be filled by the gallant fellows behind. Into the jaws of death they came, up to the very works—then, with half their number dead and dying about their feet, they broke, the left gave way—and the bloody field was won at all points. The victory was terrible and complete.

But it had cost dear, and the rejoicing in Richmond was tempered with sorrow for the loss of such as Maxcy Gregg, Cobb, and many others, lying cold upon the field of victory.

And with the first feeling of triumph the news brought, came the thought that this time *surely* the enemy would be pushed—this time he was indeed a prey! Broken and demoralized, with a deep river in his rear that he *must cross in pontoons*, the people felt that he could surely be destroyed before reaching his Stafford stronghold. But once again, as ever, the shattered and broken legions of Burnside were allowed two days to recover from their demoralization; to pass at leisure, over the trap behind them.

Great was the amaze, bitter the disappointment of the people; and the inquiry how and why this had been done, became universal. But the southern people above every other feeling had now come to cherish a perfect and unquestioning faith in General Lee; and even while they wondered at a policy that invariably left a beaten enemy to recover, and only become stronger—still they questioned with a firm reliance that there *must* be some reason, invisible to them but good and potent still.

There were no active operations immediately succeeding Fredericksburg. Picket fighting; cavalry skirmishes, severe but fruitless; and temporary raids of the enemy to devastate the country around the rear of their army, and to penetrate into that beyond their lines, occupying the winter and early spring. But there was full leisure for the people to look upon the ugliest features of the war. Fredericksburg was a ruin, riddled with shot and shell, tenanted only by the poorest classes. Her once cheerful and elegant population were ruined and starving refugees in Richmond; the smiling tracts stretching back to the Potomac were one broad, houseless waste—browned by fire, and cut with the winding wagon-roads of the enemy. Constant incursions of his cavalry—for " raiding" had now become a feature of the war—harassed the people, everywhere removed from the immediate army lines. These slaughtered and drove off their cattle, stole and consumed their supplies, burned their barns, *and destroyed their farming utensils!*—a refinement of barbarity to non-combatants, never before practiced by a civilized race.

Then, too, the news from the West, heretofore sketched, reacted on Richmond; and the gloom in the Capital grew deep and universal. Burnside had, meantime, been dismissed in disgrace for his shameful failure. The inevitable howl had again gone up in the North; then the inevitable result had come. Joseph Hooker was now the coming man—the war-gong was sounded more loudly than ever; the army was re-enforced to greater size than ever; and so equipped that its general proclaimed it the "finest army on the planet." Agog with preparation, and stuffed full with promises of certain success this time, the North forgot the many slips between its lips and the coveted cup of triumph, and waited in secure impatience for the moment when the roads would permit Hooker to advance.

And the South waited, too—not hopefully, nor with the buoyant anticipation of the past, but still with a confidence in its cause and its defenders nowise diminished; with even more fixed determination never to yield, while there were muskets left and hands to grasp them.

At last the movement came. Late in April, Hooker divided his immense army into two columns, one menacing right crossing below Fredericksburg, to hold the troops at that point; the other crossing above, to flank and pass to their rear, combining with the other wing and cutting communication with Richmond. Taking command in person of his right wing—while the left was confided to General Slocum—Hooker rapidly crossed the river, concentrating not less than 60,000 men on the Chancellorsville road, eleven miles above Fredericksburg. Grasping the situation at once, Lee ordered the small force there back to Mine Run, until re-enforced; and then, on the 2d of May, Stonewall Jackson completed that wonderful and painful circuit of the enemy—so brilliant in conception, so successful in result. Late in the afternoon he reached their extreme right and rear, secure and unsuspecting. Never stopping to rest, the Eldest Son of War hurled himself like a thunderbolt on the confident and intrenched enemy—-scattering the eleventh corps (Sigel's) like chaff, and hurling them, broken and demoralized, upon their supports. The very key of the enemy's campaign was driven out; and the "one hour more of daylight!" the hero-general prayed for—or the merciful sparing of his priceless life by the God of Battles—would have shown complete defeat, even annihilation, of Hooker's right.

But it was not so written in the Book of Life! A wise dispensation, whose object we may see, removed the best and greatest soldier of the war—sorely stricken by the hands of his own devoted men, in the darkness; the routed enemy was given, by this unequaled misfortune, and by fast falling night, opportunity for partial reorganization.

Hooker's right was turned and doubled upon his center; but he was still strong in numbers, and had the advantage of position and heavy works, abatis and rifle-pits.

Next morning General Lee assaulted in force, all along the line; and after heavy and bloody fighting, drove him from his position at all points. Sedgwick, however, had crossed the river at Fredericksburg, driving the Confederates from the town and carrying Mayre's Hill by assault. This acted as a check to Lee, who was forced to detach McLaws' division to drive Sedgwick back from his own rear. This he successfully accomplished, and—Anderson reaching McLaws just in time—on the 4th of May, the last of the series of the battles of the Rappahannock resulted in complete defeat of Sedgwick.

Still, Hooker was permitted to withdraw his army across the river; but the campaign of the week had been successful in utterly breaking his plans and clearly defeating him in every engagement.

CHAPTER XXIX.

OVER AGAIN, TO GETTYSBURG.

The campaign of the Rappahannock had shown brilliant flashes of strategy and valor. It had proved that a badly-provided army of less than 50,000 Confederates—barefooted, blanketless and half-fed, but properly led—could, even when surrounded and out-flanked, defeat and set at naught 120,000 of the best-appointed troops ever sent against them. It revived, in some degree, the droop-ing spirits of the people ; but a sorrow that rose to agony wrung the heart of the South, when what was earth of her peerless, pure and idolized Jackson was laid in the Capitol, wrapped in the flag he had made immortal.

Shattered and emaciated veterans, noble-browed matrons and pale, delicate maidens gathered around that sacred bier, in the awed hush of a common sorrow, too deep for words. Tears coursed over cheeks that had been bronzed in the fire of battle; sobs rose from hearts that had lost their dearest and nearest without a murmur, save—*Thy will be done!* And little children were lifted up to look upon what was left of him who would ever be the greatest one of earth to them. And through the coffin-lid, that calm, still face seemed hourly to grow more holy and more radiant ; the light of battle faded out from its softening lines and the seal of the God of Peace rested in plain token upon the glorified brow.

Truly did every one who looked upon it feel:

"O, gracious God ! not gainless is the loss !
A glorious sunbeam gilds thy sternest frown—
For, while his country staggers 'neath the Cross,
He rises with the Crown !"

And when the funeral procession passed the streets of the Capital, the whole people stood bareheaded and mute. Following the wail-ing notes of the dirge with unsteady feet, moved the escort of ragged and war-worn soldiers—their tattered banners furled—and every torn dress and dented gun-carriage speaking eloquently of the right they had earned to sorrow for him. It was no mocking pageant. No holiday soldiery, spruce and gay, followed that precious bier—no chattering crowds pointed out the beauties of the sight. Solemn and mourning the escort passed; sad and almost voiceless the people turned away and, going to their homes, sat with their sorrow.

After the Rappahannock fights came a lull of several weeks; and it was early in June when General Lee advanced to force the enemy out of the state. His army had been reorganized and strengthened as much as possible; General R. S. Ewell was chosen successor to Jackson; and to him, Longstreet and A. P. Hill—raised now to a full lieutenant-general—was given command of the three corps.

Diverging from the main line, after some little coquetting for position, Ewell charged Jackson's "foot cavalry" upon Winchester, capturing the town with its heavy depots of stores and munitions; while Hill kept Hooker amused, and Longstreet slowly forged his way toward the river.

Great was the joy of the poor town when it once more welcomed the gray-jackets. From the beginning it had been battle-ground and billet of both armies a dozen times. Tossed from Federal to Confederate possession—a very shuttlecock of war—it had been harassed, robbed and pillaged by the one; drained of the very dregs by free gifts to the other. But the people of Winchester never faltered in their faith; and to-day her noble women go down the roll of heroism and steadfast truth, hand in hand with the noblest ones of our history.

And the joy in Winchester was somewhat reflected at the harassed and eager-watching Capital. Undiminished by the sorrows of the last fall, undimmed by its reverses, still burned the southern desire to plant its victorious flag on hostile soil. It was neither a thirst for vengeance nor an empty boast; rather a yearning for relief—a craving for the rest from blood and battle-shocks that such a campaign would give.

It was with deep satisfaction, then, that Richmond heard that Ewell had crossed the Potomac at Williamsport, pushed on through Hagerstown and, leaving Early at York, had passed to Carlisle; that Longstreet had followed him at Williamsport; and that A. P. Hill had crossed at Shepherdstown and pushed for Chambersburg, reaching there on the 27th of June.

Hooker, falling rapidly back upon Washington—at which point he believed the movement aimed—had been sacrificed, and with more justice than usual, to popular clamor. General Geo. G. Meade replaced him in command, and strained every nerve to collect numbers of men, irrespective of quality—seeming to desire to crush the invasion by weight alone.

Wild was the alarm in the North when the rebel advance had penetrated the heart of Pennsylvania; when York was held by Early and laid under contribution and Harrisburg was threatened by Ewell. The whole North rose in its might. Governors Seymour, of New York, Andrew, of Massachusetts, and Curtin, of Pennsylvania, put their whole militia at the service of the President; the energy at Washington, momentarily paralyzed, soon recovered; and by the last day of the month, Meade had collected an army of near 200,000 men. Many of these were, of course, new levies and raw militia; but near one-half were the veterans of the armies of McClellan, Burnside and Hooker; men who had fought gallantly on southern soil and might be expected to do so on their own.

It seems that Lee's intention was to flank Meade; and leaving him in Maryland, to pass into Pennsylvania, occupy Harrisburg, destroy communications between Washington and the North and reduce Philadelphia.

Such, at least, was the universal belief of the southern people; and so rapidly did their mercurial temperament rise under it, and so great was their reliance in the army that was to accomplish the brilliant campaign, that they looked upon it already as a fixed fact. Now, at last, they felt, we will teach the Yankees what invasion really means. With their Capital leaguered, their President and Cabinet fugitives by water, and their great thoroughfare and second city in our hands, we will dictate our own terms, and end the war.

Such *might* have been the case, had Gettysburg been won, or had that battle never been fought.

If Lee's intention was to flank Meade and avoid a fight at the outset of the campaign, it was thwarted by the rapid concentration of troops in his front, near Gettysburg. To prevent being struck in detail and secure his communications, Lee was forced to recall Ewell and to concentrate his army. Hill and Longstreet were ordered up from Chambersburg; and by July 1st the opposing armies faced each other; each feeling its way cautiously and knowing that the result of this grapple of the giants must in a great measure decide the war. Meade's defeat would lose Washington, leave the heart of the North open, and demoralize the only army in that section. Lee's defeat, on the other hand, would jeopardy his very existence and probably leave Richmond an easy prey to fresh advance.

But in Richmond none of this was felt; for all that was known of the army was its victorious entry into Pennsylvania; and absurdly exaggerated stories of the dire panic and demoralization of the enemy received perfect credence.

Then the shock came.

On the 1st of July, Hill's advance encountered the enemy under Reynolds; and—after a fierce struggle, in which their general was killed—drove them back into and through the town. Here they were reformed on a semi-circular crest of hills; massing their artillery and holding their position until dark. Their loss was heavier far than Hill's, and the men not in as good fighting trim; but it was very late, and General Lee feared pressing their reserve. Had he known that it was only the advance of Meade, broken and demoralized, that held the crest, he could undoubtedly have carried and occupied it. The fearful battles of the next two days, with their terrific loss of life, doubtless hung on this lost opportunity.

By next morning the enemy had massed the remainder of his army behind these hills, now frowning with two hundred guns and blue with one dense line of soldiery. Under a fearful cannonade, through a hail of bullets that nothing living might stand, Stewart works his way slowly and steadily forward on the enemy's left; driving him from line after line of works and holding every inch gained, by dogged valor and perseverance. Hays and Hoke (of Early's) advance into the ploughing fire of the rifled guns—march steadily on and charge over their own dead and dying, straight for Cemetery Heights. This is the key of the enemy's position. That once gained the day is won; and on the brave fellows go, great gaps tearing through their ranks—answering every fresh shock with a savage yell. Line after line of the enemy gives way before that terrible charge. The breastwork is occupied—they are driven out! Melting under the horrid fire, unfaltering still—the gray-jackets reach the very hill!

Nothing mortal can stand the enfilading fire. They give way—again they charge—they are at the very works! But the fire is too heavy for their thinned ranks to stand; and night falls over the field, illumined by the red flash of cannon—drenched with blood and horrid with carnage of friend and foe. But there is no advantage gained, save a slight advance of Stewart's position on their left.

With the morning of the third day came the conviction that the vital struggle must be made for Cemetery Heights. Lee *must* win them—and then for victory!

All the artillery was massed upon this point. Then awoke the infernal echoes of such an artillery duel as the war was never to see again. The air was black with flying shot and shell, and their wild *whoo!* made one continuous song through the sultry noon. Forth from the canopy of smoke and their screen of trees, comes the chosen storming party—Pickett's division of Virginians; supported on the right by Wilcox and on the left by Heth's division under Pettigrew, its own general having been wounded in the head the day before.

Unmindful of the fire-sheeted storm into which they march—down into the Valley of the Shadow of Death stride that devoted band. Now, they emerge into the Emmetsburg road, straight on for the coveted heights. On! never blenching, never faltering—with great gaps crashing through them—filling the places of the dead with the living next to die—On! into the jaws of death goes the forlorn hope! They are at the rise—they reach the crest; and then *their batteries are suddenly silent!*

Behind them is the ghastly road, furrowed and ploughed by ceaseless shot, slippery with blood and dotted thick with their writhing, bleeding brothers. Behind them is death—defeat! Before them a hundred belching cannon—a dense, dark mass of blue, relieved only by the volleying flash that shakes and rolls along their shattered line! Still up they go! on—ever on! That small Virginia division, shattered, bleeding—*and alone* reaches the works—fights for one moment and then—*has won them!*

But there are no supports—Pettigrew has not come up; and the decimated Virginians are literally overwhelmed by the fresh masses poured upon them. Broken, torn, exhausted, they fall back—scattered into terrible death-dealing knots, that fight their way sullenly and terribly home to their own lines!

That charge—unequaled in history—has fearfully crippled the enemy. He can not pursue. But it has failed, and the battle of Gettysburg is over!

That night General Lee fell back toward Hagerstown, turning in his retreat to show front to the enemy that dared not attack. Nine days he stayed on the Maryland shore, waiting the advance that never came; then he recrossed the river, on the night of the 13th, and again fell back to the Rappahannock lines.

The second Maryland campaign had failed!

Into the midst of the general elation in Richmond crashed the wild rumors from the fight. We had driven the enemy through the town; we held the height; we had captured Meade and 40,000 prisoners. Washington was at our mercy; and Lee would dictate terms of peace from Philadelphia!

These were the first wild rumors; eagerly sought and readily credited by the people. They were determined to believe and would see no change of plan in General Lee's forced battle at Gettysburg, instead of on the plains at Harrisburg.

Then over the general joy, creeping none knew whence nor how, but rapidly gaining shape and substance, came a shadow of doubt. Crowds besieged the War Department, anxious, excited, but still hopeful. Then the truth came; tempered by the Government, but wildly exaggerated by northern sources.

Down to zero dropped the spirits of the people; down to a depth of despairing gloom, only the deeper from the height of their previous exultation. The dark cloud from Gettysburg rolled back over Richmond, darkened and made dense a hundred fold in the transit.

The terrible carnage of that field was exaggerated by rumor. Pickett's gallant division was declared annihilated; it was believed that the army had lost 20,000 men; and it was known that such priceless blood as that of Garnett, Pettigrew, Armistead, Pender, Kemper, Semmes and Barksdale had sealed the dreadful defeat.

It only needed what came the next day, to dash the last drop from the cup of hope the people still tried to hold to their lips; and that was the news of the fall of Vicksburg, on the 4th of July.

And out of the thick darkness that settled on the souls of all, came up the groan of inquiry and blame. Why had the campaign failed? they asked. Why had General Lee been forced into battle on ground of the enemy's choosing? Why had he attacked works that only an army like his would have made an effort to take, when he could have flanked the enemy and forced him to fight him on his own terms? Why had the Government—as was alleged—allowed the crucial test of liberty—the crisis campaign of the war—to be undertaken without proper transportation and supplies of ammunition?

And why, above all, had the general they still loved and trusted, spite of their doubts—why had he sent their beloved Virginians unsupported to the shambles? Why had he fought the whole Yankee army with one division?

Such were the murmurs on every side. And though they gradually died away, after the first shock of surprise and grief had passed; still they left a vague feeling behind that all was not well; that grave errors had been committed somewhere. For the southern people could not get over the feeling that there were no odds of numbers and position that could cause defeat to a southern army, properly supplied and properly handled. So, although the murmurs ceased, the conviction did not die with them that the battle of Gettysburg was a grave error; that there had been a useless waste of priceless lives; and that the campaign had been nullified, which else had ended the war.

And unlike other post-disaster conclusions of the southern people, this did not die out. It only became strengthened and fixed, the more light was thrown on the vexed questions and the more they were canvassed. The excuses of the War Department that ammunition had given out, were scornfully rejected. Then, said the people, that was your fault. General Lee could not depend—in a campaign in the heart of an enemy's country and far away from his base—upon his captures. And as to his not intending to fight a pitched battle, how could he calculate upon that, or why then did he fight it; and upon ground of the enemy's choice?

And with the other objections to the conduct of the campaign, came that of the general's treatment of the people of Pennsylvania. It was felt to be an excess of moderation to a people whose armies had not spared the sword, the torch and insult to our unprotected tracts; and it was argued—without a shadow of foundation—that Lee's knightly courtesy to the Dutch dames of Pennsylvania had disgusted his troops.

Those starving and barefooted heroes would have thought it right

17

if their beloved chief had fallen down and worshiped the makers of apple-butter! They felt he could do no wrong; and it was indirect injustice to the gallant dead that dotted Cemetery Hill—and to the no less gallant living ready to march up to those frowning heights again—to intimate that any action of their general would, or *could*, have made them fight better.

Excessive as was that moderation—ill advised as it might have proved, in case of a long campaign—it could have had no possible effect on the fortunes of the disastrous and brief one just ended.

Equally unjust as that popular folly, was the aspersion upon southern sympathizers in Maryland, that they did not come forth to aid their friends. The part of Maryland through which southern armies passed in both campaigns were sparsely settled, and that with strong Union population. The Marylander of Baltimore and the lower counties—whatever may have been his wishes, was gagged and bound too closely to express, far less carry them out. Baltimore was filled with an armed guard and was, moreover, the passage-way of thousands of troops; the lower counties were watched and guarded. And, moreover, the Confederate army was not *practically* in Maryland, but from the 20th of June to the 1st of July.

The taunt to the down-trodden Marylanders—oppressed and suffering bravely for conscience sake—we must in justice to ourselves believe only the result of grief and disappointment. Men, like goods, can only be judged " by sample;" and, from the beginning to the end of the war, Maryland may point to Archer, Winder, Elzey, Johnson and many another noble son—unhonored now, or filling, perhaps, a nameless grave—and ask if such men came from among a people who talked but would not act! And so in sorrow, disappointment and bitterness ended the second Maryland campaign.

And with it ended all hopes of carrying the war beyond our own gates in future; happy could we beat it thence, baffled and crushed as ever before.

For the short, sharp raid of General Early—penetrating to the gates of the Capital and with possible capabilities of even entering them—can hardly be considered an organized scheme of invasion. It was rather the spasmodic effort by a sharp, hard blow to loosen the tightening and death-dealing grip upon our throat, and give us time for one long, deep breath before the final tug for life.

CHAPTER XXX.

THE CONFEDERACY AFLOAT.

Measured by the popular test, success, the Confederate States Navy would, perhaps, be accorded little merit. Even cursory examination into the vast difficulties and discouragements with which it contended, will do it prompt justice.

No men who joined the southern service sacrificed more than her navy officers. The very flower of the old service, they had grown gray in their slow promotion to its positions of honor; their families depended for sole support upon the pittance of pay they received. Still they hesitated not a moment to range themselves under the banners their native states had unfurled. Once there, no men labored more faithfully—and efficiently. Subject to misconstruction, to jealousy, to petty annoyances—and later, to the most pinching straits of poverty—they were ever uncomplaining and ever ready.

Many and varied were the calls upon them. They commanded land batteries, trained raw gunners and drilled lubberly conscripts; they were bridge-builders, carpenters, wood-cutters, chemists and colliers; and, at the best, it was hard for the veteran who had, for forty years, trod the deck of a frigate, to be cooped in the contracted limits of a razeed tug, or an armed pilot boat. But once there he made the best of it; and how well he wrought in the new sphere, the names of Hollins, Lynch, Buchanan and Tucker still attest.

At the time the first Army Bill was passed by Congress, a law was also made securing to resigned naval officers the same rank they held in the United States service. But there was scarcely a keel in Confederate waters, and small indeed was the prospect for the future; so these impatient spirits, panting for active work, were put into unsuitable positions at the very outset. Later, a bill was passed for a provisional navy, but there was no fleet for their occupation. The department, therefore, used the discretion given it to confer a few honorary titles, and to appoint a vast number of subordinate officers, for shore duty in its work-shops and navy-yards.

The acceptability of Mr. Mallory to the people, at the outset of his career, has been noted. They believed that his long experience in the committee of naval affairs was guarantee for the important trust confided to him. Moreover, he was known to be relied upon by Mr. Davis as a man of solid intellect, of industry and perseverance. If his knowledge of naval affairs was entirely theoretical, it mattered little so long as he could turn that knowledge to practical account, by the counsel and aid of some of the most efficient of the scientific sailors of the Union.

Mr. Mallory took charge of the Navy Department in March, '61. At this time the question of iron-clads had attention of naval builders on both sides of the Atlantic; and deeming them indispensable to naval warfare, the Secretary's first movement was a strong memoir to Congress, urging immediate and heavy appropriations for their construction at New Orleans and Mobile. With a treasury empty and immovably averse to anything like decisive action, the astute lawgivers of Montgomery hesitated and doubted. The most that could be forced from them were small appropriations for the fitting out of privateers.

The first venture, the "Sumter," was bought, equipped and put into commission at the end of April; and in the course of a few weeks she ran out of New Orleans, in command of Raphael Semmes, and the stars and bars were floating solitary, but defiant, over the seas. The history of her cruise, the terror she spread among the enemy's shipping, and the paralysis she sent to the very heart of his commerce, are too well known to need repetition here. Badly-built craft as she was for such a service, she was still more badly equipped; but so eminently successful was she that both Government and Congress must have been incurably blind, not to put a hundred like her upon every sea where the Union flag could float.

Had one-twentieth the sum frittered away in useless iron-clads, and worse than useless "gunboats," been put into saucy and swift wasps like the "Sumter," their stings must have driven northern commerce from the sea; and the United States ports would have been more effectually blockaded, from a thousand miles at sea, than were those of the southern fleet-bound coast.

It may not be irrelevant here to allude to the finale of the Confederate cruisers; and to recall the most inane farce of all those enacted by the madmen who held power in '66.

In the January of that year, Raphael Semmes was seized and thrown into prison. He was now charged—not with having violated his parole given to General Grant, who was personally and morally responsible for his persecution—not with doing aught but "obeying the laws themselves;" but he was charged with having escaped, the year before, from the custody of a man whose prisoner he was not and had never been—with having broken from a durance that ought to have existed! From incontrovertible testimony, we know that Captain Semmes only raised the white flag, after his vessel began to sink; that he stayed on her deck until she went down beneath him; that no boat came to him from the "Kearsage," and that he was in the water full an hour, before the boat of the "Deerhound" picked him up and carried him aboard that yacht.

But radical hatred, and thirst for vengeance on a disarmed enemy, raised the absurd plea that Semmes became a prisoner of war by raising the white flag; that by so doing he gave *a moral parole!* and violated it by saving himself from a watery grave and afterward taking up arms again. It is only a proof that the country was a little less mad than the radical leaders, that the unheard-of absurdity of its Navy Department was not sustained by popular opinion. It would have no doubt been chivalric and beautiful in Raphael Semmes to have drowned in the ocean, because the boat of the "Kearsage" would not pick him up after accepting his "moral parole;" but, as he did not see it in that light, and as he was never called upon to surrender by any officer of that ship, he was perfectly free the moment his own deck left him in the waves. The white flag was but a token that he desired to save the lives of his men; and would surrender them and himself, if opportunity were given. But even granting the nonsensical claim that it made him a prisoner—the laws of war demand absolute safety for prisoners; and the fact of the "Kearsage" leaving him to drown was, in itself, a release.

There is no necessity for defense of Captain Semmes' position; but it may be well to record how blind is the hate which still attempts to brand as "*Pirate*" a regularly-commissioned officer in service, whose long career gained him nothing but respect under the northern—nothing but glory under the southern flag. If Raphael Semmes be a "pirate," then was the northern recognition of belligerents but an active lie! Then was Robert E. Lee a marauder—Wade Hampton but a bushwhacker, and Joseph E. Johnston but a guerrilla!

When the " Sumter" began her work, she was soon followed by the " Florida "—a vessel somewhat better, but still of the same class. Under the dashing and efficient Maffitt, the " Florida," too, wrought daring destruction. Her record, like that of her rival, is too familiar for repetition ; as is the later substitution of the "Alabama" for the worn-out "Sumter."

During the long war, these three vessels—and but two of them at one time—were the only cruisers the Confederacy had afloat ; until just before its close, the "Shenandoah " went out to strike fresh terror to the heart and pocket of New England. Then, also, that strong-handed and cool-headed amphiboid, Colonel John Taylor Wood, made —with wretched vessels and hastily-chosen crews—most effective raids on the coasting shipping of the Northeast.

One popular error pervades all which has been said or written, on both sides of the line, about the Confederate navy. This is the general title of "privateer," given to all vessels not cooped up in southern harbors. Regularly-commissioned cruisers, like the "Alabama " and " Florida," the property of the Navy Department, and commanded by its regularly-commissioned officers, were no more " privateers" than were the " Minnesota," or " Kearsage."

There was a law passed, regulating the issue of letters of marque ; and from time to time much was heard of these in the South. But after the first spirt of the saucy little " Jeff Davis," not more than two or three ever found their way to sea ; and even these accomplished nothing.

At one time, a company with heavy capital was gotten up in Richmond, for the promotion of such enterprises ; but it was looked upon as a job and was little successful in any sense.

So, with all the ports of the world open to belligerent ships ; with unsurpassed sailors " panting for the very lack of element" in musty offices, privateers did not increase in number ; and one of the most effective engines of legitimate warfare was but illustrated, instead of being utilized.

Meantime, the Navy Department had ceased to importune for appropriations to build iron-clads at New Orleans ; an omission that carried the grave responsibility for loss of that city, and for the far graver disaster of the closing of the whole river and the blockade of the trans-Mississippi. For had the " Louisiana" been furnished with two companion ships of equal strength—or even had she been completely finished and not had been compelled to succumb to accidents within, while she braved the terrific fire from without—the Federal fleet might have been crushed like egg-shells; the splendid exertions of Hollins and Kennon in the past would not have been nullified; the blood of McIntosh and Huger would not have been useless sacrifice; and the homes of the smiling city and the pure vicinage of her noble daughters might not have been polluted by the presence of the commandant, who crawled in after the victorious fleet.

Norfolk, however, had come into southern possession, by the secession of Virginia; and the vast resources of her navy-yard—only partly crippled by the haste of the Federal retreat—stimulated the Government. A meager appropriation was passed for the construction of the " Merrimac;" or rather for an iron-clad ship upon the hull of the half-destroyed frigate of that name. Had the whole amount necessary for her completion been given, the vessel would have been ready weeks before she was, under the dribblet system adopted. Then, indeed, it would be hard to overestimate her value; damage to shipping in Hampton Roads; or her ultimate effect upon McClellan's campaign.

No appropriation for an object of vital import could be shaken free from its bonds of red tape; and this one was saddled with an incubus, in the bill for the " construction of one hundred gunboats." The scheme to build that number of wooden vessels of small size seemed equally short-sighted and impracticable. They could only be built on inland rivers and creeks, to prevent attacks by the enemy's heavier vessels; and hence they were necessarily small and ineffective. The interior navy-yards had, moreover, to be guarded against surprises by the enemy's cavalry; and as men were so scarce, it was generally arranged that the navy-yard should follow the army lines. Constantly shifting position—caused by the rapid movements of the enemy, left these impromptu ship-yards unprotected; and then a small party of raiders would either burn them, or force their builders to do so. It was not until the appropriation was nearly spent—although *not one efficient* gunboat of this class was ever finished—that the system was abandoned as utterly worthless and impracticable.

Had the large sum thus wasted been applied to the purchase of swift and reliable cruisers—or to the speedy and energetic completion of one iron-clad at a time—it would have read a far more telling story to the enemy, both in prestige and result.

But even in the case of these, energy and capital were divided and distracted. On completion of the "Merrimac," there were in the course of construction at New Orleans, two mailed vessels of a different class—one of them only a towboat covered with railroad iron. There were also two small ones on the stocks at Charleston, and another at Savannah. The great difficulty of procuring proper iron; of rolling it when obtained; and the mismanagement of transportation, even when the plates were ready—made the progress of all these boats very slow. Practicality would have concentrated the whole energy of the Department upon one at a time; not have left them all unfinished, either to prove utterly useless at the trying moment, or to fall a prey to superior force of the enemy.

The plan of the "Merrimac" was unique, in the submersion of her projecting eaves; presenting a continuous angling coat of mail even below the water-surface. She was built upon the razeed hull of the old "Merrimac," of four-and-a-half-inch iron, transverse plates; and carried an armament of seven-inch rifled Brooke guns, made expressly for her. There was much discussion at one time, as to whom the credit for her plan was really due. It finally was generally conceded, however, that her origin and perfection were due to Commander John M. Brooke; and the terrible banded rifle-gun and bolt, she used with such effect on the "Cumberland," was his undisputed invention.

Much wonder had the good people of Norfolk expressed in their frequent visits to the strange-looking, turtle-like structure. Day by day she slowly grew; and at length, after weary work and weary waiting, took on her armament; then her crew was picked carefully from eager volunteers: her grand old captain took his place, and all was ready for the trial.

During all this time Hampton Roads had been gay with Federal shipping. Frigates, gunboats, transports and supply ships ran defiantly up and down; laughing at the futile efforts of the point batteries to annoy them, and indulging in a dream of security that was to be most rudely broken. The "Susquehanna" frigate, with heaviest armament in the Federal navy, laid in the channel at Newport News, blockading the mouth of James river and cutting off communication from Norfolk. The "Congress" frigate was lying near her, off the News; while the "Minnesota" lay below, under the guns of Fortress Monroe. The Ericsson Monitor—the first of her class, and equally an experiment as her rebel rival—had come round a few days before to watch the "Virginia," as the new iron-clad was now rechristened.

The great ship being ready, Flag-Officer Buchanan ordered the "Jamestown," Captain Barney, and the "Yorktown," Captain Tucker, down from Richmond; while he went out with the "Raleigh" and "Beaufort"—two of the smallest class of gunboats, saved by Captain Lynch from Roanoke Island. This combined force—four of the vessels being frail wooden shells, formerly used as river passenger boats—carried only *twenty-seven* guns. But Buchanan steamed boldly out, on the morning of the 8th of March, to attack an enemy carrying quite *two hundred and twenty* of the heaviest guns in the United States navy!

It was a moment of dreadful suspense for the soldiers in the batteries and the people of Norfolk. They crowded the wharves, the steeples, and the high points of the shore; and every eye was strained upon the black specks in the harbor.

Slowly—with somewhat of majesty in her stolid, even progress—the "Virginia" steamed on—down the harbor—past the river batteries—out into the Roads. Steadily she kept her way, heading straight for the "Cumberland;" and close to her stuck the frail wooden boats that a single shell might have shattered. On she went—into full range. Then suddenly, as if from one match, shipping and shore batteries belched forth the great shells hurtling over her, hissing into the water—bounding from her side like raindrops from a rock! On she headed—straight for the "Cumberland;" the crew of that ship steadily working their heated guns and wondering at the strange, silent monster that came on so evenly, so slowly—so regardless alike of shot and shell. Suddenly she spoke.

The terrible shell from her bow-gun tore the huge frigate from stern to bow; driving in her quarter, dismounting guns and scattering death along its course. Shocked and staggered, Uncle Sam's tars still stuck to their work. Once more the "Cumberland" delivered her whole broadside, full in her enemy's face at pistol range. It was her death volley. The submerged ram had struck home. A great rent yawned in the ship's side; she filled rapidly—careened —went down by the bows—her flag still flying—her men still at quarters!

On past her—scarce checked in her deadly-slow course—moved the "Virginia." Then she closed on the "Congress," and one terrific broadside after another raked the frigate; till, trembling like a card-house, she hauled down her colors and raised the white flag. The "Beaufort" ranged alongside and received the flag of the "Congress," and her captain, William R. Smith, and Lieutenant Pendergrast as prisoners of war. These officers left their side-arms on the "Beaufort" and returned to the "Congress;" when—notwithstanding the white flag—a hot fire was opened from shore upon the "Beaufort," and she was compelled to withdraw. Lieutenant Robert Minor was then sent in a boat from the "Virginia" to fire the frigate; but was badly wounded by a Minié-ball, from under the white flag; and Captain Buchanan was seriously hit in the leg by the same volley. Then it was determined to burn the "Congress" with hot shot.

There is no room for comment here; and no denial of these facts has ever been made, or attempted.

Meanwhile, the frigates "Minnesota," "St. Lawrence" and "Roanoke" had advanced and opened fire on the "Virginia;" but upon her approach to meet it, they retired under the guns of the fort; the "Minnesota" badly damaged by the heavy fire of her antagonist, while temporarily aground.

Next day the "Virginia" had a protracted but indecisive fight with the "Monitor;" the latter's lightness preventing her being run down and both vessels seeming equally impenetrable. Later in the day the victorious ship steamed back to Norfolk, amid the wildest enthusiasm of its people. The experiment had proved a success beyond the wildest expectation: and a new era seemed opened in naval warfare.

But however great the meed of praise deserved by the iron ship and her crew, at least as much was due to those of the wooden gun-boats that had so gallantly seconded her efforts. All day long had those frail shells been urged into the thickest of that terrific fire. Shot flew by, over and through them; and it seemed miraculous that they were not torn into shreds!

The success of the "Virginia," while it gave food for much comment at the North and in Europe, had the effect of stimulating the Department to renewed exertions elsewhere. At the same time it raised the navy greatly in the estimation of the people, who began now to see of what material it was composed, to accomplish so much with such limited means and opportunity. And this opinion was to be strengthened, from time to time, by the brilliant flashes of naval daring that came to illumine some of the darkest hours of the war.

Who does not remember that defense of Drewry's Bluff when Eben Farrand had only three gunboat crews and *three hastily mounted guns,* with which to drive back the heavy fleet that knew Richmond city lay helpless at its mercy?

And those desperate, yet brilliant fights off New Orleans, against every odds of metal, numbers, and worse, of internal mismanagement. Do they not illustrate the character of the navy, and bring it out in bold relief of heroism? Nor should we forget the brief but brilliant life of the "Arkansas"—born in danger and difficulty; surrounded on every side by numberless active foes; and finally dying, not from the blow of an enemy, but from the fault of those who sent her forth unfinished and incomplete!

Those trying times recall the conduct of Captain Lynch and his squadron of shells; and of the veteran Cooke in the batteries, on the dark day that lost Roanoke Island. Nor may we lose sight of the splendid conduct of that latter grim old seadog, when, returning wounded and prison-worn, he bore down on Plymouth in the "Albemarle" and crushed the Federal gunboats like egg-shells.

And conspicuous, even among these fellow-sailors, stands John Taylor Wood. Quick to plan and strong to strike, he ever and anon would collect a few trusty men and picked officers; glide silently out from Richmond, where his duties as colonel of cavalry on the President's staff chained him most of the time. Soon would come an echo from the frontier, telling of quick, sharp struggle; victorious boarding and a Federal gunboat or two given to the flames. I have already alluded to his dashing raid upon the fishery fleet; but his cunning capture of the gunboats in the Rappahannock, or his cool and daring attack on the "Underwriter," during Pickett's movement on Newberne, would alone give him undying reputation.

The United States had a navy in her waters that would class as the third maritime power of the world; and this she rapidly increased by every appliance of money, skill and energy. She bought and built ships and spent vast sums and labor in experiments in ordnance, armoring and machinery. As result of this, the Federal navy, at the end of the second year of the war, numbered some 390 vessels of all grades, carrying a fraction over 3,000 guns. Before the end of the war it had increased to near 800 vessels of war of all grades; the number of guns had doubled and were infinitely heavier and more effective; and the number of tenders, tugs, transports and supply ships would have swelled the navy list to over 1,300 vessels.

To meet this formidable preparation, the Confederate Navy Department in May, '61, had *one gulf steamer* in commission; had the fragments of the Norfolk Navy Yard; the refuse of the harbor boats of Charleston, New Orleans, Savannah and Mobile to select from; and had, besides, the neglect of Congress and the jealousy of the other branch of the service.

Spite of all these drawbacks, the rare powers of the navy officers forced themselves into notice and use.

Before the close of the war, the only two rolling-mills in the Confederacy were in charge of navy officers. They built powder-mills and supplied their own demands; and, to a great extent, those of the army. They established rope-walks and became the seekers for the invaluable stores of niter and coal that both branches of the service so much needed. More than this, they made from nothing— and in spite of constant losses from exposure to the enemy and incomplete supplies—a fleet of iron-clads numbering at one time nine vessels; and a wooden navy at the same moment reaching some thirty-five.

But these—scattered over the vast area of water courses, far from supporting each other—were unable to cope with the superior strength of metal and construction brought against them.

That much-discussed torpedo system, too—regarding the utility of which there was such diversity of opinion—had its birth and perfection in the navy. It was a service of science and perseverance; frequently of exposure to every peril. It required culture, nerve and administrative ability; and it was managed in the main with success. Still the results were hardly commensurate with the outlay involved; for though James river, some of the western streams, and Charleston harbor were literally sown with torpedoes, yet only in rare and isolated instances—such as the "De Kalb" and "Commodore Jones"—did the results equal the expectation. Thousands of tons of valuable powder, much good metal and more valuable time at the work-shops were expended on torpedoes; and, on the whole, it is very doubtful if the amount destroyed was not more than balanced by the amount expended.

Thus, with varying fortunes—but with unceasing endeavor and unfailing courage—the navy worked on. That hue and cry against it—which a brilliant success would partially paralyze—soon gathered force in its intervals of enforced inaction. Just after the triumph of Hampton Roads was, perhaps, the brightest hour for the navy in public estimation. People then began to waver in their belief that its administration was utterly and hopelessly wrong; and to think that its chief had not perhaps sinned quite as much as he had been sinned against.

The old adage about giving a bad name, however, was more than illustrated in Mr. Mallory's case. He had no doubt been unfortunate; but that he really was guilty of one-half the errors and mishaps laid at his door was simply impossible. Not taking time—and, perhaps, without the requisite knowledge—to compare the vast discrepancy of force between the two governments, the masses only saw the rapid increase of the Federal navy and felt the serious effects of its efficiency. Then they grumbled that the Confederate secretary—with few work-shops, scattered navy-yards, little money and less transportation—did not proceed *pari passu* to meet these preparations. Every result of circumstance, every accident, every inefficiency of a subordinate was visited upon Mr. Mallory's head. Public censure always makes the meat it feeds on; and the secretary soon became the target for shafts of pitiable malice, or of unreflecting ridicule. When the enemy's gunboats—built at secure points and fitted out without stint of cost, labor or material—ascended to Nashville, a howl was raised that the Navy Department should have had the water defenses ready. True, Congress had appropriated half a million for the defenses of the Tennessee and Cumberland rivers; but the censorious public forgot that the money had been voted too late. Even then it was quite notorious, that in the red-tape system of requisition and delay that hedged the Treasury—an *appropriation* and the *money* it named were totally diverse things.

When New Orleans 'fell, curses loud and deep went up against the Navy Department. Doubtless there was some want of energy in push-ing the iron-clads there; but again in this case the money was voted very late; and even Confederate machine-shops and Confederate laborers could not be expected to give their material, time and labor entirely for nothing. Had Congress made the appropriations as asked, and had the money been forthcoming at the Treasury—New Orleans might not have fallen as she did.

Later still, when the "Virginia" was blown up on the evacuation of Norfolk, a howl of indignation was raised against Secretary, De-partment and all connected with it. A Court of Inquiry was called; and Commodore Tatnall himself demanded a court-martial, upon the first court not ordering one.

The facts proved were that the ship, with her iron coating and heavy armament, drew far too much water to pass the shoal at Har-rison's Bar—between her and Richmond. With Norfolk in the ene-my's hands, the hostile fleet pressing her—and with no point whence to draw supplies—she could not remain, as the cant went, "the grim sentinel to bar all access to the river." It was essential to lighten her, if possible; and the effort was made by sacrificing her splendid armament. Even then she would not lighten enough by two feet; the enemy pressed upon her, now perfectly unarmed; and Tatnall was forced to leave and fire her.

People forgot the noble achievements of the ship under naval guid-ance; that, if destroyed by naval men, she was the offspring of naval genius. With no discussion of facts, the cry against the navy went on, even after that splendid defense of Drewry's Bluff by Farrand, *which alone saved* Richmond!

As a pioneer, the "Virginia" was a great success and fully demonstrated the theory of her projector. But there were many points about her open to grave objections; and she was, as a whole, far inferior to the smaller vessels afterward built upon her model at Richmond. Armed with the same gun, there is little doubt but the "Monitor" would have proved—from her superior lightness and obedience to her helm—no less than from her more compact build— at least her equal. Officers on the "Virginia" shared in this belief of her advantages over her terrible antagonist.

On the whole, the experience of the war tells of honest endeavor and brilliant achievement, under surpassing difficulty, for the Confederate navy. That it was composed of gallant, noble-hearted men, none who were thrown with them can doubt; that they wrought heart and hand for the cause, in whatever strange and novel position, none ever did doubt.

They made mistakes. Who in army, or government, did not?

But from the day they offered their swords; through the unequal contest of the Sounds, the victorious one of Hampton Roads; pining for the sea in musty offices, or drilling green conscripts in sand batteries; marching steadily to the last fight at Appomattox—far out of their element—the Confederate sailors flinched not from fire nor fled from duty. Though their country grumbled, and detraction and ingratitude often assailed them; yet at the bitter ending no man nor woman in the broad South but believed they had done their *devoir*—honestly—manfully—well!

Who in all that goodly throng of soldiers, statesmen and critics—did more?

CHAPTER XXXI.

THE CHINESE-WALL BLOCKADE, ABROAD AND AT HOME.

Potent factor in sapping the foundations of Confederate hope and of Confederate credit, was the blockade.

First held in contempt; later fruitful mother of errors, as to the movements and intentions of European powers; ever the growing constrictor—whose coil was slowly, but surely, to crush out life—it became each year harder to bear :—at last unbearable!

At first, Mr. Lincoln's proclamation was laughed to scorn at the South. The vast extent of South Atlantic and Gulf coast—pierced with innumerable safe harbors—seemed to defy any scheme for hermetic sealing. The limited Federal navy was powerless to do more than keep loose watch over ports of a few large cities; and, if these were even effectually closed, it was felt that new ones would open, on every hand, inviting the ventures of enterprising sailors.

This reasoning had good basis, at first; and—had the South made prompt and efficient use of opportunity and resources at hand, by placing credits abroad and running in essential supplies—the result of the first year's blockade might largely have nullified its effect, for the last three. But there seemed indurated contempt for the safety-bearing look ahead; and its very inefficiency, at the outset, of the blockade lulled the South into false security.

The preceding pages note the rapid and vast growth of the Union navy; but the South misjudged—until error had proved fatal—that enterprise and "grit" of Yankee character; that fixed steadiness of purpose which forced both, ever, into most resultful effort. And, so gradual were appreciable results of this naval growth; so nearly imperceptible was the actual closing of southern ports—that the masses of the people realized no real evil, until it had long been accomplished fact.

Already record has been made of the urgence on Government of sending cotton abroad, and importing arms, munitions and clothing, which ordinary foresight declared so needful. But—only when the proper moment had long passed—was the then doubtful experiment made.

A twin delusion to the kingship of cotton besotted the leaders as to the blockade. Arguing its illegality equal to its inefficiency, they were convinced that either could be demonstrated to Europe. And here let us glance briefly at the South's suicidal foreign policy; and at the feeling of other people regarding it.

Under the Treaty of Paris, no blockade was *de facto*, or to be recognized, unless it was demonstrated to be effectual closing of the port, or ports, named. Now, in the South, were one or two ships, at most, before the largest ports; with an average of one vessel for every hundred miles of coast! And so inefficient was the early blockade of Charleston, Wilmington and New Orleans, that traders ran in and out, actually with greater frequency than before those ports were proclaimed closed. Their Government declared—and the southern people believed—that such nominal blockade would not be respected by European powers; and reliant upon the kingship of cotton inducing early recognition, both believed that the ships of England and France—disregarding the impotent paper closure—would soon crowd southern wharves and exchange the royal fleece for the luxuries, no less than the necessaries, of life.

When the three first commissioners to Europe—Messrs. Yancey, Rost and Mann—sailed from New Orleans, on March 31, '61, their mission was hailed as harbinger to speedy fruition of these delusive thoughts, to which the wish alone was father. Then—though very gradually—began belief that they had reckoned too fast; and doubt began to chill glowing hopes of immediate recognition from Europe. But there was none, as yet, relative to her ultimate action. The successful trial trip of the "Nashville," Captain Pegram, C. S. N.—and her warm reception by the British press and people—prevented that. And, after every victory of the South, her newspapers were filled with praise from the press of England. But gradually— as recognition did not come—first wonder, then doubt, and finally despair took the place of certainty.

When Mr. Yancey came back, in disgust, and made his plain statement of the true state of foreign sentiment, he carried public opinion to his side; and—while the Government could then do

18

nothing but persist in effort for recognition, now so vital—the people felt that dignity was uselessly compromised, while their powerless representatives were kept abroad, to knock weakly at the back door of foreign intervention.

Slight reaction came, when Mason and Slidell were captured on the high seas, under a foreign flag. Mr. Seward so boldly defied the rampant Lion; Congress so promptly voted thanks to Captain Wilkes, for violating international law; the Secretary of the Navy—after slyly pulling down the blinds—so bravely patted him on the back—that the South renewed her hope, in the seeming certainty of war between the two countries. But she had calculated justly neither the power of retraction in American policy, nor Secretary Seward's vast capacity for eating his own words; and the rendition of her commissioners—with their perfectly quiet landing upon British soil—was, at last, accepted as sure token of how little they would accomplish. And, for over three years, those commissioners blundered on in thick darkness—that might not be felt; butting their heads against fixed policy at every turn; snubbed by subordinates—to whom alone they had access; yet eating, unsparingly and with seeming appetite, the bountiful banquet of cold shoulder!

It is not supposable that the people of the South realized to the full that humiliation, to which their State Department was subjecting them. Occasionally Mr. Mason, seeing a gleam of something which might some day be light, would send hopeful despatches; or before the hopeful eyes of Mr. Slidell, would rise roseate clouds of promise, light with bubbles of aid—intervention—recognition! Strangely enough, these would never burst until just after their description; and the secretary fostered the widest latitude in press-rumors thereanent, but deemed it politic to forget contradiction, when—as was invariably the case—the next blockade-runner brought flat denial of all that its precedent had carried.

Still, constant promises with no fulfillment, added to limited private correspondence with foreign capitals, begat mistrust in elusive theories, which was rudely changed to simple certainty.

Edwin DeLeon had been sent by Mr. Davis on a special mission to London and Paris, after Mr. Yancey's return; his action to be independent of the regularly established futility. In August, 1863, full despatches from him, to the southern President and State

Department, were captured and published in the New York papers. These came through the lines and gave the southern people the full and clear exposé of the foreign question, as it had long been fully and clearly known to their government.

This publication intensified what had been vague opposition to further retention abroad of the commissioners. The people felt that their national honor was compromised; and, moreover, they now realized that Europe had—and would have—but one policy regarding the Confederacy.

Diplomatically regarded, the position of the South was actually unprecedented. Europe felt the delicacy—and equally the danger—of interference in a family quarrel, which neither her theories nor her experience had taught her to comprehend. Naturally jealous of the growing power of the American Union, Europe may, moreover, have heard dictates of the policy of letting it exhaust itself, in this internal feud; of waiting until both sides—weakened, wearied and worn out—should draw off from the struggle and make intervention more nominal than needful. This view of "strict neutrality"—openly vaunted only to be practically violated—takes color from the fact of her permitting each side to hammer away at the other for four years, without one word even of protest!

Southern prejudice ever inclined more favorably toward France than England; the scale tilting, perhaps, by weight of Franco-Latin influence among the people, perhaps by belief in the suggested theories of the third Napoleon. Therefore, intimations of French recognition were always more welcomed than false rumors about English aid.

In the North also prevailed an idea that France might intervene—or even recognize the Confederacy—before colder England; but that did not cause impartial Jonathan to exhibit less bitter, or unreasoning, hatred of John Bull. Yet, as a practical fact, the alleged neutrality of the latter was far more operative against the South than the North. For—omitting early recognition of a blockade, invalid under the Treaty of Paris—England denied *both* belligerent navies the right to refit—or bring in prizes—at her ports. Now, as the United States had open ports and needed no such grace, while the South having no commerce thus afforded no prizes—every point of this decision was against her.

Equally favoring the North was the winking at recruiting; for, if men were not actually enlisted on British soil and under that flag, thousands of "emigrants"—males only; with expenses and bounty paid by United States recruiting agents—were poured out of British territory each month.

When France sent her circular to England and Russia, suggesting that the time had come for mediation, the former summarily rejected the proposition. Besides, England's treatment of the southern commissioners was coldly neglectful; and—from the beginning to the end of the Confederacy, the sole aid she received from England was personal sympathy in isolated instances. But British contractors and traders had tacit governmental permission to build ships for the rebels, or to sell them arms and supplies, at their own risks. And, spite of these well-known facts, northern buncombe never tired of assailing "the rebel sympathies" of England!

With somewhat of race sympathy between the two peoples, the French emperor's movements to feel the pulse of Europe, from time to time, on the question of mediation, kept up the popular delusion at the South. This was shared, to a certain extent, even by her government; and Mr. Slidell's highly-colored despatches would refan the embers of hope into a glow. But while Napoleon, the Little, may have had the subtlest head in Europe, he doubtless had the hardest; and the feeble handling by the southern commissioner, of that edged-tool, diplomacy, could have aroused only amusement in those subordinate officials, whom alone he reached.

The real policy of France was doubtless, from the beginning, as fixed as was that of England; and though she may have hesitated, for a time, at the tempting bait offered—monopoly of southern cotton and tobacco—the reasons coercing that policy were too strong to let her swallow it at last.

For the rest, Russia had always openly sympathized with the North; and other European nations had very vague notions of the merits of the struggle; less interest in its termination; and least of all, sympathy with what to them was mere rebellion.

And this true condition of foreign affairs, the Confederate State Department did know, in great part; should have known in detail; and owed it to the people to explain and promulgate. But for some occult reason, Mr. Benjamin refused to view the European landscape, except through the Claude Lorrain glass which Mr. Slidell persistently held up before him. The exposé of Mr. Yancey, the few sturdy truths Mr. Mason later told; and the detailed resumé sent by Mr. DeLeon and printed in the North—all these were ignored; and the wishes of the whole people were disregarded, that the line begun upon, should not be deviated from. There may have been something deeply underlying this policy; for Secretary Benjamin was clear-sighted, shrewd and well-informed. But what that something was has never been divulged; and the people—believing the Secretary too able to be deluded by his subordinate—revolted.

The foreign policy grew more and more into popular disfavor; the press condemned it, in no stinted terms; it permeated the other branches of the government and, finally, reacted upon the armies in the field. For the growing dislike of his most trusted adviser began to affect Mr. Davis; his ready assumption of all responsibility at the beginning having taught the people to look direct to him for all of good, or of evil, alike.

As disaster followed disaster to southern arms; as one fair city after another fell into the lap of the enemy; as the blockade drew its coil tighter and tighter about the vitals of the Confederacy—the cry of the people was raised to their chief; demanding the cause of it all. The first warm impulses of patriotic and inflammable masses had pedestaled him as a demigod. The revulsion was gradual; but, with the third year of unrelieved blockade, it became complete. And this was due, in part, to that proclivity of masses to measure men by results, rather than by their means for accomplishment; it was due in greater part, perhaps, to the President's unyielding refusal to sacrifice either his convictions, or his favorites, to popular clamor, however re-enforced by argument, or reason.

Mr. Davis certainly seemed to rely more upon Mr. Benjamin than any member of his Cabinet; and the public laid at that now unpopular official's door all errors of policy—domestic as well as foreign. Popular wrath ever finds a scape-goat; but in the very darkest hour Mr. Benjamin remained placid and smiling, his brow unclouded and his sleek, pleasant manner deprecating the rumbling of the storm he had raised, by his accomplishments and sophistries. When his removal was clamorously demanded by popular voice, his chief closed his ears and moved on unheeding—grave—defiant!

Calm retrospect shows that the Confederacy's commissioners were, from first to last, only played with by the skilled sophists of Europe. And, ere the end came, that absolute conviction penetrated the blockade; convincing the South that her policy would remain one of strict non-intervention.

After each marked southern success, would come some revival of recognition rumors; but these were ever coupled, now, with an important "if!" If New Orleans had not fallen; if we had won Antietam; if Gettysburg had been a victory—then we *might* have been welcomed into the family of nations. But over the mass of thinkers settled the dark conviction that Europe saw her best interest, in standing by to watch the sections rend and tear each other to the utmost. Every fiber either lost was so much subtraction from that balance of power, threatening to pass across the Atlantic. The greater the straits to which we reduce each other, said the South, the better will it please Europe; and the only faith in her at last, was that she hoped to see the breach permanent and irreconcilable, and with it all hopes of rival power die!

If the theory be correct, that it was the intent of the Great Powers to foster the chance of two rival governments on this continent, it seems short-sighted in one regard. For—had they really recognized the dire extremity, to which the South was at last brought, they should either have furnished her means, directly or indirectly, to prolong the strife; or should have intervened and established a broken and shattered duality, in place of the stable and recemented Union.

Nor can thinkers, on either side, cavil at Europe's policy during that war; calculating, selfish and cruel as it may seem to the sentimentalist. If corporations really have no bowels, governments can not be looked to for nerves. Interest is the life blood of their systems; and interest was doubtless best subserved by the course of the Great Powers. For the rumors of destitution and of disaffection in France and England—caused by the blockade-begotten "cotton famine—that crept through the Chinese wall, were absurdly magnified, both as to their proportions and their results. And the sequel proved that it was far cheaper for either nation to feed a few thousand idle operatives—or to quell a few incipient bread riots—than to unsettle a fixed policy, and that at the risk of a costly foreign war.

There was bitter disappointment in the South, immediately succeeding dissipation of these rosy, but nebulous, hopes in the kingship of cotton. Then reaction came—strong, general and fruitful. Sturdy "Johnny Reb" yearned for British rifles, shoes, blankets and bacon; but he wanted them most of all, to *win* his own independence and to force its recognition!

There are optimists everywhere; and even the dark days of Dixie proved no exception to the rule. It was not unusual to hear prate of the vast benefits derived from the blockade; of the energy, resource and production, expressed under its cruel constriction! Such optimists—equally at fault as were their pessimistic opponents—pointed proudly to the powder-mills, blast-furnaces, foundries and rolling-mills, springing up on every hand. They saw the great truth that the internal resources of the South developed with amazing rapidity; that arms were manufactured and supplies of vital need created, as it were out of nothing; but they missed the true reason for that abnormal development, which was the dire stress from isolation. They rejoiced to very elation at a popular effort, spontaneous—unanimous—supreme! But they realized little that it was exhaustive as well.

Could these life-needs the South was compelled to create within, have been procured from without, they had not alone been far less costly in time, labor and money—but the many hands called from work equally as vital had not then been diverted from it. The South was self-supporting, as the hibernator that crawls into a stump to subsist upon its own fat. But that stump is not sealed up, and Bruin—who goes to bed in autumn, sleek and round, to come out a skeleton at springtime—quickly reproduces lost tissue. With the South, material once consumed was gone forever; and the drain upon her people—material—mental—moral—was permanent and fatal.

One reason why the result of the blockade—after it became actually effective—was not earlier realized generally at the South, was that private speculation promptly utilized opportunities, which the Government had neglected. What appeared huge overstock of clothing and other prime necessities had been "run in," while there was yet time; and before they had advanced in price, under quick depreciation of paper money. Then profits doubled so rapidly that —spite of their enhanced risk from more effective blockade—private ventures, and even great companies formed for the purpose, made "blockade-breaking" the royal road to riches. Almost every conceivable article of merchandise came to southern ports; often in quantities apparently sufficient to glut the market—almost always of inferior quality and manufactured specially for the great, but cheap, trade now sprung up.

Earlier ventures were content with profit of one, or two hundred per cent.; calculating thus for a ship and cargo, occasionally captured. But as such risk increased and Confederate money depreciated, percentage on blockade ventures ran up in compound ratio; and it became no unusual thing for a successful investment to realize from fifteen hundred to two thousand per cent. on its first cost.

Still, even this profit as against the average of loss—perhaps two cargoes out of five—together with the uncertain value of paper money, left the trade hazardous. Only great capital, ready to renew promptly every loss, could supply the demand—heretofore shown to have grown morbid, under lost faith in governmental credit. Hence sprung the great blockade-breaking corporations, like the Bee Company, Collie & Co., or Fraser, Trenholm & Co. With capital and credit unlimited; with branches at every point of purchase, reshipment and entry; with constantly growing orders from the departments—these giant concerns could control the market and make their own terms.

Their growing power soon became quasi dictation to Government itself; the national power was filtered through these alien arteries; and the South became the victim—its Treasury the mere catspaw—of the selfsame system, which clear sight and medium ability could so easily have averted from the beginning!

Even when pressure for supplies was most dire and Government had become almost wholly dependent for them upon the monopoly octopus—it would not move. Deaf to urgent appeals of its trusted officers, to establish a system of light, swift blockade-runners, the Department admitted their practical necessity, by entering into a limited partnership with a blockade-breaking firm. And, it must go without saying that the bargain driven was like the boy's: "You and I will each take half and the rest we'll give to Anne!"

As noted, in considering finance, the mania for exchanging paper money for something that could be enjoyed, grew apace as the war progressed. Fancy articles for dress, table luxuries and frippery of all sorts came now into great demand. Their importation increased to such bulk as, at last, to exclude the more necessary parts of most cargoes; and not less to threaten complete demoralization of such minority as made any money. It may seem a grim joke;—the starving, tattered—moribund Confederacy passing sumptuary laws, as had Venice in her recklessness of riches! But, in 1864, a law was necessitated against importation of all articles, not of utility; forbidden luxuries being named per schedule. That its constant evasion —if not its open defiance—was very simple, may be understood; for the blockade firms had now become a power coequal with Government, and exceptions were listed, sufficient to become the rule.

And so the leeches waxed fat and flourished on the very life-blood of the cause, that represented to them—opportunity! And, whatever has been said of speculators at Richmond, they were far less culpable than these, their chiefs; for, without the arch-priests of greed, speculation would have died from inanition. The speculators were most hungry kites; but their maws were crammed by the great vultures that sat at the coast, blinking ever out over the sea for fresh gains; with never a backward glance at the gaunt, grim legions behind them—naked—worn—famished, but unconquered still!

Transportation needs have been noted, also. No department was worse neglected and mismanaged than that. The existence of the Virginia army wholly depended on a single line, close to the coast and easily tapped. Nor did Government's seizure of its control, in any manner remedy the evil. Often and again, the troops around Richmond were without beef—once for twelve days at a time; they were often without flour, molasses or salt, living for days upon corn-meal alone! and the ever-ready excuse was want of transportation!

Thousands of bushels of grain would ferment and rot at one station; hundreds of barrels of meat stacked at another, while the army starved because of "no transportation!" But who recalls the arrival of a blockader at Charleston, Savannah, or Wilmington, when its ventures were not exposed at the auctions of Richmond, in time unreasonably short!

These facts are not recalled in carping spirit; nor to pronounce judgment just where the blame for gross mismanagement, or favoritism should lie. They are recorded because they are historic truth; because the people, whom they oppressed and ruined—saw, felt and angrily proclaimed them so; because the blockade mismanagement was twin-destroyer with the finance, of the southern cause.

The once fair cities of Charleston, Savannah and Wilmington suffered most from the blockade, both in destruction of property and demoralization of their populations. The first—as "hot-bed of treason" and equally from strategic importance—was early a point of Federal desire; but the fleet had been compelled to stand idly by and witness the bloodless reduction of Sumter. Later—when strengthened armaments threatened constant attack—Lee and Beauregard had used every resource to strengthen defenses of the still open port. What success they had, is told by the tedious and persistent bombardment—perhaps unexampled in the history of gunnery; surely so in devices to injure non-combatant inhabitants.

On the 30th January, '63, the two slow, clumsy and badly-built rams, under Captain Ingraham—of Martin Koszta fame—attacked the blockading squadron and drove the Union flag completely from the harbor; but re-enforced by iron-clads, it returned on the 7th of April. Again, after a fierce battle with the fort, the Federal fleet drew off, leaving the "Keokuk" monitor sunk; only to concentrate troops and build heavy batteries, for persistent attempt to reduce the devoted city. The history of that stubborn siege and defense, more stubborn still; of the woman-shelling "swamp-angel" and the "Greek-fire;" of the deeds of prowess that gleamed from the crumbling walls of Charleston—all this is too familiar for repetition. Yet, ever and again—through wooden mesh of the blockade-net and its iron links, alike—slipped a fleet, arrowy little blockader into port. And with what result has just been seen!

Wilmington—from long and shoal approach to her proper port—was more difficult still to seal up effectually. There—long after every other port was closed—the desperate, but wary, sea-pigeon would evade the big and surly watcher on the coast. Light draught, narrow, low in the water, swift and painted black—these little steamers were commanded by men who knew every inch of coast; who knew equally that on them depended life and death—or more. With banked fires and scarce-turning wheels, they would drop down the Cape Fear, at night, to within a hundred yards of the looming blockade giant. Then, putting on all steam, they would rush by him, trusting to speed and surprise to elude pursuit and distract his aim— and ho! for the open sea.

This was a service of keen excitement and constant danger;

demanding clear heads and iron nerves. Both were forthcoming, especially from navy volunteers; and many were " the hair-breadth 'scapes" that made the names of Maffit, Wilkinson and their confreres, household words among the rough sea-dogs of Wilmington.

Savannah suffered least of the fair Atlantic sisterhood, from the blockade. The early capture of her river forts blocked access to her wharves, almost effectually; though occasional steamers still slipped up to them. Yet, she was in such easy reach of her more open neighbors, as to reap part of the bad fruits with which they were so overstocked.

These proud southern cities had ever been famed throughout the land, for purity, high tone and unyielding pride. At the first bugle-blast, their men had sprung to arms with one accord; and the best blood of Georgia and the Carolinas was poured out from Munson's Hill to Chickamauga. Their devoted women pinched themselves and stripped their homes, to aid the cause so sacred to them; and on the burning sand-hills of Charleston harbor, grandsire and grandson wrought side by side under blistering sun and galling fire alike!

How bitter, then, for those devoted and mourning cities to see their sacred places made mere marts; their cherished fame jeopardied by refuse stay-at-homes, or transient aliens; while vile speculation—ineffably greedy, when not boldly dishonest—smirched them with lowest vices of the lust for gain! Shot-riddled Charleston—exposed and devastated—invited nothing beyond the sterner business of money-getting. There, was offered neither the leisure nor safety for that growth of luxury and riotous living, which at one time possessed Wilmington.

Into that blockade mart would enter four ships to one at any other port; speculators of all grades and greediness flocked to meet them; and money was poured into the once-quiet town by the million. And, with tastes restricted elsewhere, these alien crowds reveled in foreign delicacies, edibles and liquors, of which every cargo was largely made up. The lowest attaché of a blockade-runner became a man of mark and lived in luxury; the people caught the infection and—where they could not follow—envied the fearful example set by the establishments of the "merchant princes."

Was it strange that the people of leaguered Richmond—that the worn hero starving in the trench at Petersburg—came to execrate those vampires fattening on their life-blood; came to regard the very name of blockade-runner as a stench and the government that leagued with it as a reproach? For strangely-colored exaggerations of luxury and license were brought away by visitors near the centers of the only commerce left. Well might the soul of the soldier—frying his scant ration of moldy bacon and grieving over still more scant supply at his distant home—wax wroth over stories of Southdown mutton, brought in ice from England; of dinners where the *patés* of Strasbourg and the fruits of the East were washed down with rare Champagne.

Bitter, indeed, it seemed, that—while he crawled, footsore and faint, to slake his thirst from the roadside pool—while the dear ones at home kept in shivering life with cornbread—degenerate southerners and foreign leeches reveled in luxury untold, from the very gain that caused such privation!

This misuse of that blockade-running—which strongly handled had proved such potent agency for good—bred infinite discontent in army and in people alike. That misdirection—and its twin, mismanagement of finance—aided to strangle prematurely the young giant they might have nourished into strength;—

"And the spirit of murder worked in the very means of life!"

But the Chinese-wall blockade was tripartite; not confined to closing of the ocean ports. Almost as damaging, in another regard, were the occupation of New Orleans, and the final stoppage of communication with the trans-Mississippi by the capture of Vicksburg.

The Heroic City had long been sole point of contact with the vast productive tracts, beyond the great river. The story were twice-told of a resistance—unequaled even by that at Charleston and beginning with first Union access to the river, by way of New Orleans. But, in May, '62, the combined fleets of Porter and Farragut from the South, and Davis from the North, rained shot and shell into the coveted town for six terrible weeks. Failing reduction, they withdrew on June 24th; leaving her banners inscribed—*Vicksburg victrix!*

In May of the next year, another concentration was made on the "key of the Mississippi;" General Grant marching his army one hundred and fifty miles from its base, to get in rear of Vicksburg and cut off its relief. The very audacity of this plan may blind the careless thinker to its bad generalship; especially in view of the success that at last crowned its projector's hammer-and-tongs style of tactics. His reckless and ill-handled assaults upon the strong works at Vicksburg—so freely criticised on his own side, by army and by press—were but preface of a volume, so bloodily written to the end before Petersburg.

Under ordinary combinations, Johnston had found it easy to crush Grant and prevent even his escape to the distant base behind him. But, unhappily, Government would not re-enforce Johnston— even to the very limited extent it might; and Mr. Davis promoted Pemberton to a lieutenant-generalcy and sent him to Vicksburg. But this is no place to discuss General Pemberton's abilities—his alleged disobedience of orders—the disasters of Baker's creek and Big Black; or his shutting up in Vicksburg, hopeless of relief from Johnston. Suffice it, the dismal echo of falling Vicksburg supplemented the gloom after Gettysburg; and the swift-following loss of Port Hudson completed the blockade of the Mississippi; and made the trans-river territory a foreign land!

The coast of Maine met the waters of the Ohio, at the mouth of the Mississippi; and two sides of the blockade triangle were completed, almost impervious even to rebel ingenuity and audacity. It needed but careful guard over the third side—the inland border from river to coast—to seal up the South hermetically, and perfect her isolation.

That perfection had long been attempted. Fleets of gunboats ploughed the Potomac and all inland water-approaches to the southern frontier. A shrewd detective system, ramifying from Washington, penetrated the "disaffected" counties of Maryland; spying equally upon shore and household. The borders of Tennessee and Kentucky were closely picketed; and no means of cunning, or perseverance, were omitted to prevent the passage of anything living, or useful, into the South. But none of this availed against the untiring pluck and audacity of the inland blockade-breakers. Daily the lines were forced, spies evaded, and bold "Johnny Reb" passed back and forth, in almost guaranteed security.

Such ventures brought small supplies of much-needed medicines, surgical instruments and necessaries for the sick. They brought northern newspapers—and often despatches and cipher letters of immense value; and they ever had tidings from home that made the heart of exiled Marylander, or border statesman sing for joy, even amid the night-watches of a winter camp.

Gradually this system of "running the bloc." systematized and received governmental sanction. Regular corps of spies, letter-carriers and small purchasing agents were organized and recognized by army commanders. Naturally, these also made hay while the sun shone; coming back never—whatever their mission—with empty hands. Shoes, cloth, even arms—manufactured under the very noses of northern detectives and, possibly, with their connivance—found ever-ready sale. The runners became men of mark—many of them men of money; for, while this branch never demoralized like its big rival on the coast, the service of Government was cannily mixed with the service of Mammon.

Late in the war—when all ports were closed to its communication with agents abroad, the Richmond Government perfected this spy system, in connection with its signal corps. This service gave scope for tact, fertility of resource and cool courage; it gave many a brave fellow, familiar with both borders, relief from camp monotony, in the fresh dangers through which he won a glimpse of home again; and it gave a vast mass of crude, conflicting information, such as must come from rumors collected by men in hiding. But its most singular and most romantic aspect was the well-known fact, that many women essayed the breaking of the border blockade. Almost all of them were successful; more than one well nigh invaluable, for the information she brought, sewed in her riding-habit, or coiled in her hair. Nor were these coarse camp-women, or reckless adventurers. Belle Boyd's name became historic as Moll Pitcher; but others are recalled —petted belles in the society of Baltimore, Washington and Virginia summer resorts of yore—who rode through night and peril alike, to carry tidings of cheer home and bring back news that woman may best acquire. New York, Baltimore and Washington to-day boast of three beautiful and gifted women, high in their social ranks, who could—if they would—recite tales of lonely race and perilous adventure, to raise the hair of the budding beaux about them.

But it may be that the real benefits of "running the bloc." were counterbalanced by inseparable evils. The enhancement of prices and consequent depreciation of currency may not have felt this system appreciably; but it tempted immigration of the adventurous and vicious classes, while it presented the anomaly of a government trading on its enemy's currency to depreciation of its own. For the trade demanded greenbacks; and the Confederacy bought these—often the product of illicit traffic—from the runners themselves, at from twenty to *one thousand* dollars C. S., for one U. S. !

Such is the brief, and necessarily imperfect, glance at the triple blockade, which steadily aided the process of exhaustion and ruin at the South. Such were its undeniable effects upon the Government and the people. And that these, in part at least, might have been averted by bold foresight and prompt action—while the blockade was yet but paper—is equally undeniable!

With this, as with most salient features of that bitter—gallant—enduring struggle for life; with it, as in most mundane retrospects—the saddest memories must ever cluster about the "might have been!"

CHAPTER XXXII.

PRESS, LITERATURE AND ART.

However much of ability may have been engaged upon it, the press of the South—up to the events just preceding the war—had scarcely been that great lever which it had elsewhere become. It was rather a local machine than a great engine for shaping and manufacturing public opinion.

One main cause for this, perhaps, was the decentralization of the South. Tracts of country surrounding it looked up only to their chief city, and thence drew their information, and even their ideas on the topics of the day. But there it ceased. The principal trade of the South went directly to the North; and in return were received northern manufactures, northern books and northern ideas. Northern newspapers came to the South; and except for matters of local information, or local policy, a large class of her readers drew their inspiration chiefly from journals of New York—catholic in their scope as unreliable in their principles.

These papers were far ahead of those of the South—except in very rare instances—in their machinery for collecting news and gossip; for making up a taking whole; and in the no less important knowledge of manipulating their circulation and advertising patronage. The newspaper system of the North had been reduced to a science. Its great object was *to pay;* and to accomplish this it must force its circulation in numbers and in radius, and must become the medium of communicating with far distant points. Great competition—application of *il faut bien vivre*—drove the drones from the field and only the real workers were allowed to live.

In the South the case was entirely different. Even in the large cities, newspapers were content with a local circulation; they had a little-varying clientele which looked upon them as infallible; and their object was to consider and digest ideas, rather than to propagate, or manufacture them.

The deep and universal interest in questions immediately preceding the war, somewhat changed in the scope of the southern press. People in all sections had intense anxiety to know what others, in different sections, felt on vital questions that agitated them; and papers were thus forced, as it were, into becoming the medium for interchange of sentiment.

An examination of the leading journals of the South at this period will show that—whatever their mismanagement and want of business success—there was no lack of ability in their editorial columns. Such organs as the New Orleans *Delta*, Mobile *Advertiser*, Charleston *Mercury* and Richmond *Examiner* and *Whig* might have taken rank alongside of the best-edited papers of the country. Their literary ability was, perhaps, greater than that of the North; their discussions of the questions of the hour were clear, strong and scholarly, and possessed, besides, the invaluable quality of honest conviction. Unlike the press of the North, the southern journals were not hampered by any business interests; they were unbiased, unbought and free to say what they thought and felt. And say it they did, in the boldest and plainest of language.

Nowhere on the globe was the freedom of the press more thoroughly vindicated than in the Southern States of America. And during the whole course of the war, criticisms of men and measures were constant and outspoken. So much so, indeed, that in many instances the operations of the Government were embarrassed, or the action of a department commander seriously hampered, by hostile criticism in a paper. In naval operations, and the workings of the Conscript Law, especially was this freedom felt to be injurious; and though it sprang from the perfectly pure motive of doing the best for the cause—though the smallest southern journal, printed on straw paper and with worn-out type, was above purchase, or hush money— still it might have been better at times had gag-law been applied.

For, with a large proportion of the population of different sections gathered in huge army communities, their different newspapers reached the camps and were eagerly devoured. Violent and hostile criticisms of Government—even expositions of glaring abuses—were worse than useless unless they could be remedied; and when these came to be the text of camp-talk, they naturally made the soldiers think somewhat as they did.

19

Now, the greatest difficulty with that variously-constituted army, was to make its individuals the perfect machines—unthinking, unreasoning, only obeying—to which the perfect soldier must be reduced. "Johnny Reb" *would* think; and not infrequently, he would talk. The newspapers gave him aid and comfort in both breaches of discipline; and in some instances, their influence against the conscription and impressments was seriously felt in the interior. Still these hostilities had their origin in honest conviction; and abuses were held up to the light, that the Government might be made to see and correct them.

The newspapers but reflected the ideas of some of the clearest thinkers in the land; and they recorded the real and true history of public opinion during the war. In their columns is to be found the only really correct and indicative "map of busy life, its fluctuations and its vast concerns" in the South, during her days of darkness and of trial.

These papers held their own bravely for a time, and fought hard against scarcity of labor, material and patronage—against the depreciation of currency and their innumerable other difficulties. Little by little their numbers decreased; then only the principal dailies of the cities were left, and these began to print upon straw paper, wall papering—on any material that could be procured. Cramped in means, curtailed in size, and dingy in appearance, their publishers still struggled bravely on for the freedom of the press and the freedom of the South.

Periodical literature—as the vast flood of illustrated and unillustrated monthlies and weeklies that swept over the North was misnamed—was unknown in the South. She had but few weeklies; and these were sturdy and heavy country papers—relating more to farming than to national matters. Else they were the weekly editions of the city papers, intended for country consumption. Few monthly magazines—save educational, religious, or statistical ventures, intended for certain limited classes, were ever born in the South; and most of those few lived weakly and not long.

De Bow's *Review*, the *Southern Quarterly*, and the *Literary Messenger*, were the most noteworthy exceptions. The business interests of the larger towns supported the first—which, indeed, drew part of its patronage from the North. Neither its great ability nor the taste of its clientele availed to sustain the second; and the *Messenger*—long the chosen medium of southern writers of all ages, sexes and conditions— dragged on a wearisome existence, with one foot in the grave for many years, only to perish miserably of starvation during the war.

But any regular and systematized periodical literature the South never had. The principal reason doubtless is, that she had not the numerous class of readers for amusement, who demand such food in the North; and of the not insignificant class who did indulge in it, nine-tenths—for one reason, or another, preferred northern periodicals. This is not altogether unnatural, when we reflect that these latter were generally better managed and superior in interest—if not in tone —to anything the South had yet attempted. They were gotten up with all the appliances of mechanical perfection; were managed with business tact, and forced and puffed into such circulation as made the heavy outlay for first-class writers in the end remunerative.

On the contrary, every magazine attempted in the South up to that time had been born with the seeds of dissolution already in it. *Voluntary contributions*—fatal poison to any literary enterprise—had been their universal basis. There was ever a crowd of men and women among southern populations, who would write anywhere and anything for the sake of seeing themselves in print. And while there were many able and accomplished writers available, they were driven off by these Free-Companions of the quill—preferring not to write in such company; or, if forced to do it, to send their often anonymous contributions to northern journals. These two reasons— especially the last—availed to kill the few literary ventures attempted by more enterprising southern publishers. The first of these two in a great measure influenced the scarcity of book-producers, among a people who had really very few readers among them; and even had the number of these been larger, it seems essential to the increase of authors that there should be the constant friction of contact in float-ing literature.

Good magazines are the nurseries and forcing houses for authors; and almost every name of prominence in modern literature may be traced back along its course, as that of magazinist, or reviewer.

The South—whether these reasons for it be just or not, the fact is patent—had had but few writers of prominence; and in fiction es-pecially the names that were known could be numbered on one's fin-

gers. W. Gilmore Simms was at once the father of southern literature and its most prolific exemplar. His numerous novels have been
very generally read; and, if not placing him in the highest ranks of
writers of fiction, at least vindicate the claims of his section to force
and originality. He had been followed up the thorny path by many
who stopped half-way, turned back, or sunk forgotten even before
reaching that far.

Few, indeed, of their works ever went beyond their own boundaries; and those few rarely sent back a record. Exceptions there
were, however, who pressed Mr. Simms hard for his position on the
topmost peak; and most of these adventurous climbers were of the
softer sex.

John Esten Cooke had written a very clever novel of the olden
society, called "Virginia Comedians." It had promised a brilliant
future, when his style and method should both ripen; a promise that
had not, so far, been kept by two or three succeeding ventures
launched on these doubtful waters. Hon. Jere Clemens, of Alabama,
had commenced a series of strong, if somewhat convulsive, stories of
western character. "Mustang Gray" and "Bernard Lile," scenting
strongly of camp-fire and pine-top, yet had many advantages over
the majority of successful novels, then engineered by northern
publishers. Marion Harland, as her *nom de plume* went, was, however, the most popular of southern writers. Her stories of Virginia
home-life had little pretension to the higher flights of romance; but
they were pure, graphic and not unnatural scenes from every-day
life. They introduced us to persons we knew, or might have known;
and the people read them generally and liked them. Mrs. Ritchie
(Anna Cora Mowatt) was also prolific of novels, extracted principally
from her fund of stage experience. Piquant and bright, with a
dash of humor and more than a dash of sentiment, Mrs. Ritchie's
books had many admirers and more friends. The South-west, too,
had given us the "Household of Bouverie" and "Beulah;" and it
was reserved for Miss Augusta Evans, author of the latter, to furnish
the *only* novel—almost the only book—published within the South
during continuance of the war. The only others I can now recall—
emanating from southern pens and entirely made in the South—were
Mrs. A. de V. Chaudron's translation of Mülbach's "Joseph II.," and
Dr. Wm. Sheppardson's collection of "War Poetry of the South."

This is not an imposing array of prose writers, and it may be incomplete; but it is very certain that there are not many omissions.

In poetry, the warmer clime of the South would naturally have been expected to excel; but, while the list of rhymsters was longer than Leporello's, the *poets* hardly exceeded in number the writers of prose. Thompson, Meek, Simms, Hayne, Timrod and McCord were the few names that had gone over the border. Up to that time, however, the South had never produced any great poem, that was to stand *ære perennius*. But that there was a vast amount of latent poetry in our people was first developed by the terrible friction of war.

In the dead-winter watches of the camp, in the stricken homes of the widow and the childless, and in the very prison pens, where they were crushed under outrage and contumely—the souls of the southrons rose in song.

The varied and stirring acts of that terrible drama—its trying suspense and harrowing shocks—its constant strain and privations must have graven deep upon southern hearts a picture of that time; and there it will stand forever, distinct—indelible—etched by the mordant of sorrow!

Where does history show more stirring motives for poetry? Every rood of earth, moistened and hallowed with sacred blood, sings to-day a noble dirge, wordless, but how eloquent! No whitewashed ward in yonder hospital, but has written in letters of life its epic of heroism, of devotion, and of triumphant sacrifice!

Every breeze that swept from those ravished homes, whence peace and purity had fled before the sword, the torch and that far blacker—nameless horror!—each breeze bore upon its wing a pleading prayer for peace, mingled and drowned in the hoarse notes of a stirring cry to arms!

But not only did our people feel all this. They spoke it with universal voice—in glowing, burning words that will live so long as strength and tenderness and truth shall hold their own in literature.

For reasons thus roughly sketched, no great and connected effort had been made at the South before the war. Though there had been sudden and fitful flashes of rare warmth and promise, they had died before their fire was communicated. That the fire was there, latent and still, they bore witness; but it needed the rough and cruel friction of the war to bring it to the surface.

What the southron felt he spoke ; and out of the bitterness of his trial the poetry of the South was born.   It leaped at one bound from the overcharged brain of our people—full statured in its stern defiance mailed in the triple panoply of truth.

There was endless poetry written in the North on the war; and much of it came from the pens of men as eminent as Longfellow, Bryant, Whittier and Holmes.   But they wrote far away from the scenes they spoke of—comfortably housed and perfectly secure.   The men of the North wrote with their pens, while the men of the South wrote with their hearts !

A singular commentary upon this has been given us by Mr. Richard Grant White—himself a member of the committee.   In April, 1861, a committee of thirteen New Yorkers—comprising such names as Julian Verplanck, Moses Grinnell, John A. Dix and Geo. Wm. Curtis—offered a reward of five hundred dollars for a National Hymn !   What hope, feeling, patriotism and love of the cause had failed to produce—for the lineal descendants of the " Star Spangled Banner " were all in the South, fighting under the bars instead of the stripes—was to be drawn out by the application of a greenback poultice !   The committee advertised generally for five hundred dollars' worth of pure patriotism, to be ground out " in not less than sixteen lines, nor more than forty."

Even with this highest incentive, Mr. White tells us that dozens of barrelfuls of manuscript were rejected ; and not one patriot was found whose principles—as expressed in his poetry—were worth that much money !   Were it not the least bit saddening, the contemplation of this attempt to buy up fervid sentiment would be inexpressibly funny.

Memory must bring up, in contrast, that night of 1792 in Strasbourg, when the gray dawn, struggling with the night, fell upon the pale face and burning eyes of Rouget de Lisle—as with trembling hand he wrote the last words of the *Marseillaise.*   The mind must revert, in contrast, to those ravished hearths and stricken homes and decimated camps, where the South wrought and suffered and sang— sang words that rose from men's hearts, when the ore of genius fused and sparkled in the hot blast of their fervid patriotism !

Every poem of the South is a National Hymn !—bought not with dollars, but with five hundred wrongs and ten times five hundred precious lives !

To one who has not studied the subject, the vast number of southern war poems would be most surprising, in view of restricted means for their issue. Every magazine, album and newspaper in the South ran over with these effusions and swelled their number to an almost countless one. Many of them were written for a special time, event, or locality; many again were read and forgotten in the engrossing duties of the hour. But it was principally from the want of some systematized means of distribution that most of them were born to blush unseen.

Before my little collection—"South Songs, from the Lays of Later Days"—went to press, over nineteen hundred poems had accumulated on my hands! And since that time the number has greatly increased. There were battle odes, hymns, calls to arms, pæans and dirges and prayers for peace—many of them good, few of them great; and the vast majority, alas! wretchedly poor. Any attempted notice of their authors in limits like this would be sheer failure; and where many did so well, it were invidious to discriminate. The names of John R. Thompson, James Randall, Henry Timrod, Paul Hayne, Barron Hope, Margaret Preston, James Overall, Harry Lyndon Flash and Frank Ticknor had already become household words in the South, where they will live forever.

Wherever his people read anything, the classic finish of his "Latané," the sweet caress of his "Stuart" and the bugle-blast of his "Coercion" and "Word with the West," had assured John R. Thompson's fame. The liltful refrain of "Maryland, my Maryland" echoed from the Potomac to the Gulf; and the clarion-call James R. Randall so nobly used—"There's Life in the Old Land Yet!"—warmed every southern heart, by the dead ashes on its hearth. Who does not remember "Beechenbrook," that pure Vestal in the temple of Mars? Every tear of sympathy that fell upon its pages was a jewel above rubies, in the crown of its gentle author.

Paul Hayne had won already the hearts of his own readers; and had gained transatlantic meed, in Tennyson's declaration that he was "the sonneteer of America!" And the yearning sorrow in all eyes that looked upon the fresh mound, above what was mortal of tender Henry Timrod, was more eloquent of worth than costly monument, or labored epitaph.

But not only the clang of action and the freedom of stirring scenes produced the southern war-poems. Camp Chase and forts Warren and Lafayette contributed as glowing strains as any written. Those grim bastiles held the bodies of their unconquered inmates; while their hearts lived but in the memory of those scenes, in which their fettered hands were debarred further portion. Worn down by confinement, hunger and the ceaseless pressure of suspense; weakened by sickness and often oppressed by vulgar indignity—the spirit of their cause still lingered lovingly around them; and its bright gleams warmed and lighted the darkest recesses of their cells.

That bugle blast, "Awake and to horse, my brothers!", Teackle Wallis sent from the walls of Warren, when he was almost prostrated by sickness and mental suffering. Another poem, more mournful but with a beautiful thought of hope beyond, comes from that dismal prison-pen, Camp Chase. Colonel W. S. Hawkins, a brave Tennesseean, who was held there two long years, still kept up heart and ministered to his fellow-sufferers day and night. The close of the war alone released him, to drag his shattered frame to "his own, fair sunny land," and lay it in the soil he loved so well. But he has left a living monument; and the tender pathos of "The Hero without a Name"—and the flawless poetical gem that closes his "Last of Earth," will be remembered as long as the sacrifices of their noble author. The pent walls of other military prisons sent forth plaintive records of misery, as well as stirring strains of hope unconquered; but the two here named are easily first of the rebel-prisoner poets.

Dirges for the great dead became a popular form, in which the spirit of southern song poured itself out. I had in my collection no fewer than forty-seven monodies and dirges on Stonewall Jackson; some dozens on Ashby and a score on Stuart. Some of these were critically good; all of them high in sentiment; but Flash's "Jackson" —heretofore quoted, when noting that irremediable loss—stands incomparably above the rest. Short, vigorous, completely rounded—it breathes that high spirit of hope and trust, held by that warrior people; and, not alone the finest war dirge of the South, it is excelled by no sixteen lines in any language, for power, lilt and tenderness!

Perhaps Thompson's "Dirge for Ashby," Randall's song of triumph over dead John Pelham and Mrs. Margaret Preston's "Ashby," may rank side-by-side next to the "Jackson." The modest author of the last-named did not claim it, until the universal voice of her people called for her name; and it is noteworthy that large numbers of war-song writers hid from their just meed, behind the sheltering anonymous. And the universal characteristic of this dirge-poetry is not its mournful tenderness—while nothing could be more touching than that; but its strong expression of faith in the efficacy of the sacrifice and in the full atonement of the martyrdom!

The battle-breeze bore back to the writers no sound of weak wailing. It wafted only the sob of manly grief, tempered by a solemn joyousness; and—coming from men of many temperaments, amid wide-differing scenes and circumstance—every monody bears impress of the higher inspiration, that has its origin far beyond the realm of the narrow house!

Sacred to one and all—in the Dixie of yesterday, in the southern half of the cemented Union of to-day—is the memory of that past. Sweet and bitter commingled, as it is, we clasp it to our heart of hearts and know—that were it bitterer a thousand fold—it is ours still! So I may not leave the field of southern song, unnoting its noblest strain—its funeral hymn! Father Ryan's " Conquered Banner" is so complete in fulfillment of its mission, that we can not spare one word, while yet no word is wanting! Every syllable there finds it echo far down in every southern heart. Every syllable has added significance, as coming from a man of peace;—a priest of that church which ever held forth free and gentle hand to aid the cause of struggling freedom!

In hottest flashings of the fight; in toilsome marches of winter; in fearful famine of the trenches—the Catholic soldiers of the Confederacy ever acted the motto of the Douglas; their deeds ever said —" Ready! aye, ready!"

And, in fetid wards of fever hospital; in field-tents, where the busy knife shears through quivering flesh; on battle-ground, where shattered manhood lies mangled almost past semblance of itself; at hurried burial, where gory blanket, or rough board, makes final rest for some "Hero without a name; "—there ever, and ever tender and tireless, the priest of Rome works on his labor of love and consolation! And the gentlest daughter of the eldest church was there as well. All southern soldiers were brothers, in her eyes; children of the One Father. And that noble band of Sisters of Mercy—to which our every woman belonged; giving light and hope to the hospital, life itself to the cause—that band knew no confines of ministry—no barriers of faith, which made charity aught but one common heritage!

Over the border, too; in struggling Maryland, in leaguered Missouri, and far into the North, the Catholic clergy were friends of the southern cause. They ceased never openly to defend its justice; quietly to aid its sympathizers. They helped the self-exiled soldier to bear unaccustomed hardships, on the one side; carried to his lonely mother, on the other, tidings of his safety, or his glory, that "caused the heart of the widow to sing for joy!"

Fitting, then, it was that a father of that church should chant the requiem for the dead cause, he had loved and labored for while living; that Father Ryan should bless and bury its conquered banner, when the bitter day came that saw it "furled forever."

But is that proud flag—with the glory and the pride wrought into its folds, by suffering, honor and endurance unexcelled—really "furled forever?" The dust of centuries may sift upon it, but the moth and the mold may harm it not. Ages it may lie, furled and unnoted; but in her own good time, historic Justice shall yet unfold and throw it to the breeze of immortality; pointing to each glorious rent and to each holy drop that stains it!

The war-poetry of the South has been dwelt upon, perhaps, at too great length. But it was, in real truth, the literature of the South. To sum it up may be repeated, after a lapse of twenty-five years— that sentence from the preface to my "South Songs," which raised such ire among irreconcilables of the southern press :—" In prose of all kinds, the South stood still, during the war; perhaps retrograded. But her best aspiration, 'lisped in numbers, for the numbers came!'"

Even then her poetry proved that there was life—high, brave life —in the old land yet; even then it gave earnest that, when the bitter struggle for bread gave time for thought, reason and retrospect, southern literature would rise, in the might of a young giant, and shake herself wholly free from northern domination and convention.

In art and her twin sister, music, the South displayed taste and progress truly remarkable in view of the absorbing nature of her duties. Like all inhabitants of semi-tropic climes, there had ever been shown by her people natural love and aptitude for melody. While this natural taste was wholly uncultivated—venting largely in plantation songs of the negroes—in districts where the music-master was necessarily abroad, it had reached high development in several of the large cities. Few of these were large enough, or wealthy enough, to support good operas, which the wealth of the North frequently lured to itself; but it may be recalled that New Orleans was genuinely enjoying opera, as a necessary of life, long before New York deemed it essential to study bad translations of librettos, in warmly-packed congregations of thousands.

Mobile, Charleston, Savannah and other cities also had considerable latent music among their amateurs; happily not then brought to the surface by the fierce friction of poverty. And what was the musical talent of the Capital, has elsewhere been hinted. When the tireless daughters of Richmond had worked in every other way, for the soldiers themselves, they organized a system of concerts and dramatic evenings for benefit of their families. At these were shown evidences of individual excellence, truly remarkable; while their average displayed taste and finish, which skilled critics declared would compare favorably with any city in the country.

The bands of the southern army—so long as they remained existent as separate organizations—were indisputably mediocre, when not atrociously bad. But it must be recalled that there was little time to practice, even in the beginning; literally no chance to obtain new music, or instruments; and that the better class of men—who usually make the best musicians—always preferred the musket to the bugle. Nor was there either incentive to good music, or appreciation for it, among the masses of the fighters. The drum and fife were the best they had known " at musters; " and they were good enough still, to fight by. So, recalling the prowess achieved constantly, in following them, it may be wondered what possible results might have come from inspiration of a marine band, a Grafulla, or a Gilmore!

Likewise, in all art matters, the South was at least a decade behind her northern sisterhood. Climate, picturesque surrounding and natural warmth of character had awakened artistic sense, in many localities. But its development was scarcely appreciable, from lack of opportunity and of exemplar. The majority of southern girls were reared at their own homes; and art culture—beyond mild atrocities in crayon or water-color, or terrors bred of the nimble broiderer's needle—was a myth, indeed. A large number of young men— a majority, perhaps, of those who could afford it—received education at the

North. Such of these as displayed peculiar aptitude for painting, were usually sent abroad for perfecting; and returning, they almost invariably settled in northern cities, where were found both superior opportunities and larger and better-paying class of patrons. But, when the tug came, not a few of these errant youths returned, to share it with their native states; and some of them found time, even in the stirring days of war, to transfer to canvas some of its most suggestive scenes.

Of them, the majority were naturally about Richmond; not only as the great army center, but as the center of everything else. Among the latter were two favorite pupils of Leutze, William D. Washington and John A. Elder. Both Virginians, by birth and rearing, they had the great advantage of Dusseldorf training, while they were thoroughly acquainted and sympathetic with their subjects. Some of Washington's figure-pieces were very successful; finding ready sale at prices which, had they continued, might have made him a Meissonnier in pocket, as well as in local fame. His elaborate picture, illustrating the "Burial of Latané"—a subject which also afforded *motif* for Thompson's most classic poem—attracted wide attention and favorable verdict from good critics. Mr. Washington also made many and excellent studies of the bold, picturesque scenery of his western campaigning, along the Gauley and Kanawha.

Elder's pictures—while, perhaps, less careful in finish than those of his brother student—were nothing inferior as close character-studies of soldier-life. Their excellence was ever emphasized by prompt sale; and "The Scout's Prize" and the "Raider's Return" —both horse and landscape studies; as well as a ghastly, but most effective picture of the "Crater Fight" at Petersburg, made the young artist great reputation.

Washington's "Latané" had *post-bellum* reproduction, by the graver; becoming popular and widely-known, North and South. The three of Elder's pictures, named here, were purchased by a member of the British parliament; but, unfortunately, were destroyed in the fire of the *Dies iræ*. The two first were duplicated, after the peace; and they gained praise and successful sale in New York.

Mr. Guillam, a French student, worked carefully and industriously, at his Richmond studio; producing portraits of Lee, Jackson and others; which, having exaggerated mannerisms of the French school, still possessed no little merit. A remarkable life-size picture of General Lee, which produced much comment in Richmond, was done by a deaf-mute, Mr. Bruce. It was to have been bought by the State of Virginia; possibly from sympathy with the subject and the condition of the artist, rather than because of intrinsic merit as an art-work.

But, perhaps, the most strikingly original pictures the war produced were those of John R. Key, a Maryland lieutenant of engineers; one of those decendants of "The Star Spangled Banner," early noted in this chapter. Young, ambitious and but little educated in art, Mr. Key made up that lack in boldness of subject and treatment. His school was largely his own; and he went for his subjects far out of the beaten track, treating them afterward with marked boldness and dash.

"Drewry's Bluff" was a boldly-handled sketch of what the northern army persisted in calling "Fort Darling." It showed the same venturesome originality in color-use, the same breadth and fidelity that marked Mr. Key's later pictures of Sumter, Charleston harbor and scenes on the James river.

These pictures named in common, with minor sketches from pencils less known at that time—among them that of William L. Sheppard, now famous as graphic delineator of southern scenes—illustrate both the details of the unique war, and the taste and heart of those who made it. Amid battles, sieges and sorrows, the mimic world behind the Chinese wall revolved on axis of its own. War was the business of life to every man; but, in the short pauses of its active strife, were shown both the taste and talent for the prettiest pursuits of peace. And the apparently unsurmountable difficulties, through which these were essayed, makes their even partial development more remarkable still.

The press, the literature and the art of the Southern Confederacy—looked at in the light of her valor and endurance, shining from her hundred battle-fields—emphasize strongly the inborn nature of her people. And, while there were many whom the limits of this sketch leave unnamed, that sin of omission will not be registered against the author; for the men of the South—even in minor matters —did their work for the object and for the cause; not for self-illustration.

CHAPTER XXXIII.

WIT AND HUMOR OF THE WAR.

If it be true that Sir Philip Sidney, burning with fever of his death-wound, reproved the soldier who brought him water in his helmet, that "he wasted a casque-full on a dying man," then humor borrowed largely of heroism.

Many a ragged rebel—worn with hunger and anxiety for the cause, or for those absent loved ones who suffered for it—was as gallant as Sidney in the fray; many a one bore his bitter trial with the same gay heart.

We have seen that the southron, war-worn, starving, could pour out his soul in noble song. Equally plain is it, that he rose in defiant glee over his own sufferings; striving to drown the sigh in a peal of resonant laughter. For humorous poetry abounds among all southern war-collections; some of it polished and keen in its satire; most of it striking hard and "straight-from-the-shoulder" blows at some detected error, or some crying abuse.

One very odd and typical specimen of this was the "Confederate Mother Goose;" only catch verses of which appeared in the "Southern Literary Messenger," when under editorial charge of rare George Bagby. It was born of accident; several officers sitting over their pipes, around Bagby's editorial pine, scribbled in turn doggerel on some war subject. So good were a few of these hits that they astonished their unambitious authors, by appearance in the next issue of the magazine. As a record of war-humor, a few of them may be of interest at this late day. This one shows the great terror struck to the hearts of his enemies by the war-gong of General Pope:

> "Little Be-Pope, he came at a lope,
> 'Jackson, the Rebel,' to find him.
> He found him at last, then ran very fast,
> With his gallant invaders behind him!"

"Jackson's commissary" was a favorite butt for the shafts of rebel humor. Another "Mother Goose" thus pictures him:

> " John Pope came down to our town
> And thought him wondrous wise ;
> He jumped into a 'skeeter swamp
> And started writing lies.
> But when he found his lies were out—
> With all his might and main
> He changed his base to another place,
> And began to lie again ! "

This verse on McClellan does not go to prove that the South respected any less the humane warfare, or the tactical ability of him his greatest opponents declared " the North's best general."

> " Little McClellan sat eating a melon,
> The Chickahominy by,
> He stuck in his spade, then a long while delayed,
> And cried 'What a brave general am I ! ' "

Or this, embalming the military cant of the day :

> " Henceforth, when a fellow is kicked out of doors,
> He need never resent the disgrace ;
> But exclaim, ' My dear sir, I'm eternally yours,
> For assisting in changing my base ! ' "

Perhaps no pen, or no brush, in all the South limned with bolder stroke the follies, or the foibles, of his own, than did that of Innes Randolph, of Stuart's Engineer staff; later to win national fame by his " Good Old Rebel " song. Squib, picture and poem filled Randolph's letters, as brilliant flashes did his conversation. On Mr. Davis proclaiming Thanksgiving Day, after the unfortunate Tennessee campaign, Randolph versified the proclamation, section by section, as sample :

> " For Bragg did well. Ah ! who could tell
> What merely human mind could augur,
> That they would run from Lookout Mount,
> Who fought so well at Chickamauga ! "

Round many a smoky camp-fire were sung clever songs, whose humor died with their gallant singers, for want of recording memories in those busy days. Latham, Caskie and Page McCarty sent out some of the best of the skits; a few verses of one by the latter's floating to mind, from the snowbound camp on the Potomac, stamped by his vein of rollicking satire-with-a-tear in it :

"Manassas' field ran red with gore,
   With blood the Bull Run ran;
   The freeman struck for hearth and home,
         Or any other man!
   And Longstreet with his fierce brigade
   Stood in the red redan;
   He waved his saber o'er his head,
         Or any other man!
   Ah! few shall part where many meet,
   In battle's bloody van;
   The snow shall be their winding-sheet,
         Or any other man!"

Naturally enough, with a people whose nerves were kept at abnormal tension, reaction carried the humor of the South largely into travesty. Where the reality was ever somber, creation of the unreal found popular and acceptable form in satiric verse. Major Caskie—who ever went into battle with a smile on his lips—found time, between fights, for broad pasquinade on folly about him, with pen and pencil. His very clever parody of a touching and well-known poem of the time, found its way to many a camp-fire and became a classic about the Richmond "hells." It began:

"You can never win them back,
         Never, never!
   And you'd better leave the track
         Now forever!
   Tho' you 'cut' and 'deal the pack'
   And 'copper' every Jack,
   You'll lose 'stack' after 'stack'—
         Forever!"

Everything tending to bathos—whether for the cause, or against it—caught its quick rebuke, at the hands of some glib funmaker. Once an enthusiastic admirer of the hero of Charleston indited a glowing ode, of which the refrain ran:

Beau sabreur, beau canon,
   Beau soldat—Beauregard!

Promptly came another, and most distorted version; its peculiar refrain enfolding:

Beau Brummel, Beau Fielding,
   Beau Hickman—Beauregard!

As it is not of record that the commander of the Army of

Northern Virginia ever discovered the junior laureate, the writer will not essay to do so.

Colonel Tom August, of the First Virginia, was the Charles Lamb of Confederate war-wits; genial, quick and ever gay. Early in secession days, a bombastic friend approached Colonel Tom, with the query: "Well, sir, I presume your voice is still for war?"

To which the wit replied promptly: "Oh, yes, devilish still!"

Later, when the skies looked darkest and rumors of abandoning Richmond were wildly flying, Colonel August was limping up the street. A *quidnunc* hailed him:

"Well! The city is to be given up. They're moving the medical stores."

"Glad of it!" called back Colonel Tom—"We'll get rid of all this blue mass!"

From the various army camps floated out stories, epigrams and anecdotes unnumbered; most of them wholly forgotten, with only a few remembered from local color, or peculiar point. General Zeb Vance's apostrophe to the buck-rabbit, flying by him from heavy rifle fire: "Go it, cotton-tail! If I hadn't a reputation, I'd be with you!"—was a favorite theme for variations. Similarly modified to fit, was the protest of the western recruit, ordered on picket at Munson's Hill:

"Go yander ter keep 'un off! Wy, we'uns kem hyah ter fight th' Yanks; an' ef you'uns skeer 'un off, how'n thunder ez thar goan ter be a scrimmidge, no how?"

A different story—showing quick resource, wnere resources were lacking—is told of gallant Theodore O'Hara, who left the noblest poem of almost any war, "The Bivouac of the Dead." While he was adjutant-general, a country couple sidled shyly up to headquarters of his division, one day; the lady blushingly stating their business. It was the most important one of life: they wanted to marry. So, a council of war was held, no chaplain being available; and the general insisted on O'Hara tying the knot. Finally, he consented to try; the couple stood before him; the responses as to obedience and endowment were made; and there O'Hara stuck fast!

"Go on!" prompted the general—"The benediction."

The A. A. G. paused, stammered; then, raising his hand grandly, shouted in stentorian tones:

20

" In the name and by the authority of the Confederate States of North America, I proclaim you man and wife!"

A grim joke is handed down from the winter camps before Atlanta, when rations were not only worst but least. A knot round a mess-fire examined ruefully the tiny bits of moldy bacon, stuck on their bayonet-grills, when one hard old veteran remarked:

"Say, boys! Didn't them fellers wot died las' spring jest *git* th' commissary, though!"

Another, not very nice, still points equally the dire straits of the men, from unchanged clothing, and their grim humor under even that trial. Generals Lee and Ewell—riding through a quiet road in deep consultation, followed by members of their staff—came suddenly upon a North Carolinian at the roadside. Nude to the waist, and careless of the august presences near, the soldier paid attention only to the dingy shirt he held over the smoke of some smoldering brush. The generals past, an aide spurred up to the toilet-making vet, and queried sharply:

" Didn't you see the generals, sir? What in thunder are you doing?"

"Skirmishin'!" drawled the unmoved warrior—"An' I ent takin' no pris'ners, nuther!"

After this lapse of time—when retrospect shows but the gloom and sorrow which shadowed the dark "days of storm and stress," while none of the excitement and tension in them remains—it may seem incomprehensible that the South could laugh in song, while she suffered and fought and starved. Stranger still must it be to know that many a merry peal rang through the barred windows of the fortress-prisons of the North. Yet, many a one of the exchanged captives brought back a rollicking "prison glee;" and some sing, even to-day, the legend of "Fort Delaware, Del."

The "Prison Wails" of Thomas F. Roche, a Marylander long captive, is a close and clever parody on General Lytell's " I am dying, Egypt," which came through the lines and won warm admirers South. It describes prison discipline, diet and dirt, with keen point and broad grin. From its opening lines:

"I am busted, mother—busted!
  Gone th' last unhappy check;
And th' infernal sutlers' prices
  Make my pocket-book a wreck!—"

to the human, piteous plaint that ends it:

"Ah! Once more, among the lucky,
Let thy hopeful buy and swell;
Bankers and rich brokers aid thee!
Shell! sweet mother mine, Oh! shell!—"

the original is closely followed and equally distorted.

But strangest, amid all strange humors of the war, was that which echoed laughter over the leaguered walls of scarred, starving, desperate Vicksburg! No siege in all history tells of greater peril and suffering, borne with wondrous endurance and heroism, by men and women. It is a story of privation unparalleled, met by fortitude and calm acceptance which recall the early martyrdoms for faith! And, indeed, love of country grew to be a religion, especially with the women of the South, though happily none proved it by stress so dire as those of her heroic city; and they cherished it in the darkest midnight of their cause, with constancy and hope that nerved the strong and shamed the laggard.

That history is one long series of perils and privations—of absolute isolation—sufficient to have worn down the strongest and to have quenched even

The smile of the South, on the lips and the eyes—
Of her barefooted boys!

Yet, even in Vicksburg—torn by shot and shell, hopeless of relief from without, reduced to direst straits of hunger within—the supreme rebel humor rose above nature; and men toiled and starved, fought their hopeless fight and died—not with the stoicism of the fatalist, but with the cheerfulness of duty well performed! And when Vicksburg fell, a curious proof of this was found; a manuscript bill-of-fare, surmounted by rough sketch of a mule's head crossed by a human hand holding a Bowie-knife. That memorable *menu* reads:

HOTEL DE VICKSBURG, BILL OF FARE, FOR JULY, 1863.

Soup: Mule tail.

Boiled: Mule bacon, with poke greens; mule ham, canvassed.

Roast: Mule sirloin; mule rump, stuffed with rice; saddle-of-mule, *à l'armée.*

Vegetables: Boiled rice; rice, hard boiled; hard rice, any way.

Entrées: Mule head, stuffed *à la Reb;* mule beef, jerked *à la*

Yankie; mule ears, fricasseed *à la getch;* mule side, stewed—new style, hair on ; mule liver, hashed *à l'explosion.*

SIDE DISHES : Mule salad ; mule hoof, soused ; mule brains *à l'omelette ;* mule kidneys, *braisés* on ramrod ; mule tripe, on half (Parrot) shell ; mule tongue, cold, *à la* Bray.

JELLIES : Mule foot (3-to-yard) ; mule bone, *à la* trench.

PASTRY : Rice pudding, pokeberry sauce ; cottonwood-berry pie, *à la* iron-clad ; chinaberry tart.

DESSERT : White-oak acorns ; beech-nuts; blackberry-leaf tea; genuine Confederate coffee.

LIQUORS : Mississippi water, vintage 1492, very superior, $3; limestone water, late importation, very fine, $3.75; spring water, Vicksburg bottled up, $4.

Meals at few hours. Gentlemen to wait upon themselves. Any inattention in service should be promptly reported at the office.

JEFF DAVIS & CO., *Proprietors.*

CARD : The proprietors of the justly-celebrated Hotel de Vicksburg, having enlarged and refitted the same, are now prepared to accommodate all who may favor them with a call. Parties arriving by the river, or by Grant's inland route, will find Grape, Cannister & Co.'s carriages at the landing, or any depot on the line of entrenchments. Buck, Ball & Co. take charge of all baggage. No effort will be spared to make the visit of all as interesting as possible.

This capture was printed in the Chicago *Tribune,* with the comment that it was a ghastly and melancholy burlesque. There is really a train of melancholy in the reflection that it was so little of a burlesque; that they who could endure such a siege, on such fare, should have been compelled to bear their trial in vain. But the quick-satisfying reflection must follow of the truth, the heroism—the moral invincibility—of a people who could so endure and——laugh!

But it was not only from the soldiers and the camps that the humor of the South took its color. Spite of the strain upon its better part—from anxiety, hope-deferred and actual privation—the society of every city keeps green memories of brilliant things said and written, on the spur of excitement and contact, that kept the sense of the whole people keenly alert for any point—whether serious or ridiculous.

The society of the Capital was marked evidence of this. It preserved many epigrammatic gems; often coming from the better—and brighter—half of its composition. For Richmond women had long been noted for society ease and *aplomb*, as well as for quickness of wit; and now the social amalgam held stranger dames and maidens who might have shown in any *salon*.

A friend of the writer—then a gallant staff-officer; now a grave, sedate and semi-bald counsellor—had lately returned from European capitals; and he was, of course, in envied possession of brilliant uniform and equipment. At a certain ball, his glittering blind-spurs became entangled in the flowing train of a dancing belle—one of the most brilliant of *the* set. She stopped in mid-waltz; touched my friend on the broidered chevron with taper fingers, and sweetly said:

" Captain, may I trouble you to dismount ?"

Another noted girl—closely connected with the administration—made one of a distinguished party invited by Secretary Mallory to inspect a newly-completed iron-clad, lying near the city. It was after many reverses had struck the navy, causing—as heretofore shown—destruction of similar ships. Every detail of this one explained, lunch over and her good fortune drunk, the party were descending the steps to the captain's gig, when this belle stopped short.

"Oh! Mr. Secretary!" she smiled innocently—"You forgot to show us one thing!"

" Indeed ?" was the bland query—" Pray what was it ?"

To which came the startling rejoinder :

" Why your arrangement for blowing them up !"

There was one handsome and dashing young aide, equally noted for influence at division-headquarters, which sent him constantly to Richmond; and for persistent devotion, when there, to a sharp-witted belle with a great fortune. One night he appeared at a soiree in brand new uniform, his captain's bars replaced by the major's star on the collar. The belle, leaning on his arm wearily, was pouting; when another passed and said: "I congratulate you, major. And what are your new duties ?"

The officer hesitated only one instant, but that was fatal; for the lady on his arm softly lisped: "Oh! he is *Mrs.* General ——'s commissary, with the rank of major!"

It is needless to add that the epigram—unjust as it was—had its effect; and the belle was no more besieged.

But of all the bright coteries in Richmond society—its very arcanum of wit, brilliance and culture—rises to memory that wholly unique set, that came somehow to be called "the Mosaic Club." Organization it was none; only a clique of men and women—married as well as single—that comprised the best intellects and prettiest accomplishments of the Capital. Many of the ladies were Will Wyatt's "easy goers;" ever tolerant, genial and genuine at the *symposia* of the Mosaics, as they showed behind their *chevaux-de-frise* of knitting-needles elsewhere. Some of them have since graced happy and luxurious homes; some have struggled with poverty and sorrow as only true womanhood may struggle; some have fought out the battle of life, sleeping now at rest forever. But one and all then faced their duty—sad, bitter, uncongenial as it might be—with loyalty and tender truth; one and all were strong enough to put by somber things, when meet to do so, and enjoy to the full the better pleasures society might offer.

And the men one met wore wreaths upon their collars often; quite as likely *chevrons* of "the men" upon their sleeves. Cabinet ministers, poets, statesmen, artists, and clergymen even were admitted to the "Mosaics;" the only "*Open sesame!*" to which its doors fell wide being that patent of nobility stamped by brain and worth alone.

Without organization, without officers; grown of itself and meeting as chance, or winter inactivity along army lines dictated—the Mosaic Club had no habitat. Collecting in one hospitable parlor, or another—as good fortune happened to provide better material for the delighting "muffin-match," or the entrancing "waffle-worry," as Will Wyatt described those festal procedures—the intimates who chanced in town were bidden; or, hearing of it, came to the feast of waffles and the flow of coffee—real coffee! without bids. They were ever welcome and knew it; and they were likewise sure of something even better than muffins, or coffee, to society-hungry men from the camps. And once gathered, the serious business of "teaing" over, the fun of the evening began.

The unwritten rule—indeed, the only rule—was the "forfeit essay," a game productive of so much that was novel and brilliant, that no later invention of peace-times has equaled it. At each meeting two hats would be handed round, all drawing a question from the one, a word from the other; question and word to be connected in either a song, poem, essay, or tale for the next meeting.

Then, after the drawing for forfeits, came the results of the last lottery of brain; interspersed with music by the best performers and singers of the city; with jest and seriously-brilliant talk, until the wee sma' hours, indeed.

O! those nights ambrosial, if not of Ambrose's, which dashed the somber picture of war round Richmond, with high-lights boldly put in by master-hands! Of them were quaint George Bagby, Virginia's pet humorist; gallant, cultured Willie Meyers; original Trav Daniel; Washington, artist, poet and musician; Page McCarty, recklessly brilliant in field and frolic alike; Ham Chamberlayne, quaint, cultivated and colossal in originality; Key, Elder and other artists; genial, jovial Jim Pegram; Harry Stanton, Kentucky's soldier poet— and a score of others who won fame, even if some of them lost life —on far different fields. There rare "Ran" Tucker—later famed in Congress and law school—told inimitably the story of "The time the stars fell," or sang the unprecedented ballad of "The Noble Skewball," in his own unprecedented fashion!

It was at the Mosaic that Innes Randolph first sang his now famous "Good Old Rebel" song; and there his marvelous quickness was Aaron's rod to swallow all the rest. As example, once he drew from one hat the words, "Daddy Longlegs;" from the other, the question, "What sort of shoe was made on the Last of the Mohicans?" Not high wit these, to ordinary seeming; and yet apparent posers for sensible rhyme. But they puzzled Randolph not a whit; and—waiving his "grace" until the subsequent meeting, he rattled off extempore:

> " Old Daddy Longlegs was a sinner hoary
> And punished for his wickedness, according to the story.
> Between him and the Indian shoe, this likeness doth come in,
> One made a mock o' virtue, and one a moccasin ! "

Laughter and applause were, in mid-roar, cut by Randolph's voice calling:

Corollary first: If Daddy Longlegs stole the Indian's shoe to keep his foot warm, that was no excuse for him to steal his house, to keep his wigwam.

And again he broke down—only to renew—the chorus with:

Corollary second: Because the Indian's shoe did not fit ary Mohawk, was no reason that it wouldn't fit Narragansett!

Such, in brief retrospect was the Mosaic Club! Such in part the fun and fancy and frolic that filled those winter nights in Richmond, when sleet and mud made movements of armies, "Heaven bless us! a thing of naught!"

The old colonel—that staff veteran, so often quoted in these pages —was a rare, if unconscious humorist. Gourmet born, connoisseur by instinct and clubman by life habit, the colonel writhed in spirit under discomfort and camp fare, even while he bore both heroically in the flesh; his two hundred and sixty pounds of it! Once, Styles Staple and Will Wyatt met him, inspecting troops in a West Virginia town; and they received a long lecture, *à la* Brillat Savarin, on enormities of the kitchen.

"And these people have fine wines, too," sadly wound up the colonel. "Marvelous wines, egad! But they don't know how to let you enjoy them!"

"'Tis a hard case," sympathized Styles, "I do hear sometimes of a fellow getting a stray tea, but as for a dinner! It's no use, colonel; these people either don't *dine* themselves, or they imagine we don't."

"Did it ever strike you," said the colonel, waxing philosophic, "that you *can't* dine in but two places south of the Potomac? True, sir. Egad! You may stumble upon a country gentleman with a plentiful larder and a passable cook, but then, egad, sir! he's an oasis. The mass of the people South don't live, sir! they vegetate—vegetate and nothing else. You get watery soups. Then they offer you mellow madeira with some hot, beastly joint; and oily old sherry with some confounded stew. Splendid materials—materials that the hand of an artist would make luscious—egad, sir; *luscious*— utterly ruined in the handling. It's too bad, Styles, too bad!"

"It is, indeed," put in Wyatt, falling into the colonel's vein, "too bad! And as for steaks, why, sir, there is not a steak in this whole country. They stew them, colonel, actually *stew beefsteaks!* Listen to the receipt a 'notable housewife' gave me: 'Put a juicy steak, cut two inches thick, in a saucepan; cover it well with water; put in a large lump of lard and two sliced onions. Let it simmer till the water dries; add a small lump of butter and a dash of pepper —and it's done!' Think of that, sir, for a *bonne bouche!*"

"Good God!" ejaculated the colonel, with beads on his brow. "I have seen those things, but I never knew how they were done! I shall dream of this, egad! for weeks."

" Fact, sir," Wyatt added, " and I've a theory that no nation deserves its liberties that stews its steaks. Can't gain them, sir! How can men legislate—how can men fight with a pound of stewed abomination holding them like lead? ' Bold and erect the Caledonian stood,' but how long do you think he would have been ' bold,' if they had stewed his ' rare beef' for him? No, sir! mark my words: the nation that stews its beefsteaks contracts its boundaries! As for an omelette—"

" Say no more, Will!" broke in the colonel solemnly. "After the war, come to my club and we'll dine—egad, sir! *for a week!*"

That invincible pluck of the southron, which carried him through starvation and the sweltering march of August, through hailing shot and shell, and freezing mud of midwinter camps—was unconquered even after the surrender. Equally invincible was that twin humor, which laughed amid all these and bore up, even in defeat. Some of the keenest hits of all the war—tinctured though they be with natural bitterness—are recalled from those days, when the beaten, but defiant, Rebel was passing under the victor's yoke.

Surprising, indeed, to its administrators must have been the result of " the oath," forced upon one green cavalryman, before he could return to family and farm. Swallowing the obnoxious allegiance, he turned to the Federal officer and quietly asked:

" Wail, an' now I reck'n I'm loyil, ain't I?"

" Oh, yes! You're all right," carelessly replied the captor.

"An' ef I'm loyil, I'm same as you 'uns?" persisted the lately sworn. " We're all good Union alike, eh?"

" Oh, yes," the officer humored him. " We're all one now."

" Wail then," rejoined Johnny Reb slowly, " didn't them darned rebs jest geen us hell sometimes?"

City Point, on the James river, was the landing for transports with soldiers released from northern prisons, after parole. A bustling, self-important major of United States volunteers was at one time there, in charge. One day a most woe-begone, tattered and emaciated " Johnnie " sat swinging his shoeless feet from a barrel, awaiting his turn.

" It isn't far to Richmond," suddenly remarked the smart major, to nobody in particular.

" Reck'n et's neer onto three thousin' mile," drawled the Confed. weakly.

"Nonsense! You must be crazy," retorted the officer staring.

"Wail, I ent a-reck'nin' adzact," was the slow reply—"Jest tho't so, kinder."

"Oh! you did? And pray why?"

"Cos et's took'n you'uns nigh onto foore year to git thar from Wash'nton," was the settling retort.

In the provost-marshal's department at Richmond, shortly after surrender, was the neatest and most irrepressible of youths. Never discourteous and often too sympathetic, he was so overcurious as to be what sailors describe as "In everybody's mess and nobody's watch." One day a quaint, Dickensesque old lady stood hesitant in the office doorway. Short, wrinkled and bent with age, she wore a bombazine gown of antique cut—its whilom black red-rusty from time's dye. But "Aunt Sallie" was a character in Henrico county; and noted withal for the sharpest of tongues and a fierce pair of undimmed eyes, which now shone under the dingy-brown poke bonnet. Toward her sallied the flippant young underling, with the greeting:

"Well, madam, what do *you* wish?"

"What do I wish?" The old lady grew restive and battle-hungry.

"Yes'm! That's what I asked," retorted the youth sharply.

"What do I wish?" slowly repeated the still-rebellious dame. "Well, if you *must* know, I wish all you Yankees were in —— hell!"

But not all the humor was confined to the governing race; some of its points cropping out sharply here and there, from under the wool of "the oppressed brother"——in-law. One case is recalled of the spoiled body servant of a gallant Carolinian, one of General Wheeler's brigade commanders. His master reproved his speech thus:

"Peter, you rascal! Why don't you speak English, instead of saying 'wah yo' is'?"

"Waffer, Mars' Sam?" queried the negro with an innocent grin. "Yo allus calls de Gen'ral— *Weel-*er?"

Another, close following the occupation, has a spice of higher satire. A Richmond friend had a petted maid, who—devoted and constant to her mistress, even in those tempting days—still burned with genuine negro curiosity for a sight of everything pertaining to "Mars' Linkum's men"—especially for "de skule."

For swift, indeed, were the newcome saints to preach the Evangel of alphabet; and negro schools seemed to have been smuggled in by every army ambulance, so numerously did they spring up in the captured Capital. So, early one day, Clarissa Sophia, the maid of color, donned her very best and, "with shiny morning face," hied her, like anything but a snail, to school. Very brief was her absence; her return reticent, but pouting and with unduly tip-tilted nose. After a time negro love for confidences conquered; and the murder came out.

The school-room had been packed and pervaded with odors—of sanctity, or otherwise—when a keen-nosed and eager school-marm rose up to exhort her class. She began by impressing the great truth that every sister present was "born free and equal;" was "quite as good" as she was.

"Wa' dat yo's sain' now?" interrupted Clarissa Sophia. "Yo' say Ise jess ekal as yo' is?"

"Yes; I said so," was the sharp retort, "and I can prove it!"

"Ho! 'Tain't no need," replied the lately disenthralled. "Reck'n I is, sho' nuff. But does yo' say dat Ise good as missus?—*my* missus?"

"Certainly you are!" This with asperity.

"Den Ise jess gwine out yere, rite off!" cried Clarissa Sophia, suiting action to word—"Ef Ise good as *my* missus, I'se goin' ter quit; fur I jess know *she* ent 'soshiatin' wid no sich wite trash like you is!"

And so—under all skies and among all colors—the war dragged its weary length out; amid sufferings and sacrifices, which may never be recorded; and which were still illumined by the flashes of unquenchable humor—God's tonic for the heart!

Had every camp contained its Froissart—had every social circle held its Boswell—what a record would there be, for reading by generations yet unborn!

But—when finished, as this cramped and quite unworthy chronicle of random recollections is—then might the reader still quote justly her of Sheba, exclaiming:

"And behold! the one-half of the greatness of thy wisdom was not told me!"

CHAPTER XXXIV.

THE BEGINNING OF THE END.

While neither in itself—perhaps not the combination of the two—was final and conclusive, the beginning of the end of the Confederacy may be dated from the loss of Vicksburg and the simultaneous retreat from Gettysburg. For these two disasters made all classes consider more deeply, both their inducing causes and the final results that must follow a succession of such crushing blows.

There can be little doubt that a complete victory at Gettysburg, vigorously followed up, would have ended the war; and the generally-accepted belief in the South was that the exhaustive defeat was proportionately bad. The war had been going on two years and a half. Every device had been used to put the whole numerical strength of the country into the field and to utilize its every resource. The South had succeeded to a degree that stupefied the outside world and astonished even herself. But the effort had exhausted, and left her unfit to renew it. Over and again the armies of the East and West had been re-enforced, reorganized and re-equipped—and ever came the heavy, relentless blows of the seemingly-exhaustless power, struggled against so vainly. The South had inflicted heavy loss in men, material and prestige; but she wasted her strength in these blows, while unhappily she could not make them effective by quick repetition.

The people, too, had lost their early faith in the Government. They had submitted to the most stringent levy of conscription and impressment ever imposed upon a nation. They had willingly left their fields to grow weeds, their children to run wild and perhaps to starve; they had cheerfully divided their last supplies of food with the Government, and had gone to the front steadily and hopefully. But now they could not fail to see that, in some points at least, there had been gross mismanagement. The food for which their families were pinched and almost starved, did not come to the armies. Vast stores of provision and supplies were blocked on the roads, while speculators' ventures passed over them. This, the soldiers in the trench and the laborer at the anvil saw equally.

They saw, too, that the Government was divided against itself; for the worse than weak Congress—which had formerly been as a nose of wax in Mr. Davis' fingers—had now turned dead against him. With the stolid obstinacy of stupidity it now refused to see any good in any measure, or in any man, approved by the Executive.

Under the leadership of Mr. Foote—who wasted the precious time of Congress in windy personal diatribes against Mr. Davis and his "pets"—nothing was done to combine and strengthen the rapidly sundering elements of Confederate strength. Long debates on General Pemberton; weighty disquisitions on such grave subjects as the number of pounds of pork on hand when Vicksburg was surrendered; and violent attacks on the whole *past* course of the administration, occupied the minds of those lawgivers. But at this time there was no single measure originated that proposed to stop the troubles in the future.

Therefore, the people lost confidence in the divided Government; and losing it began to distrust themselves. Suffering so for it, they could not fail to know the terrible strain to which the country had been subjected. They knew that her resources in men and material had been taxed to the limit; that there was no fresh supply of either upon which to draw. This was the forlorn view that greeted them when they looked within. And outside, fresh armies faced and threatened them on every side—increased rather than diminished, and better armed and provided than ever before.

This state of things was too patent not to be seen by the plainest men; and seeing it, those became dispirited who never had doubted before. And this time, the gloom did not lift; it became a settled and dogged conviction that we were fighting the good fight almost against hope. Not that this prevented the army and the people from working still, with every nerve strained to its utmost tension; but they worked without the cheery hopefulness of the past.

Fate seemed against them. Had they been Turks they would have said: "It is *kismet!* Allah is great!" As they were only staunch patriots, they reasoned: "It is fearful odds—but we *may* win." And so solemnly, gloomily—but none the less determined— the South again prepared for the scarcely doubtful strife.

The stringent addenda to the Conscription law—that had come too late—were put into force. All men that could possibly be spared—

and whom the trickery of influence could not relieve—were sent to the front; and their places in the Government were filled by the aged, the disabled, and by women. In the Government departments of Richmond—and in their branches further South—the first ladies of the land took position as clerks—driven to it by stress of circumstances. And now as ever—whether in the arsenals, the factories, or the accountant's desk—the women of the South performed their labor faithfully, earnestly and well. Those men who could not, possibly be spared, were formed into companies for local defense; were regularly drilled, mustered into service, and became in fact regular soldiers, simply detailed to perform other work. When the wild notes of the alarm bell sent their frequent peals over Richmond, and warned of an approaching raid—armorer, butcher and clerk threw down hammer and knife and pen, and seized their muskets to hasten to the rendezvous. Even the shopkeepers and speculators, who seemed conscription-proof, were mustered into some sort of form; driven to make at least a show of resistance to the raid, by which they would suffer more than any others. But it was only a show; and so much more attention was paid in these organizations to filling of the commissary wagon than of the cartridge-box, that the camps of such " melish," in the woods around Richmond, were converted more into a picnic than a defense.

Supplies of war material, of clothing, and of arms, had now become as scarce as men. The constant drain had to be supplied from manufactories, worked under great difficulties; and these now were almost paralyzed by the necessity for their operatives at the front. Old supplies of iron, coal and ore had been worked up; and obtaining and utilizing fresh ones demanded an amount of labor that could not be spared. The blockade had now become thoroughly effective; and, except a rare venture at some unlooked-for spot upon the coast, no vessel was expected to come safely through the network of ships. Blankets and shoes had almost completely given out; and a large proportion of the army went barefoot and wrapped in rugs given by the ladies of the cities, who cut up their carpets for that purpose.

Yet, in view of all this privation; with a keen sense of their own sacrifices and a growing conviction that they were made in vain, the army kept up in tone and spirits. There was no intention or desire to yield, as long as a blow could be struck for the cause; and the veteran and the " new issue "—as the new conscripts were called in derision of the currency—alike determined to work on as steadily, if not so cheerily, as before.

And still Congress wrangled on with Government and within itself; still Mr. Foote blew clouds of vituperative gas at President and Cabinet; still Mr. Davis retained, in council and field, the men he had chosen. And daily he grew more unpopular with the people, who, disagreeing with him, still held him in awe, while they despised the Congress. Even in this strait, the old delusion about the collapse of Federal finance occasionally came up for hopeful discussion; and, from time to time, Mr. Benjamin would put out a feeler about recognition from governments that remembered us less than had we really been behind the great wall of China.

After Gettysburg and Vicksburg, came a lull in the heavier operations of the war. But raids of the enemy's cavalry were organized and sent to penetrate the interior South, in every direction. To meet them were only home guards and the militia; with sometimes a detachment of cavalry, hastily brought up from a distant point. This latter branch of service, as well as light artillery, now began to give way. The fearful strain upon both, in forced and distant marches, added to the wearing campaigns over the Potomac, had used up the breed of horses in the South. Those remaining were broken down by hard work and half feed; so that one-half the cavalry was dismounted—belonging to "Company Q" the men called it—and the rest was scarcely available for a rapid march, or a very heavy shock.

But the cavalry of the enemy had increased wonderfully in drill, discipline and general efficiency. Armed with the best weapons, mounted upon choice horses, composed of picked men and officered by the boldest spirits in the North, Federal cavalry now began to be the most potent arm of their service. Men sadly recalled the pleasant days when the brilliant squadrons of Hampton, or Fitz Lee— the flower of the South, mounted on its best blood stock—dashed laughingly down upon three times their force, only to see them break and scatter; while many of their number rolled over the plain, by the acts of their own steeds rather than of hostile sabers. Even much later, when the men were ragged and badly armed, and the horses were gaunt from famine, they still could meet the improving horsemen of the enemy and come off victors—as witness the battles of the Fords. But now the Yankees had learned to fight—and more incomprehensible still to the Reb, they had learned to ride!

They were superior in numbers, equipment, and—to be honest—in discipline; and could no longer be met with any certainty of success. It was a bitter thing for the Golden Horse Shoe Knights; but like many ugly things about this time, it was true. So the Yankee raids—aimed as a finality for Richmond, but ever failing approach to their object—still managed to do incalculable mischief. They drove off the few remaining cattle, stole and destroyed the hoarded mite of the widowed and unprotected—burned barns—destroyed farming utensils; and, worse than all, they demoralized the people and kept them in constant dread.

As a counter-irritant, and to teach the enemy a lesson, General Morgan, early in July, started on a raid into the Northwest. With 2,000 men and a light battery, he passed through Kentucky and on to the river, leaving a line of conquest and destruction behind him— here scattering a regiment of the enemy—there demoralizing a home guard; and, at the river, fighting infantry and a gunboat, and forcing his way across into Indiana. Great was the scare in the West, at this first taste the fine fruits of raiding. Troops were telegraphed, engines flew up and down the roads as if possessed; and in short, home guards, and other troops, were collected to the number of nearly 30,000 men.

Evading pursuit, and scattering the detached bands he met, Morgan crossed the Ohio line—tearing up roads, cutting telegraphs, and inflicting much damage and inconceivable panic—until he reached within five miles of Cincinnati. Of course, with his merely nominal force, he could make no attempt on the city; so, after fourteen days of unresting raiding—his command pressed, worn out and broken down—he headed for the river once more. A small portion of the command had already crossed, when the pursuing force came up. Morgan made heavy fight, but his men were outnumbered and exhausted. A few, following him, cut their way through the enemy and fled along the north bank of the Ohio. The pursuit was fierce and hot; the flight determined, fertile in expedients, but hopeless in an enemy's country, raised to follow the cry. He was captured, with most of his staff and all of his command that was left—save the few hundred who had crossed the river and escaped into the mountains of Virginia.

Then for four months—until he dug his way out of his dungeon with a small knife—John Morgan was locked up as a common felon, starved, insulted and treated with brutality, the recital of which sickens—even having his head shaved! There was no excuse ever attempted; no pretense that he was a guerrilla. It was done simply to glut spite and to make a dreaded enemy feel his captors' power.

Meantime General Bragg, at Tullahoma, faced by Rosecrans and flanked by Burnside's "Army of the Cumberland," was forced to fall back to Chattanooga. Rosecrans pressed him hard, with the intent of carrying out that pet scheme of the North, forcing his army down through Georgia and riddling the Cotton States. It is inessential here to recount the details of these movements. Rosecrans had a heavy and compact force; ours was weak and scattered, and Bragg's urgent appeal for men met the invariable answer, there were none to send. For the same reason—insufficient force—Buckner was forced to abandon Knoxville; and a few weeks later Cumberland Gap, the key-position to East Tennessee and Georgia, was surrendered!

At this critical juncture the loss of that position could scarcely be exaggerated; and the public indignantly demanded of Government why it had been lost. The War Department shifted the responsibility, and declared that no reason existed; that the place was provisioned and impregnable, and that the responsibility rested alone with the officer in command, who was now a prisoner with his whole force.

This hardly satisfied the public clamor; and so ill-omened a commencement augured badly for the success of the campaign for position, in which both armies were now manœuvring. The real details of these preliminary movements are scarcely clear to this day. General Bragg's friends declare that he forced Rosecrans to the position ; his enemies, that Rosecrans first out-generaled him and then laid himself open to destruction, while Bragg took no advantage of the situation.

However this may be, we know that on the morning of the 19th September, '63, the battle of Chickamauga was commenced by the enemy in a series of obstinate division engagements, rather than in a general battle; Bragg's object being to gain the Chattanooga road in the enemy's rear, and his to prevent it. The fighting was heavy, stubborn and fierce, and its brunt was borne by Walker, Hood and Cleburne. Night fell on an undecided field, where neither had advantage ; and the enemy perhaps had suffered more heavily than we.

All that night he worked hard to strengthen his position; and our attack—which was to have commenced just at dawn—was delayed from some misapprehension of orders. At length Breckinridge and

Cleburne opened the fight, and then it raged with desperate, bloody obstinacy, until late afternoon.   At that time the Confederate right had been repulsed; but Longstreet's left had driven the enemy before it.   Then the whole southern line reformed; moving with steady, resistless sweep upon the confident enemy.   He fought obstinately— wavered—rallied—then broke again and fled toward Chattanooga. The rout was complete and the enemy so demoralized that Longstreet —feeling that he could be crushed while panic-struck—ordered Wheeler to intercept his flight.   It was stated that Longstreet's order was countermanded by General Bragg; but—whatever the reason— there was no pursuit!

The fruits of the hard-won victory were 8,000 prisoners, 50 pieces of artillery, near 20,000 muskets—*plus* a loss of life barren of results. For, instead of crushing the enemy and completely relieving the state and the Georgia frontier, the failure to press Rosecrans at the moment left him free communication with his rear and full time to recuperate. Instead of pressing on, General Bragg took position on Missionary Ridge; and criticism of the hour declared that he thus invested the Federals in the town, which—by a rapid advance—might already have been his, without a fight.

It is neither the intent, nor within the scope of these papers—even did their author possess the ability for it—to enter into detailed criticism of military events; far less to reopen those acrimonious partisanships, so bootless at the time and worse than useless now.   But, to comprehend the state of public feeling at the South, it is essential to have the plain data, upon which it was based; and to have plainly stated the causes to which popular opinion ascribed certain results.

After Chickamauga, there was very general—and seemingly not causeless—discontent.   The eternal policy of massing great armies, at any sacrifice; fighting terrible battles; and then failing to close the grasp upon their fruits—apparently already in hand—had worn public patience so threadbare, that it refused to regard Chickamauga as anything more than another of those aimless killings, which had so often drenched the West, to no avail.

Strong and open expression was made of the popular wish for General Bragg's removal; but Mr. Davis refused—as ever—to hear the people's voice, in a matter of policy.   He retained General Bragg, and the people held him responsible for what they claimed was the result—Lookout Mountain!

Fas est ab hoste doceri. Public clamor at the North declared that loss of command should reward Rosecrans for loss of the battle; and, in mid-October, he was superseded by General Grant.

Like all popular heroes of the war, Grant had become noted, rather through hard-hitting than strategic combination. His zenith was mounted on the capture of Vicksburg; a project which northern generals denounced as bad soldiership and possible of success, only through an enemy's weakness. At this time, he was certainly not in high estimation of his own army, because of dogged disregard of loss in useless assaults; and it will be recalled that General McClernand was court-martialed for his declaration that he "could not be expected to furnish brains for the whole army!" The estimate of Grant's compeers is not refuted by any evidence in the War Department that, from Shiloh to Appomattox, he ever made one combination stamped by mark of any soldiership, higher than courage and bull-dog tenacity. Even scouting the generally-accepted idea, in the army of Vicksburg and later in that of Chattanooga—that McPherson provided plans and details of his campaigns; and dismissing McClernand's costly taunt as mere epigram—this was the accepted estimate of General Grant's tactical power.

But he inaugurated his command at Chattanooga with boldness and vigor. He concentrated 25,000 troops in the town; opened his communications; and then—to prevent any possible movement flanking him out of them—boldly took the initiative.

Meantime, Longstreet had been detached by General Bragg, for that badly-provided, badly-digested and wholly ill-starred expedition to Knoxville; one which seemed to prove that the history of misfortune was ever to repeat itself, in impracticable diversions at precisely the wrong time. For, even had this corps not been badly equipped and rationed, while almost wholly lacking in transportation, it certainly depleted a daily-weakening army, in the face of one already double its numbers and daily increasing.

On November 18th—spite of management that forced him to subsist on precarious captures—Longstreet reached the enemy's advanced lines, at Knoxville; drove him into the city and completely isolated him from communication. Capitulation was a mere matter of time; but disastrous news from the main army drove the Confederate to the alternative of assault, or retreat. Choosing the former, he made it with the same desperate gallantry displayed at Gettysburg, or Corinth;

illustrated by brilliant, but unavailing, personal prowess. The strength of the enemy's works—and openness of approach, with wire netting interlaced among the stumps of the new clearing, was too much for the southern soldiers. Several times they reached the works, fighting hand-to-hand; but finally Longstreet fell back, in good order and carrying his subsistence. He chose his own line of retreat, too; and with such good judgment as to be within reach of any new combination of Bragg—from whom he was now cut off—or, failing that, to keep his rear open through Virginia, to Lee's army.

Meantime, Grant massed troops in Chattanooga, sufficient in his judgment to crush Bragg; and, learning of the latter's detachment of Longstreet's corps, determined to strike early and hard. On the 25th he attacked with his whole force, in two grand columns under Thomas, Sherman and Hooker. The little southern army of less than forty thousand was judiciously posted; having advantage of being attacked. The terrible shock of the double attack was successfully repulsed on the right by Hardee, on the left by Buckner. Broken, reeling—shattered—he was hurled back, only to form again with splendid courage. Once more checked and driven back, after desperate fighting on both sides, the Federals made a third advance with steady, dogged valor. Then constancy was rewarded; they broke the Confederate center; swung it in disorder upon the wings; and, holding the ground so hotly won, had the key to the position.

Still the day was not wholly lost to the South, had her men not given way to causeless panic. Left and right followed center—lost all order and fell back almost in flight. Then the scattered and demoralized army was saved from utter ruin, only by the admirable manner in which Cleburne covered that rout-like retreat, day after day; finally beating back Thomas' advance so heavily that pursuit was abandoned.

Missionary Ridge cost the South near 8,000 men; all the Chickamauga artillery and more; and the coveted key-position to the situation. But it cost, besides, what could even less be spared; some slight abatement in the popular confidence in our troops, under all trials heretofore. Reasoning from their dislike to General Bragg, people and press declared that the men had been badly handled through the whole campaign; yet—so inured were they to the ragged boys fighting successfully both the enemy and our own errors— there came general bad augury from the panic of Missionary Ridge

Mr. Davis had visited Bragg's army, after the howl that went up on his failure to press Rosecrans. On his return, the President appeared satisfied and hopeful; he authorized statement that the delay after Chickamauga was simply strategic; and the impression went abroad that Bragg and he had affected combinations now, which would leave Grant only the choice between retreat and destruction.

If these tactics meant the detaching of Longstreet—said thoughtful critics—then are combination and suicide convertible terms!

Neither was public feeling much cheered by the aspect of the war in Virginia. Lee and Meade coquetted for position, without definite result; the former—weakened by Longstreet's absence—striving to slip between Meade and Washington; the latter aiming to flank and mass behind Lee, on one of the three favorite routes to Richmond. The fall and winter wore away with these desultory movements; producing many a sharp skirmish, but nothing more resultful. These offered *motif* for display of dash and military tact on both sides; that at Kelly's Ford, on the Rapidan—where the Federals caught the Confederates unprepared—showing the hardest hitting with advantage on the Union side. The compliment was exchanged, by a decisive southern success at Germania Ford; but the resultless fighting dispirited and demoralized the people, while it only harassed and weakened the army. Both looked to the great shock to come; forces for which were gathering, perhaps unseen and unheard, yet felt by that morbid prescience which comes in the supreme crises of life.

The trans-Mississippi was now absolutely cut off from participation in the action of the eastern Confederacy; almost equally so from communication with it. Still that section held its own, in the warfare peculiar to her people and their situation. Quick concentrations; sharp, bloody fights—skirmishes in extent, but battles in exhibition of pluck and endurance—were of constant occurrence. Kirby Smith —become almost a dictator through failure of communication— administered his department with skill, judgment and moderation. Husbanding his internal resources, he even established—in the few accessible ports, defiant of blockade—a system of foreign supply; and "Kirby Smithdom"—as it came to be called—was, at this time, the best provisioned and prepared of the torn and stricken sections of the Confederacy.

Note has been made of the improvement of Federal cavalry; and of their raids, that struck terror and dismay among the people.

During the winter of '63–'64, Averill penetrated the heart of Virginia, scattering destruction in his path; and, though he retired before cavalry sent to pursue him—he even shot his horses as they gave out, in the forced flight—his expedition had accomplished its object. It had proved that no point of harassed territory was safe from Federal devastation; that the overtaxed and waning strength of the South was insufficient to protect them now!

Gradually—very gradually—this blight of doubt and dissatisfaction began to affect the army; and—while it was no longer possible to fill their places by new levies—some of the men already at the front began to skulk, and even to desert.

Though still uncondoned, the crime of these was roughly urged upon them; for imagination brought to the ears of all, the shriek of the distant wife, insulted by the light of her burning roof and turned starving and half-clothed, into the snowy midnight! And all the more honor was it to the steadfast that they held out—dogged but willing—to the bitter end; fighting as man had not fought before —not only against their enemy—not only against their own natural impulses—but against hope, as well!

For the mass of that grand, tattered and worn army never faltered; and only their enduring patriotism—backed as it was by selfless energy of their home-people—availed to make up for the lost opportunities of the Government!

In Congress was vacillation, discord, vacuity; while the people were goaded to the absurd charge, that some of its members were traitors! But the great diplomat has graven the truth, that an error may be worse than a crime; and the errors of the Confederate Congress—from *alpha* to *omega*—were born of weakness and feeble grasp on the prompt occasions of a great strife, like this which so submerged their littleness.

It is in some sort at the door of Congress that the head of the government, harassed by overwork, distracted by diverse trifles— each one too vital to entrust to feeble subordinates; buffeted by the gathering surge without and dragged down by the angry undertow within, lost his influence, and with it his power to save!

The beginning of the end had come upon the South. Her stoutest and bravest hearts still,

> "Like muffled drums, were beating
> Funeral marches to the grave!"

CHAPTER XXXV.

THE UPPER AND NETHER MILLSTONES.

From the earliest moment General Grant assumed command in the West, the old idea of bisecting the Confederacy seems to have monopolized his mind. The oft-tried theory of "drilling the heart of the Rebellion"—by cutting through to the Atlantic seaboard—had never been lost sight of, but in Grant's hands it was to be given practical power and direction.

To effect that object, it was essential to make North Georgia the objective point; and North Georgia—now as ever—offered a stubborn and well-nigh insurmountable barrier. But the northern War Department was now fully impressed with the importance of crushing the spine of the Confederacy; and the fact was as clearly realized in the North, as in the South, that the vital cord of Confederate being ran from Atlanta to Richmond! Therefore, every facility of men and material was furnished the commander, who at that moment stood out—in reflected lights from Vicksburg and Missionary Ridge—as the military oracle of the North; and he was urged to press this design of the campaign to a vigorous and speedy issue.

During the winter of 1863–64, General Grant incubated his grand scheme, and with the month of February brought forth a quadruple brood of ridiculous mice.

His plan—in itself a good and sound one—was to secure a permanent base nearer than the Mississippi. To accomplish this he must first secure Mobile, as a water base, and connect that with some defensible point inland. At the same time that this attempt was made —and while the troops guarding the passway into Georgia might be diverted—Thomas, commanding the Chattanooga lines, was to advance against that point.

The plan was undoubtedly sound, but the general's want of balance caused him to overweight it, until its own ponderousness was its destruction. On the 1st of February, Sherman, with a splendidly-appointed force of 35,000 infantry, and corresponding cavalry and artillery, marched out of Vicksburg; to penetrate to Mobile, or some other point more accessible, on the line of the proposed new base. Simultaneously a heavy force approached the city from New Orleans; Smith and Grierson, with a strong body of cavalry, penetrated Northern Mississippi; and Thomas made his demonstration referred to.

Any candid critic will see that four converging columns, to be effective, should never have operated so far away from their point of convergence, and so far separated from each other. The enterprise was gigantic; but its awkwardness equaled its strength, and its own weight broke its back.

Sherman, harassed by cavalry and skirmishers—advanced in solid column; while Polk, with his merely nominal force, was unable to meet him. But the latter fell back in good order; secured his supplies, and so retarded his stronger adversary, that he saved all the rolling-stock of the railroads. When he evacuated Meridian, that lately busy railroad center was left a worthless prize to the captor.

Meantime Forrest had harassed the cavalry force of Smith and Grierson, with not one-fourth their numbers; badly provided and badly mounted. Yet he managed to inflict heavy loss and retard the enemy's march; but finally—unable to wait the junction of S. D. Lee, to give the battle he felt essential—Forrest, on the 20th February, faced the Federal squadrons. Confident of an easy victory over the ragged handful of dismounted skirmishers, the picked cavalry dashed gaily on. Charge after charge was received only to be broken—and Forrest was soon in full pursuit of the whipped and demoralized columns. Only once they turned, were heavily repulsed, and then continued their way to Memphis.

This check of his co-operating column and the utter fruitlessness of his own march, induced a sudden change of Sherman's intent. He fell rapidly back to Vicksburg; his army perhaps more worn, broken and demoralized by the desultory attentions of ours, than it would have been by a regular defeat.

Meantime the New Orleans-Pensacola expedition had danced on and off Mobile without result. Thomas had been so heavily repulsed on the 25th, that he hastily withdrew to his lines at Chickamauga—and the great campaign of General Grant had resulted in as insignificant a fizz as any costly piece of fireworks the war produced.

On the contrary, history will give just meed to Forrest, Lee and Polk for their efficient use of the handfuls of ill-provided men, with whom alone they could oppose separate and organized armies. They saved Alabama and Georgia—and so, for the time, saved the Confederacy. There could be no doubt that the sole safety of the invading columns was their numerical weakness. General Grant's practice of a perfectly sound theory was clearly a gross blunder; and had Polk been in command of two divisions more—had Lee been able to swoop where he only hovered—or had Forrest's ragged boys been only doubled in number—the story told in Vicksburg would have been even less flattering to the strategic ability of the commander.

As it was, he had simply made a bad failure, and given the South two months' respite from the crushing pressure he was yet to apply. For the pet scheme of the North was but foiled—not ruined; and her whole power sang but the one refrain—*Delenda est Atlanta!*

And those two months could not be utilized to much effect by the South. Worn in resources, supplies—in everything but patient endurance, she still came forth from the dark doubts the winter had raised, hopeful, if not confident; calm, if conscious of the portentous clouds lowering upon her horizon.

Meanwhile, Grant, elevated to a lieutenant-generalcy, had been transferred to the Potomac frontier; and men, money, supplies—without stint or limit—had been placed at his disposal.

On the 1st February, Mr. Lincoln had called for 500,000 men; and on the 14th March for 200,000 more!

General Grant, himself, testified to the absolute control given him, in a letter to Mr. Lincoln, under date of 1st May, '64—from Culpeper C. H., which concludes: " I have been astonished at the readiness with which everything asked for has been granted without any explanation being asked. Should my success be less than I desire and expect, the least I can say is, that the fault is not with you."

With these unlimited resources, he was given almost unlimited power; and the jubilant North crowed as loudly as it had before Manassas, the Seven Days, or Fredericksburg.

In Richmond all was quiet. The Government had done all it could, and the people had responded with a generous unanimity that ignored all points of variance between it and them. All the supplies that could be collected and forwarded, under the very imperfect systems, were sent to the armies; all the arms that could be made, altered or repaired, were got ready; and every man not absolutely needed elsewhere—with the rare exceptions of influence and favoritism openly defying the law—was already at the front.

And seeing that all was done as well as might be, the Capital waited—not with the buoyant hopefulness of the past—but with patient and purposeful resolve.

And the ceaseless clang of preparation, cut by the ceaseless yell of anticipated triumph, still echoed over the Potomac—ever nearer and ever louder. Then, by way of interlude, on the 28th March, came the notorious Dahlgren raid. Though Kilpatrick was demoralized and driven back by the reserves in the gunless works; though Custar's men retired before the furloughed artillerists and home guards; and though Dahlgren's picked cavalry were whipped in the open field by one-fourth their number of Richmond clerks and artisans!—boys and old men who had never before been under fire— still the object of that raid remains a blot even upon the page of this uncivilized warfare. It were useless to enter into details of facts so well and clearly proved. That the orders of Dahlgren's men were to release the prisoners, burn, destroy and murder, the papers found on his dead body showed in plainest terms.

No wonder, then, that many in Richmond drew comfort from soothing belief in special Providence, when three trained columns of picked cavalry were turned back in disgraceful flight, by a handful of invalids, old men and boys!

The feeling in Richmond against the raiders was bitter and universal. Little vindictive, in general, the people clamored that arson and murder—as set forth in Dahlgren's orders—merited more serious punishment than temporary detention and highflown denunciation. The action of the Government in refusing summary vengeance on the cavalrymen captured, was indubitably just and proper. Whatever their object, and whatever their orders, they were captured in arms and were but prisoners of war; and, besides, they had not really intended more than dozens of other raiders had actually accomplished on a smaller scale.

But the people would not see this. They murmured loudly against the weakness of not making these men an example. And more than one of the papers used this as the handle for violent abuse of the Government and of its chief.

At last all preparations were complete; and the northern army—as perfect in equipment, drill and discipline as if it had never been defeated—came down to the Rapidan.

Grant divided his army into three corps, under Hancock, Warren and Sedgwick; and on the 5th May, his advance crossed the river, only to find Lee quietly seated in his path. Then commenced that series of battles, unparalleled for bloody sacrifice of men and obstinacy of leader—a series of battles that should have written General Grant the poorest strategist who had yet inscribed his name on the long roll of reverses. And yet, by a strange fatality, they resulted in making him a hero to the unthinking masses of his countrymen.

Lee's right rested on the Orange road; and an attempt, after the crossing, to turn it, was obstinately repulsed during the entire day, by Heth and Wilcox. During the night Hancock's corps crossed the river, and next morning received a fierce assault along his whole line. The fighting was fierce and obstinate on both sides; beating back the right and left of Hancock's line, while sharply repulsed on the center (Warren's). Still his loss was far heavier than ours, and the result of the battles of the Wilderness was to put some 23,000 of Grant's men *hors de combat;* to check him and to force a change of plan at the very threshold of his "open door to Richmond." For next day (7th May) he moved toward Fredericksburg railroad, in a blind groping to flank Lee.

It is curious to note the different feeling in Washington and Richmond on receipt of the news. In the North—where the actual truth did not reach—there was wild exultation. The battles of the Wilderness were accounted a great victory; Lee was demoralized and would be swept from the path of the conquering hero; Grant had at last really found the "open door!" In Richmond there was a calm and thankful feeling that the first clinch of the deadly tug had resulted in advantage. Waning confidence in the valor of men, and discretion of the general, was strengthened, and a somewhat hopeful spirit began to be infused into the people. Still they felt there would be a deadlier strain this time than ever before, and that the fresh and increasing thousands of the North could be met but by a steadily diminishing few—dauntless, tireless and true—but still how weak! Yet there was no *give* to the southern spirit, and—as ever in times of deadliest strain and peril—it seemed to rise more buoyant from the pressure.

Next came the news of those fearful fights at Spottsylvania, on the 8th and 9th—in which the enemy lost three to our one—preceding the great battle of the 12th May. By a rapid and combined attack the enemy broke Lee's line, captured a salient with Generals Ed John-

son and George H. Stewart and part of their commands, and threatened, for the time, to cut his army in two. But Longstreet and
Hill sent in division after division from the right and left, and the
fight became general and desperate along the broken salient. The
Yankees fought with obstinacy and furious pluck. Charge after
charge was broken and hurled back. On they came again—ever to
the shambles! Night fell on a field piled thick with bodies of the
attacking force; in front of the broken salient was a perfect charnel-
house!

By his own confession, Grant drove into the jaws of death at
Spottsylvania *over* 27,000 *men!* But his object was, for the second
time, utterly frustrated; and again he turned to the left—still dogged
and obstinate—still seeking to flank Lee.

On the 14th, Grant was again repulsed so sharply that his advance
withdrew; and then the "greatest strategist since Napoleon" struck
out still for his cherished left; and, leaving "the open door," passed
down the Valley of the Rappahannock.

Lee's calm sagacity foresaw the enemy's course, and on the 23d
Grant met him face to face, in a strong position near the North Anna.
Blundering upon Lee's lines, throwing his men blindly against works
that were proved invincible, he was heavily repulsed in two attacks—
with aggregate loss amounting to a bloody battle. Failing in the
second attack (on the 25th) Grant swung off—still to the left—and
crossing the Pamunkey two days later, took up strong position near
Cold Harbor on the last day of May.

Lee also moved down to face Grant, throwing his works up on a
slight curve extending from Atlee's, on the Central Railroad, across the
old Cold Harbor field—averaging some nine miles from Richmond.
Our general was satisfied with the results of the campaign thus far;
the army was buoyant and confident, and the people were more reliant
than they had been since Grant had crossed the Rapidan. They felt
that the nearness of his army to Richmond in no sense argued its
entrance into her coveted defenses; and memories of Seven Pines,
and of that other Cold Harbor, arose to comfort them.

In the North, great was the jubilee. It was asserted that Grant
could now crush Lee and capture his stronghold at a single blow;
that the present position was only the result of his splendid strategy
and matchless daring; and the vapid boast, "I will fight it out on this
line if it takes all summer"—actually uttered while he was blindly

groping his way, by the left, to the Pamunkey!—was swallowed whole by the credulous masses of the North. They actually believed that Grant's position was one of choice, not of necessity; and that Lee's movement to cover Richmond from his erratic advance—though it ever presented an unbroken front to him, and frequently drove him back with heavy loss—was still a retreat!

Both sides can look now calmly and critically at this campaign—seemingly without a fixed plan, and really so hideously costly in blood. When Grant crossed the Rapidan, he could have had no other intention than to sweep Lee from his front; and either by a crushing victory, or a forced retreat, drive him toward Richmond. Failing signally at the Wilderness, he abandoned this original plan and took up the Fredericksburg line. Here again the disastrous days of Spottsylvania foiled him completely; and he struck for the Tappahannock and Fort Royal line. Lee's emphatic repulse of his movement on the North Anna again sent Grant across the Pamunkey; and *into the very tracks of McClellan two years before!*

But there was one vast difference. McClellan had reached this base with no loss. Grant, with all McClellan's experience to teach him, had not reached this point at a cost of less than 70,000 men!

Had he embarked his troops in transports and sailed up the river, Grant might have landed his army at the White House in twenty-four hours; and that without the firing of a shot. But he had chosen a route that was to prove him not only the greatest strategist of the age, but the most successful as well. The difference of the two was simply this: he took twenty-six days instead of one; he fought nine bloody engagements instead of none ; he made four separate changes in his digested plan of advance ; and he lost 70,000 men to gain a position a condemned general had occupied two years before without a skirmish !

But the people of the North did not see this. They were only allowed partial reports of losses and changes of plan ; they were given exaggerated statements of the damage done to Lee and of his dire strait ; and the fact of Grant's proximity to the Rebel Capital was made the signal for undue and premature rejoicing. He was already universally declared the captor of Richmond, by a people willing to accept a fact with no thought of its cost ; to accept a result for the causes that produced it.

But Grant was now in a position when he could not afford to await the slow course of siege operations. He could not allow time for the hubbub at the North to die away and reflection to take its place. Blood to him was no thicker than water; and he must vindicate the boasts of his blind admirers—cost thousands of lives though it might. Once more he marshaled his re-enforced ranks, only to hurl them into the jaws of death. For though worn away by the fearful friction of numbers—melted slowly in the fiery furnace of battle—the little Confederate force sat behind its works, grim, defiant—dangerous as ever!

Could Grant crush out that handful by the pure weight of his fresh thousands—could he literally hurl enough flesh and blood against it to sweep it before him—then the key of every road to Richmond was in his hands! So, on the morning of the 3d of June, Hancock's corps rushed to the assault.

Impetuous and fierce, the charge broke Breckinridge's line. Fresh men poured in and, for a moment, the works were in the enemy's hands. But it was only for a moment. They rallied, relief came— the conflict was fierce and close—but it was short. When the smoke rose, Hancock's line was broken and retreating. Again and again he rallied it splendidly, only to be hurled back each time with deadlier slaughter. On the other points Warren and Burnside had been driven back with terrible loss; and along the whole southern line the death-dealing volley into the retreating ranks rang the joyous notes of victory. Grant had played the great stake of his campaign and lost it!

He had lost it completely, and in an incredibly short time. Near 30,000 men told the horrid story of that ferocious hurling of flesh and blood against earthworks. Near one-fifth of his whole force had paid for his last great blunder, while the Confederate loss was less than *one-tenth* his own!

Even McClellan's line had failed the sledge-hammer strategist, and nothing was left but to transfer his army to the south side of the James. Lingering with dogged pertinacity on his slow retreat—turning at every road leading to the prize he yearned for, only to be beaten back—Grant finally crossed the river with his whole force on the 13th of June.

The great campaign was over. It had been utterly foiled at every point; had been four times turned into a new channel only to be more signally broken; and had ended in a bloody and decisive defeat that left Grant no alternative but to give up his entire plan and try a new one on a totally different line. For the southern arms it had been one unbroken success from the Rapidan to Cold Harbor; for though sometimes badly hurt, the Confederates had never once been driven from an important position; had never once failed to turn the enemy from his chosen line of advance—and had disabled at the least calculation 120,000 of his men at the cost of less than 17,000 of their own!

Such was the southern view, at the moment, of this campaign of invasion; as unparalleled in the history of war, as was that of Stonewall Jackson in the Valley. Such is the view of southern thinkers, to-day; and it is backed by the clearest judgment and calmest criticism of the North.

That success was made the test of merit; that attrition at last wore away unre-enforced resistance; that highest honors in life, and national sorrow in death, were rewards of a man—truly great in many regards, if justly measured; all these are no proof that General Grant was either a strategist, or a thinker; no denial that his Rapidan campaign —equally in its planning and its carrying out—was a bald and needlessly-bloody failure!

And, realizing this at the supreme moment, can it be wondered that the people of Richmond, as well as the victorious little army, grew hopeful once more? Is it strange that—mingled with thanksgivings for deliverance, unremitting care of the precious wounded, and sorrow for the gallant dead of many a Virginia home—there rose a solemn joyousness over the result, that crowned the toil, the travail and the loss?

And so the South, unrefreshed but steadfast, girded her loins for the new wrestle with the foe, now felt to be implacable!

CHAPTER XXXVI.

"THE LAND OF DARKNESS AND THE SHADOW OF DEATH."

It is essential to a clear understanding of the events, directly preceding the fall of the Confederacy, to pause here and glance at the
means with which that result was so long delayed, but at last so fully
accomplished.

From official northern sources, we learn that General Grant
crossed the Rapidan with three corps, averaging over 47,000 men.
Therefore, he must have fought the battles of the Wilderness with
at least 140,000 men. At that time the total strength of General
Lee's morning report did not show 46,000 men·for duty. Between
the Wilderness and Spottsylvania, Grant was re-enforced to the extent of near 48,000 picked men; and again at Cold Harbor with near
45,000 more. Northern figures admit an aggregate of 97,000 *re-enforcement* between the Rapidan and the James! In that time, Lee,
by the junction of Breckinridge and all the fragments of brigades he
could collect, received less than 16,000 re-enforcement; and even the
junction with Beauregard scarcely swelled his total additions over
20,000.

Grant's army, too, was composed of the picked veterans of the
North—for his Government had accepted large numbers of hundred-
day men for local and garrison duty, that all the seasoned troops
might be sent him. Yet with an aggregate force of 234,000 men, opposed to a total of less than 63,000, General Grant failed signally
in the plan, or plans of his campaign—losing in twenty-six days, and
nine heavy fights and several skirmishes, *seven men for one of General
Lee's!*

Can any candid thinker analyze these results and then believe
Grant a strategist—a great soldier—anything but a pertinacious
fighter? Can one realize that anything but most obstinate bungling
could have swung such an army round in a complete circle—at a loss
of over one-half of its numbers—to a point it could have reached in

twenty-four hours, without any loss whatever? For the soldiers of the North, in this disastrous series of blunders, fought with constancy and courage. Beaten day after day by unfailing troops in strong works, they ever came again straight at those impregnable positions, against which obstinate stolidity, or blind rage for blood, drove them to the slaughter. Hancock's men especially seemed to catch inspiration from their chivalric leader. Broken and beaten at the Wilderness—decimated at Spottsylvania, they still were first in the deadly hail of Cold Harbor—breaking our line and holding it for a moment. Sedgwick and Warren, too—though the victim of unjust prejudice, if not of conspiracy—managed their corps with signal ability, in those ceaseless killings into which Grant's "strategy" sent them.

Nor was the immense superiority of numbers already shown, all. For this main advance—like every other of General Grant's—had co-operating columns all around it. Add to the men under his immediate command, those of the adjunct forces under his inspiration—Butler, 35,000, Hunter, 28,000 and Sigel, 10,000—and there foots up a grand total of 307,000 men!

We may, therefore, consider that General Lee, in the summer campaign of 1864, kept at bay and nullified the attack of 307,000 men with scarcely one-fifth their number; not exceeding 63,000!*

While Grant was engaged in his pertinacious failures to flank Lee, General Sheridan—whose fame as a cavalry leader was already in the mouths of men in such pet names as "Little Phil" and "Cavalry Sheridan"—made a raid of considerable proportions toward Richmond. Flanking Lee upon the right, he proceeded over the North and South Anna, damaging the railroads at Beaver Dam and Ashland stations. Thence he moved toward Richmond, but was met at Yellow Tavern by General Stuart with a small body of his cavalry and a hastily-collected force of infantry. A sharp engagement resulted in forcing the enemy off; when he passed down the James to Turkey Island, where he joined Butler's forces.

---

*Some time after the notes were made, from which these figures are condensed, two articles on Grant's campaign appeared in print—one in the New York "*World*," the other, by Mr. Hugh Pleasants, in "*The Land We Love*" magazine. Writing from diametrically opposite standpoints, with data gathered from opposing sources, Mr. Pleasants and the "*World*" very nearly agree in their figuring; and it was gratifying to this author to find that both corroborated the above estimates to within very inconsiderable numbers. Later historical papers have not materially changed them; save, perhaps, some southern claims still further to reduce Lee's army.

But the fight had one result far more serious to the South—the death of General J. E. B. Stuart—the gallant and popular leader of Confederate cavalry; so ill to be spared in those days of watchful suspense to come, when General Lee keenly felt the loss of "the eyes of the army."

During the whole fight the sharp and continuous rattle of carbines, broken by the clear boom of field artillery, was distinctly heard in Richmond ; and her defenseless women were long uncertain what the result would be. They knew nothing of the force that was attacking, nor of that which was defending their homes ; every man was away save the aged and maimed—and the tortures of doubt and suspense were added to the accustomed strain of watching the end of the fight. When the news came there was deep thankfulness; but it was solemn and shadowed from the sorrow that craped the victory.

Meantime, General Sigel had threatened the Valley with a heavy force ; but, in mid-May he had been met by General Breckinridge and was defeated with such loss of men and munitions, that he retreated precipitately across the Shenandoah. The co-operation of Sigel was virtually at an end.

But the more important co-operation had been equally unsuccessful. Simultaneously with Grant's passage of the Rapidan, General Butler, with an army of 35,000 men and a fleet of iron-clads, double-enders, gunboats and transports sufficient for a war with England, sailed up the James. This force was intended to proceed direct to Richmond, or to march into undefended Petersburg, as the case might seem best to warrant. The land forces disembarked at Bermuda Hundred and, after fortifying heavily on the line of Howlett's House, made serious demonstrations direct on Drewry's Bluff. Butler supposed that, the defenses being entirely uncovered by the drain of men for Lee's army, he could carry them with ease. In this hope he relied much upon the powerful aid of the fleet ; but Admiral Lee, ascending in a double-ender, lost his pioneer-boat, the "Commodore Jones" and very nearly his own flag-ship, by a torpedo, opposite Signal Station. This stopped the advance of the fleet, as the river was supposed to be sown with torpedoes.

Nowise daunted, General Butler—like the true knight and chivalrous leader his entire career proves him to be—drew his line closer round the coveted stronghold. But on the 16th of May, Beauregard sallied out and struck the hero of New Orleans so suddenly and so sharply that he drove him, with heavy loss and utter demoralization, clear from his advanced lines to Bermuda Hundred. Only the miscarriage of a part of the plan, entrusted to a subordinate general, saved Butler's army from complete destruction.

As it was, he there remained "bottled up," until Grant's peculiar strategy had swung him round to Petersburg; and then the "bottle-imp" was released.

Seeing himself thus foiled on every hand—his magnificent plans utterly crushed, and his immense numbers unavailing—Grant struck into new combinations. Hunter had already penetrated into West Virginia as far as Staunton; and hounding on his men with the savagery of the bloodhound, was pushing on for Lynchburg and the railroad lines of supply adjacent to it. Grant at once detached Sheridan with a heavy force, to operate against the lines from Gordonsville and Charlottesville.

Simultaneously he, himself, was to strike a resistless blow at Petersburg; and thus with every avenue of supply cut off, the leaguered Capital must soon—from very weakness—drop into eager hands stretched out to grasp her.

On the 16th and 17th June, there were sharp and heavily-supported attacks upon portions of the Confederate line before Petersburg. The expectation evidently was to drive them in by sheer weight; for it was known only that part of Lee's forces had crossed the river, and the line was one of immense extent—requiring three times his whole force to man it effectively.

But, as ever before, General Grant underrated his enemy; and, as ever before, his cherished theory of giving six lives for one to gain his point failed. Both attacks were heavily repulsed. Still holding to that theory, however, Grant attacked the whole Confederate front at dawn of the 18th. Driven back with heavy slaughter, the men were again sent in. Four times that day they rallied and came well up to the works; and four times they were sent back reeling and bleeding. Even Grant's obstinacy could not drive them again into certain destruction; and the assault on Petersburg had failed utterly, at the cost of 14,000 men for the experiment.

On that same day, Hunter was driven back from an assault on Lynchburg, and sent in disgraceful rout through West Virginia.

Hampton, too, had done his share as ever in the long war. He had caught Sheridan at Trevellian's Station, and compelled him to retreat and entirely abandon his part of Grant's new programme; and a little later he came upon Kautz and Wilson—in a railroad raid below Petersburg—and defeated them disastrously, capturing their trains, artillery and a large proportion of their men.

Thus, by July, these rough and repeated lessons had taught even General Grant that hammering with flesh and blood upon earthworks was too costly; that barn-burning and railroad-tearing cavalry were not effectual to reduce the city that had so laughed to scorn his brilliant tactics of the left flank!

A more disgusted, if not a wiser man, he sat down and fortified for a regular siege; as fully convinced as ever that the blood of the soldiers was the seed of the war; as fixed in his theory that he could spare seven lives for one and gradually by this fearful "swapping, with boot," reduce the capital he had failed to win by soldierly methods or skillful combination.

And the southern people felt that was the test to be applied to them now. Bayonet and steel, rapine and torch had failed; but now the process of *pulverizing* was to come. "Southern blood!" was General Grant's war-cry—"Southern blood by the drop, if it take rivers of ours. Southern lives by the score—and we can well pay for them with the hundred!"

And, looking the alternative squarely in the face, the southern people for the last time girded their loins for the shock; feeling they could do what men might and when they could no longer do— they could die!

Once more the tide of battle had rolled away from Richmond; but it surged up, redder and rougher, against her sister city. And staunch little Petersburg braced herself to meet its advancing waves —ever offering to them her dauntless breast and ever riding above them, breathless but victorious. Old men with one foot in the grave —boys with one foot scarce out of the cradle, stood side by side, with the bronzed veterans of Lee's hundred fights. Women sat quiet, the shells of Grant's civilized warfare tearing through their houses and through the hospitals. And fearless for themselves, they worked steadily on, nursing the wounded and the sick; giving from their daily-decreasing store with self-forgetfulness; encouraging the weak by their presence and their courage.

But not alone the fierce sounds immediately around them claimed the attention of the people of the Capital. From North Georgia came the hoarse echo of renewed strife; and they felt, in sober truth, more immediate anxiety for the result there than at their own doors. Inured to danger and made familiar with its near approach, the people of Virginia looked calmly forward to the most fearful shock of battle, if it was nothing more. They knew the crushing force of Grant's numbers, but the danger was tangible and they could see a possible issue out of it, through blood and sacrifice. But they knew and felt that Atlanta was the back door to Richmond. Let the enemy once enter that and divide the spinal column of the Confederacy, and what hope was there! For a brief space the maimed and dying body might writhe with final strength; the quivering arms strike fierce, spasmodic blows; but no nourishment could come—the end must be death—and death from inanition!

The people knew and felt this fully. They were perfectly aware that, should Atlanta fall and the enemy penetrate to our rear lines of communication, the cause was lost. We might make a fierce resistance for the moment; but without supplies, all organized plan must cease. And the wildest hope indulged in that event was the possibility of a detached and guerrilla warfare that would make the country untenable.

Therefore, every eye was turned toward Dalton, where Johnston's little army now was—every ear was strained to catch the first echo of the thunder about to roll so ominously among the Georgia mountains.

Upon General Grant's elevation to the chief command, General W. T. Sherman had been left in charge in the West. Not discouraged by the failure of Grant's quadruple advance, two months before, Sherman divided his army—like that operating on the Rapidan—into three corps. Thomas, leading the center, or direct advance; Schofield, the left on the North-east, and McPherson the right on the South-west—he moved upon Dalton, almost simultaneously with Grant's passage of the Rapidan. And like Grant, he essayed a flank movement; but with far different result.

There was another point of similarity—the great disparity of numbers. Sherman could not have had in all, far short of 80,000 men; while Johnston's greatest exertions could not collect at Dalton an effective force of 35,000. Many of these, too, were local troops and raw levies, green and undisciplined; while Sherman's forces were the flower of the western army.

Such were the points of similarity; but there was one great difference known to the Confederate leaders and people. Sherman would use every advantage of strategy and combination, rather than attempt the sledge-hammer style of attack developed by Grant. And there was more to be dreaded from his quiet and cautious approach—with its accompanying care for human life, that would preserve his army —than from any direct assault, however vigorous. This was proved at the very outset; for his advance on Dalton was a piece of military tact that—unlike Grant's at the Wilderness—was founded upon sound calculation. McPherson was thrown so far round to the South-west as seriously to threaten Johnston's communications; and by the 8th of June, the latter was forced to evacuate Dalton and retire down Resaca Valley toward the line of the Etowah river.

This movement was accomplished with quiet and perfect ease; keeping ever a steady front to the enemy, pressing rapidly on.

Feeling that the fate of the whole cause was now vested in the little army left him to defend the great key—Atlanta—Johnston was great enough to resist the opportunities for glorious battle; to give up, without a struggle—which could only entail resultless waste of men—the rich tracts so valuable to us; to offer himself to the condemnation of unthinking censure—all to insure the safety of that vital organ of Confederate life.

On the 14th June, the enemy pressed heavily against temporary works in Resaca Valley and was twice repulsed, with heavy loss. Then Johnston turned upon him and gained a decisive advantage— driving him two miles. On the two succeeding days, his attempts amounted to scarcely more than skirmishes; and on the third our troops resumed, unmolested, their retreat along the line of the Etowah. By the end of the month Johnston had taken up a strong position, with his center resting upon Kenesaw Mountain; while the enemy had thrown up works, at some points nearer even than those at Petersburg.

At dawn on the 27th, Sherman attacked along the whole line, directing his main strength to Kenesaw Mountain. He was repulsed decisively on both flanks and with especial slaughter in the center; losing over 3,500 men. Next day Cleburne's division defeated McPherson's corps in a severe fight, inflicting even heavier loss than it had sustained at Kenesaw Mountain. But these fights—while retarding the enemy's advance and causing him a loss three times our own— were all nullified by Sherman's effective use of that flanking process, so strangely misused by his rival in Virginia. Those movements were but those of pawns upon the board; while the serious check to Johnston at Dalton—the flank movement upon his right—was repeated here. On the 4th of July he was flanked out of his mountain fastnesses and was falling back upon Atlanta.

There is no stronger proof of the hold General Johnston had upon the masses of the people and of their respectful confidence in his great ability, than their reception of this news. They had watched his long retreat almost without a fight; had seen the enemy penetrate almost to the heart of Georgia, occupying rich tracts of our most productive land, just ready for the harvest; and finally had heard him thundering at the very gates of Atlanta—to enter which they felt were death to us. And yet the people never murmured at their general, nor at the army he commanded. There was an unshaken conviction that he was doing his best; that his best was *the* best. But the Government had not forgotten nor forgiven General Johnston; and for wholly inexplicable reasons, he was summarily transferred from his command and replaced by General Hood, on the 18th of July.

People could not see the ground for Johnston's removal; for he had followed the very same line that had earned General Lee the wildest enthusiasm of the people, even while it gave him almost supreme control of the military power of the Confederacy. Lee had fallen back to his proper base—so had Johnston. The former had faced far greater odds and had inflicted far heavier punishment upon the enemy; but the latter had contended against strategic ability rather than blind force—against human sagacity rather than brute courage. And if Johnston had inflicted less damage, his wise abstinence from battle had saved many lives, invaluable now; and in the end he had placed his army in almost impregnable works around the great prize he was to guard. Foreseeing the result of his opponent's strategy, he had nullified it by seeking the position into which he would finally have been forced.

So far, the Virginia and the Georgia campaigns had been markedly similar in conduct and result. Both armies, driven by overwhelming numbers, had drawn their lines around their last strongholds; and there kept their enemy at bay. And had General Johnston been allowed to reap the reward of his clear foresight and patient abstinence—who can tell but the festering Lazarus might yet have risen whole, and defied the vast wealth of aggression hurled against it?

The universal and outspoken disgust of the people at the removal of Johnston, was in no sense referable to their objection to his successor. General Hood had forced their highest admiration, and bought their warmest wishes, with his brilliant courageous and his freely-offered blood. They knew him to be dauntless, chivalrous and beloved by his men; and, even if untried in a great command, they were willing to give him the benefit of the doubt. His first movements, too—seemingly so brilliant and dashing, compared to the more steady but resultful ones of Johnston—produced a thrill of pride and hope with all the people, save the thoughtful few, who felt we could not afford now to buy glory and victory unless it tended to the one result—safety.

On the 20th July Hood assumed the offensive. He struck the enemy's right heavily and with success; repeating the blow upon his extreme left, on the 22d. The advantage on both days was with the Confederates; they drove the enemy from his works, captured several thousand prisoners, and killed and wounded over 3,000 men. But there was no solid gain in these fights; and, the enemy shifting his line after them further to the east, there was another furious battle on the 28th day of July.

In this Hood was less successful, losing heavily and gaining little or no ground. The results of the fights at Atlanta were briefly these: Hood had broken the long and sagacious defensive course; the people were perhaps inspirited at the cost of over 4,000 invaluable men; and the enemy was taught that we were too weak to drive him from his line, or even to make any solid impression on him.

Feeling this—and secure in a line of communication with his base —Sherman sat doggedly and grimly down before Atlanta. He felt he could wait.

But the end came, before even the Federal leader could have expected. After the fights at Atlanta, Hood feared the cutting of his communications. He was fearful, lest the system that had forced Johnston from Dalton and Kenesaw Mountain might be made available against him here; and the very means he had adopted to prevent it precipitated the disaster. He divided his forces into two distinct armies—sending one, under Lieutenant-General Hardee, to Jonesboro, twenty-two miles away!

Sherman, aware of the movement—which had in fact resulted from his threatening of Hood's flank—forced his superior numbers wedge-like into the gap, and effectually separated the wings. Then he struck in detail. Hardee, at Jonesboro, failed to make any impression upon him on the 1st of September, while Hood—weakened and unable to check his movements on the left—was forced, on the 31st August, to decide upon the evacuation of Atlanta!

This fatal movement was accomplished on the evening of the 1st of September, without further loss; but the key to the Confederate cause—the sole barrier to the onward sweep of Sherman to the ocean—was in his hands at last!

There may have been causes operating on General Hood that were not known to the people; for the results and their motive was shrouded in silence. His dispatch announcing the fall of the most important point was very brief; stating in a few lines that Hardee, having failed against the enemy at Jonesboro, while he could not oppose his flank movement at Atlanta, he had given up that city. Even later—when General Hood published his report of the Atlanta campaign—he differs in essential points from General Johnston, and neither his theories nor their carrying out are made comprehensible to the public.

There was a terrible shock to the people of the South in the fall of Atlanta. They knew its importance so fully that its loss was the more keenly felt. There came sudden revulsion from the hope that had begun once again to throb in the public pulse. The loud murmurs that had arisen after other defeats were wanting now; but a sullen and increasing gloom seemed to settle over the majority of the people. It was as though they were stunned by the violence of the shock and felt already its paralyzing influence. It was in vain that a ten days' truce was granted by the victorious enemy, during which Mr. Davis visited the army and spoke brave words of future victory. The people had now lost all faith in Mr. Davis and his methods; and they sullenly refused to accept the happy auguries of victory he drew from crushing defeat. Even the army itself—while still doggedly determined to strike its hardest to the bitter end—began to feel that it was fighting against hope.

And in that ten days' truce there was little chance for those worn and wasted battalions to recuperate. There were no fresh men to send to their aid; few, indeed, were the supplies that could be forwarded them. But they looked into the darkness ahead steadily and calmly; they might not see their path in it, but they were ready to march without the path. And even as they watched and waited, so at Petersburg and Richmond a small but sleepless David watched the grim Goliath, stretched in its huge bulk before their gates. Ceaselessly the trains flashed back and forth over the iron link between those two cities—now Siamese-twinned with a vital bond of endurance and endeavor. Petersburg, sitting defiant in her circle of fire, worked grimly, ceaselessly—with what hope she might! and Richmond worked for her, feeling that every drop of blood she lost was from her own veins as well.

And so for many weary months the deadly strain went on; and the twin cities—stretched upon the rack—bore the torture as their past training had taught the world they must—nobly and well!

CHAPTER XXXVII.

DIES IRÆ—DIES ILLA.

It is nowise within the scope of these sketches to detail that memorable siege of Petersburg, lasting nearly one year. It were needless to relate here, how—for more than ten months—that long southern line of defense, constantly threatened and almost as constantly assailed, was held. Men know now that it was not by strength, but by sleepless watch and dogged endurance, that less than 30,000 worn men—so dotted along works extending near forty miles, that at points there was one soldier to every rod of earthwork—held their own, even against the earlier onsets. Men now realize why the Federal general—failing in every separate effort to buy. a key-position, even at the cost of six lives for one—was forced to sit down sullenly and wait the slow, but sure, process of attrition.

These matters are now stamped upon the minds of readers, on both sides of the Potomac. In the North they had voluminous reports of every detail ; and the cessation of interest elsewhere gave full leisure to study them. In the South, 30,000 earnest historians from the trenches were sought, each one by eager crowds ; and the story of every cannonade and skirmish and charge, told in honest but homely words, was burned into the memory of intent listeners.

Slowly that summer wore itself away. Steadily that bloody history traced itself out; punctuated, now by many a fierce and sudden rush of crowding Federals—ever beaten back with frightful loss ; again by rare sorties from our line, when our leaders saw the chance to strike some telling blow.

But spite of care in those leaders and superhuman endurance in the men, the southern troops were worn with watching and steadily melting away. Close, ceaseless fighting thinned their ranks; there were no more men—even the youngest of the land, or its first borns —to take the places of the lost veterans. General Grant's words were strictly true—" the South had robbed the cradle and the grave!" The boasted army of the North, led by her latest-chosen champion and strategist, was kept at bay by a skeleton of veterans, barely held together by the worn-out sinews and undeveloped muscle of old age and infancy.

Then the fall of Atlanta came!

The people were not to be deceived by platitudes about "strategic purposes," or empty nothings about "a campaign to nullify it." They had gotten now beyond that; and saw the terrible blow that had been dealt them in all its naked strength. They felt that an army that had failed to check Sherman, when it was behind strong works, would hardly do so in the open field. They felt that he could now at his leisure bore into the coveted heart of our territory; that the long-attempted "bisection of the rebellion" was accomplished; that further aid, or supplies, from that section was impossible. And then the people of Richmond turned once more with unfailing pride, but lessening hope, toward the decreasing bands that still held their own gates secure. But they saw how the deadly strain was telling upon these; that the end was near.

But even now there was no weak yielding—no despairing cry among the southern people. They looked at the coming end steadily and unflinchingly; and now, for the first time, they began to speculate upon the possible loss of their beloved Capital. It was rumored in Richmond that General Lee had told the President that the lines were longer than he could hold; that the sole hope was to evacuate the town and collect the armies at some interior point for a final struggle that might yet sever the bonds, ever closing tighter and tighter upon us. And the rumor added that Mr. Davis peremptorily and definitely rejected this counsel; declaring that he would hold the city, at any cost and any risk.

For once—whatever cause they had to credit these reports—the popular voice was louder on the side of the unpopular President than on that of the idolized general. The tremendous efforts to capture the Capital; the superhuman exertions made to defend it in the last four years, *had made Richmond the cause!* People argued that if Richmond was lost, the State of Virginia was lost, too; that there was no point in North Carolina where the army could make a stand, for even that "interior line" then became a frontier. Beyond this the people felt the moral effect of such a step; and that the army, as such, could never be carried out of Virginia. And with the ceaseless discussion of this question, came the first yearnings for peace propositions. To this extremity, the South had been confident and fixed in her views. Cheated of her hopes of foreign intervention, she had yet believed her ability to work out her own oracle; through blood and toil—even ruin, perhaps—but still to force a peace at last. But now the popular voice was raised in answer to the vague words of peace that found their way over the Potomac. If there be any desire in the North for cessation of this strife, said the people, for God's sake let us meet it half way. Even the Congress seemed impressed with the necessity of meeting any overtures from the North, before it was too late and our dire strait should be known there. But it was already too late; and the resultless mission of Mr. Stephens to Fortress Monroe proved that the Washington Government now saw plainly that it could force upon us the terms it made the show of offering.

The failure of this mission, no less than the great mystery in which the Government endeavored to wrap it, produced a decided gloom among the thinking classes; and it reacted upon the army as well. The soldiers now began to lose hope for the first time. They saw they were fighting a hydra; for as fast as they lopped off heads in any direction, fresh ones sprang up in others. They began, for the first time, to feel the contest unequal; and this depressing thought—added to the still greater privations following the loss of Georgia—made desertion fearfully common, and threatened to destroy, by that cause, an army that had withstood every device of the enemy.

And so the fall wore into winter; and the news from General Hood's lines only added to the gloom. After the truce of ten days, following the fall of Atlanta, Hood had moved around and gotten almost in Sherman's rear. For a moment there was great exultation, for it was believed he would destroy the enemy's communications and then attack him, or force an attack on ground of his own choosing. Great was the astonishment and great the disappointment, when Hood moved rapidly to Dalton and thence into Alabama, leaving the whole country south of Virginia entirely open, defenseless, and at Sherman's mercy.

And, as usual, in moments of general distress, Mr. Davis was blamed for the move. He had, it was said, removed Joe Johnston at the very moment his patient sagacity was to bear its fruits; he had been in Hood's camp and had of course planned this campaign—a wilder and more disastrous one than the detachment of Longstreet, for Knoxville. Whosesoever may have been the plan, and whatever may have been its ultimate object, it failed utterly in diverting Sherman from the swoop for which he had so long hovered. For, while the small bulwark of Georgia was removed—and sent in Quixotic joust against distant windmills—the threatening force, relieved from all restraint, and fearing no want of supplies in her fertile fields, pressed down, "Marching thro' Georgia."

Meantime Hood, with no more serious opposition than an occasional skirmish, crossed the Tennessee at Florence, about the middle of November. The enemy fell back before him, toward Nashville, until it seemed as if his intent was to draw Hood further and further away from the *real* point of action—Sherman's advance. On the 30th of November, however, Thomas made a stand at Franklin ; and then resulted a terrific battle, in which the Confederates held the field, with the loss of one-third of the army. Six of our generals lay amid their gallant dead on that unhappy field ; seven more were disabled by wounds, and one was a prisoner. The enemy's loss was stated at far less than ours ; and he retired into Nashville, to which place our army laid siege on the 1st of December.

Weakened by the long march and more by the terrible losses of Franklin ; ill-supplied and half-fed, Hood's army was compelled to rely upon the enemy's want of supplies driving him out. On the 15th of December he attacked our whole line, so furiously as to break it at every point. Hood's defeat was complete; he lost his whole artillery—over fifty pieces—most of his ordnance and many of his supply trains. In the dreadful retreat that followed, General Forrest's vigorous covering alone saved the remnant of that devoted army ; and on the 23d of January, 1865—when he had brought them once more into temporary safety—General Hood issued a farewell order, stating that he was relieved at his own request.

Gallant, frank and fearless even in adversity, he did not shirk the responsibility of the campaign ; declaring, that disastrous and bitter as it had been, he had believed it best.

So ended all real resistance in the South and West. The enemy had gained the back door to Richmond, had shattered its supports and had marched on to the rear of those strongholds that had so long defied his power from the sea.

It was but a question of time, when Charleston and Savannah should fall; and even the most hopeful could see that Virginia was the only soil on which resistance still walked erect.

Meanwhile, the winter was passing in Richmond in most singular gayety. Though the hostile lines were so close that the pickets could "chaff" each other without raising their voices, still both had learned that direct attacks in front were not practicable; and such was the state of the roads all around Petersburg, that no movement out of works could be attempted. Therefore more active fighting had for the moment ceased; numbers of young officers could get to Richmond, for a few days at a time; and these came worn and tired from camp and famished for society and gayety of some sort. And the younger ladies of Richmond—ready as they ever were to aid and comfort the soldier boys with needle, with bandage, or with lint —were quite as ready now to do all they could in plans for mutual pleasure.

They only felt the strain was for the moment remitted ; they recked not that it was to come to-morrow for the final crush ; and they enjoyed to-day with all the recklessness of long restraint.

Parties were of nightly occurrence. Not the brilliant and generous festivals of the olden days of Richmond, but joyous and gay assemblages of a hundred young people, who danced as though the music of shells had never replaced that of the old negro fiddler —who chatted and laughed as if there were no to-morrow, with its certain skirmish, and its possible blanket for winding-sheet. For the beaux at these gatherings were not only the officers on leave from Petersburg ; the lines drawn close to the city furnished many an acquisition, who would willingly do ten miles in and out, on horseback through the slush and snow, for one *deux temps* with "somebody in particular."

And many a brave fellow had ridden direct from the ball-room into the fight. I can well recall poor H. now, as he looked when last I saw him in life. Ruddy and joyous, with his handsome face one glow of pleasure, he vaulted gaily to his saddle under the bright moon at midnight. Curbing his restive horse, and waving a kiss to the bright faces pressed against the frosty pane, his clear *au revoir!* echoed through the silent street, and he was off.

Next morning a country cart brought his lifeless body down Main street, with the small blue mark of a bullet in the middle of the smooth, clear, boyish brow. Never leaving his saddle, he had ridden into a picket fight, and a chance shot had cut short the life of so much promise.

But it is not meant that these parties entailed any waste of those supplies, vital alike to citizen and soldier. They were known as "Starvations;" and all refreshments whatever were forbidden, save what could be drawn from the huge pitcher of "Jeems' River" water, surrounded with its varied and many-shaped drinking utensils. Many of these, even in the houses of the best provided, were of common blown glass, with a greenish tinge that suggested a most bilious condition of the blower. The music was furnished by some of the ancient negro minstrels—so dear to the juvenile southern heart in days gone by; or more frequently by the delicate fingers of some petted and favored belle. And never, amid the blare of the best trained bands, the popping of champagne, and the clatter of forks over *paté de foies gras,* was there more genuine enjoyment and more courtly chivalry to the *beau sexe,* than at these primitive soirées.

The "Starvations" were not the only amusements. Amateur theatricals and tableaux again became the rage in midwinter; and talent of no contemptible grade was displayed on many an impromptu stage. And that especial pet horror of supersensitive godliness— the godless German cotillion—even forced itself into the gayeties of the winter. Great was the wrath of the elect against all amusements of the kind—but chiefest among outrages was this graceless German. But despite the denunciations, the ridicule, and even the active intervention of one or two ministers, the young soldiers and their chosen partners whirled away as though they had never heard a slander or a sermon.

I have already endeavored to show how a certain class in Richmond deprecated gayety of all kinds two years before. These, of course, objected now; and another class still was loud and violent against it. But, said the dancers, we do the fighting—we are the ones who are killed—and if we don't object, why in the deuce should you? Cooped up in camp, with mud and musty bacon for living, and the whistling of Miniés and whooing of shells for episode, we long for some pleasure when we can get off. This is the sole enjoyment we have, and we go back better men in every way for it.

This was rather unanswerable argument; and the younger ladies were all willing to back it; so *malgré* long faces and a seeming want of the unities, the dancing went on.

We have heard a great deal *post-bellum* bathos about that strange mixture of gay waltzes, and rumble of dead-cart and ambulance; but one must have heard the sounds together before he can judge; and no one who was not in and of that peculiar, and entirely abnormal, state of society, can understand either its construction, or its demands.

But the short spasm of gayety, after all, was only the fitful and feverish symptom of the deadly weakness of the body politic. It was merely superficial; and under it was a fixed and impenetrable gloom. The desertions from the army were assuming fearful proportions, that no legislation or executive rigor could diminish; supplies of bare food were becoming frightfully scarce, and even the wealthiest began to be pinched for necessaries of life; and over all brooded the dread cloud of a speedy evacuation of the city.

Every day saw brigades double-quicking back and forth through the suburbs; the continuous scream of steam-whistles told of movement, here and there; and every indication showed that the numbers of men were inadequate to man the vast extent of the lines. As the spring opened, this became more and more apparent. There was no general attack, but a few brigades would be thrown against some ill-defended work here; and almost simultaneously the undefended lines there would have a force hurled against them. It almost seemed that the enemy, aware of our weakness, was determined to wear out our men by constant action, before he struck his heavy blow. How dear the wearied, starving men made these partial attacks cost him, already his own reports have told.

March came, and with it, orders to remove all government property that could possibly be spared from daily need. First the archives and papers went; then the heavier stores, machinery and guns, and supplies not in use; then the small reserve of medical stores was sent to Danville, or Greensboro. And, at last, the already short

23

supplies of commissary stores were lessened by removal—and the people knew their Capital was at last to be given up!

The time was not known—some said April, some the first of May; but the families of the President and Cabinet had followed the stores; the female Department clerks had been removed to Columbia—and there was no doubt of the fact. After four years of dire endeavor and unparalleled endurance, the Capital of the South was lost!

In their extremity the people said little, but hope left them utterly. In the army or out, there were few, indeed—and no Virginians—but believed the cause was lost when the army marched away.

Richmond was Virginia—was the cause!

With Sherman already in possession of Charleston and Savannah, and the army unable to do aught but retreat sullenly before him—with Virginia gone, and the Confederacy narrowed down to North Carolina, a strip of Alabama and the trans-Mississippi—what hope was left?

After General Johnston had been relieved at Atlanta, the Department had managed, on one reason or another, to shelve him until now. The public voice was loudly raised against the injustice done the man they admired most of all the bright galaxy of the South; and even Congress woke from its stupor long enough to demand for the great soldier a place to use his sword. This was in January; but still the government did not respond, and it was not until the 23d February that he was restored to command. Then—with the shattered remnant of his army, augmented, but not strengthened by the fragments of flying garrisons—he could only fall back before the victorious progress of that "Great March" he might effectually have checked, on its threshold at Atlanta.

Deep gloom—thick darkness that might be felt—settled upon the whole people. Hope went out utterly, and despair—mingled with rage and anguish as the news from the "Great March" came in—took its place in every heart. But in every heart there was bitter sorrow, humiliation—but no fear. As Richmond became more and more empty, and the time to abandon her drew nearer and nearer, her people made what provision they might to meet the enemy they had scorned so long. One class and one alone, showed any sign of fear—the human vultures so long fattened on the dead and dying—the speculators.

With every preparation long since made for the event—with cellars and attics stored with tobacco and other merchandise—with Confederate blood-money converted into gold—these Shylocks now shivered in anticipation of the coming greenbacks, for abject dread of the bluebacks that were to bring them. There is one gleam of satisfaction through the gloom of the great fire—it partly purified the city of these vermin and the foul nests they had made themselves.

All seemed ready during March, and the people watched every movement, listened for every sound, that might indicate actual evacuation. Each morning the city rose from its feverish sleep, uncertain whether, or not, the army had withdrawn in the stillness of the night.

During all this fitful suspense there was no general fight along the lines, and from time to time hope would flicker up, and for the moment throw the shadows into shape of a possible victory—a saving blow for the storm-racked ship of state, now her decks had been cleared for desperate action. Then it would down, down again, lower than before.

With the end of March the enemy made new combinations. His whole disjointed attacks had been against the South Side road, the main artery of supply and retreat. He had ceased organized attacks on the works, and sought only to strike the communications. Now, Sheridan, with a formidable force, was sent to Five Forks ; and Richmond heard, on the first day of April, of desperate fighting between him and Pickett.

Next morning, the 2d April, rose as bright a Sunday as had shone in all Richmond that spring. The churches were crowded, and plainly-dressed women—most of them in mourning—passed into their pews with pale, sad faces, on which grief and anxiety had both set their handwriting. There were few men, and most of these came in noisily upon crutches, or pale and worn with fever.

It was no holiday gathering of perfumed and bedizened godliness, that Sunday in Richmond. Earnest men and women had come to the house of God, to ask His protection and His blessing, yet a little longer, for the dear ones that very moment battling so hotly for the worshipers.

In the midst of a prayer at Dr. Hoge's church, a courier entered softly, and advancing to Mr. Davis, handed him a telegram. Noiselessly, and with no show of emotion, Mr. Davis left the church, followed by a member of his staff. A moment after another quietly said a few words to the minister; and then the quick apprehensions of the congregation were aroused. Like an electric shock they felt the truth, even before Dr. Hoge stopped the services and informed them that Richmond would be evacuated that night; and counseled they had best go home and prepare to meet the dreadful to-morrow. The news spread like wildfire. Grant had struck that Sunday morning—had forced the lines, and General Lee was evacuating Petersburg!

The day of wrath had come.

Hastily the few remaining necessaries of the several departments were packed, and sent toward Danville, either by railroad or wagon. Ordnance supplies, that could not be moved, were rolled into the canal; commissary stores were thrown open, and their hoarded contents distributed to the eager crowds. And strange crowds they were. Fragile, delicate women staggered under the heavy loads they bore to suffering children at home; the pale wife clutched hungrily at the huge ham, or the bag of coffee, for the wounded hero, pining at home for such a delicacy. Children were there with outstretched hands, crying for what they could carry; and hoary-headed men tugged wearily at the barrels of pork, flour, or sugar they strove to roll before their weak arms.

Later in the evening, as the excitement increased, fierce crowds of skulking men, and course, half-drunken women, gathered before the stores. Half-starved and desperate, they swore and fought among themselves over the spoils they seized. Orders had been given to destroy the whisky at once; but, either from lingering tenderness, or from the hurry of the movement, they were only partially obeyed.

Now the uncontrolled swarms of men and women—especially the wharf rats at Rockett's where the navy storehouses were—seized the liquor and became more and more maddened by it. In some places where the barrels were stove, the whisky ran in the gutters ankle deep; and here half-drunken women, and children even, fought, to dip up the coveted fluid in tin pans, buckets, or any vessel available.

Meanwhile, preparation went on rapidly; the President and Cabinet left for the South—General Breckinridge, Secretary of War, alone remaining to direct the details of evacuation. Everything was ready for the few remaining troops to withdraw, leaving the works on the northern side of the James unoccupied, before daylight. Then the officer with the burning party went his rounds, putting the torch to every armory, machine-shop and storehouse belonging to the Government. By midnight these had begun to burn briskly; one lurid glare shot upward to the sky, from the river; then another and another. The gunboats had been fired, and their crews, passing to the shore equipped for camp, followed the line of the retreating army up the river bank.

Who, that was in it, will ever forget that bitter night? Husbands hastily arranged what plans they might, for the safety of families they were forced to leave behind; women crept out into the midnight, to conceal the little jewelry, money or silver left them, fearing general sack of the city and treachery of even the most trusted negroes. For none knew but that a brutal and drunken mob might be let loose upon the hated, long-coveted Capital, in their power at last! None knew but that the black rule of Butler might be re-enacted—excelled; and women—who had sat calm and restful, while the battle of Seven Pines and the roar of Seven Days, and the later Cold Harbor, shook their windows—now broke down under that dreadful parting with the last defenders of their hearths! Death and flame they had never blanched before; but the nameless terrors of passing under the Yankee yoke vanquished them now.

Pitiful were leave-takings of fathers with their children, husbands with new-made brides, lovers with those who clung to them in even greater helplessness. Ties welded in moments of danger and doubt—in moments of pleasure, precious from their rarity—all must be severed now, for none knew how long—perhaps forever! For man, nor woman, might pierce the black veil before the future. Only the vague oppression was there, that all was over at last; that days to come might mean protracted, bloody mountain warfare—captivity, death, separation eternal!

So men went forth into the black midnight, to what fate they dreamed not, leaving those loved beyond self to what fate they dared not dream!

But even in that supreme hour—true to her nature and true to her past—the woman of Richmond thought of her hero-soldier; not of herself. The last crust in the home was thrust into his reluctant hand; the last bottle of rare old wine slyly slipped into his haversack. Every man in gray was a brother-in-heart to every woman that night!

Long after midnight, I rode by a well-remembered porch, where all that was brightest and gayest of Richmond's youth had passed many happy hours. There was Styles Staple; his joyous face clouded now, his glib tongue mute—with two weeping girls clinging to his hands. Solemnly he bent down; pressed his lips to each pure forehead, in a kiss that was a sacrament—threw himself into their mother's arms, as she had been his own as well; then, with a wrench, broke away and hurled himself into saddle. There was a black frown on Staple's face, as he rode up by me; and I heard a sound—part sob; more heart-deep oath—tear out of his throat. If the Recording Angel caught it, too, I dare swear there was no record against him for it, when—thirty hours later—he answered to his name before the Great Roll-Call! For no more knightly lips will ever press those pure brows; no more loyal soul went to its rest, out of that dire retreat.

Two hours after midnight, all was ready; and all was still, save the muffled roll of distant wagons and, here and there, the sharp call of a bugle. Now and again, the bright glare, above the smoke round the whole horizon, would pale before a vivid, dazzling flash; followed by swaying tremble of the earth and a roar, hoarsely dull; and one more ship of the little navy was a thing of the past.

Later still came to the steady tramp of soldiers—to be heard for the last time in those streets, though its echo may sound down all time! The last scene of the somber drama had begun; and the skeleton battery-supports filed by like specters, now in the gloom, now in the glare of one of the hundred fires. No sound but the muffled word of command came from their ranks; every head was bowed and over many a cheek—tanned by the blaze of the fight and furrowed by winter night-watches—the first tear it had ever known rolled noiselessly, to drop in the beloved dust they were shaking from their feet.

Next came gaunt men, guiding half-starved horses that toiled along with rumbling field-pieces; voiceless now and impotent, as once, to welcome the advancing foe. And finally the cavalry pickets came in, with little show of order; passed across the last bridge and fired it behind them. Over its burning timbers rode General Breckinridge and his staff;—the last group of Confederates was gone;—Richmond was evacuated!

Dies iræ—dies illa!

CHAPTER XXXVIII.

AFTER THE DEATH BLOW WAS DEALT.

Just as dawn broke through the smoke-eddies over the deserted Capital, the morning after its evacuation, two carriages crept through the empty streets, toward the fortifications. In them—grave-faced and sad—sat the Mayor of Richmond and a committee of her council, carrying the formal surrender to the Federal commander on the northern bank of the James.

Many a sad, a few terrified, faces peered at them through closed shutters; but the eager groups about the fires, striving still to secure scraps from the flames, never paused for a glance at the men who bore the form of the already accomplished fact.

Before long, eager watchers from Chimborazo Heights saw blue-coats rise dim over the distant crest. Then came the clatter of cavalry, sabers drawn and at a trot; still cautiously feeling their way into the long-coveted stronghold. Behind followed artillery and infantry in compact column, up the River Road, through Rockett's to Capitol Square. There they halted; raised the Stars-and-stripes on the staff from which the Stars-and-bars had floated—often in their very sight —for four weary, bitter years!

It was a solemn and gloomy march; little resembling the people's idea of triumphal entry into a captured city. The troops were quiet, showing little elation; their officers anxious and watchful ever; and dead silence reigned around them, broken only by the roar and hiss of flames, or the sharp explosion as they reached some magazine. Not a cheer broke the stillness; and even the wrangling, half-drunken bummers round the fires slunk sullenly away; while but few negroes showed their faces, and those ashen-black from indefinite fear; their great mouths gaping and white eyes rolling in curious dread that took away their faculty for noise.

By the time Weitzel's brigade of occupation had been posted—and several regiments massed on the Capitol—the fire had become general. Intending only to destroy munitions and supplies of war—the firing party had been more hasty than discreet. A strong breeze sprang up, off the river, and warehouse followed warehouse into the line of the flames. Old, dry and crammed with cotton, or other inflammable material, these burned like tinder ; and at many points, whole blocks were on fire.

A dense pall of smoke hovered low over the entire city; and through it shone huge eddies of flames and sparks, carrying great blazing planks and rafters whirling over the shriveling buildings. Little by little these drew closer together; and by noon, one vast, livid flame roared and screamed before the wind, from Tenth street to Rockett's ; licking its red tongue around all in its reach and drawing the hope—the very life of thousands into its relentless maw !

Should the wind shift, that rapidly-gaining fire would sweep up-town and devour the whole city; but, while the few men left looked on in dismayed apathy, deliverance came from the enemy. The regiments in Capitol Square stacked arms ; were formed into fire-squads; and sped at once to points of danger. Down the deserted streets these marched ; now hidden by eddying smoke—again showing like silhouettes, against the vivid glare behind them. Once at their points for work, the men went at it with a will; and—so strong was force of discipline—with no single attempt at plunder reported !

Military training never had better vindication than on that fearful day ; for its bonds must have been strong indeed, to hold that army, suddenly in possession of city so coveted—so defiant—so deadly, for four long years.

Whatever the citizens may vaguely have expected from Grant's army, what they received from it that day was aid—protection—safety ! Demoralized and distracted by sorrow and imminent danger; with almost every male absent—with no organization and no means to fight the new and terrible enemy—the great bulk of Richmond's population might have been houseless that night, but for the disciplined promptitude of the Union troops. The men worked with good will; their officers, with ubiquitous energy. If the fire could not be stayed, at any particular point, a squad entered each house, bore its contents to a safe distance; and there a guard was placed over them.

Sad and singular groups were there, too. Richmond's best and tenderest nurtured women moved among their household gods, hastily piled in the streets, selecting this or that sacred object, to carry it in their own hands—where? Poor families, utterly beggared, sat wringing their hands amid the wreck of what was left, homeless and hopeless; while, here and there, the shattered remnant of a soldier was borne, on a stretcher in kindly, if hostile, hands, through clouds of smoke and mourning relatives to some safer point.

Ever blacker and more dense floated the smoke-pall over the deserted city; ever louder and more near roared the hungry flames. And constantly, through all that dreadful day, the *whoo!* of shells from magazines, followed by the thud of explosion, cut the dull roar of the fire. For—whether through negligence or want of time—charged shells of all sizes had been left in the many ordnance stores when the torch was applied. These narrow brick chambers—now white hot and with a furnace-blast through them—swept the heaviest shells like cinders over the burning district. Rising high in air, with hissing fuses, they burst at many points, adding new terrors to the infernal scene; and some of them, borne far beyond the fire's limit, burst over the houses, tearing and igniting their dry roofs.

Slowly the day, filled with its hideous sights and sounds, wore on; and slowly the perseverance of man told against the devouring element. The fire was, at last, kept within its own bounds; then gradually forced backward, to leave a charred, steaming belt between it and the unharmed town. Within this, the flames still leaped and writhed and wrangled in their devilish glee; but Richmond was now comparatively safe, and her wretched inhabitants might think of food and rest. Little had they recked of either for many a dread hour past!

The provost-marshal, that unfailing adjunct to every occupation, had fixed his office at the court-house. There a mixed and singular crowd waited gloomily, or jostled eagerly, for speech of the autocrat of the hour. Captured officers stood quietly apart, or peered out earnestly through the smoke drifts, while their commitments to Libby Prison were made out; anxious and wan women, of every sphere in life, besieged the clerk preparing "protection papers;" while a fussy official, of higher grade, gave assurance to every one that guards should be placed about their homes, For the deserted women of Richmond dreaded not only the presence of the victorious enemy, but also that of the drunken and brutalized "bummers" and deserters who stayed behind their own army.

The guards were really stationed as promptly as was practicable ; the fire-brigade men were sent to quarters; pickets in blue patroled the outskirts ; and, by nightfall, the proud Capital of the Southern Confederacy was only a Federal barrack!

For two days after their entrance the Union army might have supposed they had captured a city of the dead. The houses were all tightly closed, shutters fastened and curtains drawn down ; and an occasional blue-coated sentry in porch, or front yard, was the sole sign of life. In the streets it was little different. Crowds of soldiers moved curiously from point to point, large numbers of negroes mixing with them—anxious to assist their new found brotherhood, but wearing most awkwardly their vested rights. Here and there a gray jacket would appear for a moment—the pale and worn face above it watching with anxious eyes the unused scene ; then it would disappear again. This was all. The Federals had full sweep of the city—with its silent streets and its still smoking district, charred and blackened; where, for acre after acre, only fragments of walls remained, and where tall chimney stacks, gaunt and tottering, pointed to heaven in witness against the useless sacrifice.

For two days this lasted. The curious soldiers lounged about the silent town, the burned desert still sent up its clouds of close, fetid smoke; the ladies of Richmond remained close prisoners. Then necessity drove them out, to seek food, or some means to obtain it; to visit the sick left behind ; or to make charitable visits to those who might be even less provided than themselves.

Clad almost invariably in deep mourning—with heavy veils invariably hiding their faces—the broken-hearted daughters of the Capital moved like shadows of the past, through the places that were theirs no longer. There was no ostentation of disdain for their conquerors —no assumption of horror if they passed a group of Federals—no affected brushing of the skirt from the contact with the blue. There was only deep and real dejection—sorrow bearing too heavily on brain and heart to make an outward show—to even note smaller annoyances that might else have proved so keen. If forced into collision, or communication, with the northern officers, ladies were courteous as cold; they made no parade of hatred, but there was that in their cold dignity which spoke plainly of impassable barriers.

And, to their credit be it spoken, the soldiers of the North respected the distress they could but see; the bitterness they could not misunderstand. They made few approaches toward forcing their society—even where billeted in the houses of the citizens, keeping aloof and never intruding on the family circle.

For several days the water-approaches to the city could not be cleared from the obstructions sunk in them; all railroad communication was destroyed, and the whole population was dependent upon the slender support of the wagon trains. Few even of the wealthiest families had been able to make provision ahead; scarcely any one had either gold, or greenbacks; and suffering became actual and pinching. Then came the order that the Federal commissary was to issue rations to those needing them. Pinching themselves, as they did; preferring to subsist on the slenderest food that would sustain life, to accepting the charity of the enemy—many of those suffering women were driven by sheer hunger—by the threatened starvation of their children, or of the loved wounded ones near them—to seek the proffered bounty. They forced their way into the surging, fighting crowd of greasy and tattered negroes, of dark-faced "bummers" and "loyal" residents—and they received small rations of cornmeal and codfish; bearing them home to be eaten with what bitter seasoning they might of tears from pain and humiliation.

The direst destitution of the war had been nothing to this. With their own people around them, with hope and love to sustain them, the women of Richmond did not wince under the pinch of want. But now, surrounded by enemies, with not a pound of flour, or a cent of currency, actual starvation—as well as humiliation—stared them in the face. The few who went to draw rations, sat down in blank despair. They *could not* make up their minds to go again. The fewer still, who had the least surplus from immediate wants, distributed it freely; and a cup of sugar from a slender stock was bartered here for a few slices of the hoarded ham, or a pound or two of necessary meal.

Meantime, sutlers, peddlers and hucksters swarmed in like locusts, on the very first steamers up the river. They crowded Broad street, the unburned stores on Main, and even the alleyways, with great piles of every known thing that could be put up in tin. They had calculated on a rich harvest; but they had reckoned without their host. There was no money in Richmond to spend with them; and after a profitless sojourn, they took up their tin cans, and one by one returned North—certainly wiser and, possibly, better men. It was peculiar to note the universality of southern sympathy among these traders. There was scarcely one among them who didn't think the war "a darned shame;" they were intensely sympathetic and all came from South of the Pennsylvania line. But the supporters, either of their principles, or their trade, were the few lucky negroes who could collect "stamps," in never so small qualities; and to such the sutlers were a joy forever.

Shut off entirely from any communication with their retreating troops and mingling so little with their captors, Richmond people got only most startling and unreliable rumors from the army. Clinging, with the tenacity of the drowning, to the least straw of hope, they would not yet give up utterly that army they had looked on so long as invincible—that cause, which was more than life to them! Though they knew the country around was filled with deserters and stragglers; though the Federals had brigades lying round Richmond in perfect idleness—still for a time the rumor gained credit that General Lee had turned on his pursuer, at Amelia Court House, and gained a decisive victory over him. Then came the more positive news that Ewell was cut off with 13,000 men; and, finally, on the 9th of April, Richmond heard that Lee had surrendered. Surely as this result should have been looked forward to—gradually as the popular mind had been led to it—still it came as a blow of terrific suddenness. The people refused to believe it—they said it was a Yankee trick; and when the salute of one hundred guns rang out from forts and shipping, they still said, bitterly, it was a ruse to make them commit themselves.

Gradually they came to accept the inevitable; and, as the last ray of hope died out, its place was filled with the intense yearning to know the fate of those lost and loved ones—to know if they had died at the bitter ending, or lived to be borne away into captivity. Forgetting pride, hostility—all but their anxiety for those so precious to them now—the women caught at every shred of information; questioned ignorant soldiers eagerly; and listened patiently to the intelligible news the officers were only too willing to give. And at last these rumors assumed tangible form—there was no longer any room to doubt. General Lee, weakened by desertion and breaking down of his men—by General Ewell's capture and by the sense of hopelessness of further resistance, had on the morning of the 9th of April, surrendered 24,000 men—including the volunteer citizens, and the naval brigade of all the Richmond ship's-crews—and with them 8,000 muskets! Such, too, was the condition of the horses that the Federals refused even to drive them away from their stands. Little need, indeed, had there been for those extra brigades around the city.

Then Richmond, sitting like Rachel in her desolation, waited for the return of her vanquished—heroes still to her. News came of the general parole; and every sound across the river—every cloud of dust at the pontoon bridge—was the signal for a rush to doorstep and porch. Days passed and the women—not realizing the great difficulties of transportation—grew impatient to clasp their loved ones once more to their hearts. False outcries were made every hour, only to result in sickening disappointment and suspense. At last the evening of the third day came and, just at dusk, a single horseman turned slowly into deserted Franklin street.

Making no effort to urge his jaded beast, travel-stained and weary himself, he let the reins fall from his hands and his head droop upon his chest. It was some time before any one noticed that he wore the beloved gray—that he was Major B., one of the bravest and most staunch of the noble youth Richmond had sent out at the first. Like electricity the knowledge ran from house to house—"Tom B. has come! The army is coming!"

Windows, doorsteps and curbstones became alive at the words— each woman had known him from childhood—had known him joyous, and frank, and ever gay. Each longed to ask for husband, son, or brother; but all held back as they saw the dropped head, and felt his sorrow too deep to be disturbed.

At last one fair wife, surrounded by her young children, stepped into the road and spoke. The ice was broken. The soldier was surrounded; fair faces quivering with suspense, looked up to his, as soft voices begged for news of—"somebody's darling;" and tender hands even patted the starved beast that had borne the hero home! The broad chest heaved as it would burst, a great sob shook the stalwart frame, and a huge teardrop rolled down the cheek that had never changed color in the hottest flashes of the fight. And then the sturdy soldier—conquering his emotion but with no shame for it—told all he could and lightened many a heavy heart. And up to his own door they walked by his side, bareheaded and in the roadway, and there they left him alone to be folded in the embrace of the mother to whom he still was "glorious in the dust."

Next morning a small group of horsemen appeared on the further side of the pontoons. By some strange intuition, it was known that General Lee was among them, and a crowd collected all along the route he would take, silent and bareheaded. There was no excitement, no hurrahing; but, as the great chief passed, a deep, loving murmur, greater than these, rose from the very hearts of the crowd. Taking off his hat and simply bowing his head, the man great in adversity passed silently to his own door; it closed upon him, and his people had seen him for the last time in his battle harness.

Later others came, by scores and hundreds; many a household was made glad that could not show a crust for dinner; and then for days Franklin street lived again. Once more the beloved gray was everywhere, and once more bright eyes regained a little of their brightness, as they looked upon it.

Then suddenly the reins were tightened. On the morning of the 14th, the news of Lincoln's murder fell like a thunderclap upon victor and vanquished in Richmond. At first the news was not credited; then an indignant denial swelled up from the universal heart, that it was for southern vengeance, or that southern men could have sympathy in so vile an act. The sword and not the dagger was the weapon the South had proved she could use; and through the length and breadth of the conquered land was a universal condemnation of the deed.

But the Federal authorities—whether sincere in their belief, or not —made this the pretext for a thorough change of policy in Richmond.

First came uniform orders, that none of the insignia, or rank marks, of the South should be worn—a measure peculiarly oppressive to men who had but one coat. Then came rules about "congregations of rebels," and three Confederates could not stand a moment on a corner, without dispersion by a provost-guard.

Finally came the news of Johnston's surrender—of the last blow to the cause, now lost indeed. Still this fact had been considered a certain one from the date of Lee's surrender; and it bore none of the crushing weight that had made them refuse to believe in the latter. Confident as all were in General Johnston's ability to do all that man might, they still knew his numerical weakness; that he must ere long be crushed between the upper and nether millstones. So this news was received with a sigh, rather than a groan.

There was a momentary hope that the wise covenant between Generals Johnston and Sherman, as to the basis of the surrender, would be indorsed by the Government; but the result of its refusal and of the final surrender on the 13th—was after all little different from what all had expected. Even the wild and maddened spirits, who refused to accept Lee's cartel, and started to work their way to Johnston, could have had no hope of his final success in their calmer moments.

But Johnston's surrender did not lift the yoke from Richmond, in any degree. Police regulations of the most annoying character were imposed; the fact of a parole bearing any significance was entirely ignored; no sort of grace was shown to its possessor, unless he took the oath; and many men, caught in Richmond at this time and far from home, were reduced to distress and almost starvation by the refusal of transportation.

All this the southern people bore with patience. They submitted to all things but two: they would not take the oath and they would not mix socially with their conquerors. In that respect the line was as rigorously drawn in Richmond, at that time, as ever Venice drew it against the Austrian. Not that any attempt was omitted by the Federals to overcome what they called this "prejudice." There was music in Capitol Square, by the best bands of the army, and the ladies were specially invited by the public prints. Not one went; and the officers listened to their own music in company with numbers of lusty black emancipated, who fully felt themselves women and sisters. Next it was given out that the negroes would not be admitted; but then the officers listened alone, and finally gave it up. Failing in public, every effort—short of rudeness and intrusion, which were never resorted to—was made to effect a social lodgment in private. But no Federal uniform ever crossed a rebel threshold, in those days, save on business. The officers occupied parts of many houses; but they were made to feel that the other part, occupied by the household, was private still.

Another infliction, harder to bear, was the well-meant intrusion of old friends from the North. Pleasure parties to Richmond were of constant occurrence; and for the time quite eclipsed in popularity, with the Washington idlers, the inevitable pilgrimage to Mt. Vernon. Gaily dressed and gushing over in the merriment of a party of pleasure, these visitors often sought out their *ante-bellum* friends; and then and there would condone the crime of rebellion to them—sitting in desolation by the ashes of their household gods. It is not hard to understand how bitter was proffered forgiveness, to those who never admitted they could have been wrong; and perhaps the soft answer that turneth away wrath, was not always given to such zealously officious friends.

There was little bitterness expressed, however much may have fermented in the hearts of the captured; and, as a general thing, the people were grateful for the moderation of the Yankees, and appreciated the good they had done at the fire. But, deeper than any bitterness could have sunk, was that ingrained feeling that there were two peoples that these could never again mingle in former amity, till oil and water might mix. The men especially—and with much apparent reason—were utterly hopeless of the future; and, collecting in knots, they would gloomily discuss the prospect of emigration, as if that were the sole good the future held. There can be little doubt that had the ability been theirs, a large majority of the young men of the South would have gone abroad, to seek their fortunes in new paths and under new skies. Luckily, for their country, the commander at Richmond failed to keep his agreement with the paroled officers; and—after making out rolls of those who would be granted free permission and passage to Canada, England or South America—those rolls were suddenly annulled and the whole matter given up. Thus a number of useful, invaluable men who have ever since fought the good fight against that outrage—the imposition of negro dominance over her—were saved to the South.

24

And that good fight, begun in the natural law of self-preservation, has eventuated to the interests of a common country. For no one who does not intimately understand the character of the negro—his mental and moral, as well as his physical, constitution—can begin to comprehend the sin committed against him, even more than against the white man, by putting him in the false attitude of equality with, or antagonism to, the latter.

No one, who did not move among the negroes, immediately after conquest of the South—and who did not see them with experience-opened eyes—can approach realization of the pernicious workings of that futile attempt.

Writing upon the inner details of the war and its resulting action upon the morale of the southern people, omission can not be made of that large and unfortunate class ; driven—first by blind fanaticism, later by fear of their own party-existence—into abnormal condition by the ultra radicals. The negro rapidly changed ; "equality" frittered away what good instincts he had and developed all the worst, innate with him. It changed him from a careless and thriftless, but happy and innocent producer, into a mere consumer, at best ; often indeed, into a besotted and criminal idler, subsisting in part upon Nature's generosity in supplying cabbage and fish, in part upon the thoughtlessness of his neighbor in supplying chickens and eggs.

Yet—so powerful is result of habit ; on so much foundation of nature is based the Scythian fable—the negroes of the South, immediately succeeding the surrender, used the new greatness thrust upon them with surprising innocence. Laziness, liquor and loud asseverations of freedom and equality were its only blessings claimed ; and the commission of overt acts, beyond those named, were rare enough to prove the rule of force of habit. Lured from old service for a time, most of them followed not far the gaudy and shining Will-o'-the-Wisp ; and almost all—especially the household and personal servants—soon returned to "Ole Mas'r" once more, sadder and wiser for the futile chase after freedom's joys. But, even these were partly spoiled and rendered of far less practical use to themselves, or to their employers.

The "negro question" to-day is made merely a matter of politics, rather than one of political economy. At the date of the Confederacy's death, it is a matter of history.

Gradually—by very slow degrees—people in Richmond—as elsewhere in the South, further removed from victor's contact—began to grow so far accustomed to the chains imposed upon them, that they seemed less unbearably galling. Little by little—forced by the necessities of themselves and of those still dearer—men went to work at new and strange occupations ; doing not what they would, but what they could, in the bitter struggle with want for their daily bread. But, spite of earnest resolve and steady exertion,

"There was little to earn and many to keep—"

and every month it seemed to grow harder and harder to make the bare means of life. And not alone did the men work—hard and steadily, early and late. As the women of the South had been the counsellors, the comforters, the very life of the soldiers when the dark hour was threatened ; so they proved themselves worthy helpmeets now that it had come.

No privation was too great, no work too unaccustomed for them to undergo. Little hands that had never held even a needle until the war, now wrought laboriously at the varied—sometimes even menial—occupations that the hour demanded. And they worked, as they had borne the war—with never a murmur ; with ever a cheering word for the fellow-laborer beside them—with a bright trust in the future and that each one's particular " King should have his own again."

And here the author's task is ended—albeit far from completed ; for so little has been told, where there was so much to tell. But, there was no longer a Rebel Capital, to offer its inside view; and what followed the fall—were it not already a twice-told tale—has no place in these pages. Disjointed sketches, these have perchance told some new, or interesting, facts. Certes, they have omitted many more, well worth the telling, noted during those four unparalleled years; but plainly not compressible, within the limits of one volume.

Happily, the trials, the strain, the suffering of those years remain with us, but as a memory. That memory is, to the South, a sacred heritage which unreasoning fanaticism may not dim—which Time, himself, shall not efface. To the North that memory should be cleared of prejudice and bitterness, becoming thus a lesson priceless in worth.

Happily, too, the sober second thought of a common people,

aided by the loyalty of the South—to herself and to her plighted faith —has changed into recemented union of pride and of interest, that outlook from the crumbled gates of Richmond, which made her people groan in their hearts:

Solitudinem faciunt appellantque pacem!

FINIS.

APPENDIX.

FIRST AND LAST BLOOD OF THE WAR.

While the battle of Bethel is recorded in the foregoing pages as the first decided fight of the war between the States, it may leave erroneous impression not to note the date of "first blood" really shed in action on southern soil. In the report of the Adjutant-general of the State of Virginia, for 1866, occurs this entry:

J. Q. Marr, graduated July 4, 1846. Lawyer. Member of the Virginia Convention. Entered military service as Captain of Virginia Volunteers, April 1, 1861. Killed at Fairfax Courthouse, Virginia, May 13, 1861. First blood of the war.

Naturally, many conflicting statements as to the last effective shot of the long struggle were made and received as true. The most reliable would appear to be the following, reproduced from a paper printed by the boys of Mr. Denson's school, in the village of Pittsboro, N. C., in 1866:

The accomplished author of that series of interesting papers, "The Last Ninety Days of the War in North Carolina," published in *The Watchman*, New York, states that the last blood of the war was shed near the Atkins plantation, a few miles from Chapel Hill, on the 14th April, 1865. In a later number of the same paper, a member of the First Tennessee Cavalry says that it is a mistake ; that companies E and F, of the same regiment to which he belonged, skirmished sharply with the Federals on the 15th, and claims that this was the last blood shed. Both are in error : there was a skirmish near Mt. Zion church, two miles south-east of Pittsboro, North Carolina, between a body of Wheeler's cavalry and a party of Federals, on the 17th of April ; two Yankees were wounded, and three others, with several horses, captured. There was other skirmishing in the neighborhood about this time, and as late as the 29th (two days after General Johnston surrendered), a squad of Federal cavalry rode through Pittsboro, firing upon the citizens and returned soldiers, and receiving their fire in return. These men were pursued and overtaken near Haw river, where a skirmish occurred, in which two of the Yankees were killed and two others wounded, one mortally. This Haw river incident is a familiar and well authenticated one and most probably it really showed the last of the long bloodshed.

WHY NO PURSUIT AFTER MANASSAS.

Attention has frequently been drawn to the restiveness of the entire southern people, under alleged neglect to seize golden opportunities for pressing the enemy, after Confederate successes. Most frequently repeated of all these charges, is that which puts upon the shoulders of Jefferson Davis the onus of delay—and of all resulting evil—after the first victory on Manassas Plains. This charge receives semi-official sanction, from ex-Vice-President Stephens ; for his history of the war plainly asserts that to the President was due "the failure of the Confederate troops to advance after the battle of Manassas." The following correspondence between the two men most interested in that mooted question may therefore be read with interest by all candid thinkers :

RICHMOND, VA., November 3, 1861.
General J. E. Johnston, Commanding Department of the Potomac :

SIR : Reports have been and are being widely circulated to the effect that I prevented General Beauregard from pursuing the enemy after the battle of Manassas, and had subsequently restrained him from advancing upon Washington City. Though such statements may have been made merely for my injury, and in that view their notice might be postponed to a more convenient season, they have acquired importance from the fact that they have served to create distrust, to excite disappointment, and must embarrass the administration in its further efforts to re-enforce the armies of the Potomac, and generally to provide for the public defense.

For these public considerations, I call upon you as the commanding general, and as a party to all the conferences held by me on the 21st and 22d of July, to say whether I obstructed the pursuit of the enemy after the victory at Manassas, or have ever objected to an advance or other active operation which it was feasible for the army to undertake ?

Very respectfully yours, etc., JEFFERSON DAVIS.

(373)

HEADQUARTERS, CENTREVILLE, November 10, 1861.

To His Excellency, the President:

SIR : I have had the honor to receive your letter of the 3d instant, in which you call upon me, as the "Commanding General, and as a party to all the conferences held by you on the 21st and 22d of July, to say :

"Whether I obstructed the pursuit after the battle of Manassas.

"Or have ever objected to an advance, or other active operations which it was feasible for the army to undertake."

To the first question I reply : No. The pursuit was "obstructed" by the enemy's troops at Centreville, as I have stated in my official report. In that report I have also said why no advance was made upon the enemy's capital (for reasons) as follows :

The apparent freshness of the United States troops at Centreville, which checked our pursuit ; the strong forces occupying the works near Georgetown, Arlington and Alexandria ; the certainty, too, that General Patterson, if needed, would reach Washington with his army of more than 30,000, sooner than we could ; and the condition and inadequate means of the army in ammunition, provision and transportation, prevented any serious thoughts of advancing against the Capital.

To the second question, I reply, that it has never been feasible for the army to advance further than it has done—to the line of Fairfax Courthouse, with its advanced posts at Upton's, Munson's and Mason's Hills. After a conference at Fairfax Courthouse with the three senior General officers, you announced it to be impracticable to give this army the strength which those officers considered necessary to enable it to assume the offensive. Upon which, I drew it back to its present position.

Most respectfully your obedient servant,   J. E. JOHNSTON.

A true copy :

G. W. C. LEE, Col. and A. D. C.

THE FIRING UNDER THE WHITE FLAG, IN HAMPTON ROADS.

Reference has been made in these pages, to the peculiar circumstances of the wounding of Flag-Lieutenant Robert D. Minor, in the "Merrimac" fight on the 8th March, 1862. The official report of Fleet-Captain Franklin Buchanan distinctly states the facts and formulates the charge, accepted by the author. From this lengthy and detailed official document is reproduced verbatim this

EXTRACT FROM REPORT OF FLAG-OFFICER BUCHANAN.

NAVAL HOSPITAL,
NORFOLK, March 27, 1862.

To Hon. S. R. Mallory, Secretary of the Navy :

*   *   *   *   *   *   *   *   *   *   *

While the Virginia was thus engaged in getting her position, for attacking the Congress, the prisoners state it was believed on board that ship that we had hauled off; the men left their guns and gave three cheers. They were soon sadly undeceived, for a few minutes after we opened upon her again, she having run on shore in shoal water. The carnage, havoc and dismay, caused by our fire, compelled them to haul down their colors, and to hoist a white flag at their gaff half-mast, and another at the main. The crew instantly took to their boats and landed. Our fire immediately ceased, and a signal was made for the Beaufort to come within hail. I then ordered Lieutenant-Commanding Parker to take possession of the Congress, secure the officers as prisoners, allow the crew to land, and burn the ship. He ran alongside, received her flag and surrender, from Commander William Smith and Lieutenant Pendergrast, with the side-arms of those officers. They delivered themselves as prisoners of war on board the Beaufort, and afterward were permitted, at their own request, to return to the Congress, to assist in removing the wounded to the Beaufort. They never returned, and I submit to the decision of the Department whether they are not our prisoners. While the Beaufort and Raleigh were alongside the Congress, and the surrender of that vessel had been received from the commander, she having two white flags flying, hoisted by her own people, a heavy fire was opened upon them from the shore and from the Congress, killing some valuable officers and men. Under this fire the steamers left the Congress; but as I was not informed that any injury had been sustained by those vessels at that time, Lieutenant-Commanding Parker having failed to report to me, I took it for granted that my order to him to burn her had been executed and waited some minutes to see the smoke ascending from her hatches. During this delay we were still subjected to the heavy fire from the batteries, which was always promptly returned.

The steam frigates Minnesota and Roanoke, and the sailing frigate St. Lawrence, had previously been reported as coming from Old Point ; but as I was determined that the Congress should not again fall into the hands of the enemy, I remarked to that gallant young officer, Flag-Lieutenant Minor, "that ship must be burned." He promptly volunteered to take a boat and burn her, and the Teazer, Lieutenant-Commanding Webb, was ordered to cover the boat. Lieutenant Minor had scarcely reached within fifty yards of the Congress, when a deadly fire was opened upon him, wounding him severely and several of his men. On witnessing this vile treachery, I instantly recalled the boat and ordered the Congress destroyed by hot shot and incendiary shell.

* * * * * * * * * * * *

FRANKLIN BUCHANAN, *Flag Officer.*

DEPRECIATION OF CONFEDERATE CURRENCY.

In the chapters on Finance and Dollars and Cents, reference has been made to the rapid depreciation of C. S. Treasury notes. The condensed table appended—gathered from most reliable data—will explain this more clearly than could a volume :

RELATIVE VALUE OF GOLD FROM JANUARY 1, 1861, TO MAY 12, 1865.

1861.—January 1st to May 1st, 5 per cent.; to October 1st, 10 per cent.; October 15th, 12 per cent.; November 15th, 15 per cent.; December 1st, 20 per cent.

1862.—January 1st, 20 per cent.; February 1st, 25 per cent.; February 15th, 40 per cent.; March 1st, 50 per cent.; March 15th, 65 per cent.; April 1st, 75 per cent.; April 15th, 80 per cent.; May 1st. 90 per cent.; May 15th, 95 per cent.; June 15th, 2 for 1; August 1st, 2.20 for 1; September 1st, 2.50 for 1.

1863.—February 1st, 3 for 1; February 15th, 3.10 for 1; March 1st, 3.25 for 1; March 15th, 5 for 1; May 15th, 6 for 1; June 1st, 6.50 for 1; June 15th, 7.50 for 1; July 1st, 8 for 1; July 15th, 10 for 1; August 15th, 15 for 1; November 15th, 15.50 for 1; December 15th, 21 for 1.

1864.—March 1st, 26 for 1; April 1st, 19 for 1; May 1st, 20 for 1; August 15th, 21 for 1; September 15th, 23 for 1; October 15th, 25 for 1; November 15th, 28 for 1; December 1st, 32 for 1; December 31st, 51 for 1.

1865.—January 1st, 60 for 1; February 1st, 50 for 1; April 1st, 70 for 1; April 15th, 80 for 1; April 20th, 100 for 1; April 26th, 200 for 1; April 28th, 500 for 1; April 29th, 800 for 1; April 30th, 1,000 for 1, May 1st (last actual sale of Confederate notes), 1,200 for 1.

GENERAL LEE'S FAREWELL ORDER TO THE ARMY OF NORTHERN VIRGINIA.

HEADQUARTERS ARMY NORTHERN VIRGINIA,
April 10, 1865.

GENERAL ORDER, }
No. 9. }

After four years of arduous service, marked by unsurpassed courage and fortitude, the Army of Northern Virginia has been compelled to yield to overwhelming numbers and resources. I need not tell the brave survivors of so many hard-fought battles, who have remained steadfast to the last, that I have consented to this result from no distrust of them ; but, feeling that valor and devotion could accomplish nothing that would compensate for the loss that must have attended the continuance of the contest, I determined to avoid the useless sacrifice of those whose past services have endeared them to their countrymen.

By the terms of agreement, officers and men can return to their homes and there remain until exchanged. You will take with you the satisfaction that proceeds from the consciousness of duty well performed ; and I earnestly pray that a merciful God will extend to you His blessing and protection. With unceasing admiration of your constancy and devotion to your country and a grateful remembrance of your kind and generous consideration for myself, I bid you an affectionate farewell.   R. E. LEE, *General.*

GENERAL JOHNSTON'S FAREWELL ORDER TO THE ARMY OF TENNESSEE.

GENERAL ORDER, ⎱
  No. 18.   ⎰

[HEADQUARTERS ARMY TENNESSEE,
Near Greensboro, N. C., April 27, 1865.

By the terms of a military convention made on the 26th instant, by Major-General W. T. Sherman, United States Army, and General J. E. Johnston, Confederate States Army, the officers and men of this army are to bind themselves not to take up arms against the United States until properly relieved from that obligation, and shall receive guarantees from the United States officers against molestation by the United States authorities so long as they observe that obligation and the laws in force where they reside.

For these objects, duplicate muster-rolls will be made out immediately, and after the distribution of the necessary papers, the troops will be marched under their officers to their respective States, and there be disbanded, retaining all private property.

The object of this convention is pacification, to the extent of the authority of the commanders who made it. Events in Virginia which broke every hope of success by war, imposed on its general the duty of sparing the blood of this gallant army and saving our country from further devastation and our people from ruin.
                                                 J. E. JOHNSTON, *General.*

GENERAL SHERMAN'S ORDER ON HIS CONVENTION WITH GENERAL JOHNSTON.

SPECIAL FIELD ORDER, ⎱
   No. 65.   ⎰

HEADQUARTERS MILITARY DIVISION OF THE MISSISSIPPI.
In the Field, Raleigh, N. C., April 27, 1865.

The General Commanding announces a further suspension of hostilities and a final agreement with General Johnston, which terminates the war as to the armies under his command and the country east of the Chattahoochee.

Copies of the terms of convention will be furnished Major-Generals Schofield, Gillmore and Wilson, who are specially charged with the execution of its details in the Department of North Carolina, Department of the South, and at Macon and Western Georgia.

    *   *   *   *   *   *   *   *   *   *   *   *

General Schofield will procure at once the necessary blanks, and supply the Army Commanders, that uniformity may prevail ; and great care must be taken that the terms and stipulations on our part be fulfilled with the most scrupulous fidelity, whilst those imposed on our hitherto enemies be received in a spirit becoming a brave and generous army.

Army Commanders may at once loan to the inhabitants such of the captured mules, horses, wagons and vehicles as can be spared from immediate use ; and the Commanding Generals of Armies may issue provisions, animals and any public supplies that can be spared, to relieve present wants and to encourage the inhabitants to renew their peaceful pursuits, and to restore the relations of friendship among our fellow-citizens and countrymen.

Foraging will forthwith cease, and, when necessity or long marches compel the taking of forage, provisions or any kind of private property, compensation will be made on the spot ; or, when the disbursing officers are not provided with funds, vouchers will be given in proper form, payable at the nearest Military Depot.
              By order of   MAJOR-GENERAL W. T. SHERMAN.
L. M. DAYTON, *Assistant Adjutant-General.*

Library of Congress Cataloguing in Publication Data

DeLeon, Thomas C. (Thomas Cooper), 1839-1914.
Four years in rebel capitals.
Reprint. Originally published: Mobile, Ala.: Gossip Print. Co., 1890.
1. DeLeon, Thomas C. (Thomas Cooper), 1839-1914. 2. Confederate States of America—History.
3. United States—History—Civil War, 1861-1865—Personal narratives, Confederate.
4. Southern States—Description and travel. 5. Southern States—Biography.
I. Title.
E487.D34   1983   973.7'13   83-9280
ISBN 0-8094-4463-1 (library)
ISBN 0-8094-4462-3 (retail)

Printed in the United States of America

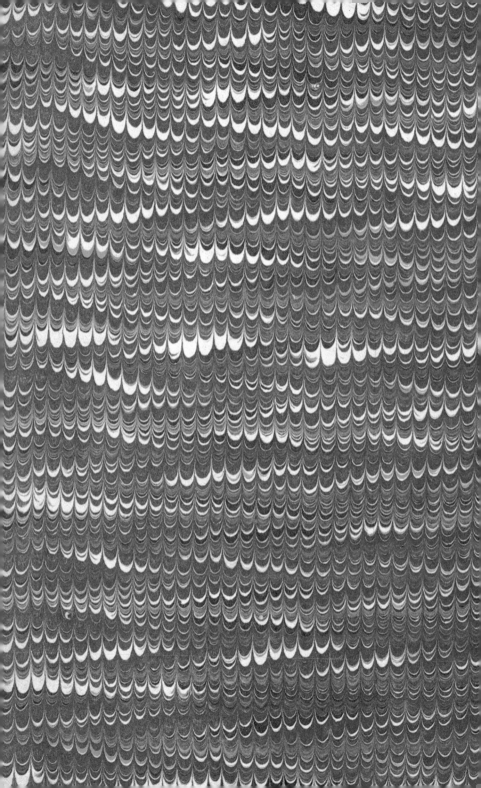